Hours of Work

WILEY SERIES IN PSYCHOLOGY AND PRODUCTIVITY AT WORK

Series Editors
D. J. Oborne and M. M. Gruneberg

The Physical Environment at Work
Edited by D. J. Oborne and M. M. Gruneberg

Computers at Work—A behavioural approach
D. J. Oborne

Hours of Work—Temporal factors in work scheduling
Edited by Simon Folkard and Timothy H. Monk

Further titles in preparation

Hours of Work

Temporal Factors in Work-Scheduling

Edited by
Simon Folkard
MRC Perceptual & Cognitive Performance Unit
University of Sussex

and

Timothy H. Monk
Department of Psychiatry
Cornell University Medical College

JOHN WILEY & SONS
Chichester New York Brisbane Toronto Singapore

Library of Congress Cataloging in Publication Data:

Main entry under title:
Hours of Work
(Wiley series in psychology and productivity at work)
Includes index.
1. Hours of labor. 2. Shift system. 3. Fatigue,
Mental. I. Folkard, Simon. II. Monk, Timothy H.
III. Series.
HD5106.H68 1985 331.25'72 84-17330

ISBN 0 471 10524 4

British Library Cataloging in Publication Data:

Hours of Work — (Wiley series in psychology and productivity at work)
1. Hours of labor
I. Folkard, Simon II. Monk, Timothy
331.25'72 HD5106

ISBN 0 471 10524 4

Phototypeset by TYPE SETTING
Printed by the Pitman Press Ltd., Bath

Contributors and Current Addresses

Torbjorn Akerstedt	*IPM and Stresslab, Korolinska Institute, Box 60 205, S–104 01 Stockholm 60, Sweden*
W. Peter Colquhoun	*MRC Perceptual and Cognitive Performance Unit, Laboratory of Experimental Psychology, University of Sussex, Brighton, Sussex, England.*
Angus Craig	*MRC Perceptual and Cognitive Performance Unit, Laboratory of Experimental Psychology, University of Sussex, Brighton, Sussex, England.*
D. Roy Davies	*Department of Applied Psychology, University of Aston in Birmingham, Birmingham, England.*
Simon Folkard	*MRC Perceptual and Cognitive Performance Unit, Laboratory of Experimental Psychology, University of Sussex, Brighton, Sussex, England.*
Jan E. Fröberg	*Department of Psychology, University of Stockholm, S–106 91 Stockholm, Sweden.*
Mats Gillberg	*National Defence Research Institute, FOA 541, Box 27322, S–102 54 Stockholm, Sweden.*
Manfred Haider	*Institut für Umwelthygiene der Univ. Wien, Kinderspitalgasse 15, A–1095, Wien, Austria.*
James A. Horne	*Department of Human Sciences, Loughborough University, Loughborough, Leicestershire, England.*
Gerard Kerkhof	*Department of Physiology and Physiological Physics, University of Leiden, Wassenaarseweg 62, 2333 AL Leiden, The Netherlands.*

Karl E. Klein	*DFVLR-Institute for Aerospace Medicine, Linder Höhe, 5000 Köln 90, West Germany.*
Kazutaki Kogi	*ILO Regional Office for Asia and the Pacific PO Box 1759, Bangkok, Thailand*
Margit Koller	*Institut für Umwelthygiene der Univ. Wien, Kinderspitalgasse 15, A–1095, Wien, Austria.*
Peretz Lavie	*Sleep Laboratory, Faculty of Medicine, Technion–Israel Institute of Technology, Haifa, Israel 32000.*
David S. Minors	*Department of Physiology, Stopford Building, University of Manchester, Manchester, England.*
Timothy H. Monk	*Institute of Chronobiology, Department of Psychiatry, Cornell University Medical College, Westchester Division, The New York Hospital, 21 Bloomingdale Road, White Plains, New York 10605, USA.*
Paula Patkai	*Department of Psychology, University of Stockholm, S–106 91 Stockholm, Sweden.*
Joseph Rutenfranz	*Institut für Arbeitsphysiologie, An der Universität Dortmund, Ardeystrasse 67, Dortmund D-4600, West Germany.*
Donald I. Tepas	*Department of Psychology, Illinois Institute of Technology, IIT Center, Chicago, Illinois 60616, USA.*
James Walker	*22 The Square, Cranbrook, Ilford, Essex, England.*
James M. Waterhouse	*Department of Physiology, Stopford Building, University of Manchester, Manchester, England.*
Hans M. Wegmann	*DFVLR-Institute for Aerospace Medicine, Linder Höhe, 5000 Köln 90, West Germany.*
Rütger A. Wever	*Max-Planck-Institut für Psychiatrie, Außenstelle Andechs, Arbeitsgruppe Chronobiologie, D–8138 Andechs, West Germany.*

Contents

Editorial Foreword to the Series

The books in this series have been written for a specific and significantly large readership; namely those who have an interest in, and the task of, improving productive output at work. Common to all the volumes is the presentation of the results of psychological research, and an account of the principles, that are concerned particularly with ways of improving organizational efficiency.

The format of the series — which contains single-authored and edited multiauthored volumes — helps greatly in this endeavour. Thus, the various aspects of this multifaceted problem of working efficiency can be addressed in a number of different ways and from different viewpoints. The list of titles already produced or in preparation illustrates this.

This volume sits very well in the Psychology and Productivity at Work Series. It considers how the temporal structure of work, either within a 24-hour period or within unbroken spells, can influence a worker's productivity. Since this is such a very wide topic the format of an edited monograph is eminently suitable, and the editors have managed to assemble a large and distinguished group of authors, with international reputations, to generate a very comprehensive work. It will be of value to any educated person who wishes to read about the significance of psychology in reducing some of the current problems at work, with implications for concommitant increases in overall productivity.

D.J. Oborne
M.M. Gruneberg

Foreword

The very large subject to which this book is devoted can be dated, in its modern manifestations, to the industrial revolution. As if in a planetary experiment hours of waking were then wrested away from the control of Nature and handed over to the control of Man, or so it was thought until recently. The vast cost of night, as night was turned into day, was most willingly borne as firstly gas-light and secondly, electricity, triumphantly bore their copies of the sun into factories, trains, streets and homes. The same trend has been intensified in this century by the displacement of much of sport and more of other entertainment from day to night; by the spread of mechanical transport which is as well attuned to the one as to the other; and, above all, by the extension into the hours of darkness of shiftwork of one form and another. In an analogous version of the same trend as vigorous an attempt has been made to transport summer's heat as well as summer's light into winter. Much of the new wealth created in the last two centuries has come from the new dispositions of working time and been used to bear the cost of colonizing the dark.

However, in spite of all the benefits that this process has bestowed, it has also imposed some burdens on any people who have been considered 'factors of production' and as capable as machines of working strange hours. This has been partly because there has not been enough systematic understanding of how people behave when working abnormal hours, or normal hours for that matter.

As the result of an explosion of knowledge in the last twenty years or so the whole situation has begun to alter. A new discipline, chronobiology, has begun to emerge with sufficient presence to have a powerful effect on psychology, geography and (slowly) sociology. The underlying relationship of human functioning to time-patterns laid down well before the industrial revolution is becoming better understood. A new light (or rather, lights) can therefore be thrown on the old subject of hours of work, as it has been in this book. All the authors are in the forefront of an international community of scholars who are speaking with increasing authority and in broad agreement with each other. The social consequences could, eventually, be very large indeed.

Michael Young
Institute of Community Studies, London 1984

Preface

The last few decades have seen substantial changes in many people's hours of work. The incidence of 'abnormal' work hours, such as those involved in shiftwork, has increased dramatically over this period, while 'normal' work hours have become less rigid due to the introduction of 'flexitime' and other alternative work schedules. These changes have been paralleled by an increased awareness that people's ability to work is not constant, but subject to temporal variations. Perhaps the most obvious of these variations are those associated with the fact that we are a diurnal species that habitually sleeps at night. Thus, unlike the machines that they operate, shiftworkers have their own internal time structure that may make them less efficient at some times than at others. Nor can this internal time structure be easily reset, like the hands of a clock, to take account of abnormal work hours.

This book thus attempts to address the question of how hours of work may best be structured so as to be more pleasant, productive and safe for the employee, and most cost-effective for the employer. The basic premise of this book is that the human body is subject to temporal variations. Many of these variations are of a rhythmic or cyclic nature, resulting in, for example, some times of day being more suitable for work than others. Other temporal variations stem from the fact that work takes place over time, and abilities may vary simply as a result of 'time on task'. The problems of 'fatigue' resulting from prolonged work are not covered in this book since they are the subject of their own volume in this series (*Occupational Fatigue* by I. Brown).

As editors, we have attempted to illustrate both the depth and breadth of this area by commissioning a fairly large number of relatively short chapters from experts in their fields. We have not limited these experts to psychologists since we believe the problems in this area to be multidisciplinary in nature. A shiftworker's productivity may be influenced not only by temporal variations in performance efficiency, but also by factors such as sleep deprivation, health and the quality of social and family life. In addition, although we hope that most chapters will be understood without reference to others, we have attempted a coherent structuring of the book as a whole. Thus, the first chapters introduce various aspects of circadian (around 24-hour) rhythms, and sleep. These are followed by chapters on non 24-hour rhythms, and on aspects of non-rhythmic temporal variations.

The second half of the book contains the more practically oriented chapters, and deals with the effects of normal and abnormal work hours. The final two chapters deal with some of the special problems encountered by the crews of ships and aircraft.

In executing our editorial duties, we have been continually impressed by the understanding, patience and enthusiasm of our fellow authors. We are extremely grateful to them, to the series editors, to the editorial staff at John Wiley, and to our colleagues for their help and support. We also wish to acknowledge the invaluable help provided by Mrs Patricia Chatfield and Miss Margaret Heyburgh in cheerfully retyping various versions of most of the manuscripts submitted by the authors. Timothy Monk further acknowledges partial funding support from the National Institute on Aging (Grant AG 04135-01), the National Institute of Mental Health (Grant MH 37814-02) and a NASA Co-operative Agreement (No. NCC 2-253). Finally, we extend our warmest thanks to our wives and children for putting up with us, and for just being there!

Simon Folkard,
Brighton

Timothy H. Monk,
New York

1984

Hours of Work
Edited by S. Folkard and T.H. Monk

Chapter 1
Introduction to Circadian Rhythms

David S. Minors and James M. Waterhouse

CONTENTS

ABSTRACT

This chapter introduces the reader to the regular 24-hour variations in physiological processes that are often disrupted by abnormal work schedules. These 'circadian rhythms' are shown to differ in the degree to which they reflect a response to our environment or an internal biological 'clock'. In either case, the precise timing of these rhythms is shown to be dependent on environmental time cues or 'zeitgebers'. The final section introduces some of the practical implications of these rhythms.

1.1 BASIC IDEAS

1.1.1 A rhythmic world

We have evolved in a world which shows many examples of rhythmicity. At different parts of the surface of the globe regular changes occur through the year as we move through the seasons, these changes being most marked at the poles. More obvious than these oscillations, because of their more rapid frequency, are the oscillations associated with the solar day which recur every 24 hours. In this case, not only are there the alternations in light intensity and environmental temperature between night and day, but also our whole social behaviour is structured to the solar day. The normal social rhythm is one of daytime work, evening leisure and night sleep. It is the problems associated with living differently from the norm, in particular working at night or on shifts, which will be concentrated upon in this book.

Not only do our environmental and social behaviour show rhythmicity; it is present also at a biological level. The study of such biological rhythms has become a science in itself, termed *Chronobiology.* In this first chapter we will discuss the basic concepts of this science and introduce the mechanisms controlling these rhythms.

1.1.2 Constancy and rhythmicity in physiological systems

When the physiology of man is studied it rapidly becomes apparent that a prerequisite for health is the maintenance of many physiological variables (e.g. blood pressure, body fluids and gases) within a very restricted range; such control is termed *homeostatis.* Thus, it is common knowledge that healthy individuals must maintain their body temperature within narrow limits in spite of climatic exigencies. The dangers of hypothermia in the aged, or excessively high temperatures during fever, are well known. Indeed, an important aspect of diagnosis consists of ascertaining if a variable (e.g. blood pressure, plasma hormone concentration) falls outside a range compatible with health, and the process of recovery can be monitored by a return of the variable to within the normal range.

Such a 'steady-state' or homeostatic picture is, however, an oversimplification, as can be seen if a succession of readings is taken frequently and over many days. When this is done, it is found that, though variables remain within narrow limits, they are not constant rather they are rhythmic. With the recent development of analytical techniques that require only small volumes of urine or minute volumes of plasma (e.g. radioimmunoassay) and of automatic recording devices, rhythmicity has been confirmed for an extremely wide range of variables. Indeed, it is difficult to find a variable that does not vary rhythmically. Furthermore, the period of these rhythms (the time taken to complete one cycle) is very diverse: ranging from only a fraction of a second (as in the electrical activity of the brain) through about one second (the rhythmic beating of the heart) to, at the other extreme, very infrequent rhythms, perhaps only one per month or per year (the human menstrual cycle and the hibernatory behaviour of some mammals, respectively). It has become evident in the last few decades that biological variables which show rhythms with a cycle length of 24 hours are very common. They are termed *circadian rhythms* (from the Latin: *circa,* about; *dies,* a day). A description of many of these rhythms can be found in Minors and Waterhouse (1981). Rhythms which oscillate with a higher frequency than this are termed *ultradian* and those which oscillate with a lower frequency, *infradian.* In this chapter, and in most others in this book, it is the circadian rhythms which will be concentrated upon, though in those chapters dealing with sleep, ultradian rhythms will also be described, while some infradian rhythms are described in Chapter 8.

1.2 CIRCADIAN RHYTHMS

Figure 1.1 illustrates circadian rhythms in a selection of physiological variables obtained from healthy subjects on a normal schedule of sleep, waking and mealtimes. It can be seen that the variables show higher values during the daytime (1200–1800) and lower values during the night, with minimum values in the small hours. The examples in this figure could be added to almost indefinitely, most of

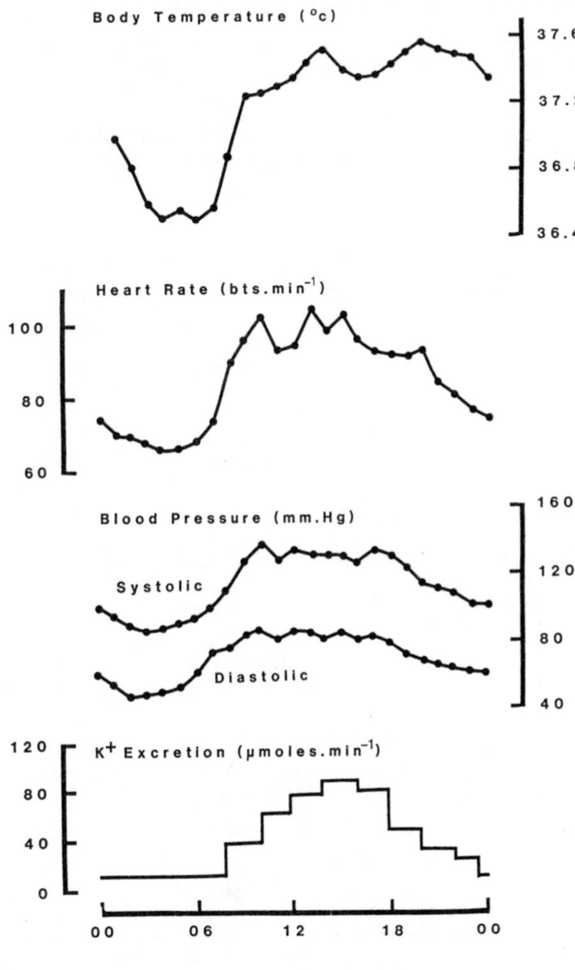

Figure 1.1 Daily changes in deep body temperature, heart rate, blood pressure and the urinary excretion of potassium. Measurements were made hourly over a single 24-h period and the data represent the means from four subjects. Unpublished data of Minors and Waterhouse

them showing the general result that daytime values are higher than those found at night. A common exception to this generalization is that of the rhythm in the concentration of some hormones in blood which tend to peak during the night, or in the hours just after waking, and show lowest values during the evening.

When one wants to describe a rhythm quantitatively one is concerned with defining: *the mean* — the level about which oscillation takes place; *the range of oscillation; the phase of the rhythm* — that is its placement in time, often described as the time when peak values are found; and *the period of the rhythm* — the time to complete one cycle (in the case of circadian rhythms this is always about 24 hours). These definitions are illustrated in Figure 1.2, top, together with the symbols used to represent them.

Though the waveforms of circadian rhythms are extremely variable, they can often be approximated by a sinusoid (e.g. those in Figure 1.1). In such a case, the rhythm can be quantified by fitting a cosine curve. Fitting a cosine curve to the data requires computation (see Nelson *et al.,* 1979), but in essence it involves minimizing the deviation between the required curve and the data in a manner analogous to minimizing the deviations of the data about the required straight line in linear regression analysis. The important parameters of the best-fitting curve

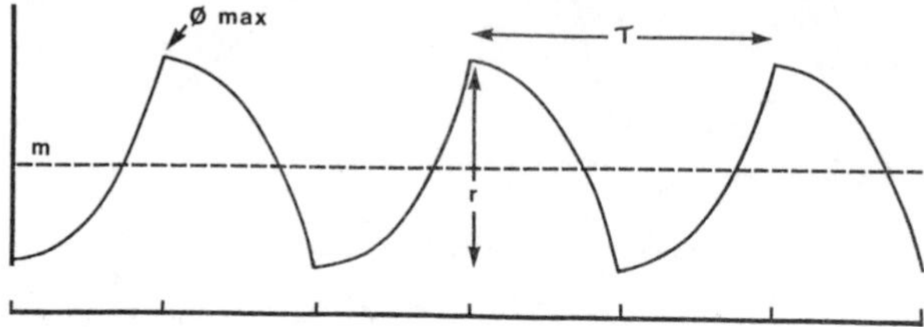

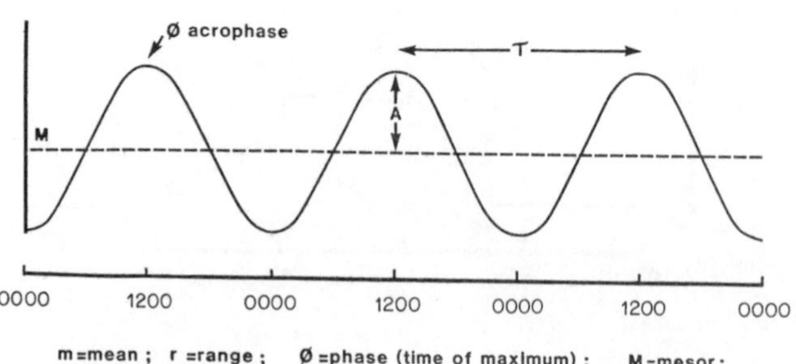

Figure 1.2 A rhythm's parameters. Above, when the raw data are presented; below, when a cosine curve has been fitted to the data

are its mean value (*mesor*), its distance between peak and mesor (*amplitude*) and the time of peak (*acrophase*). These are shown in Figure 1.2, bottom. Confidence intervals for these parameters can also be calculated.

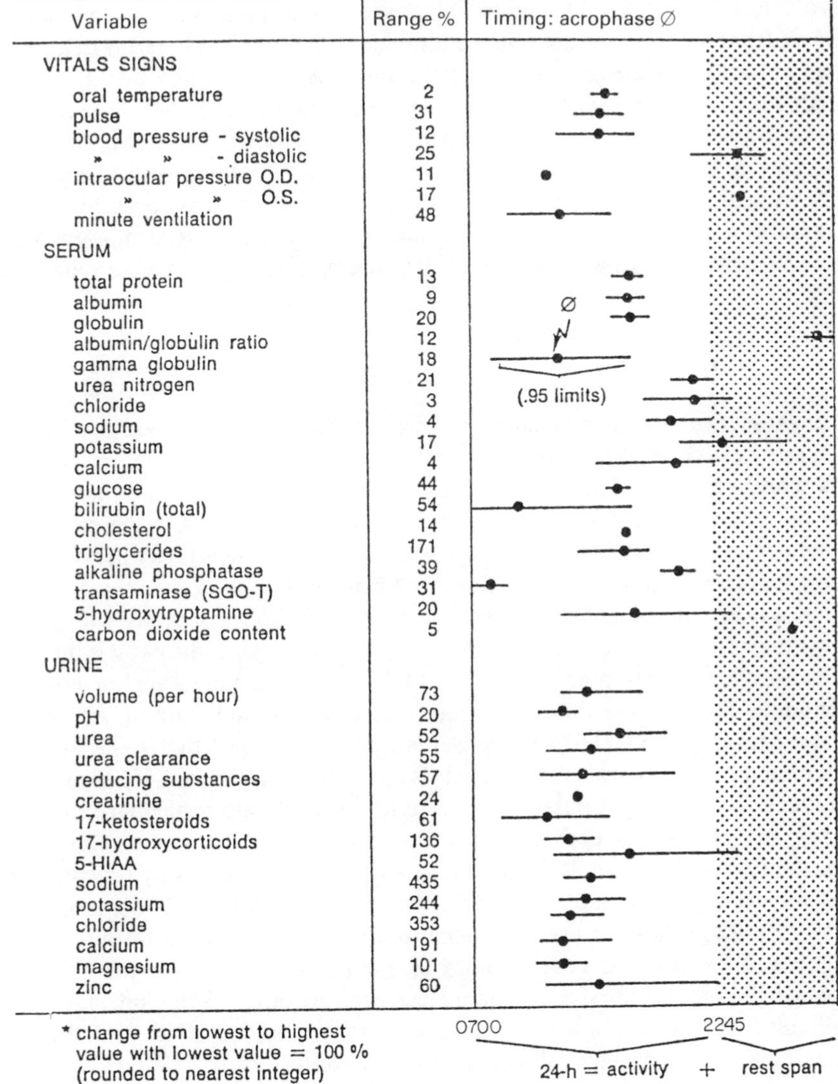

Figure 1.3 An acrophase map of 13 young soldiers. The acrophase (represented by a dot) and their confidence limits are shown with reference to the normal sleep–wakefulness cycle (hatched area represents normal sleep time). From Kanabrocki *et al.* (1973)

Many other terms are used in the study of rhythms and the interested reader can find these in the glossaries of chronobiology (Halberg and Katinas, 1973; Halberg *et al.*, 1977).

As a result of such mathematical operations, rather than plotting the raw data on a time axis (Figure 1.1), it is possible to describe an individual (or a population if data from numerous synchronized individuals are pooled) in terms of a phase diagram as shown in Fig. 1.3 in which the acrophases only are plotted. It must be made clear at the outset that such diagrams show considerable differences in detail between individuals, with rhythms tending to be phased earlier than average in some subjects, but later than average in others (see Chapter 3). Nevertheless, such a phase map is an objective and complete description of a person's (or population's) rhythmicity and can be used to assess abnormalities such as those occurring in disease or after altered sleep–wakefulness schedules.

1.3 EXOGENOUS AND ENDOGENOUS COMPONENTS OF CIRCADIAN RHYTHMICITY

It might seem at first sight that the circadian rhythms so far described (see Figures 1.1 and 1.3) could wholly result from the effects of the rhythmic environment upon an individual. Thus, during the daytime he would be awake, active and taking meals whereas at night he would be asleep and fasting; therefore, one would predict that his blood pressure, heart rate and temperature will rise during the daytime and fall at night. Such an argument could also explain the nocturnal peak of certain hormones since endocrine function is often associated with growth and repair which might take place more appropriately when the body is inactive. However, it should be noted from Figure 1.1 that body temperature, for example, continues to fall some time after sleep onset (2330) and starts to rise before waking takes place (0730), two observations that suggest that some factor in addition to the sleep–wakefulness cycle is involved. Furthermore, if our circadian rhythms were simply a passive response to our rhythmic behaviour (including mealtimes and social activity), they would disappear if this behaviour were constant throughout the 24 hours. One can test this argument by removing the rhythmic components of behaviour, viz. one can stay awake for 24 hours; one can take identical snacks at evenly spaced intervals; the effects of posture can be eliminated by constant bedrest or by remaining sedentary; and the effects of changing noise, light and social influences can obviously be minimized without difficulty. One protocol which has attempted to remove all these influences simultaneously has been called the *constant routine* or Mills's test (Halberg, 1978). In Figure 1.4 is shown the average hourly deep body temperature during such a constant routine in a group of eight subjects (broken line). Also shown in this figure is the equivalent temperature rhythm when they slept and ate at conventional times (solid line). A comparison of these two curves yields the following important results.

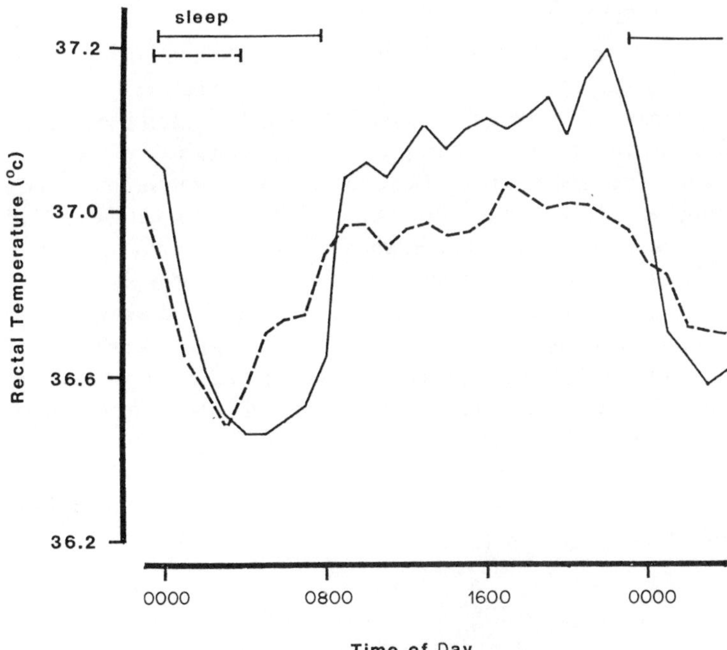

Figure 1.4 Mean circadian changes in rectal temperature measured hourly in eight subjects living a normal sleep–wakefulness cycle (solid line) and in the same subjects awoken at 0400 and spending the subsequent 24 h awake in constant light and taking hourly small identical snacks (broken line). From Minors and Waterhouse (1981)

(i) The temperature rhythm during the constant routine does not disappear; this result, found in the cases of other variables that have been studied and also when people are kept awake for several days (see Chapter 6), is taken to imply some internal or endogenous timing mechanism that is metaphorically called a biological 'clock'.

(ii) There is some effect of the normal alternation of night and day and their associated activities, i.e. of a 'nychthemeral' existence, since the two sets of data are not identical. This effect, attributed to external factors, is called the *exogenous* or *masking influence.*

(iii) In normal circumstances, the two components are in phase with one another. Thus, at night the low values are due to the body's clock, accentuated by (exogenous) inactivity and fasting during sleep; during the daytime, peak activity coincides with highest values from the endogenous clock.

Having established that normal circadian rhythms in nychthemeral conditions consist of an endogenous component and an exogenous, masking, component, it is now necessary to consider each in more detail.

1.3.1 Exogenous or Masking Component

The exogenous or masking component is due to the alternation of sleep and wakefulness and all the differences that normally exist between these two states. Many physiological variables are directly affected by sleep itself (Mills *et al.*, 1978a). Thus, for example, the act of going to sleep causes a profound fall in body temperature. The masking effect of sleep on body temperature can be deduced by comparing the rhythms obtained when the subjects remained awake during the constant routine with those obtained when they lived normally and were allowed to sleep (Figure 1.4). This indicates that sleep depresses body temperature by about 0.2°C (see Chapter 2, section 2.4). The size of the masking effect of sleep depends upon the variable under consideration, being particularly marked in the case of the rhythms found in the plasma levels of growth hormones and prolactin. For other variables the dominant masking effect will not be sleep. For example, the main masking effect upon the plasma insulin rhythm is likely to be the nychthemeral variation in food (and hence glucose) intake, while the masking influence in the case of urine flow will be daily variations in drinking (and hence water intake).

1.3.2 Endogenous component

If it is intended to study the endogenous component of a rhythm, then it is necessary to remove or minimize the exogenous component and, as with any oscillator, it is desirable to study as many consecutive cycles as possible. One method is to continue the constant routine protocol beyond 24 hours (see, for example, Froberg *et al,* 1972, and Chapter 6, in which a study of about 3 days' duration was concerned). However, this protocol suffers two disadvantages. First, three cycles are still insufficient to assess the period of the rhythm or the effects of external influences at all accurately. Second, as the experiment progresses, the effects of fatigue might begin to predominate over those of an internal clock.

The method which has yielded most information about the internal clock is the free-running experiment. With humans this consists of isolating the subject from any cues regarding the passage of time; this is done either in a cave or in a specially constructed isolation unit. The subject is allowed to take meals and sleep when he wishes, but these are monitored by the experimenter. Samples of urine and plasma can be collected and recordings of deep body temperature, performance, etc., can be made in order to estimate details of these rhythms. Such experimental protocols routinely last from 10 to 30 days, but records of several months have also been achieved.

This type of experiment has produced a mass of data, many of them complex, and they are reviewed in Chapter 2. However, at this stage it is sufficient to say that rhythms continue, and are then said to be free-running. This is strong evidence for the presence of an internal (or endogenous) clock-like mechanism. Equally important is the observation that the variables show a period not of exactly 24 hours but, in humans, of about 25 hours. It is for this reason that these rhythms are described as *circa*dian — the period is of *about* a day.

1.3.3 Entrainment and zeitgebers

Although the inherent period of the endogenous clock controlling circadian rhythms is often greater than 24 hours in humans, it is found that, when a rhythm is measured in an individual living in normal nychthemeral conditions, its period is exactly 24 hours. It follows that under normal conditions the endogenous clock must be adjusted to run with a period of 24 hours. This adjustment of the endogenous clock is termed *synchronization* or *entrainment*. Thus, although not a totally appropriate analogy, the biological clock has been likened to a watch which runs slow and which must be adjusted (entrained) to register correct time. Such entrainment of the endogenous clock is a necessity for otherwise there would be a continuing mismatch between our internal and external time.

Entrainment of the internal clock to exactly 24 hours is believed to be achieved by rhythmic changes in the external environment called synchronizers or zeitgebers (German: *Zeit,* time; *geber,* giver). Thus, the alternation of light and dark entrains leaf movements to the solar day; the alternation of food availability and scarcity entrains the activities of many predators to a 24-hour cycle; and the rhythmic buffeting caused by high tides entrains shore-dwelling creatures to a lunar day.

In principle, the ability or otherwise of an external rhythmic influence to act as a zeitgeber can be established in animals by (i) establishing a free-running, circadian rhythm in, say, activity patterns by placing the animal in a constant environment (generally continuous darkness), and then (ii) imposing the putative zeitgeber upon this environment and observing whether or not the rhythm is entrained to this cycle or continues to free-run. (The zeitgeber is normally imposed as a regular 'present:absent' schedule with a period of 24 hours, for example, '16 h light:8 h dark' (mimicking summer) or '3 h food available:21 h food unavailable'). Finally (iii), the putative zeitgeber is removed, whereupon the entrained rhythm should free-run again *starting from the entrained position.* This last point is important since it distinguishes entrainment from masking. If the imposition of external rhythmicity had acted only as a masking influence, then its removal would uncover the fact that the internal clock had free-run throughout its presence.

Although these methods have been used with considerable success in the chair-acclimatized squirrel monkey (Moore-Ede *et al.*, 1982), further comment is required. First, this method, as described, investigates if external rhythms are *individually* sufficient to entrain the internal clock or oscillator. It is quite conceivable that a group of external rhythms, together but not singly, might act as a zeitgeber. Second, although an external rhythmicity may act as a zeitgeber, it is found that entrainment is not immediate, i.e. if the phase of the zeitgeber is suddenly shifted it may be several days before the circadian rhythm shows a similar shift of phase. Third, the external rhythmicity acts as a zeitgeber provided that its period does not differ too much from the free-running period of the clock it is to entrain. (See Chapter 2, section 2.3.1). This is described as the range of entrainment of the internal clock and is found to be narrow when the zeitgeber is weak and wider when the zeitgeber is strong. Fourth, if the animal possesses more than one internal clock (see Chapter 2), then more than one set of zeitgebers would be possible, each clock possessing its own relative strength and range of entrainment with respect to each set of zeitgebers.

1.3.4 Zeitgebers in humans

The questions that arise are: what are the zeitgebers that affect humans and how do they exert their effects? There is still some controversy on this issue. It is an important one since knowledge of the most important synchronizers might enable advice to be given regarding the best way to adjust one's rhythms to a change in schedule (see Chapter 15).

Wever and his colleagues (Wever, 1979a) have advanced the view that the alternation of light and dark is a weaker zeitgeber than are rhythmic cues provided by social influences. Briefly, they found that subjects were not entrained by a light:dark schedule alone, but only when gong strokes (to summon the subject to perform tasks) were regularly superimposed. Wever believes that the subjects perceived these strokes as social contacts from the experimenters. One problem in interpreting these experiments is that subjects were free to use accessory lighting during the imposed 'night'. Thus there was no real need to make use of the rhythmic information provided by the light:dark cycle alone. However, when the gong strokes were added, and since they were more frequent in the 'day' than during the 'night', it would have been inconvenient to have ignored the information they gave. Of course, the protocol does not enable us to say if social influences (gong strokes) alone act as zeitgeber.

Moore-Ede and his colleagues (Moore-Ede *et al.*, 1982) have argued that the light:dark cycle, rather than social influences, acts as a synchronizer. Thus they showed that humans entrained to an imposed light:dark cycle when no auxiliary lighting was allowed during the dark phase. In the absence of this cycle, then, rhythms free-ran even though the experimenters maintain that the subjects could have produced their own social zeitgeber by talking to the experimenters if and when they wished. In these experiments the effects of the light:dark cycle as an entraining agent seem clear enough, but the protocol was such that it would have been inconvenient (if not impracticable) not to comply. Further, the social influences seem not to have been rhythmic because the opportunity to talk was present *all* the time, and this would not seem to be the ideal test for a zeitgeber.

It is our view that attempts to find the most important single zeitgeber are of rather limited usefulness if a whole group of zeitgebers might be more appropriate (Minors and Waterhouse, 1981a). Such an argument could run: individuals go to bed since they know that they need a certain amount of sleep to prepare for the rigours of the next day. Domestic (e.g. shopping) and business commitments dictate that one is awake during the daytime and so it is *convenient* to arrange one's waking time to coincide with daytime. Once the sleep–wakefulness cycle has been established, all other potential zeitgebers (light:dark, feeding:fasting, social mixing:social isolation, noise:quiet, etc.) will be adjusted to coincide. If this approach is correct, then to assess the potency of any individual zeitgeber might be less important (and very difficult to perform anyway). Instead, circumstances in which the synchrony that normally exists between different zeitgebers are changed (shiftwork) might become of far greater relevance to a human's well-being.

Recent work has also considered the mechanisms by which zeitgebers might affect internal clocks (Moore-Ede *et al.*, 1982). Experiments upon rodents and, more often, considerably lowlier organisms, have established that pulses of light can adjust the internal clocks, sometimes advancing and sometimes delaying them. It is possible from such results to construct schemes whereby entrainment of the circadian clock to exactly 24 hours is achieved. There is some evidence that different zeitgebers entrain different rhythms preferentially, which is further evidence for the existence of more than one clock. Finally, a substantial body of data implicate protein synthesis as at least part of the process by which the clocks' activities are manifested. To what extent all these findings apply to humans is not yet known.

The path by which zeitgebers influence the clocks have also received study recently. In a number of animal species (including man) a direct projection from the retina to the suprachiasmatic nucleus of the hypothalamus has been demonstrated. This is likely to play an important role when light:dark cycles act as a zeitgeber. The link between feeding and clock adjustment is less certain, but it is suggested that food intake produces rhythmic changes in plasma amino-acids which in turn affect brain neurotransmitter synthesis via uptake of the amino-acid precursors. When one considers the means by which other rhythmic influences act as zeitgebers (noise, quiet and social influences) one is left with speculation rather than data (Minors and Waterhouse, 1981a; Moore-Ede *et al.*, 1982).

1.3.5 The relative sizes of endogenous and exogenous components

The relative sizes of the endogenous and exogenous components of a rhythm differ between variables. One of the most successful means of measuring these components has been to require subjects to live 'days' of <22 or >26 hours (by making use of watches or clocks that run fast or slow by the appropriate amount) in an environment where there are no 24-hour cues (Arctic summer or isolation unit). In these circumstances, since the length of the 'day' is outside the range of entrainment of the endogenous clock, the clock takes up its inherent period of about 25 hours, whereas the exogenous component of any rhythm will have a period equal to the length of the artificial 'day'. As a result, two rhythmic components can be detected in a single variable (one due to the endogenous component and the other due to the exogenous component) and the amplitude of each component can be calculated (see Mills *et al.*, 1977). The relative amplitudes of these two components form the circadian amplitude ratio (CAR) which will be high for rhythms with marked endogenous components and low when the rhythms are mainly exogenous. Table 1.1 summarizes the results from some experiments performed in an isolation unit and in the Arctic. The similarity between the results is noteworthy.

Table 1.1 Rank ordering for circadian amplitude ratio of different constituents measured in Arctic and isolation unit experiments

		Arctic	Isolation unit	
		21-h day	21-h day	27-h day
Endogenous	17-hydroxycorticosteroids	1	–	–
↑	Temperature	–	1	1
	Potassium	2	2	2
	Chloride	4	3	3
	Flow	3	4	4
	Phosphate	–	5	5
	Sodium	3	6	6
↓	Urate	–	7	7
Exogenous	Calcium	–	7	8

– Not assessed

1.4 IMPLICATIONS

It can be seen that, under normal conditions, there is a multitude of circadian rhythms that interact with each other and result from the simultaneous presence of external and internal influences. These rhythms are phylogenetically ancient and are found throughout the living kingdom, with the exception of bacteria in which generation times of less than an hour render meaningless the concept of circadian rhythms. The advantage of the possession of such rhythms is taken to be that a certain independence of the outside world is achieved. Thus, an internal clock will enable the animal to emerge from its hiding place at an appropriate time after the departure of predators, and before too much time that can be used for its own activity has been wasted. Another advantage, which applies equally to man, is that the organism can 'pre-adapt' to some forthcoming event. The plant can raise its leaves ready for sunrise, and the human can change his hormone and neural status in time for waking and for the stresses of the new day. As the evening progresses, he can begin to 'tone down' in preparation for sleep (Cloudsley-Thompson, 1980). Under normal conditions the rhythms are phase-locked (that is, their relative timings are constant) both when different physiological and psychological variables are considered and when internal and external rhythms are compared. That is, there is a stability in the whole structure (as is implied by Figure 1.3).

However, such a temporal structure can be upset by modifications to sleep–wakefulness schedules and associated factors such as mealtimes and social influences (see Chapter 14). The problem arises because the endogenous clock is stable and unable to adjust its timing rapidly, while individual overt rhythms are found to adjust to a changed sleep–wakefulness schedule at different rates. This latter is because of differences in the relative importance of endogenous and exogenous components. As a result, a state of internal and external dissociation exists when the normal phase relationships between different variables and between such variables and the environment are lost. In addition, the process of adjustment to the new zeitgebers will begin so that rhythms, as well as being wrongly phased, are changing their timing with respect to 'old body' time and 'new environmental' time. Such abnormalities coincide with, and are believed to be in some way responsible for, fatigue, poor performance, feelings of general malaise and gastro-intestinal disorders. After time-zone transitions such a group of symptoms is known as 'jet-lag syndrome', but it is found also in shiftworkers who are required to sleep at abnormal times. Indeed, in the longer term, the persistence of such symptoms is one of the reasons why workers leave shiftwork, and it might be related to the observation that shiftworkers as a group are more liable than non-shiftworking controls to suffer from duodenal ulcers (Harrington, 1978).

Clearly, it is desirable to ameliorate such symptoms if possible. Many approaches to this problem have been considered (see Chapters 14, 15 and 16); one which is particularly relevant to the present chapter is to attempt to stabilize circadian rhythmicity, i.e. to minimize day-to-day changes in the timing of different rhythms. This has considerable implications both for the shiftworker and the designer of the shift system since there is evidence that individuals differ in the response of their circadian rhythms to changes in a sleep–wakefulness schedule and that different schedules alter rhythms by different amounts.

One possible means of achieving such stability is based upon the effect that sleep exerts upon circadian rhythms in general. Recent work (Minors and Waterhouse, 1981b, 1983a) has indicated that circadian rhythms can be stabilized, at least partially, by taking only 4 hours' sleep regularly each day ('anchor' sleep). The time at which such sleep is taken determines the phase at which rhythms are stabililized. It might be possible with the appropriate timing of 'anchor' sleep to stabilize rhythms with a phase that is useful to the individual concerned.

Further, it is worth remembering that nearly all studies of circadian rhythmicity have been performed upon subjects in a rhythmic environment, i.e. in the presence of external rhythmicity. The extent to which this exogenous rhythmicity masks that rhythmicity which is due to the endogenous component is poorly understood. Some evidence (Mills *et al.*, 1978b) suggests that adaptation of the internal clock to time-zone transition, simulated in an isolation unit, is less than that measured in the presence of a rhythmic environment adjusted to the new 'local' time. Preliminary data from shiftwork studies (Minors and Waterhouse, 1983b) also indicate that overestimates of the adaptation of the internal clock might have been made in earlier work (reviewed in Minors and Waterhouse, 1981a; Moore-Ede *et al.*, 1982).

Finally, the importance of sleep to circadian rhythm studies must be stressed. Although it will be argued in Chapter 5 that, on average, we take too much sleep, and that the body's physiology is little altered by sleep deprivation, it is beyond doubt that the complaints of nightworkers are often concerned with the inability to obtain 'satisfactory' sleep during the daytime. Since sleep not only 'masks' circadian rhythms, but also is an important link in the complex chain whereby internal rhythms are entrained to a 24-hour day by zeitgeber, this inability to obtain sufficient sleep during the daytime may result in asynchrony between behavioural rhythms and the internal clock. Thus the shiftworkers' rhythms may fail to shift their phase to a value completely appropriate to their nocturnal activity. As indicated above, this may be partly responsible for the malaise often experienced by such workers.

Hours of Work
Edited by S. Folkard and T.H. Monk

Chapter 2

Man in Temporal Isolation: Basic Principles of the Circadian System

Rütger A. Wever

CONTENTS

ABSTRACT

This chapter briefly reviews some of the main findings from an extensive series of studies in which individuals have been isolated from natural time cues (zeitgebers) for several weeks. These studies clearly demonstrate that circadian rhythms persist in the absence of natural zeitgebers, and can be entrained by artificial ones. They further indicate that the body temperature can run independently of the sleep–wake cycle. This finding suggests the need for a multioscillatory model of the human circadian system, and has far-reaching implications for the adjustment of circadian rhythms to abnormal work hours.

2.1 INTRODUCTION

Circadian rhythms occur in the values of nearly all measurable physiological variables in animals, including humans, and are governed by internal and external influences. A thorough understanding of the system controlling these circadian rhythms requires a separation of the action of these influences. One way to achieve this is to put subjects in temporal isolation, i.e. to exclude the natural day–

night cycle and other external influences or time cues, where any residual rhythm can only be controlled by internal influences.

Studies of this type, conducted with various species from unicellular organisms up to man, have consistently shown that circadian rhythms persist under these conditions, i.e. they 'free-run' but with periods slightly different from 24 hours. This deviation of the free-running periods from that of the Earth's rotation confirms their independence from external influences since there are no known external stimuli with periods corresponding to those of free-running rhythms. However, in the absence of such temporal isolation, all organisms show rhythms with periods of exactly 24 hours, i.e. coinciding with that of the day–night cycle. Thus the external influences accompanying the day–night alternation are not necessary for the maintenance or the generation of circadian rhythmicity, but are necessary for its synchronization with the Earth's rotation. Further, it appears that it is not only natural time cues that have the capacity to act as zeitgebers, i.e. to synchronize circadian rhythms, but also that artificial zeitgebers of various types can do so.

In order to examine the regularities in circadian rhythmicity, two types of experiment under temporal isolation will be considered. On the one hand, experiments under constant experimental conditions, where no natural or artificial time cues are present, are relevant in order to evaluate purely internal influences. On the other hand, experiments under the influence of artificial zeitgebers of various types are relevant in order to evaluate the combined influence of internal and external factors. Only by considering the results of many different types of isolation experiment can we deduce the properties of the human circadian system and their practical implications.

The experiments discussed in this chapter have all been performed in isolation units that have been described in detail elsewhere (Wever, 1979a). In these units, the subjects are isolated from all known natural time cues, including environmental noise. Various types of stimuli can be introduced into the units, either operating continuously or varying according to any predetermined schedule to give artificial time cues. Some of these stimuli can be introduced without the knowledge of, or being perceptible to, the subjects. In order to guarantee a 'steady state' in the parameters observed, and hence to ensure the consistency of the results, the experiments need to be long-term, and typically are of about 4 weeks' duration.

2.2 FREE-RUNNING RHYTHMS

Under constant conditions, i.e. without any time cues, human circadian rhythms free-run (see Figure 2.1) and are remarkably resistant to various stimuli. The mean free-running period from 156 subjects who have been tested under constant conditions is 25.00 ± 0.50 hours (for reasons to be discussed later, the periods of sleep–wake rhythms can show different values). This small interindividual

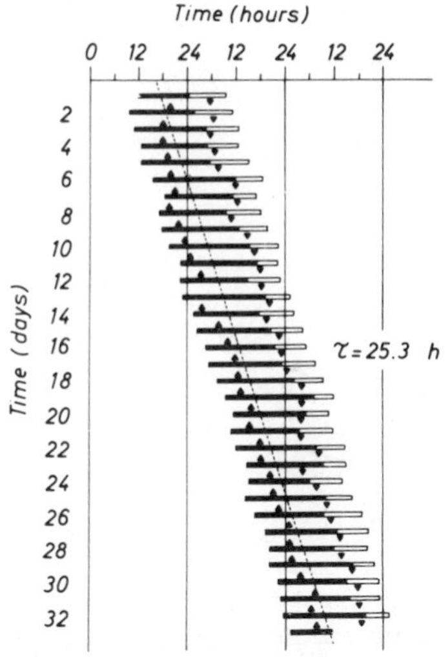

Figure 2.1 An example of free-running human circadian rhythms, under constant environmental conditions. Wake (solid bars), sleep (open bars), and the maximum (▲) and minimum (▼) of the continuously recorded rectal temperature are plotted as a function of time of day (abscissa). Successive days are plotted beneath one another. After transients lasting a few days (in which temperature phase advanced relative to the sleep–wake cycle), all the measured rhythms ran in synchrony with a period of 25.3 h

variability in the periods is all the more remarkable since it includes data from subjects living under various experimental conditions. Thus, for example, studies in which groups of subjects have been isolated together, and have had social contacts with one another, have yielded the same results as experiments with singly isolated subjects (Wever, 1975b). It has also been shown that the relative deprivation of physical activity due to limited space does not influence the results. Thus, requiring subjects to perform hard physical work on a bicycle ergometer during one section of a study, and to refrain from any avoidable activity during another section of the same study, had no effect on the free-running period (Wever, 1979b).

It has also been shown that the small interindividual range of free-running periods is considerably larger than the intraindividual range obtained from a number of subjects who have taken part in more than one experiment at intervals of 1–5 years. Indeed, not only were the free-running periods remarkably similar in these studies, but so were all the other rhythm parameters including the individual shape; so much so that the rhythm pattern could be used as an individual characteristic in a similar manner to a finger-print (Wever, 1983b).

When the transition from a 24-hour day to free-running rhythms with a period of about 25 hours occurs, the phase relationship between most overt rhythms varies over the course of several days (cf. Figure 2.1). For example, on a 24-hour day, the maximum of deep body temperature of healthy subjects occurs during the second half of the wake episode, and the minimum during the last part of the sleep episode, such that the decrease in deep body temperature occurs mainly during sleep (see Figure 2.2). However, in a free-running state the temperature maximum consistently occurs during the first half of the wake episode and the minimum at the beginning of the sleep episode, or even at the end of the wake

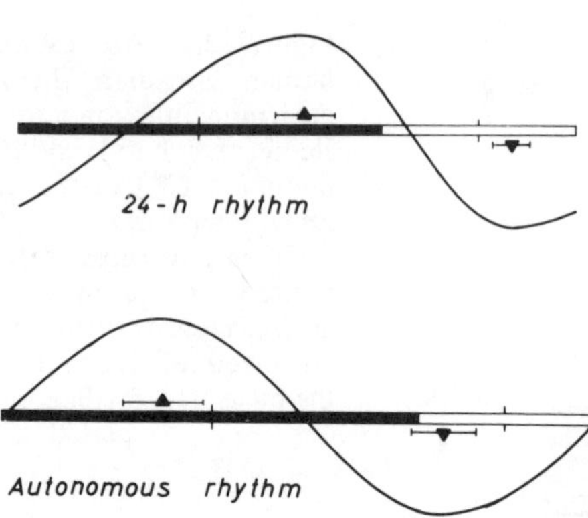

Figure 2.2 Average cycles (over many subjects and many days each) of sleep–wake and rectal temperature, on a 24-h day (upper), and free-running under constant conditions (lower). The midpoints of the sleep and wake episodes are indicated, as are the means and standard deviations of the positions of the maximum and minimum temperature values

episode, with the consequence that deep body temperature increases during sleep (as it does in the 26-hour day; see below). This reversal in the course of body temperature during sleep has consequences with respect to the structure of sleep. On a 24-hour day, REM sleep propensity is smallest at the beginning of sleep and increases over the period of sleep with decreasing body temperature. However, in a free-running state REM sleep propensity shows the opposite trend and is largest at the beginning of sleep and decreases over the sleep period with increasing body temperature (Wever, 1982).

One might suppose that the internal phase shift accompanying the transition between synchronized 24-hour rhythms and free-running rhythms is due to the considerable change in all living circumstances, combined with the experimental transition between a 24-hour day and constant conditions under temporal isolation. This argument, however, can be rejected by considering experiments where the transition was induced by a zeitgeber that was imperceivable to the subjects (e.g. weak electromagnetic fields). Even when a subject does not consciously perceive this transition his rhythms clearly show these internal phase shifts. Thus, it would appear that these transitions are not due to a behavioural change.

When in a steady state free-running sleep–wake rhythms show a number of regularities (Figure 2.1). One of these concerns the relative variability of different measures of the sleep–wake cycle. Sleep onset fluctuates around the mean fairly consistently, and to a far greater extent than wake onset or the midpoint of sleep which is the least fluctuating measure of phase. Thus sleep and wake onset do not fluctuate independently of one another but show a negative relationship. A wake episode that is longer than the average for a particular subject is typically followed by a shorter than average sleep episode and vice versa. Other serial correlations concern the whole sleep–wake cycle, measured from one wake onset to the next, from one sleep onset to the next, or from some other reference phase. Any deviation in the duration of a cycle from the long-term average is subsequently corrected by opposite deviations in the duration of the following, and even of the following but one, cycle. This constitutes a stabilization mechanism which can also be observed in other overt rhythms such as that in deep body temperature. These negative serial correlations, between adjacent sleep and wake episodes, and between successive sleep–wake cycles, are very highly significant ($p<10^{-12}$) (Wever, 1984a).

If any given parameter of a free-running rhythm changes as a result of an experimental manipulation such as a change in the magnitude of a continuously operating controlling stimulus, various other rhythm parameters will also change systematically. Thus, if the period shortens, the fraction of sleep decreases, the variability in wake (and to a lesser extent sleep) onset decreases, the mean value and amplitude of the rhythm in deep body temperature increases, the variability of this rhythm decreases, and the shape of this rhythm changes from being skewed to the right to being skewed to the left. A lengthening of the period is accompanied by opposite changes in all these parameters (Wever, 1979a). In contrast to these numerous intraindividual relationships, interindividual relationships are rather rare, and to date only a significant correlation between the amplitude of the temperature rhythm and the fraction of sleep, such that subjects with large amplitudes sleep longer has been established (Wever, 1981).

2.3 ENTRAINED RHYTHMS

2.3.1 Artificial zeitgebers

Various types of stimuli can influence the circadian system. These can be of a physical nature such as light, which is the most effective stimulus in most species but is only effective in man if it exceeds an intensity threshold of several thousand lux, or electromagnetic fields which are effective in man, as well as other species, despite the fact that they are imperceptible. Effective stimuli can also be of a chemical nature, and in animal studies various hormones and substances such as heavy water (D_2O) have been shown to influence circadian rhythms. Behavioural stimuli, such as social contacts, are particularly salient in man, and may also affect the circadian rhythms of lower species.

In the case of human circadian rhythms it has been shown that those stimuli which are able to operate as zeitgebers can also modify free-running rhythms when presented continuously (Wever, 1979a). Such modification affects all rhythm parameters simultaneously, and can result in arrhythmicity of the system. However, even in this extreme case it can be shown that the feedback mechanism (i.e. the 'clock' or 'oscillator') continues to operate, despite the fact that it has insufficient strength to compensate for the dissipation of oscillatory energy, and hence to result in measurable self-sustaining rhythms (Wever, 1980b). Finally, it is interesting to note that the removal of certain organs, in particular the pineal in birds, or the suprachiasmatic nuclei (SCN) in mammals, can also result in a similar arrhythmicity.

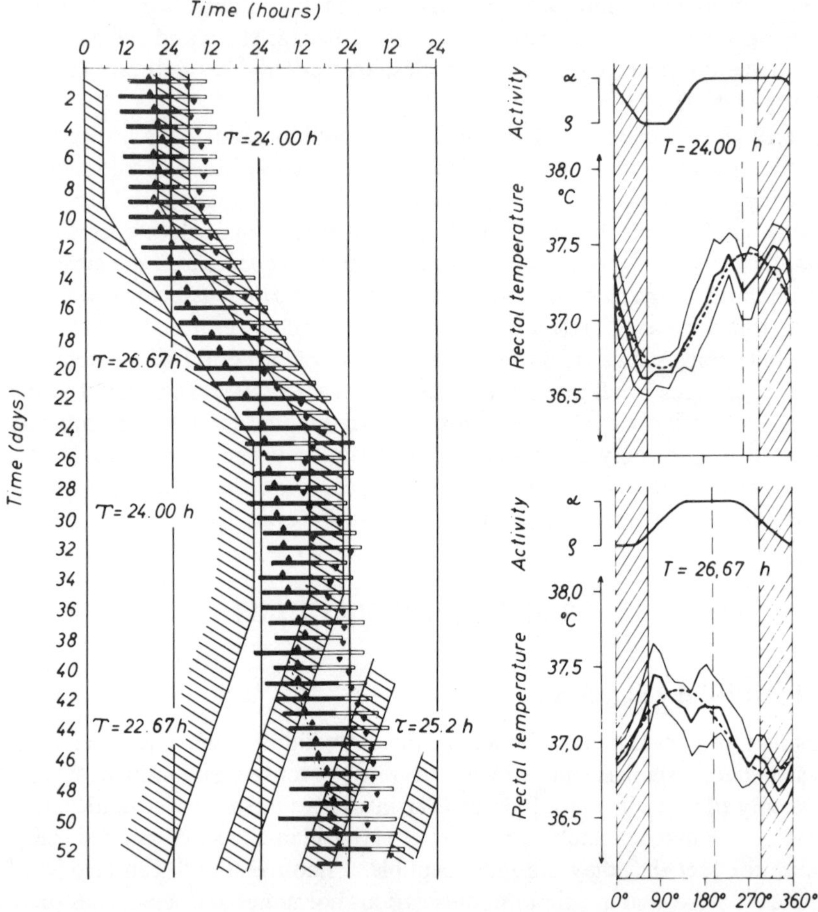

Figure 2.3 An example of a human circadian rhythm under the influence of an artificial zeitgeber, with different periods in the four successive sections. The left-hand panel shows the successive wake episodes (solid bars) and sleep episodes (open bars) and the maximum (▲) and minimum (▼) values of the rectal temperature rhythm. All the rhythms were synchronized to the zeitgeber in the first three sections, but free-ran (in spite of the zeitgeber) in the fourth section. The right-hand panels show the educed cycles of sleep–wake and rectal temperature (with standard deviations) and the best-fitting sine wave (dotted line), calculated from the first two sections and plotted relative to the zeitgebers

Under the influence of external zeitgebers, circadian rhythms remain synchronized as long as the period of the zeitgebers is within a limited 'range of entrainment' (see Figure 2.3), which for human rhythms is from about 23 to 27 hours. Within this range of entrainment, the phase relationship of the rhythms to the zeitgeber, and most internal phase relationships between different overt rhythms, vary systematically with the period. Thus, the shorter the zeitgeber period, the later is the phase of all rhythms relative to the zeitgeber, the later is the phase of the rhythm in deep body temperature relative to the sleep–wake cycle, and the larger is the fraction of sleep (Figure 2.3, right diagram).

In a 24-hour day where sleep is relatively long, the minimum of deep body temperature consistently occurs close to the end of sleep, but in a 26-hour day where sleep is relatively short it occurs shortly after sleep onset. However, in a 25-hour day, where the zeitgeber period coincides more or less with the intrinsic period, the temperature minimum does not occur in the middle of the sleep episode as might be expected, but fluctuates in an irregular fashion from one sleep episode to the next, and is often difficult to determine. The same changes in these internal phase relationships would occur if the zeitgeber period remained constant, but the intrinsic period of the rhythm changed. Thus, if people had intrinsic periods close to 24 hours, the phase position of their temperature minima would be unstable under the natural 24-hour day. The significant deviation of the free-running period of healthy subjects from 24 hours may be of adaptive value in avoiding this instability that occurs with coinciding intrinsic and zeitgeber periods.

If the period of the zeitgebers is outside the range of entrainment, circadian rhythms free-run (Figure 2.3, fourth experimental section), but not completely independently of the zeitgeber. Rather, they show the phenomenon of 'relative coordination' in which all phase relationships to the zeitgeber may occur over successive cycles, but not with equal frequencies, resulting in the rhythm's phases showing a scalloping pattern. If the zeitgeber period is close to the limit of entrainment, 'relative entrainment' may occur in which a rhythm is, on average, synchronized with the zeitgebers, but shows periodically fluctuating phase relationships.

2.3.2 Phase-shift studies

The use of artificial zeitgebers enables us to simulate shiftwork and 'jet-lag' by shifting the phase rather than changing the period (Wever, 1980a). If the subject is informed of the shift, and consequently is aware that he is living in temporal disagreement with the environment, shiftwork is simulated. If, however, the subject is not informed of the shift, and fails to become aware of it, he will falsely assume that he continues to live in temporal agreement with the environment and transmeridian flights are simulated. The latter type of experiment in particular leads to highly reliable results which, in principle, are in agreement with those of real flight experiments. All rhythms adapt to the shifted zeitgebers within a few days, but the rhythms of different variables adjust at different rates such that, for example, the sleep–wake rhythm adjusts faster than the rhythm in deep body temperature. The relationship between reentrainment behaviour and rhythm parameters measured before the shift, allows certain predictions to be made: (i) the larger the circadian temperature amplitude of a subject and hence the larger his sleep fraction (see above), the longer complete reentrainment will take, and (ii) the earlier the phase of a subject's temperature rhythm, or the more he is a 'morning type' (see Chapter 3), the greater the impairment of his objectively measured performance and his subjectively scored well-being. Similar results have been obtained from shiftwork studies (Reinberg *et al.*, 1978).

2.4 INTERNAL DESYNCHRONIZATION

2.4.1 Spontaneous desynchronization

All the results of isolation experiments discussed so far have originated from experiments in which the measured overt rhythms all ran in mutual synchrony, at least after the dissipation of any initial dissociation. Most experiments are, in fact, of this type although in some subjects (51 out of 156 in the present experimental series) the overt rhythms of different variables spontaneously ran with different periods (Figure 2.4). This state of 'spontaneous internal desynchronization' can

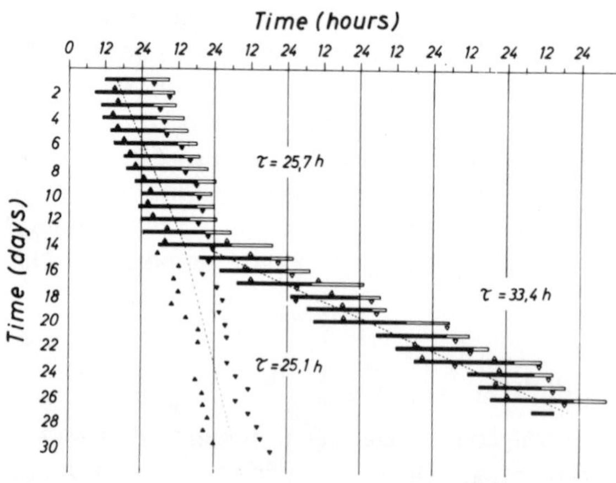

Figure 2.4 An example of spontaneous internal desynchronization of human circadian rhythms. After several cycles in which the rhythms were synchronized and ran with a period of 25.7 h, the sleep–wake cycle lengthened to a mean period of 33.4 hours, while the temperature rhythm shortened to a period of 25.1 h. Other details as for Figure 2.1

occur either from the beginning of an experiment, or from some point during the course of it. This state is characterized by the overt rhythm of deep body temperature running with a period close to 25 hours (as in internally synchronized rhythms), but the overt sleep–wake rhythm running with a greatly deviating period (ranging from 12 to 65 hours in the present experiments).

The period of most other overt rhythms coincides with that of the temperature rhythm or with that of the sleep–wake rhythm. The propensity to desynchronize in this manner depends to some extent on the experimental conditions. It is, for example, significantly greater when a subject lives in a self-controlled light–dark cycle, and switches the lights on when he gets up and off when he goes to sleep, than under constant illumination. However, individual differences are also important, with internal desynchronization being considerably more likely in older subjects, and in subjects with higher neuroticism scores (Wever, 1979a).

2.4.2 Individual differences

The subjects who exhibit spontaneous internal desynchronization during the course of a study have reliably shorter or longer synchronized free-running periods than those who do not exhibit this phenomenon. Further, those with shorter periods than normal show a strong tendency to desynchronize by a shortening of the sleep–wake cycle, while those with longer periods than normal desynchronize by a lengthening of their sleep–wake cycle. Thus, shortly after the beginning of a study it is possible to predict not only whether internal desynchronization will occur, but also whether it will be achieved by a shortening or lengthening of the sleep–wake cycle, simply by examining the free-running period.

It is commonly assumed that morning and evening types differ in their free-running period (see Chapters 3 and 18), and thus morning types should be more likely to desynchronize by a shortening of the sleep–wake cycle, while evening types do so by lengthening it. Unfortunately, this prediction has yet to be tested, although a similar pattern of results *has* recently been established for sex differences. Under internally synchronized conditions the free-running period of females is on average 28 minutes shorter than that of males (Wever, 1984a). Further, although females are more likely to desynchronize by a shortening of their sleep–wake cycle than males, there is no subsequent difference in the period of their desynchronized free-running temperature rhythms. Hence, it would appear that the main difference between the sexes is in the intrinsic period of their sleep–wake cycles rather than in their temperature rhythm (Wever, 1984b). Indeed, under internally synchronized conditions the sleep fraction of females is on average 18 per cent larger than that of males (Wever, 1984a), but this difference disappears under internal desynchronization due to a greater change in the sleep fraction of females. Taken together, these findings suggest that females may be more prone to various rhythm disorders than males.

2.4.3 Multioscillatory control

These phenomena are most compatible with a multioscillator model of the human circadian system (Wever, 1975a). In this model the various overt rhythms are jointly controlled by a few basic oscillators (in the simplest case by two oscillators) which have different oscillatory strengths, and which have been designated as type I, type II, etc., according to their strengths. Each overt rhythm is assumed to be controlled by all these basic oscillators but to very different extents. For example, deep body temperature is assumed to be predominantly controlled by the (stronger) type I oscillator, but is also influenced by all the other oscillators, while the sleep–wake is predominantly controlled by the (weaker) type II oscillator, but again all the other oscillators influence it.

These basic oscillators are in turn controlled by external stimuli, and influence one another. If their intrinsic periods are close enough together, they synchronize and, hence, appear outwardly as only one oscillator. The period of this 'combined oscillator' is a compromise between the intrinsic periods of the individual participating oscillators, with the contribution of each oscillator depending on its oscillatory strength. Thus, when internal desynchronization occurs, the period of the temperature rhythm changes in the opposite direction to that of the sleep–wake cycle, but to a much smaller extent. If the differences between the intrinsic periods of the different basic oscillators exceed a certain limit, i.e. the mutual range of entrainment, their mutual interaction is insufficient to synchronize them and they free-run separately.

The residual interaction between the oscillators is manifested in the phenomenon of 'internal relative coordination' in which both the phase and amplitude of different overt rhythms, and especially the sleep–wake cycle, vary systematically. Although any internal phase relationship between the rhythms of sleep–wake and deep body temperature can occur during internal desynchronization, phase relationships that are similar to those in internal synchronization are more frequent than others. Consequently, the duration of a wake or sleep episode depends on its phase position within the temperature cycle. An episode of wake or sleep that starts during the ascending section of the temperature cycle will be longer than one that starts during the descending section of the temperature cycle. Sleep onset occurs most frequently shortly before a temperature minimum, while wake onset most frequently occurs during the ascending section of the temperature cycle. Similarly, the parameters of the temperature rhythm, including its amplitude, depend on its temporal relationship to the sleep–wake cycle (Zulley and Wever, 1982). It is also noteworthy that the sleep fraction is on average about 13 per cent smaller than normal during internal desynchronization (Wever, 1982).

2.4.4 Induced internal desynchronization

It is clear from the results discussed so far that the state of internal desynchronization is of particular importance in throwing light on the nature of the circadian system. Fortunately, although only about a third of the subjects spontaneously show internal desynchronization, it can be *induced* by means of artificial zeitgebers in all subjects. If the period of these zeitgebers is within the range of entrainment of one oscillator, but outside that of another, rhythms predominantly controlled by the former will remain entrained, while those predominantly controlled by the latter will free-run, i.e. a state of 'partial synchronization' will occur.

Thus a strong zeitgeber with a period of less than 22 hours or more than 28 hours is outside the range of entrainment of the 'temperature oscillator' but within that of the 'sleep–wake oscillator'. Consequently, the temperature rhythm free-runs, with a scalloping phase pattern reflecting relative coordination, while the sleep–wake cycle remains entrained. Alternatively, the zeitgeber period can be changed at certain points within the study. A study might start with a zeitgeber period to which all the measured overt rhythms remain entrained, but which is subsequently shortened or lengthened beyond the limit of entrainment of some, but not all, of the rhythms under consideration. The extreme case of this type of study is one in which the period of the zeitgebers is shortened or lengthened by a small amount (e.g. 5 minutes) on each sleep–wake cycle.

In these 'fractional desynchronization' studies each overt rhythm follows the zeitgebers down or up to a certain period after which it free-runs (see Figure 2.5).

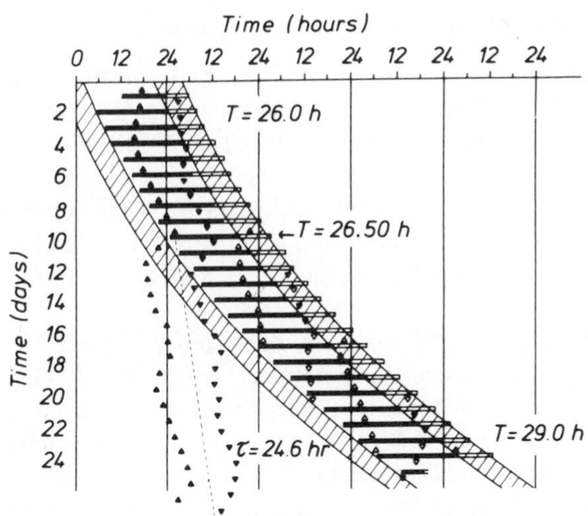

Figure 2.5 An example of a 'fractional desynchronization' study in which the artificial light–dark cycle (dark = shaded area) was progressively lengthened by 10 min per cycle from 26.0 h to 29 h. The sleep–wake cycle remained entrained up to 29 h, while the temperature rhythm broke out at a period of 26 hours 50 minutes, and subsequently free-ran with a period of 24.6 h

This allows a very precise determination of each rhythm's limit of entrainment to be made, and also allows us to determine whether or not any two given rhythms can be separated from one another. Thus we can examine the relationship between two variables by seeing whether the rhythms that occur in them can be separated. In general, it transpires that many of the physiological rhythms that have been studied to date can be separated, e.g. temperature, sleep–wake, and the urinary excretion of sodium and potassium, suggesting some independence of these variables.

The fractional desynchronization method also allows us to examine the relative effectiveness of different zeitgebers. For example, if the level of illumination of an artificial light–dark cycle is increased beyond a threshold of several thousand lux, the range of entrainment of the temperature rhythm is increased considerably (Wever *et al.*, 1983). In addition, we can examine the internal interaction between the oscillators within the circadian system by determining the degree to which one oscillator can act as a zeitgeber for another. Thus, simply giving motivated subjects auditory signals as to when to sleep and wake in otherwise constant conditions, has been shown to operate as an 'internal zeitgeber' on all the other overt rhythms that were measured. Indeed, the limit of entrainment of these latter rhythms was very similar to that obtained with normal external zeitgebers (Wever, 1983a).

2.4.5 Performance rhythms and masking effects

One advantage of these induced internal desynchronization studies is that the subject is not in a 'time-free' environment, and can thus be given regular signals or cues to rate his mood or do performance tests, etc. (although, of course, not on a 24-hour timescale). Indeed, the subject can even be woken from sleep to do these tests, and thus relatively continuous data can be obtained. Not surprisingly, performance readings taken during the sleep period in this manner tend to be depressed relative to those taken at other times, and this is partially due to what is known as a 'masking' effect.

In fact, masking effects occur in many other rhythms, including body temperature, and indeed occur in internally synchronized subjects. However, they are particularly obvious in internally desynchronized subjects where circadian variations can be separated from masking-induced variations (evoked by sleep–wake alternations) since they run with different periods. In general, deep body temperature is fairly consistently higher during wake than during sleep, with overshoots and undershoots in temperature occurring at the transitions between wake and sleep of about 50 per cent of the steady state changes (Figure 2.6, upper left). Moreover, educed average cycles can be calculated from temperature data obtained exclusively during the wake episodes and compared to those for temperature data obtained exclusively during the sleep episodes (Figure 2.6, upper right). While both curves are very similar in shape they are typically separated from each other by about 0.3°C due to a masking effect of sleep. There

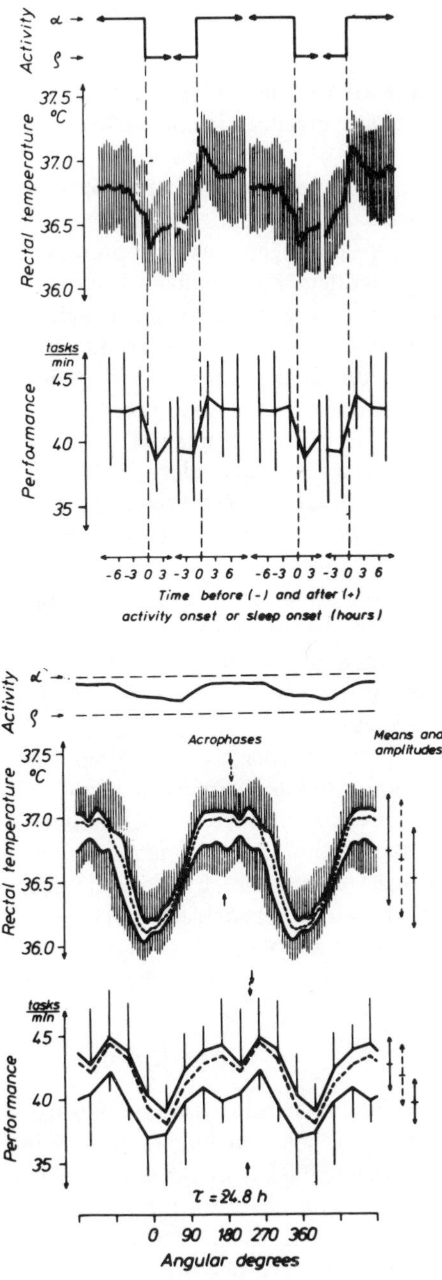

Figure 2.6 The educed cycles of sleep–wake, rectal temperature and performance (computation speed) from an experiment in which a subject lived under the influence of a strong 28-h zeitgeber for 4 weeks and, hence, showed partial synchronization. Left: The data plotted relative to sleep onset and wake onset for several hours before and after these points. Right: The data plotted according to the dominant period of the temperature rhythm, calculated from data obtained exclusively during wake episodes (upper trace) or exclusively during sleep episodes (lower traces), or both (dotted lines)

is also a slight phase dependence of the masking effect in that the sleep temperature curve is phase advanced in comparison to the wake curve by about 1 hour.

Very similar effects can be seen in the comparable performance scores (Figure 2.6, lower panels), with the sleep performance curve being fairly consistently lower than the wake one. The magnitude of this masking effect in performance is, however, typically smaller than the circadian variation. There also appears to be a 'post-lunch dip' in performance in both curves, despite the fact that these curves represent a 24.8-hour rhythm while the eating of lunch took place once every 28 hours. Clearly, this is strong evidence for the view that at least part of the 'post-lunch dip' has nothing to do with the ingestion of food but rather is controlled by the body temperature rhythm (see Chapter 4).

Masking effects of this type, which are largely associated with the sleep–wake activity cycle of the subject, are important in the context of shiftwork and jet-lag since they can lead to spurious conclusions regarding the adjustment of rhythms. It is thus clearly necessary to distinguish between the masking effect of an altered sleep–wake cycle, and the more fundamental rhythmic effect that might result from the adjustment of the 'sleep–wake' oscillator. In practical situations it is often difficult to obtain adequate data to allow us to distinguish between these two effects. However, as we have seen, such a distinction is possible in induced desynchronization studies.

Circadian rhythms in performance are considered in more detail in Chapter 4. However, it is worth noting that in many of the studies discussed in this chapter subjects have been required to perform a computation test (the Pauli-test) and the results indicate that the rhythm in performance on this task is approximately equally likely to follow the temperature rhythm or the sleep–wake cycle. Which of these it follows varies from subject to subject, and from one condition to another. The most consistent, but somewhat paradoxical, finding is that both performance on this task, and the subject's mood, tend to be better when the subject is internally desynchronized.

2.5 CONCLUSIONS

The main conclusion to be drawn from the studies discussed in this chapter is that man's physiological and psychological circadian rhythms seem to be controlled by a multioscillatory system. This is in agreement with a simple mathematical model originally proposed to account for the results from animal studies, and allows us to account for a wide range of findings in terms of basic laws of oscillatory systems. There is a strong need for further studies of the kind discussed in this chapter to enable further refinement of this model. Such refinement will not only have important theoretical implications, but may have tremendous practical application in the field of abnormal work hours. In the future, basic principles derived from this type of model may allow us to predict the likely adjustment to any given shift system, and to develop counter measures or coping strategies that minimize the detrimental effects of such systems.

Hours of Work
Edited by S. Folkard and T.H. Monk

Chapter 3

Individual Differences in Circadian Rhythms

Gerard Kerkhof

CONTENTS

ABSTRACT

This chapter presents an overview of studies that have been conducted in an attempt to determine and categorize individual differences in circadian rhythms. The results of a diurnal study on selected morning-type and evening-type subjects are presented. In addition, differences related to personality, age and sex are discussed, although the emphasis is placed on morningness–eveningness in view of indications that strongly suggest a relationship with fundamental properties of the circadian system. Finally, attention is given to studies which have revealed a relationship between individual differences in the steady state, and individual differences in the circadian response to external temporal changes.

3.1 INTRODUCTION

One of the essential characteristics of the circadian system is the persistence of its rhythmicity in the absence of rhythmic influences from the outside (see Chapters 1 and 2). Variations in the value of the free-running period may be due entirely to error of measurement. They may, however, also contain a systematic component. If this is the case, it is theoretically possible to relate this systematic component to individual differences in various rhythm parameters. This has been corroborated for the activity rhythm in animal studies which have shown that differences in the free-running period (even of the order of half an hour) lead to differences in the shape, the amplitude, and the external phase position of the rhythm when it is observed under normal light–dark conditions (Aschoff, 1965; Aschoff, Saint Paul and Wever, 1971). The relationship between the free-running period and the external phase position of a rhythm under normal conditions has led some authors to postulate a relationship between the free-running period and the score of people on a morningness–eveningness questionnaire. So-called morning-type (M-type) people, characterized by a relatively advanced sleep-wake rhythm, would then have a shorter free-running period than eveningness-type (E-type) people, known by their relatively delayed sleep–wake rhythm (see Kerkhof, 1985).

Differentiating people according to their degree of morningness–eveningness, however, does not cover all individual differences that have been observed. Differences associated with personality, sex and age have also been found in rhythm parameters. It is as yet, however, unclear how these factors may relate to the functioning of the circadian system. In evaluating their impact, the possibility has to be considered that they exert their influence directly upon the rhythmic variable(s), and do not relate to the functioning of the circadian system itself. Whatever the case, it appears impossible to reduce all individual differences to a common cause on the basis of the available evidence. In the following, these differences will thus be discussed under separate headings.

3.2 MORNING TYPES AND EVENING TYPES

3.2.1 Selection

Typically, M-type and E-type subjects are selected on the basis of a questionnaire which consists of items relating to habitual arising and bedtimes, preferred times of physical and mental performance, and subjective fatigue after arising and before going to bed. For samples of a few hundred subjects, the questionnaire scores are usually normally distributed. Studies which specifically address themselves to the question of morningness–eveningness typically select only subjects with extremely high and extremely low scores. For a random sample of subjects this means that when, for example, the widely used questionnaire of Horne and Östberg (Horne and Östberg, 1976) is employed, on average only 5 per cent 'extreme M-types' and 5 per cent 'extreme E-types' will be encountered. When these extreme groups have been asked to record their sleeptimes for several weeks, it has been found that M-types go to bed at night and arise in the morning about 80 minutes earlier than E-types (Horne and Östberg, 1977; Foret *et al*, 1982; Kerkhof, 1984; Webb and Bonnet, 1978). Studies of similarly selected groups have shown reliable differences between the two types of subjects in the course of a day of various rhythmic variables. This is illustrated in the next section with some results of a diurnal study recently conducted by the present author.

3.2.2 A diurnal study

Figure 3.1 summarizes the results of a study of eight extreme M-type and eight extreme E-type subjects who performed an auditory reaction time task at six different times of day, one session per day. In this task, subjects were given 30 presentations of a warning tone, followed after 1.5 seconds by an identical second tone. The subjects were instructed to make a fast button press in response to the second of each pair of tones.

The mean values of measurements of oral temperature just before and after the task showed an increment over the day for both groups of subjects (Figure 3.1A).

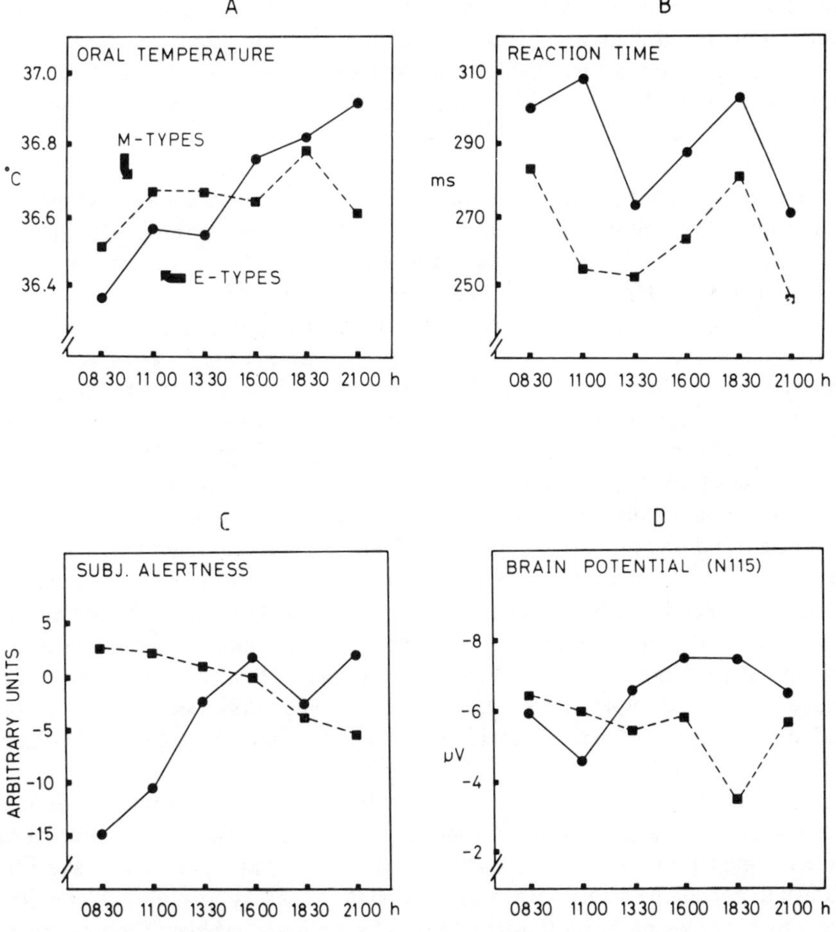

Figure 3.1 Mean values of (A) oral temperature; (B) reaction time; (C) subjective alertness; and (D) the amplitude of the N115 brain potential component elicited by the warning tone, as a function of the time of day. Values have been separately averaged across eight M-types (broken lines) and eight E-types (solid lines)

For the M-types, however, the range of values over which the temperature increased was considerably smaller than the range for the E-types. During the morning sessions the M-types attained higher values than the E-types, while for the evening sessions the reverse applied. Thus, at least with regard to the morning and the evening sessions, the two groups could be differentiated on the basis of their temperature values. The trends of reaction speed were very similar for the two groups (Figure 3.1B). The fastest responses were recorded during the late morning and during the evening, with the morning peak being somewhat advanced for the M-types as compared with the E-types.

The curves of Figures 3.1A and 3.1B diverge considerably, suggesting that they may not be driven by the same internal circadian process. In this type of study, however, it is impossible to exclude the possibility that the two variables are affected unequally by endogenous and exogenous factors, i.e. by factors which are internal or external to the circadian system. In particular, human performance is known to be very susceptible to fluctuations in motivation, which may in turn have a rhythmic component. An unequal influence of endogenous and exogenous components on two variables may obscure a common endogenous influence. Temporal isolation studies have, however, shown fairly convincingly that the rhythms of body temperature and computational performance can sometimes run independently of each other (Wever, 1979a).

A circadian rhythm of arousal is often assumed to underlie diurnal variations in performance (see Chapter 4). In an attempt to assess the level of arousal at different times of day, the subjects in the present study were asked to complete a questionnaire consisting of arousal-descriptive adjectives against which they rated their momentary level of subjective alertness. Figure 3.1C presents the mean values for the two groups of subjects. The M-types showed a maximum in the morning and a decreasing trend over the day, while the E-types showed the opposite trend. In comparing Figures 3.1B and 3.1C it is evident that subjective alertness is a bad predictor of reaction time performance. However, as will be seen in Chapter 4, it is becoming increasingly clear that the particular form of the performance rhythms is determined by the load that is placed upon the various aspects of performance, such as the sensory, perceptual, cognitive and motor processes. For example, tasks which depend heavily upon speed follow a rather different time course from those which have a large memory component (Folkard and Monk, 1980).

The recording of electrical brain activity (the so-called brain potentials) promises to be a valuable tool in the identification of the brain processes involved in performance rhythms. Some components of these brain potentials have been shown to correlate closely with specific modes of sensory, perceptual, cognitive and motor processes. In particular, the N115 amplitude has been shown to relate to the behaviour of orienting towards stimuli, and to vary with the amount of stimulus-related arousal (Näätänen and Michie, 1979; Öhman and Lader, 1977). In the present study, recordings were made of the N115 component elicited by the warning tone. For the M-types the mean values of the N115 amplitude showed a general decrement over the day, while the mean values for the E-types tended to increase over the day (see Figure 3.1D). The correspondence between the curves of Figures 3.1C and 3.1D suggests that the observed variations in subjective alertness may apply mainly to perceptual processes and not to other (e.g. response-related) processes. In fact, behavioural measures of perceptual accuracy have been observed to follow a course which closely resembles the courses of subjective alertness and the N115 amplitude as recorded in the present study (Horne *et al.*, 1980).

3.2.3 Rhythm parameters

More insight into individual differences in rhythm parameters may be gained from recordings over one or more periods of 24 hours. Figure 3.2 summarizes the temperature findings of eleven studies which have employed M-type and E-type subjects (Akerstedt and Fröberg, 1976a; Breithaupt *et al.*, 1981; Fröberg, 1977; Hildebrandt and Strattman, 1979; Horne and Östberg, 1976; Horne *et al.*, 1980; Kerkhof, 1982; Kerkhof *et al.*, 1984; Östberg, 1973b; Östberg and McKnicholl, 1973; Patkai, 1971b).

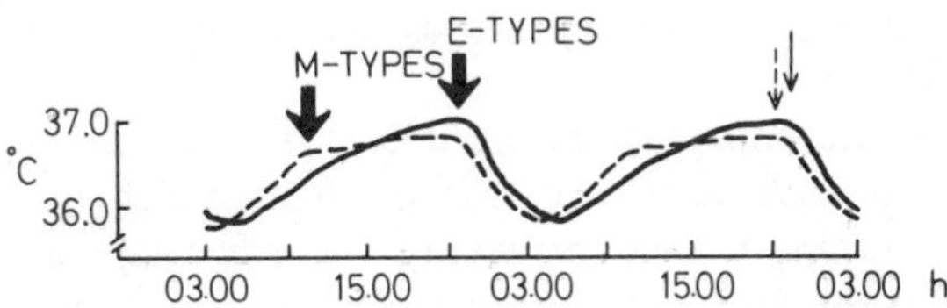

Figure 3.2 The daily course of body temperature for M-types (broken line) and E-types (solid line). The curves have been drawn on the basis of the compiled results of eleven studies. For the sake of clarity two periods of 24 hours have been depicted. The small arrows indicate the times at which the M-types and the E-types reach their respective maximum values

The results have been double plotted, i.e. plotted for two successive periods of 24 hours. Clearly, a difference in time of temperature maximum between M-types and E-types appears to be a rather incomplete description of the two curves depicted in Figure 3.2. Rather there appears to be a substantial difference between the shapes of the two curves, with the curve for the E-types being more negatively skewed (to the right) than that for the M-types. Indeed, a detailed consideration of all rhythm parameters for M-types and E-types suggests the existence of a difference in fundamental properties of the circadian system (Kerkhof, 1985). Subjective alertness peaks for the two types differ by an average of 171 minutes, for example.

3.3 PERSONALITY, AGE AND SEX

It has already been suggested in the foregoing that personality variables may be responsible for some of the individual differences in circadian rhythms. Various studies have indeed shown a relationship between personality variables and sleep parameters, of which the times of retiring at night and awakening in the morning appear to be the most relevant (Taub *et al.*, 1978). In fact, early studies of individual differences concentrated almost exclusively upon the trait of introversion-extraversion. The general finding implied that introverts have an earlier phase position than extraverts with regard to the rhythms of sleeping and waking, body temperature and performance. A leading hypothesis holds that introverts are chronically more aroused or have a higher level of arousability than extraverts. On the basis of this hypothesis, and the notion that the level of arousal varies over the day, attempts have been made to understand the differences between introverts and extraverts with respect to their diurnal trends of performance. These attempts, however, have been complicated by findings indicating the multivariate nature of arousal as well as that of performance (Eysenck and Folkard, 1980). Indeed, there is some evidence showing that the trait of introversion–extraversion may not be totally independent of that of morningness–eveningness. Not only has a weak correlation between the two measures been found, but also there appears to be some correspondence with regard to the tonic level of arousal. Thus, M-types have been observed to have a greater overall autonomous responsiveness than E-types (Hildebrandt, 1980; Kerkhof *et al.*, 1981).

With regard to the impact of ageing upon the circadian system, the most consistent finding across studies concerns the reduction of rhythm amplitude with age. This has been reported predominantly for body temperature, as e.g. in a recent study from the group of Weitzman (Weitzman, Moline, Czeisler and Zimmerman, 1982). These authors also report evidence of an age-dependent change in the temporal order of the circadian system. As compared with a group of 6 young subjects, 6 older subjects had their temperature rhythm advanced relative to mid-sleep, a result which agrees well with the finding of a positive correlation between age and morningness (Akerstedt and Torsvall, 1981a). The signs of a reduced strength of circadian control with age are in accordance with the common observation of greater susceptibility to the occurrence of rhythm disturbances.

The results of studies on sex differences in circadian rhythmicity are scanty and inconsistent. For rhythm parameters such as mean level, amplitude, shape and phase position contradictory findings have been reported. Recent reports by Wever (1984b), however, give indications of a sex difference in the temporal organization of the circadian system, leading to the prediction that females will show more M-type behavior than males.

3.4 CONCLUDING REMARKS

It is apparent from the results presented in this chapter that in the steady state people differ in their functioning at different times of day, as assessed by subjective, behavioural and physiological measures. These differences have been discussed in relation to diurnal type, personality, sex and age. Considering the available evidence, the most consistent individual differences appear to be those associated with morningness–eveningness. Variables related to personality, sex and age seem to be of secondary importance in this respect. It remains uncertain, however, to what extent these categories may be interrelated. Some studies have presented indications of correlation, in particular between morningness and introversion. Others have observed a relationship between the internal temporal order of the circadian system and measures of neuroticism and depression. An important question in this context is whether individual differences in the characteristics of the circadian system accentuate or even underlie the development of particular personality traits.

A second question concerns the effects of changes in the external time cues. A 6-hour phase advance of the light–dark cycle, for example, appears to be effective in causing bipolar depressive patients to change from a state of depression into one of hypomania (Wehr *et al.*, 1979). Whether these effects are mediated by the circadian system is, however, still open to discussion. Some findings suggest that it may even be possible to predict individual differences in the effects of changing temporal conditions. Thus, the larger the amplitude, and/or the earlier the phase position, of the temperature rhythm in the steady state, the longer it has been found to take the circadian system to adjust to a phase shift, e.g. as caused by transmeridian flights (Colquhoun, 1979; Wever, 1980a). Similar results have been reported for conditions prevailing in shiftwork. For example, in permanent shiftworkers, the mean amplitude of the temperature rhythm has been found to be negatively correlated with its phase adjustment after the first nightshift (Reinberg *et al.*, 1978). Further, indications have been found of a positive correlation between subjective well-being and the mean level of the temperature rhythm (Wever, 1980a). It might well be that individual differences in the response pattern of the circadian system following time-shifts are causally related to differences in subjective well-being. The study of individual differences may thus eventually lead to the realization of a means of predicting an individual's tolerance for time-shifts. In this context, it is worth noting the finding that a disproportionately large number of those who give up shiftwork turn out to be M-types (Akerstedt and Fröberg, 1976b).

Hours of Work
Edited by S. Folkard and T.H. Monk

Chapter 4
Circadian Performance Rhythms

Simon Folkard and Timothy H. Monk

CONTENTS

ABSTRACT

This chapter briefly reviews the evidence concerning circadian rhythms in human performance. It points to some of the problems met with in examining such rhythms, and the difficulties encountered in separating endogenous circadian rhythm effects from the masking effects of the sleep–wake cycle. It is shown that the effects of time of day on performance can be fairly substantial, and that the trend over the day depends on the nature of the task under consideration. The task demands also appear to determine which oscillator is dominant in controlling performance rhythms.

4.1 INTRODUCTION

Not surprisingly, the systematic and wide-ranging differences in physiological make-up that result from the circadian system are reflected in corresponding changes in mood and performance efficiency. These rhythms are not merely the step function that would result from poor performance at night being compared with better performance during the day, nor are they necessarily of trivial magnitude or peculiar to the individual. They can result in robust fluctuations of significant magnitude that are sometimes relatively predictable in form, given knowledge of the task being tested (Folkard and Monk, 1983). Even over the normal waking day, fluctuations in performance efficiency can be as much as ± 15 per cent of the daily mean.

4.2 PROBLEMS IN EXAMINING PERFORMANCE RHYTHMS

While the study of *any* circadian rhythm poses problems for the experimenter, this is particularly true in the case of performance rhythms. Thus, unlike physiological measures, performance measures show more or less marked practice or 'learning' effects over successive sessions. These can result in totally spurious conclusions being drawn with regard to the trend in performance over the day unless they are controlled for in some way. Two main approaches have been used to avoid these problems. The first, and most common, is to use a counterbalanced design such that level of practice is balanced over the times of day studied. The main disadvantages of this approach are that it assumes different subjects to show similar 'time of day' and 'practice' trends, and that the resultant 'normative' trend may only apply to relatively unpractised subjects. The second approach is to encourage subjects to practise to the point where any residual practice effects are of negligible magnitude in comparison with the time of day effects. The main disadvantages here are the cost in subject time, resulting in limited numbers of subjects being tested, and the fact that large numbers of parallel versions of each performance test are needed. This latter requisite effectively rules out many potentially useful measures of performance.

The second main problem encountered in studying performance rhythms stems from the inherent inaccuracy of performance testing. In order to obtain reliable measures, large numbers of trials need to be given and averaged over. This makes performance-testing relatively time-consuming and intrusive, requiring subjects to interrupt their ongoing activities. As a result, it is seldom possible to obtain more than about six readings in each 24-hour period, and indeed, some studies have been limited to two, despite the fact that an absolute minimum of four approximately equally spaced readings are required to estimate the phase and amplitude of a rhythm. This requirement for equal spacing raises the third major problem in this area, namely how to obtain performance measures when a subject would normally be asleep. Obtaining such readings requires either keeping subjects awake, or waking them up, to perform the task. In either case, this will result in disturbed sleep which may affect the subject's circadian rhythms (see Chapters 1 and 2). Our preferred solution for establishing normative trends is to obtain rather more than four readings spread over the whole of the normal waking period. This ensures that sleep is not disturbed, but means that no information is obtained as to the individual's potential for performance during the sleep period.

4.3 'TIME-OF-DAY' EFFECTS IN PERFORMANCE

Until recently, most research in this area examined variations in performance only over the normal *working* day, i.e. from about 0900 to 1800. Nor was any attempt made to distinguish variations in performance due to endogenous circadian factors from those associated with the exogenous masking effects of living on a normal day-oriented, or 'nychthemeral' routine (see Chapters 1 and 2). From a practical viewpoint, such a distinction may be relatively unimportant when one is considering variations in performance over the 'normal' day, but it *is* important when abnormal work hours are considered (see Chapter 19). It is also important when considering the underlying processes responsible for time-of-day effects.

4.3.1 Early educational research

Interestingly, studies of time-of-day effects in performance predate the coinage of the term "Circadian" by over half a century. Thus, in the later part of the nineteenth century, Ebbinghaus was aware of time-of-day differences in performance, and controlled for them in his pioneering work on memory. Much of the early work was concerned with the applied problem of determining the optimal time of day for the teaching of academic subjects, and while some of it was rather poor, much of it was very good (e.g. Laird, 1925). In view of the educational nature of the research, the tasks were usually more cognitive ones such as mental arithmetic and memory for prose. Although the results were far from uniform, the general trend was towards a morning superiority. Thus, Gates (1916) concluded that 'in general, the forenoon is the best time for strictly mental work... while the afternoon may best be taken up with school subjects in which motor factors are predominant'. The mechanism for these effects was held to be a build up in 'mental fatigue' over the day, thus (in our modern parlance) tying the performance rhythm to the sleep–wake oscillator. As we shall see below, this is in direct contrast to later approaches to the problem which were more concerned with the relationship between performance and temperature.

4.3.2 The arousal theory

In contrast to the earlier work, studies carried out in the 1930s by Kleitman in Chicago, and reported in his seminal book *Sleep and Wakefulness* (Kleitman, 1939, revised 1963), were concerned mainly with simple repetitive tasks such as card-dealing, which had a comparatively small cognitive load. Perhaps because of the tasks chosen, there was strong evidence for a parallelism between time-of-day effects in performance and the circadian rhythm in body temperature. Kleitman felt that there was a causal relationship between the two, even going as far as to assert that one could simply infer variations in performance from those in oral temperature, thus avoiding the use of 'time consuming performance tests which, in themselves, interfere with, or disrupt, the scheduled activities of the persons studied' (Kleitman and Jackson, 1950b). Subsequently, when Colquhoun and his co-workers at Cambridge addressed the problem of circadian performance rhythms, the emphasis was still very much on simple repetitive tasks, and a parallelism between temperature and performance. However, the notion of a causal relationship between the two was carefully avoided, a mechanism involving a rhythm in 'basal arousal' (or the inverse of sleepiness) instead being invoked as a mediating factor (e.g. Colquhoun, 1971).

This arousal rhythm was never specified in any fine detail, but was held to parallel the temperature rhythm, and to mediate changes in performance level through an 'inverted U' relationship, whereby rises in arousal level are associated with improvements in performance up to a certain optimal arousal level, after which performance starts to decline. Further, the Yerkes-Dodson law postulated that the optimal arousal level for a task is dependent upon its complexity, with more complex tasks having a lower optimal arousal level. Thus body temperature, basal arousal and performance on many simple tasks were seen as increasing over the waking day to reach a maximum in the evening.

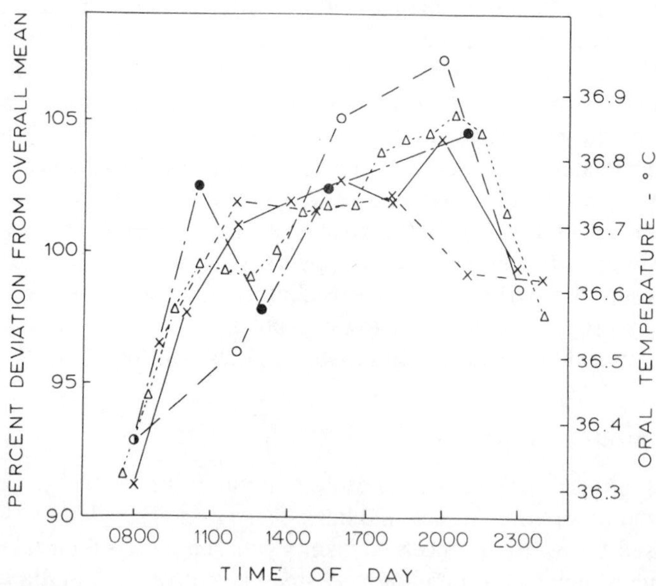

Figure 4.1 The trend over the day in serial visual search speed after Blake, 1967 (0 – . – 0); Klein *et al.*, 1972 (X– – –X); Fort and Mills, 1976 (X——X); and Hughes and Folkard, 1976 (0 – – 0). Also shown is the trend in oral temperature after Colquhoun *et al.*, 1968a (Δ– – –Δ)

The main exception to this trend was the *decline* in performance over much of the waking day which was observed in the short-term memory task of digit span (Blake, 1967). However, by invoking the arousal model, this apparent anomaly could be explained by postulating that digit span had a low optimal arousal, with the time-of-day variation thus occurring on the *falling* arm of the inverted U. A further advantage of the arousal model was that time-of-day could then be regarded as yet another arousing agent like white noise, or knowledge of results. A series of experiments involving the combination of these agents was carried out, and the various interactions explored in detail (see Blake, 1971, for a partial summary). In general, these experiments produced results that were in agreement with the model, but in view of the problems involved in devising precise predictions from it, these positive results are perhaps not entirely surprising (see Folkard (1983) for a more detailed review).

Thus, until recently, the notion was of a single performance rhythm that paralleled that in temperature. For some tasks, including serial search tasks in which subjects are required to detect a certain character in prose or random alphanumeric characters, this parallelism is indeed striking (see Figure 4.1).

Two exceptions to this parallelism were recognized. First, performance on memory tasks such as digit span was known to show a decrease over the day, and this was explained in terms of super-optimal arousal. However, before discussing this first 'exceptional' finding, it is worth considering the second exception, namely the 'post lunch dip'.

4.3.3 The post-lunch dip

In their series of studies conducted on naval ratings, Colquhoun and his colleagues (e.g. Colquhoun, 1971; Blake, 1971) found evidence for a temporary decrease in performance in the afternoon that was *not* paralleled by a similar decrease in temperature. In order to account for this decrease, Colquhoun (1971) postulated a 'post-lunch dip' in basal arousal level, an idea that agrees well with the 'siesta' enjoyed by many societies and the evidence that naps may be particularly beneficial at this time of day (Naitoh, 1981; see also Chapter 7). Colquhoun viewed this post-lunch dip as good evidence for the lack of a causal relationship between temperature and arousal, warning that 'we cannot take body temperature as an index of the level of arousal throughout the day except at times where changes in the former happen to coincide with fluctuations in the latter' (Colquhoun, 1971, p.51).

While this argument appears to be somewhat circular, there are a number of studies that *have* found a post-lunch dip in performance. These range from the laboratory studies of Blake (1967) and Colquhoun (1971) to the 'real job' measures collected by, for example, Wojtczak-Jaroszowa and Pawlowska-Skyba (1967) and Hildebrandt *et al.* (1974) (see also Chapter 19, Figure 19.1).

Unfortunately, there are also studies that have failed to find any evidence of a post-lunch dip, even when very similar measures of performance are considered (see Figure 4.1).

When a post-lunch effect *is* found, the available evidence supports the view that it is due to a decrease in arousal level. Thus, as would be predicted from the arousal theory, the effect appears to be more marked in relatively sleep-deprived subjects (Hildebrandt *et al.*, 1975), and takes the form of an *increase* in performance for tasks thought to have a low optimal level of arousal (Folkard and Monk, 1980; see Figure 4.2 below). Further, studies comparing 'lunch' and 'no lunch' conditions have found lunch to result in increased lassitude or 'deactivation' (Christie and McBrearty, 1979) and, much to the authors' surprise, a decreased ability to detect signals rather than simply a change in the criterion for responding (Craig *et al.*, 1981; see also Chapter 10). These latter studies, in which 'lunch' and 'no lunch' conditions have been compared, have also shown the ingestion of food to result in increased blood glucose and pulse rate, and decreased core (but not oral) temperature (Christie and McBrearty, 1979). Thus, these studies suggest that the 'post-lunch dip' is due to an exgenous 'masking' effect of the ingestion of food, rather than to an endogenous circadian effect.

There is also evidence for an endogenous contribution to the post-lunch dip. Thus Blake (1971) reports some evidence suggesting the occurrence of a dip when no meal was taken. However, the strongest evidence for an endogenous component comes from isolation studies in which subjects are internally desynchronized. In these circumstances, the ingestion of food typically shows the same periodicity as the sleep–wake cycle, while performance often follows the temperature rhythm. A temporary dip in the performance rhythm can be observed despite the fact that this rhythm is running with a distinctly different period from that of food ingestion (see Chapter 2, Figure 2.6). This type of finding fits well with the suggestion of some authors that the post-lunch dip reflects a bimodality of circadian rhythms due to a 12-hour harmonic of the circadian system (Hildebrandt *et al.*, 1975).

It would thus appear that the post-lunch dip, like other time-of-day effects, is not a simple effect, but has both endogenous and exogenous components. It seems probable that these components contribute differentially to any given post-lunch effect, depending on such factors as the type of task under consideration, the size and composition of the lunch taken, and individual differences in both the exogenous response to the ingestion of food and the endogenous circadian component. In view of this, the failure of some studies to find a post-lunch dip is perhaps not surprising, nor is the finding that the post-lunch dip in performance interacts with other factors such as sex (Christie and McBrearty, 1979) and personality (Craig *et al.*, 1981). At present, the only real conclusions that can be drawn are that the 'post-lunch dip' is both complex and, at least partially, inappropriately named.

4.4 THE INFLUENCE OF TASK DEMANDS

4.4.1 Memory tasks

As mentioned above, the most dramatic exception to the claimed parallelism between the temperature and performance rhythms concerns performance on memory tasks. Even from the early studies, it was clear that the time-of-day function for memory was very different from that for other tasks. Later research, by Baddeley *et al.* (1970) and Hockey *et al.* (1972), confirmed that for relatively 'pure' tasks of immediate memory (i.e. memory tested within a few minutes of presentation), performance was better in the morning than in the afternoon or evening.

Studies using digit span type memory tasks have, in fact, found performance on the normal day (see Folkard and Monk, 1980). However, on more complex tests of immediate memory, in which subjects have been required to recall the information presented in passages of prose, the trend over the day is precisely the reverse of that postulated in basal arousal level (see Figure 4.2). Thus both Laird

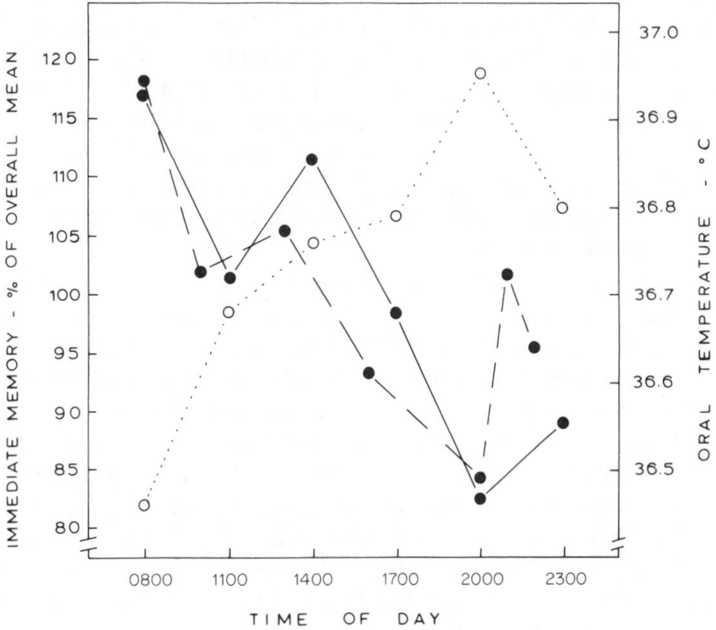

Figure 4.2 The trend over the day in immediate memory for information presented in prose after Folkard and Monk, 1980 (●——●), and Laird, 1925 (● – – ●); and in oral temperature after Folkard and Monk,1980 (0 .... 0)

(1925) and Folkard and Monk (1980) found performance on this type of task to show a general decrease over the day, with the exception of a more or less pronounced post-lunch *increment* (see above) and an increase late in the evening when body temperature, and hence presumably basal arousal, has started to fall.

The trends over the day in immediate memory performance are thus in general accord with the view that they may be mediated by the same underlying rhythm in basal arousal level as that responsible for performance on more simple tasks. Indeed, there is some evidence from outside the time-of-day area that arousal-inducing manipulations such as anxiety or noise may impair immediate memory performance (see review by Craik and Blankstein, 1975). This effect is, however, rather less consistent than the beneficial effect of such manipulations on delayed retention, a finding that suggests that delayed retention should be better following afternoon or evening presentation.

Recent studies have tested this suggestion for both random lists of digits or words (Baddeley *et al.*, 1970; Hockey *et al.*, 1972) and the information presented in a short story or in-service training film (Folkard *et al.*, 1977; Folkard and Monk, 1980). In general, the results of these studies have supported the prediction that although immediate memory may be better in the morning, delayed retention is better following afternoon or evening presentation. Indeed, it would appear that the more realistic the material used, the greater the effect of time of presentation on subsequent delayed retention (see Folkard, 1982, for a detailed review of these studies). However, Folkard and Monk (1980) also found evidence suggesting that the effect of time of presentation on delayed retention may adjust to shiftwork at a different rate from that on immediate retention. This creates problems in interpreting these findings within the arousal theory which necessarily predicts that all performance rhythms should adjust at the *same* rate (see below and Chapter 19).

These recent studies of delayed retention have examined only two times of day and have thus been unable to establish the precise trend over the day. However, in an unpublished study by Monk and Folkard, 24 undergraduate students were given 10 minutes to study a different article from a popular scientific magazine at six different times of day. Their delayed retention was tested at a constant time of day (1200–1400) a week later since the studies of Folkard *et al.* (1977) and Folkard and Monk (1980) had failed to find any time-of-retrieval effect (but see below). There was a reliable trend over the day (see Figure 4.3) which was clearly different from that for immediate retention (Figure 4.2) but was *not* the reverse trend predicted by the arousal theory. The most discrepant point from this hypothetical reverse trend was the 0800 reading. Delayed retention was particularly good following presentation at this time, despite the fact that the arousal theory predicts that this should be the worst time of day. The subsequent points fit better with the arousal theory, although the maximum was reached somewhat earlier (1400–1700) than the minimum in immediate memory (2000).

One possible explanation of the good performance following presentation at

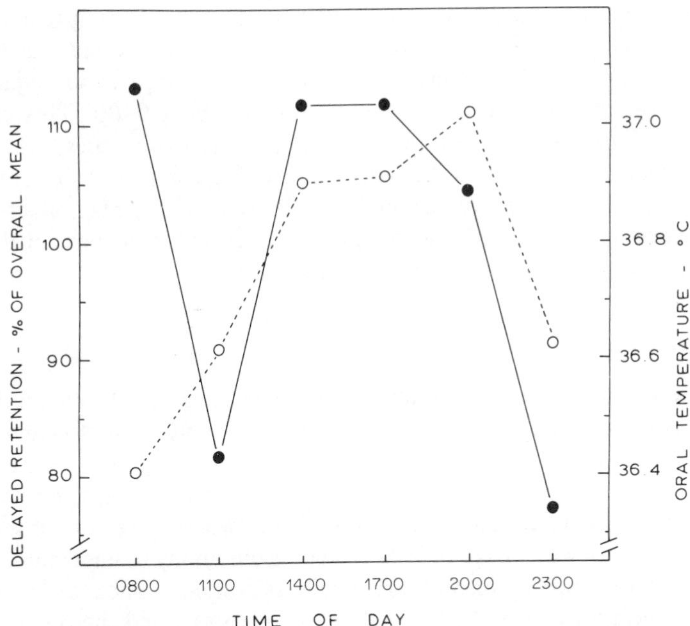

Figure 4.3 The trend over the day in the effect of time of presentation on delayed (7-day) retention (●——●) and in oral temperature (0 - - 0) from an unpublished study by Monk and Folkard

0800 is that it reflects a masking effect of the sleep–wake cycle rather than an endogenous circadian effect. The students had awoken only shortly before this 0800 session and there was thus less potential for a build-up of proactive interference. Clearly, this matter deserves further study, although the results shown in Figure 4.3 do indicate that time of day of presentation may have a fairly substantial effect on delayed retention. They further suggest that such retention is good following afternoon or evening presentation despite low immediate memory scores at this time.

The design of the studies of Folkard *et al.* (1977) and Folkard and Monk (1980) was such that time-of-retrieval effects in delayed retention could be separated from those of time of presentation. In neither study was any evidence obtained for either a main effect of time of retrieval, or a state-dependent effect such that retrieval might be better at the same time as the original presentation. However, subsequent studies *have* found evidence of an effect of time of day on retrieval using category instance tasks. These tasks, which may be more sensitive to retrieval effects, require subjects to recognize dominant (e.g. Apple) or non-dominant (e.g. Mango) instances of a category (e.g. Fruit).

Performance speed on this category instance task has been found to improve over most of the normal day (Millar, Styles and Wastell, 1980; Tilley and

Warren, 1983), and to decrease over the night to reach a minimum at about 0400 (Tilley and Warren, 1984). Further, these studies have found the effect of dominance on recognition latency to reduce over the day, and subsequently to increase over the night to reach a maximum at about 0400. This effect of dominance, it has been argued, reflects changes in retrieval efficiency over the day, such that retrieval is most efficient in the evening, but it could simply reflect a ceiling effect. Thus, these studies indicate that time of day may affect at least some aspects of retrieval efficiency, but it is unclear how important this is in comparison with the effects of time of presentation.

4.4.2 'Working memory' tasks

In most practical situations, the ability to remember a list of random digits or words immediately after being exposed to them is probably relatively unimportant. However, it has been argued that the memory stores and processes involved in performing such tasks may also be involved in performing cognitive or 'working memory' tasks (Baddeley and Hitch, 1974). Thus 'working memory' is seen to be involved in a very wide range of tasks including our ability to understand speech or text, or to perform mental arithmetic operations. Such tasks may be characterized as involving both the short-term storage, and the processing, of

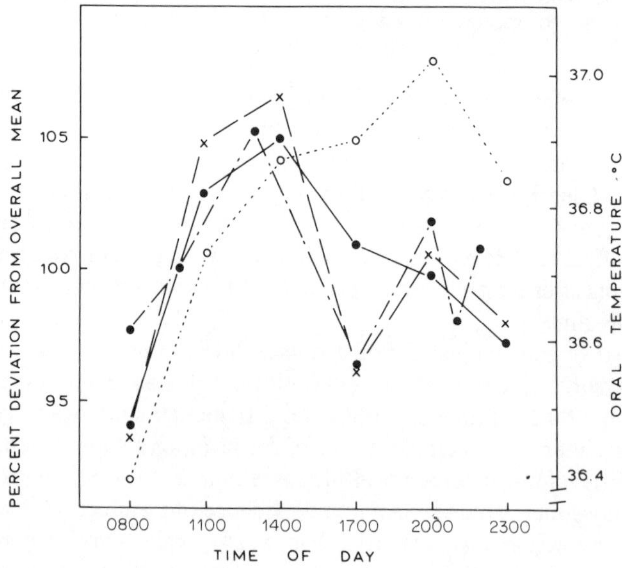

Figure 4.4 The trend over the day in working memory performance speed after Folkard, 1975a (X - - X and ●——●), and Laird, 1925 (●—·— ●); and in oral temperature after Folkard, 1975a (0......0)

information. Thus they might be expected to show a rather different function over the day from the decrease found for 'pure' short-term storage tasks, or the increase found for simple processing tasks.

The trend over the day for the performance speed of undergraduate students on a mental arithmetic task (Laird, 1925) and on two verbal reasoning tasks (Folkard, 1975a) is shown in Figure 4.4. Clearly, there is some agreement between these trends, with performance reaching a maximum at about midday. This is considerably later than that for immediate memory (Figure 4.2) but earlier than that for some simple processing tasks (Figure 4.1). Other time-of-day studies of working memory performance have, however, found somewhat different trends. Thus Rutenfranz and Helbruegge (1957) found schoolchildren's mental arithmetic performance to reach a maximum rather earlier than that shown in Figure 4.3, while Blake (1967) found a late peak in this type of performance in very highly practised young adults.

It seems probable that the reason for these inconsistencies is that the effective memory load imposed by a given task will vary according to the subject's age, intelligence and level of practice (Folkard, 1983). Thus the greater the effective memory load imposed by a task, the earlier in the day performance on that task should reach a maximum. Some evidence to support this view was obtained by Folkard *et al.* (1976) who systematically varied the memory load involved in the performance of a visual search task that was similar in other respects to those described above. With a low memory load, performance on this task paralleled body temperature quite closely, but as the memory load was increased, this relationship broke down, and was reversed with the highest memory load used (see Chapter 19, Figure 19.5).

These results suggest that, for a given subject, manipulations of the memory load involved in the performance of a task will affect the trend over the day. Unfortunately, no studies appear to have tested the alternative prediction that, for a given task, the trend over the day will depend on the subject's mental abilities, such that the performance of subjects with low abilities should reach a maximum earlier than that of more able subjects. The only suggestive evidence to support this notion comes from a study reported by Colquhoun (1971, p.82) in which the peak in performance on a mental arithmetic task appeared to become progressively later with increased practice.

The results from these studies of working memory performance thus indicate that there may be reliable and non-trivial variations in such performance over the day. However, it would appear that it may never prove possible to establish a normal trend over the day, or a best time for such tasks to be performed, since this will depend rather crucially on both the precise demands of the task and the abilities of the individual performing it. It may only prove possible to establish such 'normative trends' when the demands of the task are either so low as to be well within the capabilities of all subjects (e.g. Figure 4.1) or so high that no subject can perform the task perfectly (e.g. Figure 4.2).

4.4.3 Underlying changes in information-processing

Although the arousal theory can to some extent 'explain' the trends in performance over the day discussed above, it has little predictive power. Given a novel task or job, it would be extremely difficult to derive any prediction from the arousal theory as to the likely trend in its performance over the day. An alternative approach, which may eventually allow us to achieve this end on the basis of a task analysis, has been to attempt to determine the nature of the changes in information-processing over the day that mediate these trends. Studies of this type have been largely confined to rather artificial memory tasks and were reviewed by Folkard (1982). It would appear that the quantitative trends in memory performance over the day may reflect *qualitative* changes in the manner in which people attempt to commit information to memory. In the morning they seem to place more reliance on maintenance processing or rote rehearsal, while in the afternoon they may make more use of the meaning of the material and of elaborative processing. Changes of this type are far more difficult to demonstrate

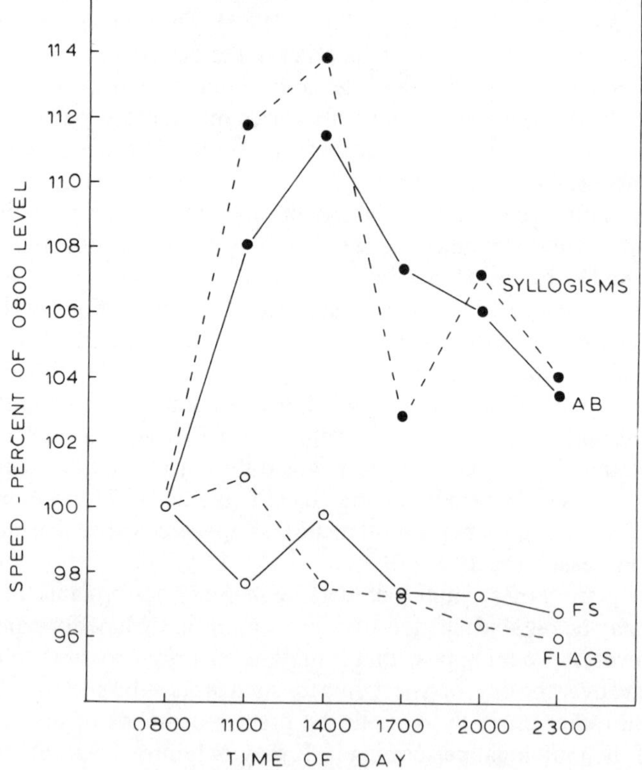

Figure 4.5 The trend over the day in performance speed on two normal verbal reasoning tasks (AB and Syllogisms), on an acoustically confusable version of one of those tasks (FS), and on a visuo-spatial reasoning task (Flags)

for more realistic memory tasks, but the evidence available to date suggests similar underlying changes (Folkard, 1980; Adam, 1983).

We also have some unpublished evidence that the trends in working memory performance over the day may be mediated by a qualitative change in information-processing. In an otherwise strict replication of the study by Folkard (1975a), subjects performed both an acoustically confusable version of one of the verbal reasoning tasks used in that study, and a visio-spatial reasoning task (after Thurstone and Jeffrey, 1956). The results, together with those of Folkard (1975a), are shown in Figure 4.5. There was no reliable trend over the day in the performance of either of these tasks. Further, a comparison of the time-of-day trend for the acoustically confusable verbal reasoning scores with the non-confusable ones of Folkard (1975) indicated that this difference was reliable.

These results suggest that variations in working memory performance over the day may be limited to those tasks that normally benefit from the use of the articulatory loop (Baddeley and Hitch, 1974). However, the effect of acoustic confusability could have been due to a change in the difficulty (or effective memory load) of the task rather than to a disruption of the use of the articulatory loop. Further, although the results shown in Figure 4.5 suggest different trends for visio-spatial tasks and non-acoustically confusable verbal tasks, rather more similar trends have been reported for schoolchildren when a more complex visio-spatial task was used (Testu, 1982). In sum, despite the practical importance of working memory performance, little is known about the changes in information-processing that mediate the trends in such performance over the day. Although, to date, the results suggest that these changes may be similar to those responsible for changes in pure memory performance, this evidence is far from convincing. Nevertheless, it would be unwise to assume that the nature of the working memory task under consideration is unimportant in determining the trend in its performance over the day.

4.4.4 Other tasks

Most recent studies of time-of-day effects in sensory and motor performance have, as indicated above, tended to emphasize the parallelism with body temperature. In the case of serial search performance, this parallelism seems fairly convincing (Figure 4.1), and has been found by many authors. However, when motor tasks are considered a less consistent picture emerges. Some authors (e.g. Blake, 1967, 1971) report that this type of performance shows a similar trend to that of serial search, while others have found a rather earlier peak at about midday. These latter studies have been reviewed by Monk and Leng (1982) who suggest that time-of-day effects in the performance of simple repetitive tasks, like those in short-term memory, may reflect a change in strategy over the day. These authors argue that an increase in speed over the day may only be achieved as a result of a reduction in accuracy, and that such a reduction may slow down motor but not serial search performance. Using a computer analogy, Monk and Leng

(1982) likened the strategy change to a reduction in the number of program steps taken to complete the task, rather than an increase in the speed with which each step is executed. The observed time-of-day trend then depends upon the impact of that strategy change on the particular performance measure taken. Although the evidence to support this argument is not conclusive, it does suggest that, like those for working memory, rather inconsistent trends are to be expected for motor performance. What is clear is that it is not only the memory load involved in the performance of a task that may affect the time-of-day trend. Other factors, such as motor involvement, may also be important, but have, as yet, received relatively little attention.

4.5 OSCILLATORY CONTROL

The arousal theory of time-of-day effects in performance essentially assumes trends in performance over the day to be mediated by a single underlying circadian rhythm in basal arousal that parallels that in temperature. Thus, in terms of the multioscillatory model discussed by Rütger Wever in Chapter 2, variations in performance are linked to the 'temperature' oscillator rather than to *either* an endogenous oscillatory *or* masking influence of the sleep–wake cycle.

It is certainly the case that in the absence of a sleep–wake cycle, i.e. under prolonged sleep deprivation (see Chapter 6), some performance rhythms persist, suggesting that they are at least partially controlled by an endogenous oscillator. On the other hand, studies of the adjustment of performance rhythms to nightwork (see Chapter 19) indicate that the rhythms in different performance measures may adjust at different rates. This finding is particularly damaging to the arousal theory since any theory that assumes all performance rhythms to be mediated by a single underlying rhythm must predict that they would all adjust at the same rate. Rather, it suggests either the need for a multioscillatory model of performance rhythms similar to that proposed by Rütger Wever for physiological ones, or that performance rhythms differ in the degree to which they are masked by the sleep–wake cycle (see Chapter 2).

In many of his pioneering studies, Rütger Wever included one of three different measures of performance efficiency. The tasks used were computation speed (i.e. a working memory task), reaction time (a motor speed task) and time estimation, although published reports have tended to concentrate on computation speed (e.g. Wever, 1979a). In all three cases, the circadian performance rhythm of internally desynchronized subjects was sometimes found to follow that in body temperature and sometimes the sleep–wake cycle. In some individuals performance consistently followed one or other of these 'marker' rhythms, while in others it appeared to change from dominant control by one of these two, to dominant control by the other. Thus, although the results were somewhat inconsistent, they provided strong support for the view that performance was influenced both by the 'temperature oscillator' and by *either* the 'sleep–wake oscillator' *or* a masking effect of the sleep–wake cycle.

With hindsight, it is possible to view the use of these particular tasks as unfortunate. Thus, whereas relatively little is known about time-of-day effects in time estimation, what *is* known about motor speed and working memory performance suggests that inconsistent trends over the day are likely (see above). Recent studies have attempted to rectify this state of affairs. Thus, in a series of seven fractional desynchronization studies (see Chapter 2), Folkard *et al.* (1983) found that performance on a serial search task consistently followed temperature rather than the sleep–wake cycle, suggesting dominant control of this performance rhythm by the temperature oscillator. There is also evidence from a similar study of Monk *et al.* (1983) that this oscillator may be dominant in controlling manual dexterity.

However, when working memory tasks are considered, the situation becomes less clear. Monk *et al.* (1983) and Folkard *et al.* (1983) examined their subjects' performance on one of the verbal reasoning tasks used by Folkard (1975a). In the Monk *et al.* study, the performance rhythm on this task showed two components, the major one corresponding to the sleep–wake cycle, and a minor one following the temperature rhythm. Thus, the verbal reasoning rhythm of this subject behaved in a similar manner to the computation rhythm of some of Wever's subjects (e.g. Wever, 1979a). In contrast, in four out of seven of the subjects studied by Folkard *et al.* (1983), the verbal reasoning performance rhythm clearly followed the temperature rhythm, while in the other three it showed evidence of separating from both the temperature rhythm *and* the sleep–wake cycle. In doing so, it appeared to run with a period of about 21 hours, implying the presence of a separate oscillator with an endogenous period distinctly different from that of either the 'temperature oscillator' or the 'sleep–wake oscillator'.

The fact that evidence for this '21-hour oscillator' was only found for three of the seven subjects on this verbal reasoning task could reflect individual differences in the oscillatory control of circadian rhythms. However, it could alternatively result from individual differences in the effective memory load imposed by this particular task. Some evidence to favour this latter interpretation was obtained from two of the subjects who also performed low, medium and high working memory load versions of a search and memory (SAM) task. Both subjects showed evidence of a 21-hour rhythm in their performance of the high memory load version despite the fact that one of them had shown no evidence of such a 21-hour component in his logical reasoning performance. Thus, it would appear that if the effective working memory load of a task is sufficiently high, the performance of that task can be controlled by a 21-hour oscillator. Which other physiological and psychological rhythms may be controlled by this oscillator is unclear, and awaits further study. However, Reinberg *et al.* (1984) have recently found that the temperature rhythm can run with this period in people intolerant of shiftwork, while Monk *et al.* (1984) have confirmed that verbal reasoning performance can free-run with a shorter period than that of simple repetitive tasks.

These results from temporal isolation studies indicate quite clearly that at least some types of performance rhythm are controlled by endogenous oscillators, and are not simply a result of 'masking' effects of the sleep–wake cycle. To date, the available evidence suggests that simple performance such as serial search and manual dexterity is predominantly controlled by the temperature oscillator, while highly memory-loaded performance may be controlled by an oscillator with an endogenous period of 21 hours. In addition, there is good evidence for an exogenous masking effect of the sleep–wake cycle on performance (see Chapter 2), and some recent evidence for an endogenous influence of the 'sleep–wake oscillator' (Monk *et al.*, 1984). Thus, it is clear both that the arousal theory is oversimplistic, and that different types of performance rhythm might adjust to abnormal work hours in very different manners (see Chapter 19).

4.6 CONCLUSIONS

Perhaps the main conclusion to be drawn from the studies reviewed in this chapter is that there is not a single performance rhythm, but many. Task demands, and in particular the working memory load, appear to be important in determining both the trend in performance over the normal day, and the behaviour of rhythms in abnormal sleep–wake situations. Further, the available evidence indicates that quantitative changes in performance efficiency over the day may reflect qualitative changes in the manner in which people process information.

From a practical viewpoint, there are two ways in which time-of-day effects in performance may be taken into account when scheduling work over the 'normal day'. First, if a single task is being performed, it may prove desirable to advance or delay the hours of work to take account of known time-of-day effects. Second, and perhaps more importantly, if an individual performs many different work tasks, overall efficiency might be improved by scheduling some for the morning and others for the afternoon. It is this latter idea that resulted in much of the early educational research in this area, although the conclusion of these researchers that the more academic school subjects should be scheduled for the morning is clearly questionable in view of more recent evidence showing long-term retention to be inferior following presentation at this time. In addition, there are other areas, such as clerical work (Monk and Conrad, 1979), where a variety of tasks are performed and where efficiency might be improved by taking account of time-of-day effects.

In fact, recent researchers have tended to ignore normal work hours and to emphasize the practical implications of time-of-day effects in performance for abnormal work schedules such as shiftwork (see Chapter 19). Since it is now clear that, even over the normal working day, performance efficiency can vary by up to ±15 per cent of the daily average, it is perhaps time to redress this bias. Important benefits could accrue from the judicious scheduling of work even within our normal working day.

Hours of Work
Edited by S. Folkard and T.H. Monk

Chapter 5

Sleep Loss: Underlying Mechanisms and Tiredness

James A. Horne

CONTENTS

ABSTRACT

Human sleep seems to be governed by at least two mechanisms. One is an obligatory requirement, probably for tissue repair and restitution following the 'wear and tear' of wakefulness. This restitution seems oriented towards the brain, as most other organs seem to obtain their restitution 'on line' during wakefulness. The other is a more facilitatory ('facultative') sleep mechanism mostly under the influence of a sleep drive governed by circadian influences as well as behaviours such as habit and boredom. 'Obligatory sleep' is primarily regulated by the length of prior wakefulness, and occupies the first part of sleep, with the remaining sleep being made up mostly by facultative sleep. Consequently, tiredness due to shortened sleep may not be due to any loss of restitutive benefit, but to the facultative sleep drive which manifests itself through a decline in motivation to perform at tasks, rather than through a failing of the inherent capacity to perform. This drive seems amenable to change, with this tiredness manageable by methods other than obtaining more sleep. Sleep loss which intrudes into obligatory sleep produces additional CNS impairments.

5.1 INTRODUCTION AND OVERVIEW

Tiredness under non-pathological conditions (i.e. excluding the more serious disorders and organic/psychiatric illnesses) is often seen to be simply due to a need for more sleep. If the usual sleep quota is not being obtained, the apparent cure is to get more sleep. Shiftworkers are particularly prone to this problem, with sleep being 'made up' on rest days, during the usual night sleep period. Although the individual may feel better for this recovery sleep, which is usually longer than the norm, this sleep may not be in the long-term interests of the shiftworker since it further encourages not only the habit of sleeping at night, but also the taking of more sleep than is usual at this time. Consequently, from the perspective of the shiftworker overcoming tiredness during work through adjustment to sleeping for shorter periods at abnormal hours, poor management of sleep on recovery days may make this adjustment more difficult.

Many people believe that they need their 8 hours sleep per day, otherwise there will be serious but ill-defined consequences. This concern with sleep is reflected in the large quantity of sleeping tablets taken nowadays, not just to overcome the distress of lying in bed awake for what often mistakenly seems to be hours, but to allay fears of what might be the physical and mental consequences of not getting 'enough' sleep.

The aim of the ensuing discussion is to point out that (i) the restorative benefits of sleep are more oriented towards the brain than the body; (ii) the effects of sleep loss on the body and the brain are not so consequential as many would believe; and (iii) a significant amount of the feeling of tiredness produced by reduced sleep is not so much due to a lack of this restitutive benefit, but to some form of sleep drive which is amenable to change.

The question why man sleeps is still very much a matter for debate. The consensus of opinion is that it is of restitutive benefit, allowing some form of tissue repair following the 'wear and tear' of wakefulness. The term 'restitutive' is used to refer to certain recovery processes, not fully understood, which occur either wholly in sleep, or to a degree which is far more efficiently carried out during sleep than during wakefulness. Although many researchers believe that both body and brain need sleep for restitutive purposes, few indicate how much sleep may be necessary for this. Sleep promotes rest and, to some extent, energy conservation. But this latter function is probably of only limited value, as man, unlike many mammals, can attain similar levels of relaxation during wakefulness (Horne, 1977, 1983a, 1983b). However, what is now becoming more evident is that a major role of sleep is to occupy constraining and unproductive hours, especially those of darkness. This role may underlie the form of sleep which causes the shiftworker most problems.

This short review will explore some of these issues further. In particular, it will become apparent that the body obtains little restitution from sleep; it is the brain (probably the cerebrum) which is the most likely target for this form of sleep function. Also, it will be pointed out that only a portion of sleep (designated 'obligatory sleep') seems necessary for this particular restitution, with the remainder of sleep being of the 'facultative' nature just mentioned, mostly for the purpose of extending sleep in order to occupy the unproductive hours of darkness.

This facultative sleep seems to be under circadian influences, unlike obligatory sleep, which simply accumulates with the quantity, and perhaps quality, of wakefulness. At sleep onset, both obligatory and facultative mechanisms are seen to be active, with a tail-off of the former well within the usual sleep period, leaving the latter to continue sleep up to the habitual sleep length; the termination of which seems largely to be temperature dependent (see Gillberg and Akerstedt, 1982a). Given time for adjustment, facultative sleep is seen to be relatively amenable to change, particularly to reduction, unlike obligatory sleep.

Tiredness, then, under non-pathological conditions, is considered here to be largely a function of these two sleep mechanisms, being related to the quantity and perhaps quality of wakefulness (i.e. an obligatory sleep need), and to a circadian factor which is also coupled to boredom and lack of productivity (i.e. a facultative sleep drive). There is also a complex interplay between sleep disturbances and restlessness (as distinct from sleep shortening) and subsequent tiredness, which relates to both mechanisms. Unfortunately though, such a topic is beyond the scope of this short review.

5.2 SLEEP AND BODY RESTITUTION

As will be seen later, there is reasonable evidence to suggest that sleep provides some form of brain restitution; however, evidence favouring a body restitutive role is limited. One of the key findings appearing to support this latter role is that certain hormones, which amongst their various activities appear to have restitutive effects, display a heightened release during sleep, and prominent within this group is human growth hormone (hGH). The substantive sleep-hGH output is mostly associated with deep sleep stages 3 and 4 (collectively called slow wave sleep–SWS). However, the significance of this release for body restitution starts to become obscure when it is noted that: (i) such a release is a rare event amongst other mammals; and (ii) other hormones integral to restitution, such as insulin, display no sleep-related release.

Several other findings have been taken as evidence of this body restitutive role for sleep, which on further analysis also turn out to be misleading. In fact, it is beginning to appear that for the majority of tissues, excluding the brain, sleep may well be a state of tissue degradation, owing to the nighttime fast.

For adult man, the reference to 'growth' in the term hGH is now generally seen to be misleading (Kostyo and Nutting, 1974; Martin, 1977; Merimee, 1979). The actions of this hormone are many, and its roles during wakefulness, let alone during sleep, are far from clear. Much of what is known about GH function has been obtained not from humans, but from animal studies using the hormone in high (pharmacological) doses, and not from more normal physiological amounts (Kostyo and Nutting, 1974; Merimee, 1979).

Tissue protein is in a continuous state of turnover; that is, breaking down into its building blocks (amino-acids), which are either disposed of as urea or re-used together with other amino-acids from recent food intake, for further protein synthesis. If an excess of 'wear and tear' were present during wakefulness, then presumably the rate of synthesis would be exceeded by the rate of breakdown, leading to a decrease in the protein content of the body. Those who believe that sleep is restitutive for the body consider that sleep redresses this imbalance, allowing synthesis to proceed at a high rate — faster than that of breakdown — leading to 'repair' and a net increase in tissue protein. However, this viewpoint can be disputed on several counts, with the main criticism stemming from the substantive review on protein metabolism by Waterlow *et al.* (1978).

These authors concluded that the main cause of heightened protein synthesis and of an increase in the body's protein content is feeding (particularly of high-protein foods) and food absorption from the gut. Hence, because of man's fasting state over the sleep period, often lasting 12 hours from evening meal to breakfast, protein synthesis during sleep should be low. Clugston and Garlick (1982) have now thrown further light on this topic, through the investigation of circadian trends in whole-body protein turnover over 24 hours. Subjects were fed during the daytime, but fasted at night (as was their normal feeding habit). Food absorption following an hour or so after feeding led to an increased tissue protein synthesis rate and reduced breakdown, causing an increase in the protein content of tissue (i.e. restitution). By 4–5 hours after the last meal of the day (at about an hour into sleep) synthesis had fallen substantially and breakdown had increased, leading to a condition of a loss of body protein (i.e. body dissolution, not restitution). This state continued throughout sleep until morning feeding, whereupon the situation reverted to an increase in body protein content. It should be noted, though, that these protein turnover trends relate to the whole individual, and the authors point out that, perhaps for the brain, there may be an exception, with sleep being more 'restitutive'.

Another index of body restitution has been seen to be rate of cell division (mitosis). For at least some human tissues, the circadian peak in mitosis appears within the usual sleep period (Scheving, 1959; Fisher, 1968). Although such findings appear to support a body restitutive hypothesis for human sleep function, it has been shown by Scheving that these peaks are not sleep dependent, as they are also present in the absence of sleep. Other circadian data on growth and mitosis can easily be perceived to favour a sleep and body restitution viewpoint, even though this may not be the correct interpretation. For example, Valk and Van den Bosch (1978) measured the circadian changes in bone growth amongst boys, and concluded that the length, and hence growth, were greatest at night (between the hours of 1800 and 0800). However, what appears to be the case is that bone length decreases during the day with respect to the nighttime value, probably due to physical activity and bone compression. This factor masked growth rates, which in fact could not fully be determined by the study.

More doubt is cast on a body restitutive role for human sleep by the large number of nil findings on the physiological effects of total sleep deprivation, although there are clear signs of CNS impairment. Unfortunately, most of these studies have been oriented towards a stress perspective and no measures have been made of other, more direct aspects of body restitution. From what indications are available, however, this restitution does not appear to be failing under total sleep deprivation.

A recent detailed review (Horne, 1978) of the physiological effects of total sleep deprivation in man reported on the literature up to 1976, and found, for example, that out of the (nine) studies assessing urinary corticosteroid output over 24–205 hours of continuous wakefulness, none reported any significant changes. Although two subsequent investigations reported increases in output (Palmblad *et al.*, 1976; Francescioni *et al.*, 1978), both also involved military battle simulation. Of the ten studies monitoring urinary catecholamine levels, only one reported a significant increase (Kuhn *et al.*, 1973), but again, the battle simulation study (Palmblad *et al.*, 1976) found an increase. Of the more psychophysiological measures reviewed (Horne, 1978), heart rate increased in three studies, decreased in five and showed no change in nine, and systolic blood pressure decreased in three studies and remained unchanged in nine. Most of these measures retained their circadian rhythms during sleep deprivation, and this particular aspect of sleep deprivation is reviewed in Chapter 6.

If sleep deprivation were to impair muscle restitution, then the physiological ability to perform physical work (i.e. physical work capacity) might be affected. Studies reporting on this index over 36–120 hours without sleep have found no decrement (Brodan *et al.*, 1969; Martin and Gaddis, 1981; Horne and Pettitt, 1984). Recent findings by Martin (1981) have shown that apparent reductions in exercise endurance during sleep deprivation are due to failing psychological motivation rather than to physiological factors. It is remarkable how well subjects can endure sustained exercise given the motivation. For example, 92 hours of near-continuous football playing in five subjects (Reilly and Walsh, 1981) resulted in only minor physical effects, although there was obvious but not serious behavioural impairment; there were no sequelae.

There remain several body systems where the effects of sleep deprivation are relatively unexplored, so the picture is far from complete. For example, it is commonly assumed that sleep loss heightens susceptibility to infection. Although two investigations (Palmblad *et al.*, 1976, 1979) have demonstrated that 72 hours of sleep deprivation produced statistically significant, but not clinically significant, changes to certain aspects of the immune response system, the authors would not interpret these changes as being adverse, but of unknown consequence.

Corticosteroid output usually increases whenever the body or mind are stressed (Bush, 1962; Henry, 1980), e.g. when an organ malfunctions. If any of these events occurred during those sleep deprivation studies which also assessed corticosteroid output, then this output would have increased; but this was not the case. Overall, then, the most parsimonious conclusion which can be made about physiological activation during total sleep deprivation is that there are few signs of any emergency reaction (Horne, 1978; Akerstedt *et al.*, 1980). However, apprehension by sleep deprived subjects about their ability to cope, or the addition of demanding conditions such as battle simulation, seem to be potent elevators of this output. It must be remembered that subjects in laboratory studies can be tired but not necessarily stressed, and that most of the sleep deprivation experiments have used mentally and physically healthy young adults, who are well looked after, and are encouraged to take a sanguine approach to the deprivation. For other types of individual, particularly older people, and under 'real world' conditions, sleep deprivation may be more consequential, but little is known about these aspects. However, inasmuch as these findings can be related to the effects on body functioning of long periods of partial sleep loss, e.g. that experienced by the shiftworker or insomiac, it would seem that there is little cause for concern over possible sequelae in relation to body function and restitution. Unless, of course, there are additional psychological stressors, e.g. adverse social and family consequences of the lifestyle of the shiftworker, or worrying about not getting enough sleep. Finally, it should be noted that the account given here on body restitution and sleep has been brief, and that more detailed accounts are available elsewhere (Horne, 1978, 1983a, 1983b, 1985).

5.3 SLEEP AND BRAIN RESTITUTION

Two or more nights of sleep deprivation bring psychological performance detriments, behavioural irritability, suspiciousness, speech slurring, usually only minor misperceptions (seldom full hallucinations), enhancement of paroxysmal EEG activity in epileptics, but few other neurological effects (Wilkinson, 1965; Naitoh, 1976; Ross, 1966; Sassin, 1970; Horne, 1978; Johnson, 1982). Whilst these changes indicate some form of CNS impairment and a need for the brain to sleep rather than to rest, they are not so extensive as might be expected if man needed 8 hours of sleep per day for brain restitution. Even the longest documented studies, of 8–11 nights of total sleep loss, did not report serious neurological or psychiatric impairment (Ross, 1966; Sassin, 1970; Gulevich *et al.*, 1966; Johnson *et al.*, 1965; Naitoh *et al.*, 1971; Pasnau *et al.*, 1968). Subjects become more suggestible during sleep deprivation, and, for example, if they are led to expect hallucinations, then such events will occur more readily.

Tiredness in the first 1–2 days of deprivation primarily affects motivation to perform at tasks, rather than the inherent cognitive 'capacity' of the individual to perform (Wilkinson, 1965; Naitoh, 1976; Johnson, 1982). The extent of performance detriment during sleep deprivation depends heavily on the type of task and its duration. Kjellberg (1977a) has gone so far as to declare that sleep deprivation is not de-arousing alone, but that it potentiates the de-arousing effects of such situational variables as simple, repetitive and long-duration tasks. Surprisingly, the more cognitive demanding tasks such as IQ performance and battle games are amongst the last to be impaired by sleep loss. This finding is perhaps somewhat contrary to a brain (cerebral) restitutive hypothesis for sleep function, because these tasks, being cerebrally 'demanding', are not the first to fail, as this hypothesis might predict. However, such tasks are inherently interesting, demanding and varied, and this encourages the subject to put in more effort to combat the tiredness. After 2–3 nights of deprivation, though, the inherent 'cognitive capacity' shows a more substantial decline, despite the best attempts by the subject to compensate for this. On the other hand, the undemanding, uninteresting and simple tasks which involve little 'cerebration' are soon adversely affected by sleep loss, even after one night, as the tedium accentuates the lack of willingness. However, given some form of reward or added encouragement to offset the motivational decline, performance decrement at these latter tasks can be reduced for the first 1–2 days of deprivation.

Many 'real world' sleep loss conditions incorporate tedium and require prolonged inspection or vigilance of standard material. Although reviewers of the performance effects of sleep deprivation (Wilkinson, 1965; Naitoh, 1976; Johnson, 1982) point out that added incentive is effective for these tasks, there have been relatively few sleep deprivation studies in this area. Probably the most notable were by Wilkinson, who performed a series of studies on the effects of added incentive (mainly knowledge of results–KR). In his first experiment, Wilkinson (1958) gave 25 minutes of five–choice reaction time after one night of sleep loss, with and without KR, on separate deprivation occasions. Also, the overall results were publicized at the end of each test, to produce a competitive spirit. These methods largely overcame the performance detriment due to sleep deprivation. In an expanded version of this study, Wilkinson (1961a) required subjects to repeat both forms of deprivation (with and without KR) on three occasions. KR remained effective for the first and second occasions. Wilkinson (1962) further reported that the detrimental effects of one night of sleep deprivation on a 20-minute addition test could be overcome when KR was added. Of particular interest was the fact that the degree of increased effort or arousal, as demonstrated by EMG level, was inversely related to the degree of performance impairment. Finally, Wilkinson (1964a) measured the effect of two nights of sleep deprivation on 20 minutes of serial reaction time, and on 30 minutes of vigilance performance, both with and without KR. The detriment in both tasks was reduced significantly by KR, particularly on the final day of deprivation.

Williams *et al.* (1959) measured daily the effects of three nights of sleep deprivation on a battery of tasks, with two types of task also being assessed for incentive effects: (i) 30 minutes of two-choice reaction time with and without KR (the subject had to look at and reset the timer after each response); (ii) 10 minutes of visual and tactile vigilance with intrasubject and intersubject competition varied. Results from both situations were inconclusive. It should be noted, however, that in the former task the experimenters gave little encouragement to the subjects to act on the KR, and in the latter task there were procedural differences between the KR and no KR conditions. Also, the task duration may have been too short for any incentive effect to become apparent.

In these studies by Wilkinson and by Williams *et al.*, measurements were only performed once during 24 hours and to date nothing is known about possible time-of-day effects with the efficacy of added incentive. Another methodological factor is that all these studies relied mostly on KR as the main incentive. However, with increasing sleepiness, coupled with the subject's increasing familiarity with the task as sleep deprivation progresses, the subject's perceived value of this form of incentive will probably decline, and it is possible that some form of compensatory increase in incentive might produce near-optimum performance levels for long periods of sleep deprivation.

Horne and Pettitt (1985) recently conducted a study to explore the effect of attractive monetary incentive on vigilance performance during 72 hours of sleep deprivation. The incentive schedule adopted was designed to be appropriate to a working environment, by minimizing errors and maximizing hits. Each day of deprivation the monetary incentive was doubled, in an attempt to counter the increasing tiredness. Incentive was able to maintain performance at baseline levels for up to 36 hours without sleep, and although deprivation began to have its effect thereafter, incentive was able to maintain performance significantly above no-incentive conditions for a further 24 hours. By the third day, incentive had no effect, despite the possibility of subjects being able to earn £12.00 in half an hour of testing. The main effect of incentive was to reduce lapsing behaviour. It was particularly interesting that under no-incentive conditions, and on the second and third days of incentive, the main detrimental effect of sleep deprivation over each 24-hour period was at night, during the normal sleep period. Over the daytime, performance levelled off, to fall again the following night. Such a finding was also made in an earlier no-incentive sleep deprivation study from the same laboratory (Horne, Anderson and Wilkinson, 1983). It seemed that the daytime circadian rise in performance counteracted the sleep deprivation effect, but at night the circadian fall added to this effect.

Horne and Pettitt (1985) also noted that only 8 hours of recovery sleep was sufficient to produce a return of performance baseline levels. Sleep quality and not sleep quantity seems to be the key. The suggestion that not all of sleep may be necessary for optimal cerebral functioning, and by inference that not all of sleep may be necessary for brain restitution, will be discussed in more detail in the next section.

Despite the presence of tiredness during sleep deprivation, it appears that from the performance findings relating to demand, stimulating and motivating tasks, the cerebrum still has the 'capacity' to perform at near optimal levels for 1–2 days of deprivation. This, together with the relatively minor neurological changes even in the longest studies, indicates that the effect of sleep deprivation on the CNS is not so severe as many might expect. Tiredness, then, might not necessarily indicate a need for brain restitution, but might be more of a circadian phenomenon relating to some form of basic sleep drive not oriented to restitution *per se.* However, one possibility which to some extent counters this interpretation, that cerebral impairment and/or a lack of cerebral restitution does occur to a significant extent early on during sleep deprivation, is as follows. There may be more capacity in the cerebral neural networks subserving performance tasks, such that as certain circuits become impaired by sleep deprivation and/or a lack of restitution, rerouting to unimpaired circuits may occur, without any overt effect on performance itself. With increasing deprivation, more circuits become impaired to the extent that the spare circuits are used up and performance overtly becomes reduced. Although this reduction may initially appear minor, the extent of the overall circuit failure may be major. Perhaps increased motivation can encourage utilization of these putative spare circuits.

5.4 FACULTATIVE SLEEP

5.4.1 Sleep reduction

Indications that not all of human sleep is essential, e.g. to brain restitution, comes from several sources. Apart from the findings of Horne and Pettitt (1985), there are several other reports that the psychological performance and behavioural impairments produced by sleep deprivation are reversed after only 1–2 nights of recovery sleep, even in the longest deprivation studies (Pasnau *et al.*, 1968; Johnson *et al.*, 1965). Also, following total sleep deprivation, it appears from studies of *ad lib* recovery sleep that only about one third of the sleep lost is in fact reclaimed (Gulevich *et al.*, 1966; Williams *et al.*, 1964; Berger *et al.*, 1971; Horne, 1976; Benoit *et al.,* 1980; Borbely *et al.*, 1981). This extra sleep seems to consist of SWS and to some extent REM (dreaming) sleep. Much of the lost SWS is reclaimed together with about half of the lost REM sleep, and it is the lost stage 2 sleep (which usually constitutes about 45 per cent of total sleep) that seems to be lost for good.

A third indicator of what appears to be some redundancy in human sleep comes from the two studies (Johnson and MacLeod, 1973; Friedman *et al.*, 1977) where sleep was systematically reduced over a period of weeks. Volunteer subjects successfully acquired the habit of taking 1–2 hours less sleep per day for at least 6–10 months (the length of the follow-up period), without any consequences such as increased daytime sleepiness. Another shorter-term chronic partial sleep deprivation study, by Webb and Agnew (1974a), required subjects to reduce their sleep to 5½ hours per day, from their usual 7½–8 hours per day, and maintain this regimen for 60 days. Few psychological performance deficits were found. However, one problem common to all three of these studies was that practice effects could not be assessed, as there was no control group undergoing regular performance assessment without sleep deprivation. Hence, any performance detriment due to sleep loss may have been offset by an improvement due to practice. A very recent study by Horne and Wilkinson (1984) attempted to redress this drawback in a 2-month sleep reduction study whereby one group of subjects reduced their sleep to 6 hours per night, from the norm of 8 hours. These subjects were matched with a control group who continued to sleep normally. Both groups were assessed for daytime tiredness at weekly intervals by (i) 1 hour of auditory vigilance testing, and (ii) an EEG assessment of the ability to remain awake for ½ hour during a fixed daytime period, with the subject lying on a bed in a quiet and darkened room. Although practice/adaptation effects were evident for both tasks for both groups, there was no significant difference between the two groups for these tests over the experimental period.

All four of these longer-term partial sleep deprivation studies provided data on the quality of the restricted sleep, and all indicated that sleep had become shortened rather than condensed. That is, subjects responded by demonstrating a loss of the latter part of sleep rather than *pro rata* reductions in all of the sleep stages. For example, Mullaney *et al.* (1977) (which is the sister paper to Friedman *et al.*, 1977) reported that the absolute level of stage 4 sleep was unaffected, but was reduced for REM sleep. In relative terms, stage 4 sleep increased and REM sleep remained about the same, and it should be noted that these findings also applied to the later follow-up sleep.

To summarize these findings, it appears that the first part (approximately 5 hours) of sleep (which, coincidentally or otherwise, is the portion occupied by SWS) represents an obligatory quota. Providing this can mostly be reclaimed or retained, it is possible for psychological performance and daytime tiredness to be maintained at normal or near-normal levels. This hypothesis does depend on a regular sleep schedule, though, as in all the sleep reduction studies just cited subjects had to maintain regular hours of sleep and wakefulness, having first decided how the sleep was to be constrained time-wise. People who are forced to take less sleep because of their employment, but who cannot maintain sleep regularity, for example shiftworkers, *will have increased difficulty in learning to take less sleep because of insufficient time to adapt through weekends off or rapidly rotating shift systems.* Also there is the tendency, here, for *longer than normal sleep to be taken on rest days,* in order to 'make up for lost sleep'. This action may begin to *prime the system into learning to take more sleep,* thus making any successful adaptation to reduced sleep more difficult.

5.4.2 Extended sleep

Not only can man learn to sleep less, but also he can sleep longer, simply by going back to sleep after the usual morning awakening (Verdone, 1968; Aserinsky, 1969, 1973; Webb and Agnew, 1975; Feinberg *et al.*, 1980). This is easily accomplished by most people, and the length of this oversleep is usually 1–2 hours. Although it could be argued that man may be chronically sleep deprived (Webb and Agnew, 1975), there is little other evidence to support such a hypothesis, and it is more likely that this extra sleep is superfluous. All of these extended sleep studies reported that the extra sleep contained mostly stage 2 sleep and about 25–30 per cent REM sleep, with little or no SWS.

The 24-hour sleep quota can also be extended by daytime napping; subjects not used to taking daytime naps can usually nap quite easily (Evans *et al.*, 1977). Karacan *et al.* (1970a) reported that naps taken in the morning contained a preponderance of REM sleep and little SWS (an observation confirmed by Agnew and Webb, 1973; Moses *et al.*, 1975; Hume and Mills, 1977; Akerstedt and Gillberg, 1981), whereas afternoon naps contained more SWS and less REM sleep. Although subjects had taken extra sleep during the day, there was no shortening of the subsequent night's total sleep time, again suggesting, like the findings from the extended sleep studies, that this extra nap sleep was in many respects superfluous. Karacan *et al.* also observed important qualitative changes in the subsequent sleep. Whilst the extra REM sleep of both the morning and afternoon naps resulted in no *pro rata* reductions in the following night's REM sleep, there were such reductions for SWS. Similar findings were reported by Whitehead *et al.* (1969). The daily amount of SWS cannot be extended by taking extra sleep; quite the reverse in fact, as this sleep is positively correlated with the length of prior wakefulness (Webb and Agnew, 1971a).

Flexibility of sleep length makes sense if one considers man before the advent of artificial lighting. In the UK the daily ratio of light hours to dark goes from 16:8 to 8:16 from summer to winter. Given that we are visually oriented animals, requiring reasonably good light to interact with the environment, the ability to alter sleep length by a few hours over the year may well have helped to overcome the boredom of the long hours of winter darkness and have kept us out of harm's way. Relaxation and lack of stimulation in the daytime also promotes sleep, and it would seem that this further addition to facultative sleep also acts as a time filler.

One factor which should not be overlooked is that oversleep and daytime naps can easily occur in people who are not suffering from lack of sleep, or are not tired prior to the extra sleep episode. It seems that lack of stimulation or a conscious decision to go to sleep is all that may be required. It is likely that this form of tiredness can be eliminated by stimulation, as well as by sleep. On the other hand, whilst stimulation can be effective in overcoming the tiredness associated with sleep loss, this stimulation (which has to be more intense and frequent than in the former condition) seems only to offset sleep, and not to substitute for it (as would be the case if sleep was not reallyrequired).

5.4.3 Naturally long and short sleepers

Total sleep time amongst healthy human sleepers follows a normal distribution within any age group. For example, in young adults the mean and standard deviation are about 7½ and 1 hour respectively. Webb and Agnew (1970) reported on the sleep stage characteristics of long (8½ hours and above) and short

(6½ hours and below) good sleepers. The amount of SWS in both groups was about the same, but the differences lay in the amounts of REM sleep and other non-REM sleep stages. A later study by Webb and Friel (1971) of sleepers taking 9½ hours and above versus sleepers taking 5½ hours and below produced similar findings with regard to these sleep stages.

The most recent study of such sleepers was by Benoit *et al.* (1980). Short and long sleepers had mean sleep times of 5 hours and 9 hours respectively, and again the sleep stage differences between the two groups were similar to those reported by Webb and Agnew (1970). In particular, REM and stage 2 sleep differed between the two groups by a factor of two. Interestingly, Benoit *et al.* (1980) also deprived the two groups of sleep for 36 hours. Whilst the average recovery sleep length of the short sleepers was significantly lengthened, this was not so for the long sleepers; SWS increased to a similar extent in the two groups, with REM sleep also increasing (by 30 per cent) in the short sleepers, but not in the long sleepers. It might seem as though the long sleepers had more facultative sleep in their usual sleep than did short sleepers, and that this has the capacity to take up any extra obligatory sleep need.

Individuals naturally sleeping less than 3–4 standard deviations below the norm (e.g. less than 3½ hours sleep in the case of middle-aged adults) will be very rare. No non-sleepers have ever been found, although a few particularly short, natural, non-insomniac sleepers have been reported. Jones and Oswald (1968) found two male subjects, aged 30 years and 54 years, who averaged 164 minutes sleep per day between them, and Stuss and Broughton (1978) described one 57 year-old male who slept on average 97 minutes per day. All three subjects had similar absolute amounts of SWS, which occupied about 50 per cent of total sleep, and although in relative terms this was about three times the age-related norm, it was normal in absolute terms. They exhibited little absolute and relative amounts of REM sleep, ranging from an average of 14 per cent with the subjects of Jones and Oswald to 16 per cent with the other subject. What is of particular importance with all three subjects is that the absolute and relative amounts of REM sleep, stage 2 and SWS were akin to what would be expected from similar lengths of sleep taken from usual sleep onset in age-related normal sleepers. One might speculate, therefore, that these very short sleepers are down to their obligatory minimum of sleep and have little facultative sleep.

5.5 CONCLUSIONS

Although the body's restitutive need for sleep is doubtful, sleep, particularly SWS, may be the only state wherein the cerebrum can obtain some form of off-line recovery. As far as it is known, no organ apart from the brain enters an essential physiological state during sleep which is unique to sleep and cannot be attained during wakefulness. For example, voluntary musculature can rest to a similar extent during relaxed wakefulness to that found in sleep. However, for the brain the situation is different; for example, during waking states the EEG indicates that even while a subject is lying relaxed in a sound-dampened and darkened room, the cerebrum is in a condition of quiet readiness, prepared to act on sensory input, and seeming not to display any marked diminution in responsiveness (i.e. 'rest'). Only sleep allows some form of cerebral shutdown, increased thresholds of responsiveness to sensory input and release from the constraining state of quiet readiness, typical of wakefulness, (see Livingstone and Hubel, 1981). In man, SWS seems to reflect a relatively profound degree of shutdown, greater than in any other sleep state, to the extent that the cerebrum appears to be functionally disconnected from subcortical mechanisms (Sato *et al.*, 1975).

If the cerebrum does need off-line recovery during sleep, as a result of waking activity, then the faster the neurochemical changes that occur in the brain during wakefulness, presumably the greater is the need for recovery. Gross cerebral metabolism runs at a high level during wakefulness, almost regardless of the degree of mental load (see Siesjo, 1978). This is because the state of readiness of the waking brain necessitates a high rate in its metabolism (Livingstone and Hubel, 1981). Factors which can produce a rise in cerebral metabolism are increased brain temperature (which can be the result of exercise — see Horne and Staff, 1983) and emotional states, possibly including sustained and demanding attention (see Siesjo, 1978). Our own findings indicate that many hours of this sustained attention during the daytime lead to increased tiredness at night and in SWS (Horne, 1976; Horne and Minard, 1985). However, the issue remains whether these sleep effects are simply a withdrawal response from the 'demanding' day (see Murray, 1966) or the result of an increased need for brain restitution.

Hours of Work
Edited by S. Folkard and T.H. Monk

Chapter 6

Sleep Deprivation and Prolonged Working Hours

Jan E. Fröberg

CONTENTS

ABSTRACT

This chapter deals with the effects on performance of continuous work for 24 hours or more. Many performance functions deteriorate under such conditions, and the degree of this detrimental effect depends on a number of factors inherent in the task or situation and on certain characteristics or attitudes of the person at work. Some of the empirical results of research in this field and on recovery from and countermeasures against performance decline will be discussed.

6.1 INTRODUCTION

This chapter considers what happens to people when they are requested to work continuously for very long spells, i.e. 24 hours or more. How do such abnormal work conditions influence humans with respect to efficiency and motivation for work? How fast is recovery, and are there any methods of ameliorating a decrease in efficiency?

In order to illustrate the complexity and multidisciplinary nature of this field of research, Figure 6.1 will be taken as a point of departure. The figure depicts results from a series of studies performed in our laboratory (see Fröberg *et al.*,

1975a,b; Fröberg, 1977; Akerstedt and Fröberg, 1977; Gillberg and Akerstedt, 1981a) on the effects of three days of continuous work at different tests or simulated tasks. The subjects of these investigations were not allowed any sleep or rest for the duration of the experiments.

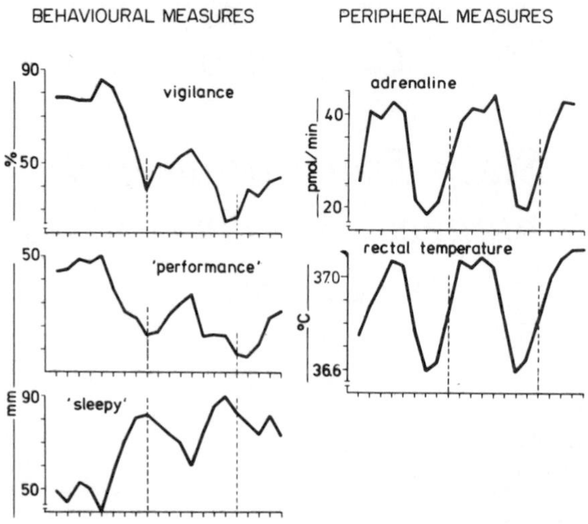

Figure 6.1 Performance, self-ratings and physiological variables of a group of subjects exposed to two nights of sleep deprivation

The data represented in Figure 6.1 show several things: (i) There is a general decreasing trend both in objective performance (a vigilance task) and in the subjects' ratings of their performance efficiency, (ii) The decline in performance efficiency is not monotonic, but cycles with time of day. This cycling is correlated with the physiological variables, i.e. when adrenaline excretion and body temperature are high, performance is better than when the physiological measures are low, (iii) Self-ratings of sleepiness increase with time of continuous work, and a very clear rhythmic component is present here, too.

In conditions like those of our experiments several factors have to be considered in order to understand and evaluate the effects of such extremely long spells of continuous work. While there are comparatively few reported studies in which subjects are required to work continuously for 24 hours or more, there is quite a large volume of research on the effects of one or several nights of sleep deprivation in which subjects were tested at different intervals throughout the vigil. Moreover, there is evidence that results from the two kinds of conditions differ very little as far as performance effects are concerned (Wilkinson, 1964a). Results from both types of studies will thus be used in the following discussion. We will take into consideration the fact that different types of tasks may change differently, that motivation may play an important role for performance efficiency, that there is a cycling in wakefulness with time of day, and that the worker is subjected to deprivation of sleep. Finally, we will consider the rate and extent of recovery of performance after a period of continuous work and the possibilities of ameliorating the downward trend in performance.

6.2 TYPE OF TASK

One of the most commonly observed effects of continuous work and sleep deprivation on performance efficiency is so-called 'lapses' or 'gaps', i.e. periods of no response (see Williams *et al.*, 1959; Wilkinson, 1969). The performance lapses are short periods of lowered arousal or light sleep, which can be traced in a simultaneously recorded EEG (see Stocker and Jovanovic, 1973). Different characteristics of the task influence the degree to which lapses appear in performance records.

One such factor is the *duration* of the task in hand, a prolonged task (half an hour or more) being more sensitive to sleep loss than a short one. It has also been shown that when a task is replicated, performance becomes worse at each successive replication (Wilkinson, 1969), and thus that a *novel* task is less affected. The latter observation accords well with the fact that *monotonous* tasks like simple reaction time and vigilance tests have been found to be very sensitive to sleep deprivation. In fact, a simple reaction time task with only one kind of stimulus, the same response every time and short intervals between stimuli may reveal a decrement in performance after a night without sleep, even though the testing period is of rather short duration (Lisper and Kjellberg, 1972).

A complex task is more vulnerable than one low in complexity. One example of this is shown in Figure 6.2 (data from Fröberg, 1978). The task was a simple coding test which was varied in complexity by having an increasing number of

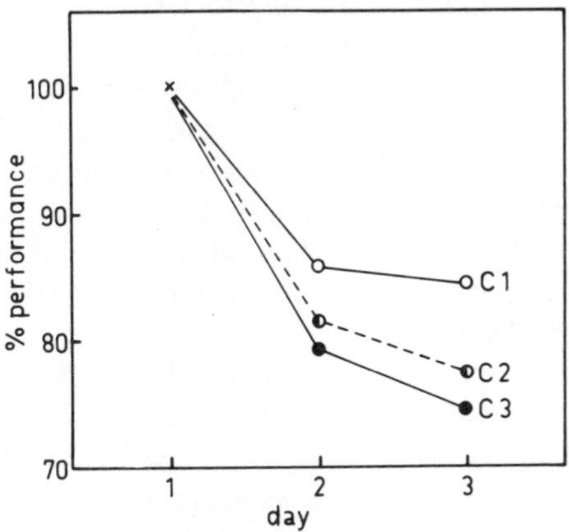

Figure 6.2 Performance in tasks differing in complexity during three nights of continuous work and sleep loss. C1 to C3 corresponds to respectively 3, 6 and 9 digits to be converted to letters. Means of 15 subjects

digits (three, six or nine) to be coded into letters. The diagram shows that the more complex the coding task was, the more performance declined during the three days of sleep loss with continuous work.

In another experiment the subjects sorted cards into either four or ten categories. Performance in the latter, more complex, task deteriorated more than that in the former (Wilkinson, 1964a).

Pacing of the task also affects the decline in performance. Tasks that are work-paced, i.e. where the stimulus is present for a restricted time and the response must be made within a certain interval, deteriorate more than self-paced tasks. In the latter, accuracy may be high with sleep loss lengthening the time taken to complete the task.

If lapses or gaps, instances of very low arousal or sleep, were the only factor which determined performance in prolonged work shifts, then one would expect a normal performance level between the lapses. There is, however, some evidence of a gradual arousal decrease, which may affect behaviour even when there are no lapses. In a simple reaction time task, lapses would lead to some very long response times whereas the rest of the distribution of performance latencies would remain unchanged. However, Lisper and Kjellberg (1972) have shown that even the fastest response times were influenced by lack of sleep. In a choice reaction time task, a significant slowing of the fastest reaction times has also been reported and was interpreted as a slowing of the response selection process (Tharp, 1978). Other results that cannot be predicted from the lapse hypothesis are that the focus of attention is diminished, and that sleep deprived subjects are less able to discard irrelevant stimulation (Hockey, 1970; Norton, 1970).

There are rather few investigations which have used more complex situations and performance tasks. One example is the experiment on continuous activity by Wilkinson (1964a) in which the subjects were working in spells of 4.5 hours followed by a 1.5 hours rest (no sleep) over a total duration of 60 hours. One of the tasks that Wilkinson used was a 'battle game' which involved rather complex decision-making and the manipulation of symbolic ships in several channels, and which produced immediate knowledge of results. In this task there was no decrement in performance at all. On the other hand, a different complex decision-making task which was used in the same investigation was seriously impaired. The latter task was disliked by the subjects, whereas the former was very popular with them. The author's conclusion was that complexity of the task has an adverse effect on performance whereas interest, reward or incentive is beneficial (see next section). When the two are combined, interest is the more potent factor.

Memory has been reported to degrade in people who are required to stay awake. In one experiment a list of words was presented one at a time, and written down by the subject. After this the subject was asked to report all the words that he could remember. Since the experimenter corrected all *writing* errors at the time that they were made, the observed deterioration in this test could hardly be an effect of lapses. Rather, it was considered to be due to a difficulty with the formation of memory traces as a result of sleep deprivation (Williams and Williams, 1966).

There are also a few studies showing detrimental effects of sleep loss on short-term memory, although the mechanisms underlying this impairment are not clear (see Wilkinson, 1964a; Donnell *et al.*, 1969). Figure 6.3 shows data on short-term memory performance from a study where 15 female subjects were working on different paper-and-pencil tests continuously for 72 hours (Fröberg, 1979).

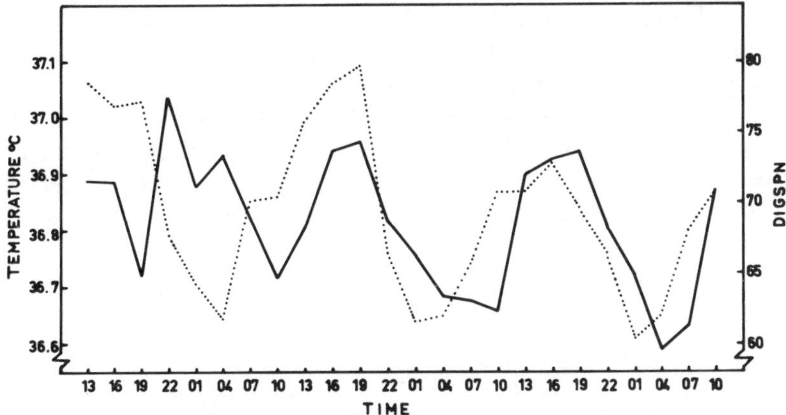

Figure 6.3 Digit span performance (continuous) and oral temperature (dotted) in 15 subjects exposed to three nights of sleep loss with continuous activity

There is a clear decreasing trend over the three days, although the circadian cycling is very strong, leading to steep rises in performance every day and an equally steep decline during the night. The graph also shows that the subjects were able to keep their performance at a relatively high level the first night without sleep, whereas after that short-term memory tended to follow the rhythm of body temperature with low levels in the small hours and early morning.

In short, then, tasks of 30 minutes or more in duration, low in novelty, interest or incentive, or high in complexity, are deemed to deteriorate in a situation of prolonged work duty and no sleep. This is the case especially if the task is often repeated.

Practical examples of vulnerable tasks might be simple sorting operations, the recording of coded messages, copy typing, display monitoring and industrial inspection. On the other hand, tasks that involve behaviour such as decision-making, problem-solving or concept formation, and which are highly interesting or rewarding to the subject, seem to be resistant.

Effects of sleep loss and continuous activity on *physical performance* have also been reported. Young people who were exposed to a night of sleep loss had a lower 'endurance' index (Copes and Rosentsweig, 1972). In another investigation a group of subjects were trained to a high physical condition, after which they were subjected to one night of sleep loss. Physical work capacity deteriorated dramatically (Olree *et al.*, 1973).

6.3 THE ROLE OF MOTIVATION

The most persuasive factor influencing performance under continuous activity and sleep loss is probably motivation for the task. Indeed, it has been argued that the deleterious effects of sleep loss might all be seen as motivational effects (Murray, 1966). Kjellberg (1977a) in his review of sleep deprivation concludes that sleep loss may have no effect on performance capacity, if by capacity we understand performance under optimal motivational conditions.

The effect of an incentive is illustrated in Figure 6.4 (data from Fröberg, 1978). The most complex version of the coding task was used with an incentive in the form of a monetary reward, which would be given to the subject if she increased her performance in relation to the score of the preceding trial. Immediate

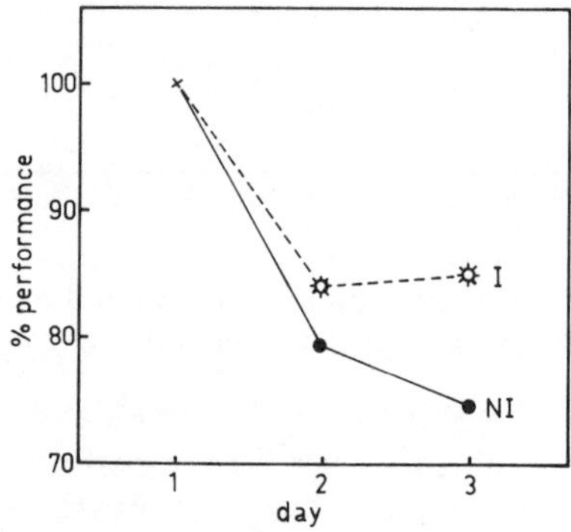

Figure 6.4 Coding task performance with (I) and without (NI) incentive in 15 subjects exposed to three nights of sleep loss with continuous activity

knowledge of results was not provided. Performance deteriorated whether an incentive was given or not, but the decrement was less in the former condition.

When a person is given knowledge of the results or 'feedback' about his work the negative effect may be diminished or even abolished (Wilkinson, 1961a, 1964b; Williams *et al.*, 1959). If the task is experienced as interesting or challenging the decline in performance is also less. Wilkinson (1965) had his subjects rate different tasks in terms of how interesting they found them. The interest ratings correlated well with vulnerability to sleep loss — vigilance and serial reaction being examples of low interest/high vulnerability tasks, while rote-learning and decision-taking tasks were rated high in interest and did not deteriorate at all with sleep loss.

One possible mechanism of this effect of sleep loss is that the subject lowers his standards of performance, i.e. is more ready to accept errors or failures (Williams *et al.*, 1959; Kjellberg, 1977b). In Kjellberg's experiment the subjects spent a shorter time on the task, left more items unsolved and gave fewer incorrect solutions in a problem-solving situation when they were informed that there were insoluble items.

6.4 THE IMPORTANCE OF SLEEP: MICROSLEEPS

If a subject who is required to work continuously does not get any sleep, many performance functions are significantly lowered after one night without sleep, and have definitely deteriorated after two nights. After the third or fourth night of total sleep deprivation very few people are able to stay awake and perform at all if their motivation is not extremely strong. This holds for conditions of *total* sleep loss, but there is a reservation which must be made with regard to the total sleep deprivation paradigm. With increasing time at work and loss of sleep 'microsleeps' will occur more and more often. Thus, the subject falls asleep for a few seconds (compare the discussion on 'lapses' or 'gaps' in section 6.2). These very short sleeps do not have the recuperative value of normal sleep, however, and the subject still feels sleepy and his performance still degrades even though there may be a large number of microsleep periods (Naitoh, 1976).

An interesting question is what happens to performance efficiency if we allow the subject a few hours of sleep per day. Studies comprising such *partial* sleep deprivation schedules show that people can tolerate them and are able to keep up their performance level with sleep periods shorter than normal. The limit of tolerance for prolonged spells of reduced sleep seems to be around 4–5 h of sleep per day (Naitoh, 1976). Even shorter sleeps may, however, be beneficial. This was dramatically evident in a field study (Haslam, 1982) in which groups of infantry soldiers worked with no sleep, 1.5 h and 3 h sleep per day. The no-sleep group withdrew from the experiment after 4 nights, whereas about 50 per cent of the 1.5 h and 90 per cent of the 3 h sleep group completed the nine days of the experiment. Performance decrements occurred for all three groups.

Other studies have shown that naps may be beneficial to performance efficiency (see Lubin *et al.*, 1976; Hartley, 1974), even though there is a tendency towards even greater deterioration of performance immediately after a short period of sleep (referred to as sleep inertia). A study by Naitoh (1981) showed that the beneficial effect of a nap on performance depended on the duration of the nap, the times of day it was taken and the number of hours of sleep loss preceding it. A 2-h nap in the early morning after 45 h of sleep loss thus had no recuperative effect on performance, whereas an equally long nap after 53 h, taken in the afternoon, restored performance efficiency significantly.

6.5 RECOVERY

In the field study of infantrymen referred to above (Haslam, 1982), one group worked for 90 h without any sleep and then the subjects were allowed 4 h of sleep per day for the following 3 days. After having thus slept a total of 12 h their average performance was close to 90 per cent of pretest values as compared to 50 per cent at the end of the total sleep deprivation period. Thirty hours of rest, of which about 19 h were spent asleep, took the subjects back to the pretrial performance levels.

Several other investigations have shown that (i) a short period of sleep (a 'nap') leads to improvements in performance (see Chapter 7); and (ii) after a full night's sleep which, if undisturbed, usually lasts several hours longer than normal sleep (12–14 h after 2–4 days of sleep loss), performance efficiency is almost fully restored.

In a series of investigations by Morgan and co-workers (summary report by Lyddan *et al.*, 1974), the effects of interrupted recovery were studied after 36–44 h of continuous activity. Two, three or four hours of rest were allowed. The recovery of performance was incomplete in all cases and ranged from 40 per cent recovery in the 44 h continuous work/4 h rest (44/4 h) condition to 73 per cent in the 36/4 h condition.

A further study by the same group of researchers showed that the performance decrement and the rate of recovery interacted with the time of day. When the 36-h period of continuous work started during the declining portion of the circadian cycle, performance decrements were larger and recovery after 4 h of rest was less complete. The authors conclude that the circadian rhythm is an important determinant of our ability to work continuously for long periods, and to recover from the effects of such conditions.

6.6. COUNTERMEASURES

What means are there of reducing or abolishing the deleterious effects of prolonged work spells and sleep loss on performance efficiency? Several factors inherent in the design of tasks, instructions and situational circumstances which may counteract performance degradation have already been mentioned. Thus, if a task is made high in interest or incentive, not too complex and not too monotonous, performance may be kept at a high level even though the duration of the continuous work period exceeds 60 hours.

One further countermeasure, which has also been mentioned above, is of course sleep. Even short naps of 1 or 2 hours may have a large effect if given at the right time of day.

When none of these remedies is possible and we have a rather monotonous task, low in interest or reward with no possibility of sleep, there are still a few things that may be invoked to counteract the decline in performance.

One such factor may be *physical exercise.* Subjects who used a bicycle ergometer during a sleep loss experiment performed better (Hasselman *et al.*, 1960). Even when the physical activity took place immediately before testing, the performance decrement was less (Lybrand *et al.*, 1954). In his review of sleep deprivation effects Wilkinson (1965) says that he has observed that a walk or some other physical activity is the best way to revive a deprived person. There are also negative results, however. Webb and Agnew (1973) deprived eight subjects of sleep for two nights under two different conditions, either bedrest or work on an ergometer bicycle for 15 minutes every other hour. Performance deteriorated in both groups and there was no difference between conditions. An increased performance decrement as a result of exercise when combined with sleep loss has also been reported (Lubin *et al.*, 1976). In this case the subjects bicycled during as much as 60 minutes each 220 minutes. Thus there may be a dose dependent effect of exercise.

Noise is usually expected to have a detrimental effect on performance efficiency. When it is combined with sleep loss, however, it may result in an improvement, as was shown by Wilkinson (1963). In normal sleep conditions white noise impaired serial reaction test error scores. Sleep loss increased the proportion of errors even more, but in the 'sleep loss plus noise' condition errors were somewhat reduced.

One further way of depressing the effects of continuous activity and sleep loss is to use *drugs*. The most effective drug seems to be amphetamine, which may restore performance in a serial reaction test to a normal level even when given after three nights without sleep (Kornetsky *et al.*, 1959).

Even though there are ways of counteracting the decrement in performance efficiency by arousing or motivating the person, we know very little about the 'costs' of such efforts. There is evidence that body systems such as hormonal and immunological defences are influenced by sleep loss and continuous work. This in turn might lead to a lowered resistance to external stressors and/or a higher accident proneness.

6.7 CONCLUSIONS

Many performance functions deteriorate under conditions of continuous work and sleep loss, and the degree of these decrements depends mainly on characteristics of the task and the motivation of the person at work. Task duration, monotony and complexity thus tend to reinforce the negative efffect, while incentive and high interest may result in no performance decrement at all. Sleep, even in the form of a short 'nap', may have a beneficial effect in certain circumstances, and a full night's recovery sleep usually restores performance to a normal level. Other means of ameliorating a decline in performance at continuous work are moderate physical activity, noise and the use of certain drugs.

Hours of Work
Edited by S. Folkard and T.H. Monk

Chapter 7

Effects of Naps on Performance

Mats Gillberg

CONTENTS

ABSTRACT

This chapter deals with the effects of single naps on performance. Naps are considered to be sleep periods between 30 minutes and 2 hours in duration. The habits of taking naps are first discussed. Then follows a review of the effects of naps on performance efficiency. This is divided into three categories: (i) daytime naps with no preceding sleep deprivation, (ii) nighttime naps taken to counteract the late night performance trough, and (iii) studies of fragmented sleep. The latter two types of nap seem to be effective in enhancing performance. However, little can be said about the effects of daytime naps. The reason for this might be that they occur (and are thus measured) during the rising phase of the circadian rhythm of performance. Also discussed are negative effects of 'sleep inertia', which are considered to be consequences of sleep deprivation.

7.1 INTRODUCTION

In spite of the fact that napping is a universal phenomenon, there seems to be no single definition of it. Not even in the scientific literature is the word 'nap' strictly defined. According to two dictionaries, a nap is 'a short sleep (esp. in the daytime)' or 'a brief sleep, often during a period other than one's regular sleeping hours'. These definitions tell us at least that a nap is not as long as a normal sleep.

But exactly how short, or rather, how long can a nap be? There is no definitive answer to that question but an inspection of the scientific literature shows that sleep periods ranging from about 30 minutes to 2 hours in duration have been referred to as naps. These limits seem roughly to be applicable also to the everyday use of the word, and will be adopted here.

7.2 NAPPING HABITS: THE INCIDENCE, TIMING AND DURATION OF HABITUAL NAPS

7.2 1 The incidence of naps

What, then, is the function of naps — why do people take naps? First of all, it is well known that naps in some specific areas of the world are parts of the cultural pattern — the siesta. This habit has been studied by Taub (1971) in a Mexican community. He found that 78.5 per cent of his subjects took four or more naps per week. A perhaps surprising finding was that these naps were not used to compensate for lost sleep, but rather that they were added to the 'normal' 7–8 hours of sleep during the night. Taub had no definitive explanation of the siesta habit other than that it is an important social occasion, perhaps tied to a traditional heavy noon-time meal. Even in 'non-siesta' cultures, there are people who take naps so frequently that they can be spoken of as habitual nappers. It seems that habitual nappers often are found among young people. Evans and Orne (1975) found that more than 50 per cent of college students could be considered habitual nappers. These researchers were also able to establish primarily two groups of habitual nappers. The first group was comprised of people who used naps to make up for lost sleep, or in anticipation of lost sleep ('replacement nappers'), while the other group took naps for more psychological reasons ('appetitive nappers'). There were no differences between nappers (in either group) and non-nappers with regard to self-reported night sleep habits, although the replacement nappers had somewhat more irregular sleep–wake habits than the appetitive nappers.

Generalization of these results to other populations, e.g. day-working adults, might, however, be risky. The subjects were young college students, a group who might have more opportunities to organize their time as they please than adults who have the more strict demands of a 9-to-5 job. Also, one might speculate whether young people, for other than occupational and social reasons (i.e. biological reasons), have less rigid sleep–wake behaviour and are less sensitive to violations of the normal sleep–wake pattern than somewhat older age groups. There is, however, no solid support for this speculation in the scientific literature.

Another group of people who habitually take naps, but for different reasons, are shiftworkers. In one of our own studies of steelworkers (Akerstedt, Torsvall and Gillberg, 1981) we found that more than 30 per cent of a population of 300 shiftworkers working three shifts (afternoon, night and morning shifts) regularly took naps during periods when they were working night and morning shifts, although almost none took naps in connection with the afternoon shift. The naps taken in connection with the nightshift were on average 2 hours in duration and taken at around 1700 h, while naps taken in connection with the morning shift averaged about 90 minutes in duration and occurred at around 1430 h. The occurrence of the naps in the steelworkers seemed to be linked to the length of the major sleep episodes. Napping occurred most frequently in connection with the two shifts that interfered most with the normal sleep, suggesting that napping fulfilled a compensatory role. Another interesting finding was that 'morning-type' persons (see Chapter 3) more often took naps associated with the nightshift than did 'evening-type' persons. For the morning shift this was reversed.

7.2.2 The timing of naps

From the above studies it is obvious that naps predominantly occurred during the afternoon. In the Dinges *et al.* (1981b) study the incidence of nap onsets peaked at around 1530 h. Evans and Orne (1975) found that their subjects, both appetitive and replacement nappers, preferred to nap at around 1600 h. College students studied by Bertelson (1979) preferred to take their naps around 1430 h. In the Mexican study by Taub (1971) naps taken by young adults typically started sometime between 1400 h and 1500 h, with the starting point becoming earlier with increased age. As mentioned earlier, data from our own study of shiftworkers showed that naps started at around 1700 h in connection with the nightshift and at around 1430 h in connection with the morning shift. In all of these studies napping seemed to occur sometime between 1430 h and 1700 h. One reason for this might be that this habit is connected to a latent biphasic pattern of sleep, since the period 1430–1700 h is roughly midway between the normal times of awakening and retiring. This is discussed by Dinges *et al.* (1981b). This pattern might also underlie the 'post-lunch dip', a period of sleepiness occurring during the afternoon. In one of our own studies, increased sleepiness during that period was shown to appear irrespective of whether the subjects had previously slept for a full 8 hours or only for 4 hours (Akerstedt and Gillberg, 1982).

7.2.3 The duraton of naps

The subjects in the above studies differed little in their reported nap durations. For habitual replacement nappers Dinges *et al.* (1981b) report a mean duration of 73 minutes and Evans and Orne (1975) reported 74 minutes, while nap durations for appetitive nappers were somewhat shorter: 58 and 62 minutes, respectively. The subjects studied by Bertelson (1979) had typical durations around 90 minutes with the extreme limits at 34 and 174 minutes. In the Mexican population the naps also lasted around 90 minutes, depending somewhat on the age group considered (Taub, 1971). As mentioned above, our shiftworkers napped 2 hours in connection with the nightshift and about 90 minutes during morning shift periods of work.

In conclusion, napping habits seem to be remarkably similar among the populations studied, even though they differ with regard to age, occupation and cultural background. The typical habitual napper prefers to sleep for about 90 minutes some time between 1430 h and 1700 h.

7.3 NAPS AND PERFORMANCE

Considering the relatively widespread use of naps for (presumably) recuperative purposes, surprisingly few studies have dealt directly with this issue. Studies of the effects of naps on subsequent performance seem to fall into three main categories. The first category includes studies of the effects of daytime napping, predominantly afternoon naps, mainly in habitual nappers. The second category includes studies of how nighttime naps can be used to alleviate the effects of different degrees of sleep loss. finally, there is the category where different kinds of fragmented sleep have been studied. This category can only be partly considered as comparable to nap studies but is nevertheless discussed because such studies illustrate methods of counteracting sleep deprivation. The primary interest of this chapter is, however, in single naps.

There are a number of questions to bear in mind that might be important when reviewing studies which deal with changes in performance due to naps, e.g. At what time of the day (or night) was the nap taken? How much time has elapsed between the last major sleep period and the nap? What was the duration and structure of the nap ('depth' of sleep) as judged through the EEG sleep stages? How soon after the nap was performance measured? Which method or methods were used to measure the effect?

7.3.1 Daytime naps

Regarding the time of day at which the nap is taken, the previously defined three categories of study form three natural groups. In the four day nap studies that will be reviewed, the timing of the naps ranged from 0935 h to 2135 h. These extreme limits occurred in the same study by Taub (1979). He concluded that there were no differences between the two timings of the day because both naps had positive effects on reaction time performance, short-term memory and subjective ratings of sleepiness, as compared to the success of control subjects who were measured in parallel but did not sleep. Positive effects on these measures were also found in another study by Taub *et al.* (1977) with naps (of different durations) in the time interval 1500 h to 1700 h. Bertelson (1979) failed to show positive effects on performance (reaction time) with naps scheduled between 1330 h and 1500 h, but found that the subjects were more relaxed and had reduced anxiety after the nap. Dinges *et al.* (1981a) studied subjects who napped in either quiet or disturbed surroundings. The two nap conditions did not differ appreciably. Furthermore, no really positive effects emerged when performance was measured 35 minutes after the nap.

The above results are somewhat contradictory in that Taub (1979) showed that naps, disregarding timings, had positive effects on performance, while Dinges *et al.* (1981a) and Bertelson (1979) found no performance improvements. This difference cannot be explained by the difference in nap duration (2 hours in the first case and 1 hour in the latter two studies) since Taub, in another of his studies (Taub *et al.*, 1977), has found there to be almost no differences between a 30-minute nap and a 2-hour nap with regard to their effect on performance. Neither do differences in sleep structure or duration give clues to the discrepant results. Nor can the contradictory results be explained by the method with which performance was measured. All four studies compared used reaction time tasks or similar psychomotor tasks.

Another possible explanation involves the time between awakening from a nap and performance measurement. In the study by Dinges *et al.* (1981a) the major question was in fact not how effective, but rather, how detrimental, the nap was. It is well known that sudden awakening from sleep is related to low performance capacity (for discussions see Dinges *et al.*, 1981a and Naitoh, 1981), a phenomenon often called sleep inertia. The purpose of Dinges *et al.* (1981a) was to study how long this sleep inertia remained and to see if it disappeared more quickly if the nap was taken in a disturbed environment rather than in a quiet one. Their conclusion was that sleep inertia had disappeared (at least) after 35 minutes. At that time performance was back to pre-nap levels, which also means that there was no *improvement* due to the nap. In the other three studies performance measurements were made 15 minutes (Bertelson, 1979) or 20 minutes (Taub *et al.*, 1977; Taub, 1979) after the nap. It does seem unlikely, though, that such small differences in timing should explain the discrepant results.

Perhaps the most plausible explanation lies in the fact that naps were taken, and the effects of them were measured, during the rising phases of the circadian rhythm and when there was no sleep deficit. There is convincing evidence that performance efficiency varies with time of day so that for most simple tasks it is rising during the day and falling during the night (e.g. Colquhoun, 1971, and Chapters 4 and 19). It is, then, only to be expected that performance should improve during the day over a period of 1 or 2 hours, even if there is no nap. The circadian upswing during the day can be so strong that it counteracts even the effects of two nights without sleep, i.e. performance is higher during the day after two nights without sleep than during the second or even the first night of deprivation (Gillberg and Akerstedt, 1981b). If there is to be an increase due to a nap during the day, when there is no sleep deprivation, this can only be small since there is not much room left for improvement. The effects of naps must always be evaluated against the background of circadian rhythms which may vary from one person to another. This implies that nap studies, especially if naps are taken when only small effects are expected, should involve designs where the subjects are their own controls so that the performance of a subject after a nap can be compared to his own performance at the same time *without* a preceding nap. This approach was only used in one of the four studies, the one by Taub *et al.* (1977). Furthermore, as circadian influences on performance will always be present, these are best controlled by allowing them to appear in their 'pure' form, unaffected by external factors (e.g. knowledge of time of day, particular activities or meals occurring at certain times of day). This kind of experimental control was not used in any of the four studies.

Strangely enough, there is no study where the effect of a daytime nap is measured during the night, i.e. when the circadian rhythm of performance is falling. The lack of measurable immediate effects of daytime naps does not exclude the fact that there might be such effects. They may remain unnoticed because they are obscured by the circadian upswing of performance. It could, therefore, very well be that the daytime naps only show their effects several hours later — when the circadian rhythm swings downward again. The study of the possible long-term effects of daytime naps would, apart from being experimentally more 'clean', also have important practical implications, since afternoon naps are often taken as 'investments' in preparation for a coming night of activity or work. Probably many of the shiftworkers in our study (Akerstedt, Torsvall and Gillberg, 1981) used naps that way, and it would be interesting to know if these 'investments' are worthwhile. Also surprising is the fact that none of the daytime nap studies had designs involving sleep deprivation, i.e. with the preceding night totally or partially sleepless. Such designs would seem natural if the functions of daytime naps are thought to be recuperative. Even if the strong circadian upswing will bring performance back to near normal levels, there is probably more room for improvement than when there is no sleep deprivation. Naitoh (1981) has studied the effect of a nap after a considerably longer period of wakefulness (53 hours) and his results are discussed below.

7.3.2 Nighttime naps

Naps taken during the night fall into a different category since they occur when 'normal' sleep occurs and, hence, when there is a 'natural' need for sleep. It has been mentioned earlier that there is a deterioration of performance at simple tasks during the night. If this performance decrement can to some extent be reduced or even completely eliminated by a nap, it can be more safely concluded that this is due to the nap itself than is the case with afternoon naps. Very few studies have explored different aspects of nighttime naps and their effects on performance: Angiboust and Gouars (1972), Naitoh, (1981) and Gillberg (1984). In the first study a 2-hour nap was scheduled to start at 2400 h, i.e. after 17 hours of continuous wakefulness. The subjects were tested between 0300 h and 0500 h. Their results were compared with those of another group which was tested at the same time but which did not have any nap, and with those of a third group tested during the day (1000–1200 h). The group that had had no nap had the worst performance on the visual vigilance task (used as a performance measure) while the nap group was considerably better, in fact quite close to the group that was tested during the day (with no sleep deprivation). Naitoh (1981) used a somewhat different design that enabled him to compare the effects of a nap scheduled from 0400 h to 0600 h after 45 hours of continuous wakefulness and a nap scheduled from 1200 h to 1400 h after 53 hours of wakefulness. He found that the early morning nap had *detrimental* effects on performance which remained for several hours. The midday nap, on the other hand, did not have this negative effect, in spite of the fact that another 8 hours of wakefulness had passed. Finally, in our own study (Gillberg, 1984) we wanted to investigate the relative merits of two different nap schedules (2100–2200 h versus 0430–0530 h), with the aim of counteracting the early morning performance trough. We found that both naps had positive effects on performance changes between 1900 h and 0700 h and that the late nap was most efficient in that it brought performance level (on a 10-min visual reaction time task) back to the same level as that at 1900 h. Results from measurements of sleep latencies were similar to the performance findings.

Obviously, the findings of Naitoh (1981) are contradictory to those of Angiboust and Gouars (1972) and Gillberg (1984). The study of Naitoh (1981), however, differs in one important aspect from the other two studies — his subjects had been awake for about 24 hours longer when they were tested during the early morning. The marked sleep inertia noted in connection with the early morning nap in this study might be attributed to this longer period of sleep deprivation. The existence of such a connection between sleep inertia and long periods of sleep deprivation was supported in one of our own studies (Akerstedt and Gillberg, 1979). We tested for memory in short waking periods during recovery sleep after 64 hours of wakefulness, and found performance was seriously affected as compared to baseline conditions.

Due to differences in design and methods of measurement it is difficult to say whether a 2-hour nap is better than a 1-hour nap. But both in the study of Angiboust and Gouars (1972) (2-hour nap) and in our own study (Gillberg, 1984) (1-hour nap) performance after the naps was nearly back to daytime or early evening levels. This seems to suggest that a 1-hour nap might very well be enough to achieve the desired positive effects. In his study Naitoh (1981) explains the lack of effect of the early morning nap not only with the existence of sleep inertia, but also with the notion that 2 hours was too *short* for the nap to have any positive effect. An alternative explanation might be that there is a critical length of sleep, relative to the cyclical variation of sleep depth, such that when the length of nap produces an awakening which coincides with a period of deep sleep, sleep inertia appears. This is to some extent supported by Dinges *et al.* (1981a) who found that signs of sleep inertia in reaction time performance were related to awakening in stage 4 (deep sleep), and that decrements in a descending subtraction task were related to increased amounts of the sleep stages 2, 3 and 4.

It was mentioned earlier that the results of daytime naps, without preceding sleep deprivation, are difficult to interpret because an increase in performance is to be expected anyway due to diurnal variation. In the experiment by Naitoh (1981), this strong diurnal influence is reflected in the fact that sleep inertia appeared only initially (within the first hour) in connection with the midday nap, compared to the long-lasting sleep inertia in connection with the early morning nap.

In connection with a nightshift, it is often not possible to take a nap close to the critical hours during the early morning, as it then would interfere with work. Naps then have to be taken during the preceding afternoon or evening, several hours before the 'critical period'. It is therefore important to know how long the effects of a nap last. As mentioned earlier, none of the day nap studies investigated the long-term effects. Hence, little can be said about the extent to which possible effects of daytime naps carry over into the night. A nap taken in the evening (2100–2200 h) did, however, have clear positive effects on performance measured 8 hours later (Gillberg, 1984), thus giving some support to the notion of a long-term carry over.

7.3.3 Multiple naps (fragmented sleep)

In the studies belonging to this category, short episodes of sleep are regularly spaced over one or several days. Most of these studies have had the purpose of examining variations of sleep structure within these sleep periods (Carskadon and Dement, 1975, 1977; Weitzman *et al.*, 1974), and include no measurement of performance. Such measurements were, however, made in a study by Lubin *et al.* (1976). The design of this experiment allowed for a comparison between subjects who slept for 1 hour per 3 hours and 40 minutes and subjects who rested in bed without sleeping during the same hours (and also with a third group who pedalled ergometer bicycles during these periods). The performance of the nap group suffered significantly less than both the bedrest and the exercise group during the 40 hours that the experiment lasted. The particular design used in this study does not, however, answer the question of what the immediate effect of a *single* nap is, or what the long-term effects of a nap might be, because if performance is measured after one of these naps (i.e. between two naps) one can never be sure if one is measuring the immediate effect of the latest nap or the sum of the long-term effects of all the other preceding naps. The results, however, support the other nap studies in showing that performance can be maintained at a reasonable level with different sleep schedules (and less sleep) than the 'normal' 8-hour nighttime sleep.

The study by Hartley (1974) falls somewhere between the fragmented sleep studies and the single nap studies. In this study, comparisons can be made between three groups: one group slept the 'normal' 8 hours, another group slept 4 hours and a third group had three 80-minute sleep periods evenly distributed over each 24-hour period. Performance (on a visual vigilance task) deteriorated more in the 4-hour group than in the group with three 80-minute sleep periods. Hartley concluded that the superiority of the 3 x 80-minute group was due to performance measurements occurring closer to these sleep periods than to the 4-hour sleep periods (7 h 45 min versus 16 h 30 min). The results from this study are, however, somewhat difficult to relate to those of single nap studies since there were three 80-minute sleep periods but only one measurement of performance per 24 hours.

7.4 CONCLUSIONS

It is obvious from the results reviewed above that there is no simple answer to the question of how naps in general affect performance. For the purpose of summarizing this review it might be appropriate to return to some of the questions put earlier. With regard to the time of day at which naps are taken, very little can be said about the immediate effects of daytime naps. Probably less confusing results would be achieved if the effects were measured during the following night, when the circadian rhythm is falling.

Late evening or nighttime naps obviously have positive effects which remain for several hours, providing the amount of preceding sleep loss is moderate (one night without sleep). In situations with considerable sleep loss (two or more nights without sleep) naps may result in sleep that is too 'deep', making the individual mentally confused upon awakening and hence negatively affecting performance. This negative effect may persist for several hours.

The duration of a nap does not seem critical. At least, 1-hour and 2-hour naps have roughly the same effects. Naps might, however, have critical durations with regard to when during the sleep cycles awakening occurs. If the person is awakened during the 'deep' sleep phases of the sleep cycle, sleep inertia might appear.

The interval between nap and performance measurement is important. With short intervals (less than about 20–30 minutes) there is a risk of sleep inertia. This critical interval can increase to several hours in subjects suffering from sleep loss. Outside of this critical interval the positive effects are largest relatively close to the nap, after which the effect slowly fades. In connection with nightshifts, this would mean that a nap taken before the start of the shift may keep performance at an acceptable level over the early morning trough.

In the experimental studies, most of the tasks used as a performance measure were of a relatively simple psychomotor kind. Therefore little can be said about whether naps affect some mental functions more than others. One speculation receiving some support might be that a nap can positively influence feelings of well-being and alertness, even though performance remains little affected.

In spite of napping seeming to be a widespread habit, especially during the afternoon, remarkably little is known about its effects on performance.

Hours of Work
Edited by S. Folkard and T.H. Monk

Chapter 8

The Menstrual Cycle

Paula Patkai

CONTENTS

ABSTRACT

A critical review of past research on the menstrual cycle is provided. Available evidence indicates that the premenstrual and menstrual periods are associated with some negative moods and somatic complaints in a majority of women. Results are, however, conflicting regarding the pattern, incidence and severity of symptoms. Similarly, data are inconclusive regarding the location of peaks and troughs in female sexual activity. There is evidence of an increase in negative social behaviours during the premenstrual/menstrual phases. The hypothesis concerning a decrement in perceptual-motor or intellectual capacity during these phases is, at present, not well supported.

8.1 INTRODUCTION

The menstrual cycle is regulated through a close cooperation between the hypothalamus, pituitary and ovary. On the basis of morphologic and hormonal changes, the cycle is usually divided up into five phases: (i) preovulatory or follicular, (ii) ovulatory, (iii) postovulatory or luteal, (iv) premenstrual and (v) menstrual. The preovulatory phase involves the growth of a number of ovarian follicles under the influence of the follicle-stimulating hormone secreted by the pituitary gland. The maturing follicles secrete estrogen and the endometrium in the uterus becomes thicker. At ovulation the egg from one (or two) follicle(s) is released and begins its journey through the fallopian tube to the uterus. In the postovulatory phase, the collapsed follicle forms a corpus luteum which produces progesterone. If fertilization does not occur, the corpus luteum regresses then, and the levels of both estrogen and progesterone decline leading to menstuation: the loss of sloughed off tissue and blood from the wall of the uterus. The main hormonal changes during the cycle involve a peak of both estrogen and progesterone around day 21, counted from the onset of menstruation, and a dip to low levels during the premenstrual phase. In addition, estrogen shows a second peak at ovulation.

There has been a deeply rooted assumption that hormonal changes during the menstrual cycle have profound effects on women's psychological state. Although not always stated explicitly, cyclical variations in behaviour during the menstrual cycle are often assumed to be *caused* by physiological changes. In spite of the fact that correlational designs, used in investigations of cyclical changes, are weak in demonstrating causal relationships, the possible influence of confounding psychological and social factors or the directionality of cause are not always considered. In recent years, this strict physiological perspective has been heavily criticized, interestingly enough mostly by women researchers (e.g. Ruble *et al.*, 1980). Their sometimes slightly ironical critique may be understood in view of the generalizations made by some researchers on the basis of scientifically poor or scanty data, depicting women as helpless victims of the ebb and flow of their hormones.

As Sherif (1980) has pointed out, the theoretical schism between biological determinism on the one hand and sociocultural determinism on the other is also present in the body of research on the menstrual cycle, where both extremes may be criticized for researcher bias. However, those researchers of a more balanced, intermediate position are anxious to point out that the menstrual cycle is characterized by a close interplay of physiological and psychological factors, thus constituting a fruitful field for studying psychophysiological relationships (Sommer, 1973).

8.2 RESEARCH ON THE MENSTRUAL CYCLE

The bulk of the research on this topic has dealt with self-reported changes in mood and somatic complaints. The influence of estrogen and progesterone on female sexual behaviour has also been a subject of considerable interest. Relatively little data are available concerning changes in arousal and objective measures of performance. In the following, an attempt will be made to summarize the major findings in these and related areas.

8.2.1 Subjective reactions: mood and somatic complaints

In general, retrospective questionnaires have yielded more evidence for consistent cyclic effects in subjective reactions than concurrent measures such as daily self-ratings. In nearly all studies that have included both types of instrument there has been considerable discrepancy or no relationship between the two scores (e.g. Golub, 1976; Abplanalp, Donnelly and Rose, 1979). The most likely explanation for this disparity is that questionnaire data are more influenced by stereotypic beliefs about menstruation (Parlee, 1974).

A wide variety of physical and psychological symptoms have been associated with the menstrual cycle. According to a review of the literature (Moos, 1969) in the late 1960s over 150 symptoms had been linked predominantly to the premenstrual and/or menstrual phases. Sometimes a distinction is made between dysmenorrhea — pain accompanying menstruation — and the premenstrual syndrome characterized by a diversity of negative symptoms like anxiety, depression and tension. There is some evidence suggesting that dysmenorrhea is of primarily physiological origin, while the premenstrual syndrome is less hormone dependent (Parlee, 1973; Patkai and Pettersson, 1975) and thus more susceptible to the influence of psychological factors.

Estimates of occurrence of premenstrual symptoms have ranged between 25 and 100 per cent (Moos, 1968). According to five large-scale investigations summarized by Sommer (1978), a majority of women report pain, water retention and negative moods in connection with the premenstrual and/or menstrual phases. There is also some evidence for an ovulatory peak in positive mood (e.g. Moos *et al.*, 1969). Results are, however, conflicting regarding the pattern, incidence and severity of symptoms, partly due to the diversity of assessment techniques and interindividual differences. Pain and water retention have been the most consistently found symptoms around menses, while data on mood changes give a much more conflicting picture (Wilcoxon *et al.*, 1976).

Several theories have been proposed concerning physiological mechanisms to account for phase-related changes (Smith, 1975). The prevailing view is that monoamine oxidase (MAO) increases during the premenstrual phase as a response to decreased estrogen and progesterone activity. MAO in turn affects neurotransmitter activity in the central nervous system (CNS). This theory is partly based on the assumption that CNS neurotransmitters are involved in the etiology of affective disorders characterized by a symptomatology resembling premenstrual and menstrual distress. Thus, the supporting evidence is indirect and several assumptions must be validated before affective fluctuations may be linked to biochemical changes (Parlee, 1973).

As an alternative to hormonal explanations, various external factors, such as social expectations, have been suggested as equally plausible causes of menstruation-related affective changes (e.g. Ruble *et al.*, 1980; Paige, 1973). The methodological shortcomings of research on the menstrual cycle have been summarized by Parlee (1973) and Sommer (1973). They point out that the failure to control the demand characteristics of the research situation, the omission of an adequate control sample, and the use of retrospective questionnaires may maximize the risk of socially mediated responses. The significance of this critique is illustrated by the results of Ruble (1977) who found a significantly higher degree of reported physical symptoms such as pain and water retention (i.e. those symptoms that in other studies had shown the strongest relation to premenses) in women who were led to believe that they were premenstrual as compared to those believing they were intermenstrual. However, menstruation-related affective fluctuations have also been demonstrated by more projective techniques which are less susceptible to response biases. For example, by analyzing women's verbal behaviour, Ivey and Bardwick (1968) found significantly higher levels of anxiety, hostility and depression in the premenstrual phase as compared with those at ovulation.

In more recent studies attempts have been made to minimize most of the methodological problems of earlier research. Paige (1971) studied the levels of anxiety and hostility in verbal samples from women with natural menstrual cycles and those taking combination or sequential oral contraceptives. The real purpose of the study was disguised. It should also be noted that both types of pill maintain high levels of female sex hormones during the cycle, except during menstruation, but only combination brands reduce significantly the amount of menstrual bleeding. In agreement with the results of Grant and Pryse-Davies (1968), non-pill women showed curvilinear fluctuations in anxiety and hostility, while affective changes did not occur in the combination group. More detailed data analysis, however, suggested that the absence of fluctuations in anxiety was related to reduced menstrual flow, while changes in hostility were considered to be hormonally dependent. The notion that menstrual bleeding might itself be a stressor eliciting negative emotions, is supported by the results of Beaumont *et al.* (1975) showing larger cyclic fluctuations in normally menstruating women as compared to hysterectomized women who presumably have unaltered hormonal cycles but do not menstruate.

In the study by Wilcoxon *et al.* (1976) both males and women with contraceptives were used as control groups. Increased pain and water retention were reported by both female groups before or during menses, while males maintained a stable level. Although negative mood also peaked during the premenstrual and menstrual phases, it was found to be more closely associated with environmental stress than with cycle phase. Englander-Golden *et al.* (1977) found no significant phase-related differences in tension between females taking, and those not taking, oral contraceptives. Similarly, Abplanalp, Donnelly and Rose (1979) found practically no relationship between cycle phase and daily ratings of mood or enjoyment of activities, although the Moos' Menstrual Distress Questionnaire (the only standardized retrospective questionnaire) yielded significant phase-related negative effects. This study (Abplanalp, Rose, Donnelly and Livingston-Vaughan, 1979) is especially interesting since it belongs to those few studies on menses where concurrent endocrine and psychological measures were taken. In disagreement with the classic work of Benedek and Rubenstein (1942), no association was found between psychological variables and the reproductive hormones estradiol and progesterone. The authors pointed out that the possibility of detecting the delicate psychoendocrine relationships involved might be enhanced by studying women with marked menstrual symptoms. A similar approach, using homogeneous subgroups, was also suggested by Sommer (1978).

8.2.2 Sexual behaviour

Lower mammals with estrous patterns only show sexual behaviour in response to periodic secretion of estrogen. In contrast, most species of female primates have menstrual cycles and mate throughout the cycle. However, they show a periodicity in sexual behaviour which increases at ovulation — thus enhancing the probability of conception — and during the premenstrual phase (Michael, 1965, referred by Kane *et al.*, 1969). Michael (1971) has also shown that progesterone treatment of female rhesus monkeys has a deleterious effect on their sexual behaviour.

With regard to humans, it is generally hypothesized that estrogen is related to an increase, and progesterone to a decrease, in the probability of sexual behaviour; although it is recognized that sexual hormones may be weak determinants of human sexuality as compared to the influence of sociopsychological or cognitive factors (Udry and Morris, 1968; Spitz *et al.*, 1975). Thus, sexual arousal is expected to be highest around the ovulatory peak in estrogen and lowest during the luteal phase when progesterone reaches its highest level.

Data are still inconclusive regarding the location of the peaks and troughs in female sexual arousal and behaviour. According to an unpublished review of 32 studies (Schreiner-Engel *et al.*, 1981), the peaks of sexual activity were distributed as follows: 8 at ovulation, 17 premenstrually, 18 postmenstrually and 4 during menstruation (the sum of peaks exceeds 32 since in some studies two or more peaks were reported). These conflicting data might be due to several factors, such as (i) the possibility that the subtle influences of female sex hormones are overridden by more potent determinants, (ii) the diversity of assessment methods including various retrospective questionnaires, daily reports and dream analyses, and (iii) differences in conceptualization of sexual behaviour, whether it is defined as, for example, sexual arousal, sexual arousability or coitus.

Englander-Golden *et al.*, (1980) have suggested that subjects' awareness that their menstrual cycle is being studied might bias their self-reports according to cultural beliefs. Indeed, in their study, sexual arousal was found to follow the hormonal pattern only in the 'unaware' condition. However, more direct tests of the hormonal hypothesis, involving concurrent measures of both hormonal and sexual activity, have failed to find any relationships. Thus, Persky *et al.* (1978) found no correlation between plasma estradiol and any of the measures of sexuality used — coitus frequency, sexual gratification and sexual arousal. In the study of Schreiner-Engel *et al.* (1981) sexual arousal in response to erotic stimuli was measured both by self-reports and by vaginal photoplethysmography. Levels of vaginal vasocongestion were significantly higher during the follicular and luteal phases than around ovulation. Subjective arousal showed a similar though non-significant trend. Neither measure, however, showed any significant correlation with plasma levels of gonadal hormones. Negative results were also obtained by Abplanalp, Rose, Donnelly and Livingston-Vaughan (1979) regarding correlations between reproductive hormones and the number and enjoyment of sexual activities either with a partner or alone.

There is also a possibility that sexual desire during the follicular phase might differ from sexual desire during the luteal phase (Singer and Singer, 1972). The study of Benedek and Rubenstein (1942) gives some support for this suggestion. Benedek found that the first part of the menstrual cycle was characterized by active object-directed heterosexual tendencies, while the progesterone phase was associated with passive-receptive sexuality, a more self-centred state. It is important to note that the estrogen and progesterone phases were objectively defined by assessing reproductive hormone activity. Thus, these positive results contrast with those enumerated above. Apart from differences in methods of assessment of endocrine functions, Benedek and Rubenstein studied neurotic patients and the psychological data consisted of psychoanalytical interpretation of dreams and other unconscious material. Stimulated by the study of Benedek and Rubenstein, Luschen and Pierce (1972) showed that ovulatory women were more other-directed than premenstrual women. In addition, the former were more responsive to sexually arousing stimuli.

According to the hormonal hypothesis, the use of oral contraceptives should eliminate cyclic changes in sexual arousal. Most research on oral contraceptives and sexuality, however, has been concerned with alterations in overall sexual desire, disregarding cyclic variations. In a double-blind study, Udry and Morris (1970) found no luteal decline in sexual activity in women on oral contraceptives, while non-pill women did show a decline. A tendency to more stability in sexual arousal in women taking oral contraceptives was also shown by Silbergeld *et al.* (1971). On the other hand, Englander-Golden *et al.* (1980) found an unexpected trough in sexuality 5–6 days before menstruation in pill-taking women.

8.2.3 Arousal and performance

There is now biochemical and neurophysiological evidence that estrogen and progesterone affect brain function (Hamburg, 1966; Kopell, 1969; Messent, 1976). On the whole, these two hormones seem to have antagonistic effects on the central nervous system, with progesterone inhibiting and estrogen stimulating its function. In accordance with these observations Kopell *et al.* (1969) proposed a hormonal/arousal hypothesis regarding the menstrual cycle.

Only a few studies have included measures of subjective arousal. Using the Nowlis Mood Adjective Check List, Moos *et al.* (1969) showed a sharp rise in pleasantness and activation around mid-cycle with lowest values in the menstrual and premenstrual phases. In another study using the same method of assessment (Little and Zahn, 1974), the midcycle rise was confirmed. On the other hand, in a normative study using the Menstrual Distress Questionnaire, practically no variation was found in the arousal factor (Moos, 1968). Bell (in Bell *et al.*, 1975) obtained significant changes in Thayer's Activation-Deactivation factors, showing a decrease in activation during the menstrual phase.

It is interesting to note that in these studies arousal — defined in positive 'action' terms like active, energetic, vigorous — tended to decrease before and during menstruation and increase at ovulation. On the other hand, during these phases, especially in the premenstrual period, anxiety and tension are often reported (see section 8.2.1), i.e. negative affect states usually associated with heightened autonomic arousal. This resembles the results of Altmann *et al.* (1941) who studied ten college women daily for a period of 5 months. The most universal cyclic phenomenon observed was an outburst of physical and mental activity in the premenstrual phase, accompanied by tension and irritability. As their case studies reveal, the physical activity spells before the onset of menstruation had in some women an almost compulsive character, involving, for example, an 'intense urge' to clean the whole house. Another outburst of activity was observed at ovulation, but this activity 'was free from nervous tension and generally bore the character of an elation' (p.224). Somewhat similar qualitative differences between the two phases were also observed by Ivey and Bardwick (1968) and Benedek and Rubenstein (1942). These results suggest that studies of 'general arousal' during the menstrual cycle cannot cover all the major changes involved. Apart from a distinction between cortical and autonomic arousal, the use of more qualitative data also seems to be necessary.

Objective measures of arousal have not yielded consistent data. Kopell *et al.* (1969), who first proposed the arousal hypothesis of the menstrual cycle, used four measures of arousal. Time estimation showed a significant fluctuation over the cyle with higher values during the premenstrual phase. Two-flash threshold showed a similar, though non-significant, trend. Galvanic skin potential and simple reaction time, however, did not vary significantly with menstrual phases. Negative findings regarding simple, and choice, reaction time have been obtained in several studies (e.g. Pierson and Lockhart, 1963; Zimmerman and Parlee, 1973). However, Gamberale *et al.* (1975), examining twelve women with severe menstrual distress, obtained a significant increase in reaction time during menstruation. No performance changes were observed in the other five tests used for measuring mental capacity. Hunter *et al.* (1979) also found a performance decrement during the premenstrual/menstrual phase in a choice-reaction time task requiring a judgement of stimulus intensity before response selection. This result is interesting since, in replicating the findings of Kopell *et al.* (1969) on two-flash thresholds with a signal-detection procedure, it was found that both sensory sensitivity *and* criterion scores changed; the subjects tended to adopt a more cautious attitude in the premenstrual period (De Marchi and Tong, 1972; Wong and Tong, 1974). Phase-related variations in sensory sensititivity have been reported for several types of stimuli (Diamond *et al.*, 1972), with lows during the premenstrual and/or the menstrual phase and highs at ovulation. The study of Diamond *et al.* (1972) on visual sensitivity also included four men, and four women on oral contraceptives, as control groups. Since cyclic changes could only be observed in non-pill women, the authors concluded that phase-related changes are probably due to the effect of endocrine changes on the CNS.

More direct evidence of the effect of gonadal hormones on the CNS has been provided by Vogel *et al.* (1971). They found an increase in EEG driving response to photic stimulation in the progesterone phase of the cycle as compared with the estrogen phase. Work on autonomic activity was reviewed by Weineman (1971). She concluded that the activity of the sympathetic nervous system is lower (Wenger's A-score higher) during the follicular than during the luteal phase. The function of the adrenals does not seem to vary in relation to the menstrual cycle (cortisol: e.g. Abplanalp *et al.*, 1977; catecholamines: Patkai *et al.*, 1974).

Redgrove (1971) and Sommer (1973) reviewed the effects of the menstrual cycle on behaviour and performance. While Redgrove focused on performance in industrial settings, Sommer was mainly interested in congitive functions and perceptual-motor behaviour. One of Sommer's conclusions was that a small percentage of women (about 8–16 per cent) do report an impairment of their mental capacities before or during menstruation. However, when objective measures of performance were used, the majority of the studies reviewed failed to demonstrate significant phase-related changes. One of the three exceptions in Sommer's review was Dalton's (1968) study of schoolgirls' examination performance. Dalton found that the girls' average mark was 5 per cent lower when examinations occurred before or during menstruation. Sommer (1973) pointed out that because of several methodological shortcomings the conclusion drawn by Dalton was completely unjustified. In a later paper (1978) Sommer also mentioned the possibility that the trauma of examination may provoke menstrual bleeding. In fact, Dalton (1968) reported a sudden rise in the number of girls menstruating during examination days, because the stress of examination altered the length of the menstrual cycle in 42 per cent of the girls. Nevertheless, she seemed to attribute the lower mark to menstruation, without considering the possibility that examination stress might effect the onset of menstruation *and* affect performance.

The same critique might be relevant to several studies by Dalton and others where an increase in negative behaviours — crimes, accidents, psychiatric crises — was reported to occur during the premenstrual/menstrual phase. Nevertheless, Sommer (1973) concluded that the evidence available still points to an effect of menstruation on negative social behaviours. Particularly convincing are the consistent results regarding suicide and suicide attempts, where all studies reviewed showed lows during the preovulatory phase.

Redgrove (1971) found the evidence concerning performance variations during the cycle somewhat conflicting. Her main conclusion was: 'it seems that the menstrual cycle does affect the capacity to carry out certain tasks, but that the extent to which these effects will be manifest in changes in performance depends on the extent to which decreases in capacity can be offset by increased effort' (p.235). As evidence of higher effort, i.e. higher motivation, during menstruation she referred to two studies from the 1930s. Her own studies included eight women in a laundry, three secretaries and nine punch-card operators. No significant phase-related changes in performance were found. For two of the three secretaries, however, a significant relationship was obtained between speed of typing and day of the menstrual cycle. The highest performance occurred just before the onset of menstruation and during the first three menstrual days! The hypothesis about higher effort was rejected for these subjects since they were considered to be working at full capacity all the time. Finally, the higher-effort hypothesis is also contradicted by the results of Patty and Ferrell (1974) showing that women in the intermenstrual phase are more motivated to achieve success than premenstrual women.

Subsequent research does not support the hypothesis that performance fluctuations parallel menstrual cycle phase. Golub (1976) studied several intellectual functions assumed to be vulnerable to affective changes. The test battery used comprised 15 measures of intellectual performance. Golub referred to Sommer's review (1973) and pointed out that the negative results were, in most studies, obtained from young women. Since premenstrual symptoms usually increase with age (Moos, 1968), her own sample was selected to consist of women between 30 and 45 years of age. Although the subjects felt significantly more depressed and anxious premenstrually, none of the performance measures showed a significant menstrual cycle effect. Rodin (1976) showed that menstruating women performed significantly better than non-menstruating women if they attributed task-produced arousal to menstruation. There was no difference between the groups in reported effort, hence Redgrove's (1971) suggestion was not supported.

8.3 CONCLUSIONS

It can be concluded that the occurrence of some negative moods and somatic complaints in a majority of women before and during menstruation is relatively well established. There is also some evidence of positive moods at ovulation. However, the precise nature of the so-called premenstrual syndrome has yet to be determined. It is possible that there is a kind of 'negative potential' associated with the premenstrual period which can be 'filled up' by various emotions depending on the psychological-social context.

The research on sexual arousal and behaviour gives a somewhat conflicting picture. However, the suggestion that there may be qualitative differences in sexual desire during the cycle is provocative and should be followed up.

There is evidence of the effect of menstruation on negative social behaviours, probably mediated by social and psychological factors. However, the adverse influence of the premenstrual and the menstrual periods upon performance is not well supported. Available tests may not be sensitive enough to detect possible small and subtle changes in intellectual or perceptual-motor capacity, although if these occur they may be of little practical interest. However, the reported criterion change in the two-flash fusion test suggests a possible influence of emotional factors on tasks involving judgement and decision.

Hours of Work
Edited by S. Folkard and T.H. Monk

Chapter 9

*Ultradian Cycles in Wakefulness — Possible Implications for Work–Rest Schedules**

Peretz Lavie

CONTENTS

ABSTRACT

Data accumulated in recent years have demonstrated cycles in diverse physiological and behavioural processes with a dominant periodicity of about 1½ h, similar to the periodicity of the REM–NONREM sleep cycles. Some of these findings have confirmed that part of Kleitman's Basic Rest–Activity Cycle (BRAC) hypothesis which predicts 1½-h cycles in waking alertness. Based on the observations that in sleep-deprived subjects the phase and period of the ultradian cycles in alertness are under voluntary control, it is hypothesized that the phase of the underlying ultradian 1½-h cycle can also be determined by motivational variables. This leads to the suggestion that the 1½-h periodicity can be seen as an endogenous 'biological working unit'.

*The research reported in this document has been made possible by Contract number DA-ERO-77-G-057 from the US Army Research Institute for the Behavioral and Social Sciences through its European Liaison Office at the European Research Office of the US Army, London, England. The opinions expressed are those of the author and do not necessarily represent those of the US Army.

9.1 INTRODUCTION

The major groups of biological rhythms have evolved in close synchrony with the temporal structure of the environment. The four circarhythms — circadian, circatidal, circalunar and circa-annual (Aschoff, 1967) — all correspond to geophysical cycles in the environment. These cycles are the day–night, tides, phases of the moon and seasons.

It has been shown that most of these rhythms persist with periods slightly deviating from the corresponding geophysical cycles when the organism is isolated from the environment.

Ultradian rhythms, which are rhythms with periods shorter than circadian (Halberg, 1967), are different from the four classes of circarhythms in not having a known corresponding environmental cycle. This chapter will summarize the evidence for the existence of ultradian rhythms in physiological and behavioural activities, and their possible relationship with the sleep REM–NONREM cycles, and will examine their possible practical implications. Although the term *ultradian* can be applied to any rhythm with a period of less than 20 h, in the present chapter the term will be used only for rhythms with a period of circa 1½ h.

9.2 THE REM–NONREM 1½-h SLEEP CYCLE

The REM–NONREM sleep cycle is no doubt the most known and best investigated ultradian cycle. Sleep is conveniently divided into two separate phases: REM (rapid eye movement) sleep and NONREM sleep. Each of the sleep phases is characterized by a distinct set of physiological changes and governed by separate neuroanatomic structures. Physiological changes associated with each of the alternating sleep states (e.g. low-voltage, fast electroencephalographic activity, rapid eye movements, irregular breathing and heart rate in REM sleep, and high-voltage, slow electroencephalographic activity, regular and slow breathing and heart rate in NONREM sleep) indicate that the cyclic changes in sleep phases actually represent a rather dramatic change in the CNS state of organization. This most probably requires complex temporal synchronization between diverse brain regions as well as between peripheral effectors.

It should be emphasized, however, that although the term REM–NONREM cycle is widely used, it is not always appreciated that it is far from being a precisely timed event. While the mean length of the cycle is close to 1½ h, this mean value is generally associated with a large between- and within-subject variability. Also, there is evidence that the REM–NONREM sleep cycle is not stationary. There is a progressive shortening of cycle length across the night and a systematic increase in the REM-NONREM ratio within each cycle (see a discussion of these data in Webb and Dube, 1981).

9.3 KLEITMAN'S BRAC MODEL

Are the 1½-h cyclic reorganization of brain activities exclusive sleep phenomena? Kleitman (1963) was the first to suggest that a cyclic process, analogous to the sleep REM–NONREM cycles, exists in waking as well. He termed this hypothesized cycle the Basic Rest–Activity Cycle (BRAC). He viewed the sleep and waking cycles as a continuous cycle, governed by the same oscillator. Kleitman hypothesized that:

> The basic rest–activity periodicity which appear in advanced sleep as a series of dreaming episodes may also manifest itself in the advanced wakefulness phase of the 24-hour rhythm in recurrent fluctuations in alertness. Postprandial letdowns and bouts of weariness at the end of the working day, often coinciding with the crest of the 24-hour rhythm, would be difficult to explain but for the relief afforded by a 15–30 min catnap, which may be long enough to tide one over the lowest part of the 80–100 min periodicity. (p.365)

9.4 ULTRADIAN RHYTHMS DURING WAKEFULNESS

Data accumulated during the last two decades have both supported Kleitman's intuitive hypothesis and expanded it. While Kleitman's model predicts ultradian cycles in waking alertness continuous with the sleep REM–NONREM cycle, several studies have shown that the 1½-h cyclicity can be traced in several behavioural and physiological processes such as renal secretions, gastric motility and eating behaviour, which are unrelated to variations in arousal.

Friedman and Fisher (1967) first reported that isolated humans, allowed free access to food, display about 1½-h cycles in their eating behaviour. Their findings were later replicated by Oswald *et al.* (1970) and by Kripke (1972). Eating cycles were also found in cats, with cycle lengths close to the length of cat REM–NONREM cycle, which is about 20 min (Sterman *et al.* 1972).

Historically, 1½-h cycles in gastric motility were among the first cycles to be documented in humans. Early in the century, Wada (1922) described a 1½-h cycle in gastric motility of sleeping humans. Recent research has indeed confirmed these observations. Hiatt and Kripke (1972) demonstrated similar cycles in waking, fasting humans, and Lavie *et al.* (1978) replicated Wada's original findings by demonstrating such cycles during sleep. This latter study, however, failed to demonstrate a consistent phase relationship between cycles in gastric motility and the sleep REM–NONREM cycles. Similarly, a lack of relationship between cyclic gastric motility and the sleep cycles was reported by Tassinari *et al.* (1973). Furthermore, dogs, sheep and rabbits were also shown to have about 1½-h cycles in gastric motility although their REM–NONREM cycles are much faster (Grievel and Ruckebusch, 1972).

Renal excretions also show high amplitude ultradian cycles having the same dominant periodicity of about 1½ h. Lavie and Kripke (1977) first showed that voluntarily urinating humans, who consumed a constant amount of fluids, secreted urine cyclically. Peak volumes occurred every 1½ h. Urinary osmolality and the concentration of Na^+ and K^+ also varied cyclically with similar periodicity, 180° out of phase to the cycles in volume. Subsequent studies have shown that the degree of synchronization among the various urinary cycles and their amplitude are dependent on the level of hydration and on posture (Luboshitzky *et al.*, 1978). Furthermore, nocturnal cycles in urine flow in sleeping humans were only partially synchronized with the sleep REM–NONREM cycles (Lavie *et al.*, 1979). Dissociation between cycles in renal activity and the REM–NONREM cycles was also demonstrated in dogs. Gordon and Lavie (1982) showed 2–2½-h cycles in dogs' urine and osmolality, which are much slower than the ½-h REM–NONREM cycles in dogs. As in humans, posture, circadian phase and the level of hydration appeared to influence the synchronization between various cycles in renal activity in the dog.

In the light of the above data, it can be concluded at this stage, even before discussing the evidence supporting the ultradian cyclicity in alertness, that the 1½-h cycles are generated by a multioscillatory system. This conclusion expands the BRAC hypothesis, which viewed the waking and sleep cycles as fragments of a single oscillatory process.

However, the experimental data confirm that part of the BRAC model which predicts orderly fluctuations in waking levels of alertness. These may affect human behaviour.

9.5 ALERTNESS OR 'SLEEPABILITY'

Kleitman's intuition that the BRAC during the waking state would be manifested in orderly fluctuations in alertness has been supported by several independent studies. In isolated subjects under partial sensory deprivation, Kripke (1972) reported significant ultradian cycles in electroencephalographic activity at various frequencies that were most prominent in the delta frequency band (0.5–3.0 cycles per second). Later, Kripke and Sonnenschein (1978) investigated the relation between fluctuations in electroencephalographic activity and daydreaming in isolated subjects. They reported that daydreaming, resembling the hypnagogic hallucinations during sleep onset, occurred at about 1½-h intervals. These were correlated with increased alpha activity and diminution of eye movements. Gertz and Lavie (1983) also showed ultradian cycles in electroencephalographic parameters. Diurnal EEG and subjectively appraised arousal measures were recorded from eleven subjects on a 5-min recording–5-min recovery schedule, continuously over 7½ h. Subjects returned to the laboratory for another 7½-h experimental period during which they attempted either to raise or to lower the frequency of their EEG with the aid of biofeedback. Significant 1½-h cyclicity was observed in the EEG measures and in the subjectively appraised arousal during both the baseline and biofeedback sessions.

Lavie (1979) investigated daytime variations in pupillary size and stability. Both are sensitive indices of sleepiness and fatigue. In this study, pupillary measures were sampled every 15 min for 10 continuous hours. Ultradian variations were found in pupillary size and stability, which were 180° out of phase with each other. That is, pupillary dilation was associated with increased stability of the pupils.

Lavie and Scherson (1981) hypothesized that ultradian cycles in alertness, if present, should be reflected in subjects' ability to fall asleep at different times during the day. To test their hypothesis, they instructed subjects to attempt to fall asleep every 20 min for 5 min, for 10 continuous hours. Electro-physiological recordings were performed during each of the 30 5-min sleep attempts. Significant 1½-h cycles in stage 1 sleep were found (Figure 9.1). The ultradian variations in the appearance of sleep stage 1 were also modulated by a circadian cycle. There was a gradual increase in wake time towards the afternoon and early evening hours and an increase in sleep stage 2 around midday at the expected 'post-lunch dip'. In the second part of this study, subjects were sleep deprived before the daytime study. Under sleep deprivation conditions, the ultradian cyclicity in 'sleepability' was modified. These results will be described in greater detail later on in this section.

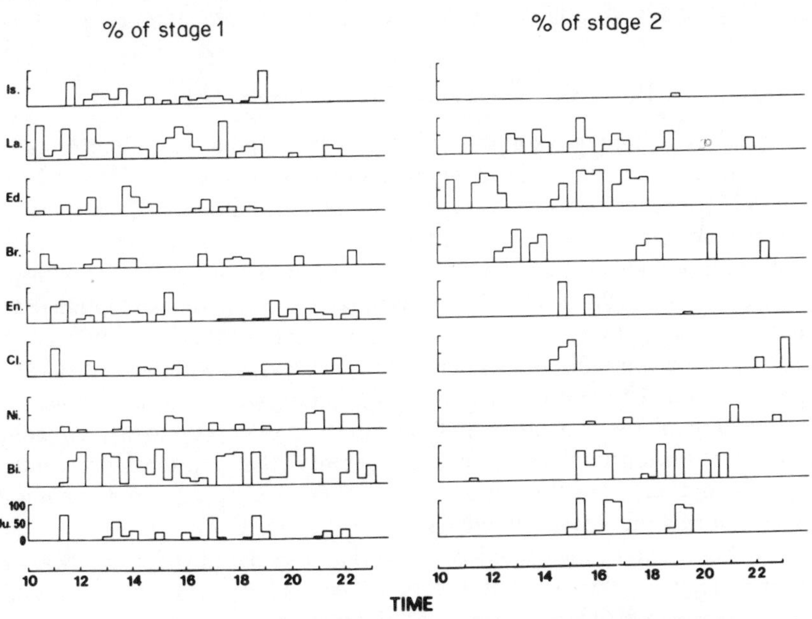

Figure 9.1 Twenty-minute distributions of stage 1 and stage 2 during the day in a 15-min waking – 5-min sleep schedule. Reproduced with permission from Lavie and Scherson (1981)

In a recent extension of the Lavie and Scherson study, Zomer and Lavie (1981) attempted to determine if the waking cyclicity in the ability to fall asleep is continuous with the sleep REM–NONREM cycles, as predicted from the BRAC hypothesis. On two separate days, subjects were awakened from sleep, either from REM or from NONREM sleep, and began a 15-min waking – 5-min sleeping schedule for 8 continuous hours. The post-awakening cycles in sleepability were only weakly synchronized with the sleep REM–NONREM cycles. When awakened from NONREM sleep, subjects showed more sleep during the first two or three sleep attempts than when awakened from REM sleep. However, because of the large between-subject variability, this difference only bordered statistical significance. In agreement with the results reported by Lavie and Scherson, there was a marked circadian modulation of the ultradian cycles in sleepability. The ultradian cyclicity was most prominent during the morning hours.

In summary, the accumulated evidence provides support for that part of the BRAC hypothesis which predicts the existence of diurnal fluctuations in alertness and arousal. The data collected so far suggest that there are short-term cycles in the ability to fall asleep. Although it could be argued that these cycles may equally reflect fluctuations in the central nervous system 'wakeability', e.g. the ability to maintain the waking state, there are preliminary data suggesting that cycles in 'sleepability' and 'wakeability' are not complementary processes (see 9.7).

9.6 PERCEPTUAL-MOTOR PERFORMANCE

Some of the most impressive ultradian cycles in perceptual-motor performance were shown in the perception of apparent motions. Lavie *et al.* (1974) and Lavie *et al.* (1975) investigated the perception of the spiral aftereffect, an apparent motion produced by a fixation on a rotating spiral, at 5-min intervals for 8-h day and 8-h night periods. They reported 1½-h cycles in the duration of the illusion during the day and night. Similar cycles were later found in the perception of the phi-phenomenon (Lavie, 1976). Furthermore, the ultradian cycles in the perception of the spiral aftereffect appeared synchronized with the cycles in the phi-phenomenon. This suggests a common oscillatory regulating mechanism for the perception of two apparent motions. In a similar way to the circadian modulation of the ultradian cyclicity in 'sleepability', the cycles in the perception of apparent motions were also not stationary. There was a gradual lengthening of the cycles during the afternoon-evening hours (Lavie, 1977).

Although it would be logical to look for ultradian cycles in vigilance, there has been surprisingly little work in this direction. The reason is that, because most, if not all, experimental interest in cycles in vigilance has focused on circadian variations, experimental designs generally employ sampling rates which are too slow to detect ultradian variations. Studies employing fast sampling rates that were sufficient for the detection of ultradian cycles lasted no more than 1–2 h, which is obviously too short to register 1½-h cycles.

The first attempts to search for ultradian cyclicity in vigilance performance were made by Globus *et al.* (1971). They described equivocal 1½-h cycles in performance of a 6-h continuous vigilance task. However, those cycles were rather weak and there was evidence of fluctuations at other frequencies as well. Orr *et al.* (1974) also reported on similar cycles in prolonged complex vigilance performance.

Gopher and Lavie (1980) investigated the possible existence of ultradian cyclicity in the linear positioning task. In this perceptual-motor task, subjects are required to move a lever to a distance of 20 cm along a metal rod, relying only on auditory and proprioceptive stimuli. Subjects were tested every 20 min or every 10 min from 0800 until 1800. In both sampling frequencies, positioning errors varied in 1½-h ultradian cycles. No significant cycles were found, however, in the speed of performance, and there was no consistent phase relationship between the cycles in performance and cycles in the flow of urine, although both cyclic phenomena showed the same cyclicity of about 1½ h. Providing subjects with immediate knowledge of results suppresses the ultradian cyclicity in positioning errors. It is interesting to note that Lavie *et al.* (1981) and Kripke *et al.* (1975) also failed to find cycles in a reaction time task.

9.7 THE EFFECTS OF SLEEP DEPRIVATION

Most of the studies investigating ultradian cyclicity in alertness and performance investigated subjects living under normal conditions during the habitual waking day. Preliminary results show, however, that sleep deprivation modifies the ultradian cyclic structure of alertness. Lavie and Scherson (1981) made some preliminary investigations on the effect of sleep deprivation on the diurnal cycles in 'sleepability'. Following one night of either total sleep deprivation or selective REM sleep deprivation, the 1½-h ultradian cycles in 'sleepability' were changed to much slower cycles of about 4–5 hours.

In the light of these preliminary results, additional experiments were conducted to investigate the effect of sleep deprivation on the temporal structure of diurnal 'sleepability' and 'wakeability' (paper in preparation). The experimental protocol was similar to the one used by Lavie and Scherson (1981). Following one night of total sleep deprivation, subjects began at 0720 a schedule of 13-min waking – 7-min sleep for either 16 or 24 hours. In addition to 'sleepability', the subjects' ability to resist sleep was also investigated. In this experimental condition, subjects began at 0720 a schedule of 13-min active waking outside the bedroom – 7-min passive waking in bed for either 16 or 24 hours after one night of total sleep deprivation. During the 7-min passive waking in bed, subjects were required to lie in bed with eyes closed and to attempt to resist sleep.

In agreement with our previous results, sleep deprivation modified the temporal structure of daytime alertness towards periodicities much slower than 1½ h. Unexpectedly, however, the temporal structure of subjects' 'wakeability' — that is, their ability to resist sleep — was different from the temporal structure of their 'sleepability'. The cyclic changes in alertness, as measured by the amount of sleep in each 7-min 'sleep attempt' or 'resisting-sleep attempt', were much more prominent in the resisting-sleep condition. Figure 9.2 presents the mean

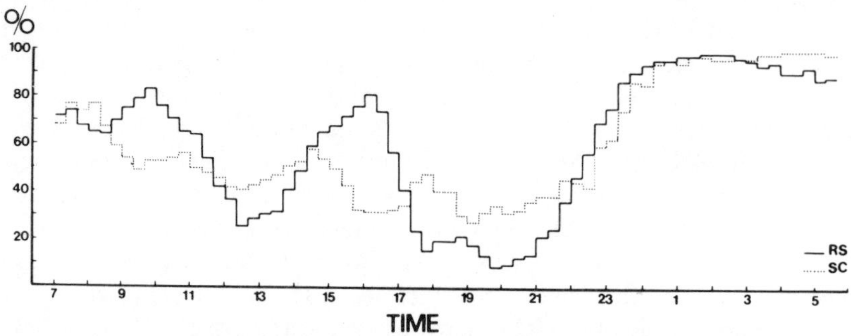

Figure 9.2 Mean data (N=4) for total sleep in each 7-min sleep attempt in the 13-min active waking – 7-min sleep schedule (dotted line) and in the 13-min active waking – 7-min passive waking in bed schedule (continuous line)

data for total sleep in each of the 72 7-min trials for four subjects investigated for 24 hours. When attempting to resist sleep, there were two sleep-irresistible periods during the day, at around 1000–1100 and at 1500–1600. Sleep, however, could be easily avoided at 1200–1400 and at 1800–2100. This 6-h cycle is not seen when subjects attempt to fall asleep.

As will be discussed later on, these last results may have important theoretical and practical implications. The fact that subjects, motivated to remain awake following one night of sleep deprivation, displayed cyclic alternations of increased and decreased 'wakeability', which does not correspond in time to fluctuations in their 'sleepability', suggests that the cyclic processes during the day may be at least partially under subjects' voluntary control.

9.8 THEORETICAL IMPLICATIONS

The data collected so far provide support for the BRAC model that circa 1½-h cycles can be measured in waking arousal. However, the findings that there are several unrelated cycles with a similar dominant periodicity strongly suggest that not only one, but several oscillators modulate functions with cycles averaging about 1½ h. We have little understanding of the functional manifestations of such cycles. Based on preliminary studies in primates (Bowden *et al.* 1978; Lewis *et al.* 1977; Delgado-Garcia *et al.*, 1976), Lavie and Kripke (1981) have recently suggested that the role of at least some of the ultradian cycles must be sought within the complex adaptation of group-living animals to their environment. Lavie and Scherson (1981) have speculated that the ultradian cyclicity in sleepiness can be seen as multiple 'sleepiness gates' during the waking state which facilitate the transitions from waking to sleeping. The main function of these 'gates' may be to provide the circadian sleep–waking cycle with a high degree of flexibility and hence adaptability to changes in sleep schedule on demand.

9.9 ULTRADIAN RHYTHMS AND WORK–REST SCHEDULES

More than a decade ago, Kleitman (1970) envisioned a practical utilization of the BRAC model: 'We can perhaps utilize the existence of this biological hour to schedule classes, units of work in factories and offices, coffee breaks, and in general arrange our activities on a rational physiological basis' (p.14). In the light of the data supporting some aspects of the BRAC model, is there any evidence supporting its possible practical utilization?

Ideally, daily activities could be optimized by synchronizing job breaks or rest periods with the recurrent 'sleepiness gates' shown, for instance, by Lavie and Scherson (1981). According to such a synchronicity, the working day would be comprised of five or more 1½-h 'working units'. The brief rest periods at the end of each 'unit' would, in Kleitman's words, 'tide one over the lowest part of the 80–100 minute periodicity'. A well-known example of such synchronicity between a presumably hypoaroused period and diurnal behaviour is the prevailing habit of taking a nap during the post-prandial dip. Increased sleepiness around midday was shown by Webb and Agnew (1977), Carskadon and Dement (1979) and Lavie and Scherson (1981) and decreased performance around this time was shown by Blake (1967).

Assuming that the ultradian cycle is an endogenous free-running cycle, accurate information about its periodicity and phase are required in order to achieve such a synchronicity. Such information is not yet available. As described previously, the periodicity of the ultradian cycle is not stationary, and the phase of the cycle is only weakly related to the REM–NONREM cycle.

Our most recent results, demonstrating a different time course for 'sleepability' and 'wakeability' of sleep-deprived subjects, raise the possibility that under certain conditions the phase of the ultradian cycle may be under voluntary control. Therefore, it is possible that starting a continuous or repetitive task, which requires high levels of alertness, resets the phase of the underlying alertness cycle. Thus, a worker beginning a repetitive and demanding task at a certain time of the day is able to maintain a constant level of performance for no more than 1½ h. A dip in performance is expected after about 1½ h, followed by a subsequent spontaneous improvement in performance and so on. In fact, there are some experimental data supporting the possibility that a 'biological working unit' of about 1½ h indeed exists. Murrel (1971), who extensively studied industrial work rythms, tested subjects for 3½ continuous hours on a task simulating the checking of electrical components. He observed that after work had continued for a period of time there was a phase of irregularity in the performance. This was followed by a surprising improvement in regularity and a second deterioration. Murrel stated that 'over a period of 6 years, 22 subjects were tested and they showed this effect fairly consistently'. He further concluded that the timing of the onset of irregularity may be related to the nature of the job and 'will not normally show a big intersubject variation'.

Although Murrel did not explain his observations in terms of resetting the phase of an underlying 1½-h ultradian cycle in alertness, he viewed these performance cycles as reflecting regular variations in arousal which may be partly under voluntary control. Based on these data, he suggested that a high level of sustained arousal cannot be maintained by operators for more than 2 h. Although he found it technically difficult to test his hypothesis in field studies, he described a preliminary study demonstrating that operators in a factory increased their production when they took a fixed rest period of 10 min every 60 min, in comparison with the irregularly occurring rests of varying length that they were accustomed to.

In conclusion, in the light of the accumulated evidence, the possible existence of a 1½-h biological 'working unit' is fascinating and merits further investigation. Synchronizing the rhythms of work with underlying biological rhythms may increase production and decrease errors and workers' attrition, particularly in highly demanding tasks.

Hours of Work
Edited by S. Folkard and T.H. Monk

Chapter 10

Vigilance: Theories and Laboratory Studies

Angus Craig

CONTENTS

ABSTRACT

This chapter reviews the success met by theories of vigilance in explaining not only the characteristic problems of vigilance, the low performance levels and especially the performance decrement with time on task, but also the fact that vigilance tasks are so particularly susceptible to the decrement. The four most prominent theories — inhibition, arousal, expectancy and attention — are evaluated, and it is concluded that only the first mentioned provides a reasonable explanation for the decrement, although the others give adequate accounts for the low performance levels. It is left to two contemporary views to account for the decrement, the one in terms of a detectability deficit, the other in terms of an active criterion adjustment; they also help to explain why decrements are so particularly evident in vigilance tasks.

10.1 INTRODUCTION AND BACKGROUND

This chapter is about vigilance, involving the sustained detection or recognition of a specified, infrequent event, as in radar or industrial inspection. Like other chapters in the volume, then, this too is about the effects of temporal factors on performance. However, unlike the material covered in Chapters 4 and 8, any performance fluctuations during vigilance are time-locked to the task itself, rather than stemming from any fundamental oscillations in the operator's functional state.

10.1.1 The problems of vigilance

Figure 10.1 illustrates a characteristic vigilance decrement function. In the case shown, operators alerted to the occurrence of a specified signal could detect its

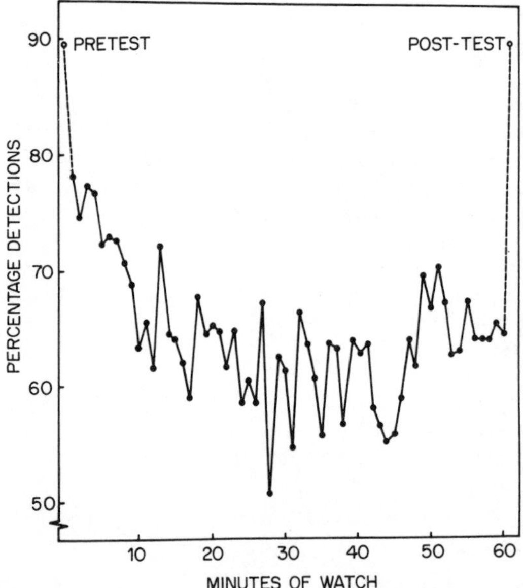

Figure 10.1 The classic vigilance decrement: mean percentage detections in 1-minute intervals as a function of time on watch, N=54. From Buckner *et al.* (1960)

presence about 90 per cent of the time. But in the unalerted conditions of vigilance, their detection level rapidly declined to 60 per cent. Immediately the vigil was over, and a return made to the alerted conditions, the original 90 per cent detection level was reinstated. These data reveal a fourfold increase in the risk of detection failure within a matter of minutes from the start of the vigil. Such substantial decrements are common in vigilance research; and the typical tasks where a failure of vigilance is most likely to occur are often ones where the consequences of a detection failure can be most serious; they include, for example, patient monitoring in intensive therapy units, radar monitoring in air traffic control and in early warning systems, nuclear plant process control monitoring, and quality control inspection in the pharmaceutical and aerospace industries. In other words, vigilance has to do with a non-trivial problem that has non-trivial consequences.

The 'vigilance decrement' can also be reflected by an increase in response latency: sometimes the latency distribution becomes progressively more skewed over time, and the lengthening is particularly evident in the longer latencies, shorter ones remaining unaltered, or even speeding up (see Davies and Parasuraman, 1982). These effects on correct detections and latencies should be integrated in an explanation of the decrement, as should the observation that false detections (reporting the occurrence of the signal when it is not there) sometimes decline over time too.

The importance of false detections in detection and recognition was conclusively demonstrated in the development of signal detectability theory (Green and Swets, 1966). Because of data or sensory limitations, an observer is often faced with the task of having to reach a decision under conditions of considerable uncertainty. If a signal is present and he judges incorrectly, he makes an error of omission — i.e. he misses, or fails to detect, the signal. On the other hand, if a signal is not present, and his judgement is in error, he makes a false detection, or false alarm. The clearer the signal, or the less noise in the internal and external systems, the higher the quality of the sensory evidence and the less likely it is that such confusions will arise. However, where such confusion does exist so that errors are inevitable, it is clear that the observer can modify his judgements, biasing them one way or another so as to affect the balance of errors, depending on his subjective evaluation of the relative weights of a miss and a false alarm. As applied to vigilance, the issue becomes one of determining whether the decrement involves a decline in the quality of the evidence (i.e. a detectability decrement) or merely a shift in the balance of errors (a criterion shift). As will be seen, apart from a narrow subset of tasks identified by Parasuraman and Davies (1977), the more common finding is that the vigilance decrement represents a shift in the balance of errors.

10.1.2 Central or peripheral?

The vigilance decrement clearly exists and is sufficiently serious to be worrying. It may or may not diminish over repeated sessions, but it does not get worse. These are among the key issues that have to be explained by any adequate theory of vigilance. As a preliminary, one can infer from the immediate reinstatement of the pre-vigil detection level on the return to the alert condition, that the decrement is probably central rather than peripheral in origin; the role of decision processes that was alluded to in the above section also supports this interpretation. The involvement of peripheral motor functioning is virtually eliminated by Adam's

(1955) observation that the usual, restorative benefits of a rest break are negated if the observer has to spend the rest break watching someone else perform the task; and by the finding that the decrement is unaffected by requirements to respond differently to all events presented rather than to respond to the infrequent signals only (Guralnick and Harvey, 1970; Whittenburg *et al.*, 1956). Any involvement of peripheral sensory functioning is contra-indicated by Mackworth *et al.*'s (1964) findings which show that failure to report (and hence detect) could occur even when the ocular system actively hunted for and fixated a signal.

10.1.3. Requisites of a theory of vigilance

If we accept that the vigilance decrement is central in origin, we still have to explain why the decrement occurs so readily in vigilance, whereas other central processes (e.g. semantic coding, mental arithmetic) have proved so remarkably resistant to decrement with time on task (see, for example, Robinson, 1938; Thorndike, 1926). The most obvious step is to seek the answer in the task variables of vigilance research, and these will feature prominently in the account presented here. By way of a complement to this emphasis, Chapter 11 focuses on the personal variables that distinguish most clearly between those observers who are likely to exhibit a substantial vigilance decrement, and those who are not.

10.2 THEORIES OF VIGILANCE

The present aim is to provide the flavour of the ideas that have guided research on vigilance over the past three or four decades. The major explanations of the decrement have attributed it to accumulated inhibition, declining expectancy, lowered arousal and increasing distraction. These are considered in turn.

10.2.1 Inhibition theory

The training and test stages of vigilance experiments resemble the acquisition and extinction phases in studies of response conditioning: in each case responses are reinforced during the former stage, but not during the latter; and in each case the unreinforced responses gradually become slower and less frequent, as if the response is inhibited or extinguished.

This notion that the level of vigilance declines because of a progressive increase in the strength of an inhibitory state, was originally advanced by N.H. Mackworth (1950) to account for the decline in detections of a relatively inconspicuous signal, and was championed more recently by McCormack (1962, 1967) to explain the decrement in response speed to a highly discriminable light-flash signal. Sufficient parallels can be drawn to ensure that this inhibition theory merits serious consideration, particularly if one recognizes the possibility that the inhibition stems primarily from the extinction of the signal response in the presence of non-signal events, events which closely resemble the signals.

These parallels between vigilance and extinction may be enumerated (see Broadbent, 1953). The main points of correspondence include:

(i) Whereas without reinforcement (knowledge of results, verbal encouragement) the detection response to signal occurrence declines and slows down over time (*extinction, inhibition*), with knowledge of results, detection response probability and latency are typically invariant with time on task (*reinforcement*) (McCormack, 1967; Warm, 1977), sometimes even when the KR is false (non-contingent reinforcement) (*disinhibition*) (Boakes, 1973; Warm, 1977).
(ii) Detection rates and latencies both improve following a brief rest pause (*dissipation of inhibition*) (Colquoun, 1959; Jenkins, 1958), and, between sessions, may recover to their original levels (*spontaneous recovery*) (Adams *et al.*, 1962; Wiener, 1964).
(iii) The introduction of a novel, extraneous stimulus event can re-establish pre-decrement levels of responding (*disinhibition*) (Mackworth, 1950; McCormack, 1962).
(iv) In conditions of low to medium temporal uncertainty, detection rates tend to be higher, and response times faster, the longer the interval between signals (*dissipated inhibition*) (Jerison, 1967; McCormack, 1967).
(v) At the same time as responding to a primary signal declines, responding to a secondary signal may improve (*behavioural contrast*) (Craig and Colquhoun, 1977).

However, inhibition theory is less able to account for the following common observations:

(i) Detection levels may be suboptimal, right from the start of the vigilance session (see Figure 10.1).
(ii) Responses may fail to become fully extinguished. Mackworth (1950) invoked the notion of expectancy to account for this partial extinction; McCormack (1962) stressed the role of motivation or drive level.
(iii) In an important minority of cases, response probability and latency remain invariant with time on task, despite the presence of features conducive to extinction.
(iv) The *more* probable the occurrence of the signal event, the *higher* is the probability of the detection response, and the *less* susceptible it is to decrement, despite being more frequently elicited without subsequent reinforcement (Craig, 1981).
(v) The likelihood of the detection response being elicited increases following an increase in signal frequency between training (acquisition) and test (extinction) phases, but declines when the signal frequency is lowered (Colquhoun and Baddeley, 1967).

The main problematic findings for inhibition theory would seem to be (i) the persistence of the detection response and the failure to achieve complete extinction of it, even with repeated non-reinforcement sessions, and (ii) the elevation rather than reduction in the rate of responding in circumstances of increased signal frequency.

These findings may be more adequately explained by expectancy theory, to which consideration is now given.

10.2.2 Expectancy theory

Expectancy theory consists of two distinct aspects, tonic and phasic. The tonic aspect relates the level of vigilance to signal frequency; the phasic aspect relates the time course of momentary fluctuactions in detection readiness to the arrival times of signal events, and relates the decrement to mismatches between these two temporal functions.

The original version of expectancy theory was stated by Deese (1955, p.362):

> (a) the observer's expectancy or prediction about the search task is determined by the actual course of stimulus events during his previous experience with the task, and (b) the observer's level of expectancy determines his vigilance level and hence his probability of detection.

Thus, when signal frequency is low, detections will be low also, and will continue to be made at this low level.

As Deese acknowledged, it is a theory about the level of vigilance, not about the decrement; if the task remains invariant, the expectancy level should also. Expectancy theory is not intended to explain the decline depicted in Figure 10.1.

However, the hypothesis does offer an account for those findings that were considered to be problematic for inhibition theory: the maintenance of a low but persistent level of responding, and the positive link between the level of responding and signal frequency.

Expectancy provides one explanation for those observations that detection probability and response speed are increasing functions of signal frequency, and that false alarm proportions may be also (Jenkins, 1958). Not surprisingly, the expectancy hypothesis also provides a ready explanation for those instances in which tailor-made transfer or carry-over effects from one level of signal or non-signal frequency to another have been demonstrated (Colquhoun and Baddeley, 1964, 1967; Krulewitz *et al.*, 1975). Mention may also be made here that it seems to be the signal's relative frequency of occurrence (i.e. the signal probability), rather than its absolute frequency, that is important in determining detection probability (Colquhoun, 1961; Jerison *et al.*, 1965; Loeb and Binford, 1968).

Shifts in the total stimulus event rate will obviously produce shifts in signal frequency without affecting signal probability, but in these instances, detection probability has generally been found to be a decreasing function of the stimulus rate (see, for example, Howell *et al.*, 1966; Loeb and Binford, 1968; McGrath and Hatcher, 1961), and although the effects of signal probability and stimulus event rate have been found to interact (see, for example, Jerison, 1967; Krulewitz and Warm, 1977), the general impression is that the overall stimulus event rate is the more potent factor of the two (see, for example, Loeb and Binford, 1968; Taub and Osborne, 1968). The usefulness of the tonic aspect of expectancy is therefore of somewhat limited value.

Unfortunately, rather much the same has to be said about the phasic aspect of the hypothesis, as elaborated by Baker (1959, 1963a).

Detection readiness could be a declining function of intersignal interval, being highest immediately after a signal has occurred, due to the latter's reinforcing properties (see, for example, Deese, 1955; Holland, 1958; Jenkins, 1958), or it could be an increasing function, being low immediately following a signal, then gradually recovering due to the dissipation of inhibition (see, for example, McCormack, 1962). In fact, Baker thought that expectancy would peak at a point in time equivalent to the mean of the intervals experienced in the past, and so would be low both immediately after a signal, and after a longer than average interval of time had elapsed. Tenuous support for each of these hypotheses can be found, but failures to find any effect indicate that one might fare as well by predicting that, within a session, detection readiness is independent of intersignal interval (Deese, 1955; Jenkins, 1958; McCormack and Prysiazniuk, 1961). McGrath and Harabedian (1963) have demonstrated that any simple effect of intersignal interval is probably obscured by whether or not the previous signal was detected, or a false alarm intervened, whether the signal frequency is high or low, and whether the observer perceives this signal rate to be faster or slower than it really is; but even allowing for these factors, support for Baker's expectancy hypothesis remains thin.

Baker's hypothesis implies that expectancy will be lower the more variable the interval between signals. In addition, he suggested that when signals failed to arrive at the peak expected moment, these failures to confirm expectancies would lead to a reduction in expectancy level, and hence in detection probability and response speed. In this way, almost as an afterthought, expectancy theory provides an attempted explanation for the vigilance decrement.

Once more, the evidence provides less than adequate support for the hypothesis. A number of studies have failed to find any particular influence of signal arrival-time regularity on detections or latencies (see, for example, Boulter and Adams, 1963; Smith *et al.*, 1966). Apart from Baker's (1963a) own evidence, only a few studies (e.g. Dardano, 1962; McCormack and Prysiazniuk, 1961) have found the predicted effect of signal regularity on response latency, but they have failed to confirm that it affects the decrement.

One is left therefore with the paradox of a major theory about vigilance whose relevance to the central phenomenon of vigilance still has to be demonstrated.

Whether that same criticism can also be levelled against arousal theory provides a focal issue for the next section.

10.2.3 Arousal theory

Deese (1955) acknowledged that the maintenance of the excitatory state of vigilance would depend on stimulation provided by the task, but felt that this might be inadequately varied to maintain even the minimal arousal level necessary for normal functioning.

Some support for this arousal interpretation has come from a number of studies that have presented varied stimulation (VS) in another modality, extraneous to the vigilance task itself. Generally, detection probability or latency improves (McGrath and Hatcher, 1961; Tarriere and Wisner, 1962; Ware *et al.*, 1964); occasionally, the decrement is reduced too (see, for example, Davies *et al.*, 1973; Fox, 1975). The elevated detections are sometimes gained at the cost of increased false alarms (see, for example, Davies *et al.*, 1973; McGrath, 1960), implying a shift in the criterion rather than in detectability; contrariwise, in a study by Davies *et al.* (1969), the only effect of the VS was a reduction in false alarms, and even this was confined to extraverted personality types. McGrath (1960) had shown that when individuals could choose how long they were exposed to VS, the improvement in detections was highly correlated with the exposure duration chosen, and Davies *et al.* (1969) had shown that extraverts, who seemed to benefit most from VS, were precisely the ones who elected to be exposed for longest to it. In accordance with arousal theory, extraverts, who seem less capable than introverts during vigilance (see, for example, Colquhoun, 1960), have been regarded as chronically less highly aroused than introverts (Broadbent, 1963a; Corcoran, 1965). (A more elaborate treatment of these individual differences is presented in Chapter 11 by Roy Davies.)

An interesting study by McGrath and Hatcher (1961) showed that the decrement on a visual task only benefited from auditory VS when the stimulus frequency was low; when it was high, VS actually enhanced the decrement. This again is consistent with arousal theory, but could equally be due to the interesting conglomeration of music, voices and other sounds distracting attention from the very demanding high-paced task (see Poulton, 1977).

Complementary to these effects, Zuercher (1965) found that conversation or mild exercise, engaged in after performance had declined, served to eliminate the decrement. This would not be surprising to the early researchers investigating the 'work decrement' on sustained cognitive tasks (e.g. Robinson and Bills, 1926), and to those currently working on the problems of monotonous work in industry, where increased self-stimulation from fidgeting and other forms of subsidiary behaviour seems to have a compensatory effect, relieving the monotony of the task, and preventing a decline in the level of functioning (e.g. Kishida, 1973).

A different approach to questions about the role of arousal in vigilance stems from the argument that, since arousal is presumed to have a physiological basis, the decline should be measurable on some recognized activation index. But this approach has been hampered by the lack of agreement on the means of objectively defining differences in arousal level, and by the known dissociations in activation level between different physiological functions, or between them and behavioural arousal (e.g. Lacey, 1967). In any case, the requisite controls have too often been lacking, so that it is impossible to say whether 'arousal' is declining due to the vigilance situation in particular, or merely to the general inactivity the situation usually demands — but in common with numerous other non-vigilance situations (see Parasuraman, 1984). In an all too rare example with adequate control, O'Hanlon (1964) demonstrated that an on-task decline in the level of plasma adrenaline by people who exhibited a vigilance decrement was completely absent from a comparable group of 'decrementers' who spent the duration of the vigil watching films. However, the data indicate, not a decline *from* the stable level of the film-watchers, but a decline *to* their level, suggesting that task-related arousal was initially higher than usual, then declined towards a 'normal' level by the end of the vigil.

It is often assumed that arousal changes as a function of time of day, increasing between early and later parts of the day, and there is fairly consistent evidence that the level of vigilance (detections, latencies) increases *pari passu* with the assumed changes in arousal, although admittedly usually with a concomitant increase in false alarms (Craig *et al.*, 1981). However, there is no parallel evidence of a consistent relation between the decrement and diurnal arousal levels (Colquhoun *et al.*, 1968a, 1968b).

Sleep deprivation is held to be de-arousing (by, for example, Johnson, 1982; Kjellberg, 1977a; Wilkinson, 1965) and the major studies of the effects on vigilance do reveal a drop in signal detectability (Poulton *et al.*, 1972, 1974; Wilkinson, 1958, 1972). But effects on the decrement are inconsistent, being absent in the study by Poulton *et al.* (1972) but present in the earlier study by Wilkinson (1958) — although only in so far as a decrement that did not occur under normal conditions was observed in the sleep-deprived state. Other reports of an effect on the decrement stem from studies involving a task with an unusually high event rate, and with a duration of only 10 min. (e.g. Williams *et al.*, 1959).

So, once again, there seems to be ample evidence that arousal influences the level of vigilance, but considerably less support for the fundamental proposition that it effects the decrement.

One of the specific hypotheses put forward to explain the effects of sleep deprivation was that it increased the incidence of momentary lapses of attention (Warren and Clarke, 1937; Williams *et al.*, 1959). This brings us on to the last of the major theories about vigilance.

10.2.4 Attention theory

Broadbent (1958, 1971) and Jerison (1970; Jerison *et al.*, 1965), in particular, both emphasized that, to be detected, a signal had first of all to be observed. Any failure to be paying attention when a transient signal arrived would result in a detection failure.

Broadbent assumed that (i) information from the environment was selectively filtered, only a restricted portion being adequately received at any one time, and that (ii) the filter was biased in favour of novelty, and against redundant information. In vigilance, any novelty associated with the occurrence of signal events will soon decline, reducing with it the probability of efficient, directed attention and of the detection of signals.

Broadbent linked his filter theory notion to evidence of 'blocks' in sustained, attention-demanding, cognitive tasks (Bills, 1931). 'Blocks' appear as momentary hesitations during an otherwise smooth flow of efficient information processing, may be identified as instances where the processing of an item takes twice as long as usual, and apparently function to dissipate fatigue (Bertelson and Joffe, 1963). Data from vigilance studies that have revealed a decrement in response latency confined to the longest latencies alone, without a corresponding shift in mean latency (e.g. Howell *et al.*, 1966; Thackray *et al.*, 1977) are consistent with Broadbent's hypothesis.

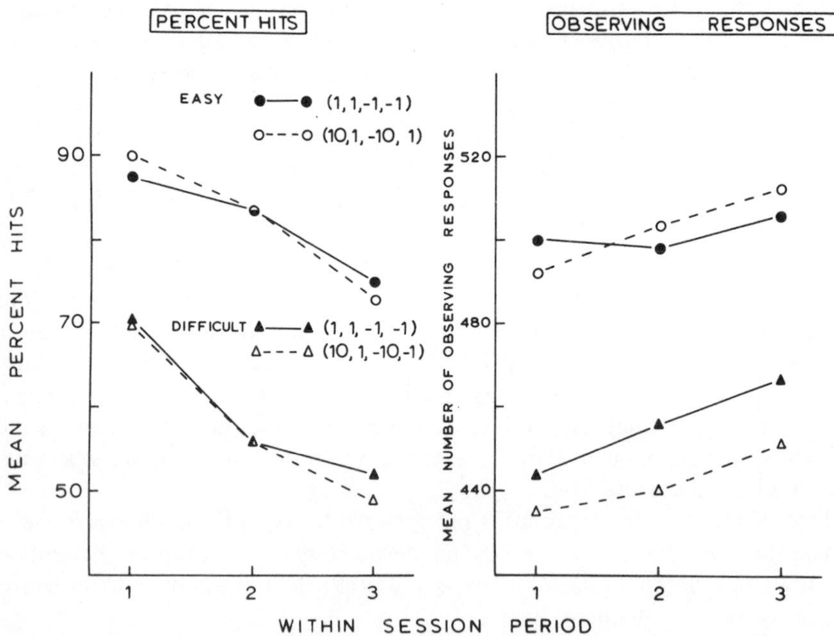

Figure 10.2 The decline in hits and the simultaneous increase in observing responses with time on task for an easy and for a difficult signal under symmetric (1, 1, –1, –1) and asymmetric (10, 1, –10, –1) pay-off conditions. From Guralnick, (1972). Copyright 1972 by the American Psychological Association. Adapted by permission of the publisher and author

Jerison says that because vigilance tasks contain uninteresting stimulus material, the observer has to make a deliberate effort to be continuously watchful. An easier strategy might be to report every event as a signal, but that is too costly in terms of false alarms. Thus, initially, an alert observing strategy is adopted. But there will be rapid adaptation, with a consequent inhibition of the observing responses and a drift towards less effortful, blurred and distracted observing. Thus, again, detections decline because of the drop in appropriate, alert observing.

There is little support for these elegant notions. Indeed, in studies where observing responses have been elicited, they generally increase over the duration of the vigilance session, even although detections or latencies are deteriorating (Broadbent, 1963b; Guralnick, 1972, illustrated in Figure 10.2); and they tend to increase when the signal's probability is reduced (Weiner and Ross, 1962).

With visual displays, the naturally occurring eye movements and fixations that may be regarded as observing responses are invariably found to be unrelated to the detection of signals (see, for example, Baker, 1960; McGrath *et al.*, 1962; Mackworth *et al.*, 1964). Against such evidence, even the natural attractiveness of these theories begins to wilt and it is small comfort to find that self-estimates of distractibility are correlated with the extent of the decrement in signal detectability (Thackray *et al.*, 1974b), the latter being, of course, an implication of non-observing.

10.2.5 Comment

The explanations of the vigilance decrement that have been considered appear less than adequate, and none has provided plausible reasons as to why sensory-perceptual tasks seem particularly susceptible to the decrement with time on task. However, some light has been shed by contemporary research workers, as outlined in the next section.

10.3 CONTEMPORARY MODELS

10.3.1 Detectability decrements: a taxonomic approach

Over the past two decades, various researchers have asked if the vigilance decrement was due to a shift in detectability or in response criterion, but only unsuccessful attempts have been made at identifying the conditions conducive to the occurrence of a detectability decrement. In part, this confusion has been due to lack of empirical evidence, stemming from the low likelihood of the phenomenon.

The confusion has only recently been resolved, by Parasuraman and Davies (1977). They pursued a taxonomic approach, guided by the abilities classification system developed by Fleishman and his colleagues (Fleishman, 1972; Levine *et al.*, 1973). This led them to distinguish between simultaneous discriminations, when both signal and non-signal are present at the same time, and successive discriminations, when they are not.

The ability of the system devised by Parasuraman and Davies (1977) to differentiate between instances in which a detectability decrement will be found, and those where it will not, is clearly shown in Figure 10.3; and has been experimentally confirmed for both auditory and visual tasks by Parasuraman (1979).

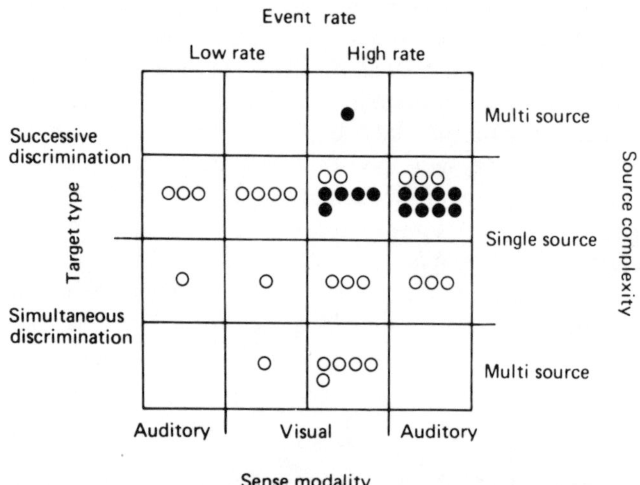

Figure 10.3 A classification of vigilance tasks according to the presence (filled circles) or absence (open circles) of a reliable decrement in perceptual sensitivity over time. Each circle represents a task used in a study of sustained attention reporting data in terms of d' or a related index. Reproduced with permission from Parasuraman, *Science,* 205, 924–926. Copyright 1979 by the AAAS

The figure reveals that increasing the opportunities for not looking at the right place at the right time (multiple sources), and presenting events in the more loosely coupled visual mode, in which it is easier to be inattentive to the displayed information, do not increase the likelihood of obtaining a detectability drop.

However, stimulus frequency (event rate: 'high' >24 events per minute) is clearly implicated, but only in conjunction with the requirement for a successive discrimination.

This systematic collation of evidence is important since it pinpoints the source of decrements that are due to a deterioration in the quality of the evidence, and implies that the most likely explanations will be based on the clear difference in processing requirements between successive and simultaneous discriminations. Davies and Parasuraman suggest that a successful account will probably focus on the differences in memory load imposed by the tasks, in conjunction with the time pressure created by the high rate, and the amount of effort the observer is willing to expend on the maintenance of efficiency. An emphasis on the information-processing demands of the task has also been expressed by Fisk and Schneider (1981), who reported detectability decrements when subjects had continually to allocate control-processing resources, but an absence of any decline when effortless automatic processing was possible. We may note that Broadbent's filter model, which implies a detectability drop, would be particularly applicable to just the sort of high processing load tasks described here.

This failure by the observer to sustain efficient performance when he is being driven to the limits of his capabilities is not surprising, and clearly belongs to a wider domain than the limited context of the vigilance experiment. It is instructive to note that the negligible work decrements with sustained cognitive tasks, referred to at the beginning of this chapter, were found with self-paced performance. Thus, the occasional use of very high paced vigilance tasks, involving successive discrimination, may provide one reason why vigilance tasks seem more prone to decrement.

However, detectability decrements are a minority occurrence, and so do not provide the whole story; changes in response bias constitute the major source of the decrement in correct detections. The next section considers some recent approaches.

10.3.2 Response rate shifts: empirical evidence

As recently as 1971, Broadbent remarked that, in a vigilance experiment, the total of hits and false alarms was usually less than the total of signals. This, in fact, is not the case, as Craig's (1978, 1979, 1980) collated evidence shows: novice observers tend to over-report on signal occurrence at the beginning of a session, and, on average, to equate signal reports with signal occurrence at the end of a session. Later, with experience, a more stable pattern presents itself. Where there is little initial disparity between signal and report rates, there is at most only a negligible decrement in the rate of reporting between beginning and end of a session. A typical example is shown in Figure 10.4. Craig found the early pattern to be characteristic of individual subjects in his own experiments, as well as of group mean data in a cross-sectional sample from the literature. It is important to realize that these changes in report frequency are independent of any detectability changes that might be taking place; detectability was not invariant with time in some of Craig's (1979, 1980) experiments, nor in the later stages of the study by Binford and Loeb (1966) from which Figure 10.4 derives.

Frequency, or probability matching, is a common enough feature of behaviour on detection or recognition tasks, and when a naive observer first encounters a task employing an extremely high or extremely low signal probability, it not unnaturally takes him a little while to adjust to the situation — particularly if, as in

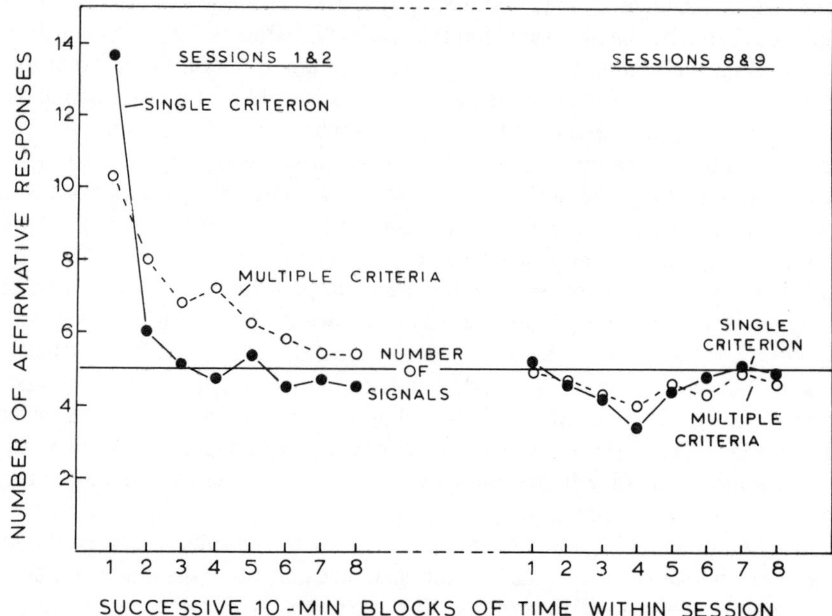

Figure 10.4 Asymptotic frequency matching as a function of time on task and task experience under conditions of single and multiple response criteria. Derived from Binford and Loeb (1966)

many vigilance studies, nobody informs him of the actual probability level (Craig, 1980; see also Williges, 1976).

Any adjustment resulting in asymptotic matching behaviour implies the operation of a self-feedback loop. Plausible processes that would integrate changes in detections, false alarms and response latencies might be based on error corrections, the response criterion being adjusted up or down to accommodate the nature of the error detected (miss or false-alarm), on report rate, adjustments being made to correct for any disparity between current and past average rates; or on event intensity, the criterion being set equal to the average intensity of the signals and non-signals experienced (Vickers, 1979; Vickers and Leary, 1983; Vickers *et al.*, 1977).

The idea that the novice observer is actively adapting his behaviour to meet the demands of the low signal probability situation contrasts markedly with the classic image of the passive observer whose vigilance is subject to involuntary decline, and leads to a radical revision of traditional views — e.g. introverts may exhibit less of a decrement than extraverts, not because they maintain vigilance better, but because they adapt less well to external circumstances (Vickers *et al.*, 1977).

As with the detectability decrement discussed in the preceding section, the reduction of the report rate towards the matching asymptote is a general phenomenon, not confined to the vigilance context. However, since it has no obvious relevance for such operations as reading or mental arithmetic — both of which were involved in the early work decrement research — it provides yet another clue as to why the vigilance task seems so particularly susceptible to the shift in performance over time.

10.4 CONCLUSIONS

A common observation from laboratory research is that, during vigilance, there is a non-trivial performance deficit that could have serious practical consequences. Previous attempts to explain the deficit as due to low arousal, low expectancy, increased distraction and accumulated inhibition have not proved particularly successful; but contemporary approaches attributing it to a decline in processing capacity and to an adaptive shift in the criterion for responding seem more promising. In addition, the recent evidence on detectability and criterion shifts helps to explain the special vulnerability of vigilance tasks to performance decrement, and encouragingly suggests that man may be more able to sustain attention than was previously supposed.

Hours of Work
Edited by S. Folkard and T.H. Monk

Chapter 11

Individual and Group Differences in Sustained Attention

D. Roy Davies

CONTENTS

ABSTRACT

This chapter focuses upon individual differences in performance in vigilance situations, and places particular emphasis upon the vigilance decrement. In the first part of the chapter a distinction is made between successive and simultaneous discrimination tasks in vigilance, and it is concluded that individual differences in vigilance performance are task-type specific. In the second part of the chapter vigilance performance is considered in relation to intelligence, sex, age and personality. It is concluded that sex and intelligence are minimally related to detection efficiency, that vigilance improves with age in childhood but deteriorates in late middle age (after about the age of 60), and that the performance of introverts is generally superior to that of extraverts. Some implications of these results for selection are briefly discussed.

11.1 INTRODUCTION

As Angus Craig points out in Chapters 10 and 12, the ability to sustain attention is important in many practical situations, including radar and sonar monitoring and surveillance, industrial inspection, process control and vehicle operation. In the laboratory the vigilance task has been regarded as providing 'the fundamental paradigm for defining sustained attention as a behavioural category' (Jerison,

1977, p.29), and since substantial individual differences in the performance of such tasks are routinely observed, numerous attempts have been made to relate scores on a variety of tests of ability and personality to efficiency in vigilance situations, frequently as a preliminary step to devising a selection battery which would discriminate between 'good' and 'bad' monitors.

In this chapter two questions are addressed:

(i) How consistent is the performance of individuals within the same vigilance testing session, across different sessions and across different monitoring tasks?
(ii) Does the ability to sustain attention in vigilance situations relate to such characteristics as personality, intelligence, age or sex?

11.2 INDIVIDUAL DIFFERENCES IN VIGILANCE PERFORMANCE

Most vigilance tasks are either visual or auditory, although a few are vibrotactile or cutaneous, and in some studies combined audiovisual presentations have been employed. Large individual differences in the performance of both auditory and visual vigilance tasks have been consistently reported, although for cutaneous and audiovisual tasks comparatively little evidence concerning individual differences is available. Detection efficiency, measured by the proportion of signals correctly detected, is generally quite consistent across time periods within the same task, whether visual or auditory (Baker, 1963a,b; Buckner, 1963; Buckner *et al.*, 1960, 1966; Mackworth, 1950), and also across testing sessions with the same task (Buckner *et al.*, 1960; Jenkins, 1958; Kennedy, 1971; Parasuraman, 1975; Sverko, 1968). Test–retest reliability coefficients for a variety of different vigilance tasks are thus usually fairly high, often reaching 0.70 and sometimes exceeding 0.90. Significant correlations have also been reported between detection efficiency measures obtained under 'alerted conditions' prior to the main vigilance session and those obtained during the session itself (Benedetti and Loeb, 1972; Buckner *et al.*, 1966; Loeb and Binford, 1971).

In a number of studies conducted in the early 1960s, correlations between measures of detection efficiency across tasks presented to different sensory modalities were found to be considerably lower than those obtained within or across sessions with the same task (see, for example, Baker, 1963a,b; Buckner *et al.*, 1960, 1966; Pope and McKechnie, 1963). Such findings cast doubt on the existence of a common factor underlying vigilance performance and were interpreted as indicating that individual differences in detection efficiency were likely to be task specific (Buckner and McGrath, 1963). In several subsequent studies attempts were made to determine those features of vigilance tasks contributing to intermodal and intramodal performance consistency. Among the task features that have been examined from this perspective are the degree to which the task is 'coupled' to the observer (i.e. the degree to which the subject is unable to ignore the stimulus), the difficulty of the discrimination required to detect signals, and the type of signal discrimination involved in the task (i.e. whether successive or simultaneous; see below and Chapter 10). One major difference between auditory and visual tasks is that the former are more tightly coupled to the observer's perceptual apparatus than are the latter since one can 'look away' or 'close' one's eyes (Elliott, 1960). It might therefore be expected that higher correlations would be obtained for measures of detection efficiency between closely coupled visual tasks and auditory tasks than between loosely coupled visual tasks and auditory tasks. Although such an expectation is confirmed by the results of one study (Hatfield and Loeb, 1968), in other studies, if anything, the reverse has been found (Hatfield and Soderquist, 1970; Loeb and Binford, 1971). In any case, there are some inconsistencies between the intercorrelations obtained for different performance measures. It thus seems unlikely that the degree of task–observer coupling makes an important contribution to intermodal performance consistency in vigilance.

A number of studies have attempted to match the difficulty of signal discrimination across tasks by equating group or individual values of signal detectability (d') prior to the main testing session through adjustments of task parameters such as signal intensity and/or duration. In the great majority of cases, such manipulations produce significant intramodal and intermodal correlations for several measures of detection efficiency, including the proportion of correct detections, the false alarm rate, detectability (d'), and response bias or criterion ($\log^{\beta}$) (see, for example, Colquhoun, 1975; Loeb and Binford, 1971; Sverko, 1968; Tyler *et al.*, 1972). The type of signal discrimination required to detect signals, as well as the difficulty of the discrimination involved, is an important determinant of performance consistency in sustained attention. In most studies of individual differences in vigilance, *successive* discrimination tasks have been employed. In these tasks comparison must be made between successively presented signal and non-signal events in terms of their identity or degree of similarity. Examples of widely used successive discrimination vigilance tasks are those in which the observer is presented with a series of brief-duration light flashes and has to detect the occasional brighter, or dimmer, flash (see, for example, Broadbent and Gregory, 1963a; Davies, Lang and Shackleton, 1973; Hatfield and Loeb, 1968), or, from a series of tones, has to detect the occasional louder, or shorter, tone (see, for example, Deaton *et al.*, 1971; Hatfield and Soderquist, 1970). Successive discrimination vigilance tasks may be contrasted with *simultaneous* discrimination vigilance tasks in which one is required to identify a previously specified stimulus configuration that forms part of a more complex sensory field. Examples of such tasks are those in which the requirement is to detect the presence of a disc of specified hue in a display of six simultaneously presented discs (see, for example, Colquhoun, 1961, 1962), or the presence of a faint tone embedded in bursts of white noise (see, for example, Hartley, Olsson and Ingleby, 1973).

Parasuraman and Davies (1977) obtained performance indices from six pairs of vigilance tasks differing in presentation modality (visual and auditory) and in type of discrimination required to detect signals (simultaneous or successive). They found that within task pairings, in which neither the presentation modality nor the discrimination requirement was the same, correlations for both performance measures were low and non-significant, whereas when both task dimensions were compatible, the correlations observed were highly significant, varying between +0.80 and +0.90. The type of discrimination also appeared to be a more important determinant of performance consistency than did presentation modality. These results, when considered in conjunction with the results from studies which have equated individual and group values of signal detectability, suggest that individual differences in vigilance are neither completely task specific nor mediated by a common vigilance factor. Instead, it appears that such differences are task-type specific, and that one of the major task characteristics determining performance consistency across tasks is the *type* of discrimination involved in signal detection.

11.3 GROUP DIFFERENCES IN VIGILANCE PERFORMANCE

11.3.1 Personality

The aspect of group differences which has been most thoroughly explored in relation to vigilance performance is undoubtedly personality, and the personality dimension which has received most investigation is that of introversion-extraversion. There are at least 13 studies which have examined the vigilance performance of introverts and extraverts (see Davies and Parasuraman, 1982, for a detailed review). The results of these studies are now summarized with respect to (i) overall performance and (ii) changes in performance over time. Of the twelve investigating possible overall differences in hit rate between introverts and extraverts, six obtained a significant difference in detection efficiency, the performance of introverts being consistently better. Introverts also appear to make fewer false alarms than do extraverts, and the few studies utilizing decision theory analyses report both that the perceptual sensitivity of introverts is superior to that of extraverts, and that the criterion for responding is more stringent (Carr, 1969; Harkins and Geen, 1975). The fact that some studies report significant differences in the detection efficiency of introverts and extraverts, while others do not, may be due, at least in part, to procedural factors. There are, for instance, considerable differences between studies in the type of task employed and its relative difficulty, in the criterion cut-off scores adopted for the purpose of selecting introverted and extraverted groups, and in the extent to which neuroticism (an additional measure provided by the Maudsley and Eysenck Personality Inventories) was controlled for. There are also differences with respect to whether the personality test used sampled only sociability scores, as in the case of Part II of the Heron Inventory, or impulsivity scores as well, as in the case of the Eysenck Personality Inventory. There are some grounds for believing that impulsivity is a more important correlate of performance decrement in monotonous tasks than is sociability (see, for example, Thackray *et al.*, 1974a).

Although reliable differences in the detection efficiency of introverts and extraverts have thus been obtained in about half the relevant studies, the principal inspiration for investigations of the relation between extraversion and detection efficiency comes from various theoretical speculations during the 1950s concerning the vigilance decrement. These suggested that introverts were better equipped for work on prolonged and monotonous tasks than were extraverts because of their higher cortical arousal and greater resistance to the establishment of inhibitory processes (Broadbent, 1958; Claridge, 1960; Eysenck, 1957). Despite some differences of emphasis among these theoretical positions, they were in agreement in predicting that extraverts should manifest a greater decrement in vigilance performance over time. However, the available evidence provides only limited support for this prediction. At least ten studies have looked for a possible differential decrement in detection rate between introverts and extraverts. Of these, two employed simultaneous discrimination tasks (both visual) and the remainder high event rate successive discrimination tasks (five auditory, three visual). A reliable differential decrement was observed in only four of the ten studies, extraverts exhibiting the greater decrement in each case. In all four studies a high event rate successive discrimination task was used and subjects were selected from the two extremes of the distribution of introversion–extraversion scores. It thus appears that differential decrements in detection efficiency may only occur when subjects are selected so as to maximize differences between introverts and extraverts, and when the task makes heavy demands on working memory and the speed at which information must be processed. The differential decrement between extreme groups of introverts and extraverts would seem to be primarily attributable to a difference in the rate at which perceptual sensitivity declines with time on task, although this possibility has not been tested directly. In the only relevant study (Hastrup, 1979), it was indeed found that extraverts exhibited a greater sensitivity decrement than did introverts, the difference being marginally significant, although this difference was only observed when the discrimination requirement was relatively easy. Hastrup's subjects were classified as introverts and extraverts on the basis of the median extraversion scale score. Clearly this experiment merits replication using extreme groups.

In summary, individuals classed as extraverts manifest reliably lower detection rates in about half the relevant studies, and signal detection theory analyses indicate that this reduction in detection efficiency is associated with lowered perceptual sensitivity and a more relaxed response criterion. Such results have been obtained with both simultaneous and successive discrimination tasks, and with non-extreme groups of introverts and extraverts. In contrast, reliable differential decrements in detection rate have so far been reported for extreme groups of introverts and extraverts performing high event rate successive discrimination tasks and would appear to reflect differential decrements in perceptual sensitivity. The generally poorer performance of extraverts in vigilance situations may be a consequence of the greater boredom that extraverts apparently experience during monotonous work (see Davies, Shackleton and Parasuraman, 1983, for a review). This may be attributable to greater 'stimulus hunger' on the part of the extraverts (Gale, 1969), coupled with the tendency to generate more vivid and more frequent visual imagery (Gale *et al.*, 1972; Morris and Gale, 1974), which is likely to result in attention being less completely and less consistently focused on task-relevant events. The probable outcome would be an overall reduction in the level of sensitivity, as has been shown in divided attention experiments involving vigilance (Broadbent and Gregory, 1963b), and also, perhaps, a steeper decline in detection rate with time at work (Antrobus, Coleman and Singer, 1967). Extraverts may thus allocate fewer attentional resources to the display being monitored, and this may be related to differences in the level of arousal. Carr (1969), for example, found that the skin resistance of extraverts was reliably higher than that of introverts throughout a 40-minute visual vigilance task, and Gange, Geen and Harkins (1979) observed the heart rate of extraverts to be lower than that of introverts during the performance of a vigilance task. Extraverts therefore appear to be less aroused than introverts in vigilance situations and if, as has been suggested (Davies, 1983; Hockey, 1983), there is a link between increases in arousal level and increases in attentional selectivity, then it is possible that introverts may exhibit greater attentional selectivity during vigilance.

Extraversion is related, albeit loosely, to two other personality measures, 'field dependence' and 'autonomic lability'. Extraverted subjects are more likely to be field dependent (Evans, 1967; Kennedy, 1977) and autonomically 'stabile' (Coles *et al.*, 1971; Crider and Lunn, 1971; Lader and Wing, 1966; Mangan and O'Gorman, 1969). The field dependence–independence dimension is generally assessed by means of the rod-and-frame test, or the Gottschaldt embedded figures test, and can be considered as a measure of 'perceptual independence'. The autonomic lability dimension refers to the frequency with which spontaneous electrodermal responses (EDRs) are emitted during rest or during stimulation (Lacey and Lacey, 1958). This measure is inversely related to the speed with which the electrodermal orienting response habituates to a series of affectively neutral, above threshold, stimuli (see, for example, Katkin and McCubbin, 1969) and can be considered as a measure of 'receptivity'. Crider and Lunn (1971) reveiwed a number of studies of electrodermal lability and suggested that lability should be regarded as a dimension of personality, measurable in terms of either the number of spontaneous EDRs or the rate of habituation of the orienting response. These two measures were subsequently labelled 'spontaneous' and 'trial' lability respectively (Sostek, 1978).

Very few studies have investigated the relationship of field dependence to detection efficiency in vigilance situations, and while there is some indication that the detection efficiency of field independent subjects is superior to that of field dependent subjects (Cahoon, 1970; Moore and Gross, 1973) it seems likely that performance differences between these two groups are affected by task type (Kennedy, 1977). On the other hand, several studies have examined the detection efficiency of stabile and labile subjects, so classified either by measures of spontaneous or trial lability or by some combination of the two (Coles and Gale, 1971; Crider and Augenbraun, 1975; Hastrup, 1979; Parasuraman, 1975; Siddle, 1972; Sostek, 1978). All these studies employed auditory successive discrimination tasks in which the event presentation rate was relatively high. In every case where a vigilance decrement was reported, stabiles showed a greater decline in detection efficiency with time than labiles. Further, in two experiments (Sostek, 1978; Hastrup, 1979), they showed a greater decrement in perceptual sensitivity (d' or P(A)), although in Hastrup's study this finding was only obtained in the more difficult version of her task. In general, measures of trial lability seem to be more closely related to detection efficiency than do measures of spontaneous lability, and labiles tend to detect more signals and to make more false alarms than do stabiles. To some extent, therefore, the vigilance performance of labiles and stabiles resembles that of introverts and extraverts, although, as indicated earlier, a reliable correlation between extraversion and autonomic lability has not been consistently observed.

11.3.2 Age

The ability of children to sustain attention, as assessed by indices of vigilance performance, appears to improve with age. In one of the most thorough investigations of the development of vigilance in children, Gale and Lynn (1972) administered a 40-minute auditory vigilance task, requiring the detection of the occasional digit in a series of letters, to 612 schoolchildren of average intelligence with an age range of 7 to 13.5 years. The results indicated that detection efficiency improved with age, for both boys and girls, up to the age of 11 years. A particularly marked improvement took place between the ages of 8 and 9 years in boys. Girls detected significantly more signals than boys at ages 7, 8 and 12, but neither sex nor age differences were obtained in the extent of the vigilance decrement. Anderson *et al.*, (1974) also reported an improvement in detection efficiency on a vigilance task for children aged 9 years and over compared to children between the ages of 6 and 8 years, and Sykes *et al.* (1973) obtained a significant correlation between age and detection rate on the Continuous Performance Test (a test originally developed to aid in the diagnosis of brain damage; see Rosvold *et al.*, 1956) for children in the age range 5 to 11 years.

Cross-sectional studies of adult age differences in vigilance, in which different cohorts are compared, suggest that detection efficiency tends to decrease with age. At least 11 studies, with a total of 15 separate experiments, of age and vigilance have been conducted. In six of these the detection rate of older individuals was reliably lower, in four the false alarm rate was higher, and in four detection efficiency declined at a faster rate with time at work. In a longitudinal study of age changes in vigilance, Quilter *et al.* (1983) reported a significant reduction in detection rate in a group of older men over an 18-year period, and suggested that a marked fall in detection efficiency occurs at or around the age of 70 years. Age differences seem equally likely to occur in successive and simultaneous discrimination tasks, although there is a tendency for such differences to be found more frequently in visual tasks than in auditory ones. Age differences in at least one performance measure were obtained in five out of six experiments in which a visual task was used, but in only four out of nine cases where an auditory task was employed. Older adults also show poorer performance in selective attention tasks (see Davies, Jones and Taylor, 1983, for a review) and their relative inefficiency in situations involving the deployment of attention may be related to the amount of attentional resources available, and to the way in which available resources are utilized.

Adult age differences in vigilance performance have thus been reported fairly frequently, and the detection efficiency of individuals over the age of 60 tends to be poorer than that of individuals in lower age groups, especially in tasks where the event presentation rate is high (Davies, 1968; Talland, 1966; Thompson *et al.*, 1963). Although decision theory measures have seldom been employed in such studies, there are some indications that the perceptual sensitivity of the observer may decline with age (Canestrari, 1962, Experiment 2; Davies and Davies, 1975; Tune, 1966a). However, any such reduction in sensitivity is likely to be fairly small and to occur quite gradually (Sheehan and Drury, 1971) unless brain damage is also present (see Davies and Parasuraman, 1982, for a review). Older people also seem to adopt more cautious response criteria in some signal detection and industrial inspection tasks (see Craik, 1969). Paradoxically, the scanty evidence from vigilance situations suggests that older individuals may sometimes adopt more risky criteria than younger ones (Bicknell, 1970; Tune, 1966a). While some reduction in perceptual sensitivity probably occurs with age, therefore, it is less clear what effect the ageing process has on criterion placement in monitoring tasks. It is possible that personality factors may exert some influence on age differences in criterion placement in vigilance. Tune (1966b), for example, found that older extraverts made over three times as many false alarms as older extraverts, although detection rates were about the same in both groups. Younger extraverts also made more false alarms than younger introverts but the difference was much less marked.

11.3.3 Mental abilities

In the development of possible selection tests for vigilance and monitoring tasks, researchers have used a variety of tests aimed at providing information about different psychological functions, in the hope that one of these would prove useful as a predictor of vigilance performance. In general, however, standard psychological tests of reasoning, of memory span and of various aptitudes, both general and specific, have not been very successful in providing consistent and valid correlates of vigilance performance (Buckner *et al.*, 1966). Thus, although the most comprehensive study yet conducted indicated that tests measuring clerical abilities might be useful predictors of within-session decrement scores (McGrath *et al.*, 1960), this finding was not upheld in a subsequent cross-validation study (McGrath, 1963b).

Likewise, attempts to establish a relationship between monitoring performance and general intelligence have not been particularly fruitful. A number of studies have failed to find differences between the vigilance performance of adults achieving relatively high and relatively low scores on standard intelligence tests (Halcomb and Kirk, 1965; McGrath *et al.*, 1960; Sipowicz and Baker, 1961; Ware, 1961). Incidental findings from several other experiments provide support for this negative result (Bakan, 1959; Colquhoun, 1959, 1962; Jenkins, 1958; Mackworth, 1950; Wilkinson, 1961a), although one or two studies have found indications of a positive relationship between intelligence and vigilance (Cahoon, 1970; Kappauf and Powe, 1959). Thus, in general, the contribution of intelligence to the efficiency with which tasks requiring sustained attention are carried out seems to be slight and, indeed, in one study no differences between the detection scores of young mental deficients, with a mean IQ of 58.1, and those of normal intelligence groups were reported (Ware *et al.*, 1962).

11.3.4 Sex

Similarly, little evidence has been found to support the view that sex differences account for a significant proportion of the variance in detection efficiency in vigilance (see Davies and Tune, 1970, for a review of early studies). This conclusion is supported by the results of more recent studies conducted both with adults (Gale, Bull, Penfold, Coles and Barraclough, 1972; Parasuraman, 1975; Tolin and Fisher, 1974) and with children (Kirchner and Knopf, 1974; Sykes *et al.*, 1973). However, in most experiments sex differences have been only of incidental interest to the experimenter and sample sizes have been relatively small. The most comprehensive investigation of vigilance performance in which sex was the sole independent variable was carried out by Waag *et al.* (1973), who tested 220 male and 220 female college students on a visual successive discrimination task lasting for 1 hour. Although Waag *et al.* found that men detected 10 per cent more signals than women, and made significantly fewer false alarms during the first 20 minutes of the task, sex accounted for only 4 per cent of the variance in detection rate and for less than 10 per cent of the variance in false alarms.

11.4 CONCLUSIONS

Although performance in vigilance situations exhibits a high degree of consistency, the prospects for developing a selection battery for use in monitoring situations do not at present seem particularly bright, despite the fact that some people are clearly more efficient monitors than others.

Differences in the demands on information-processing mechanisms, and in particular on working memory, make a considerable contribution to the consistency of performance in vigilance situations. Thus, it is likely that different abilities are involved in the performance of successive discrimination and simultaneous discrimination tasks. One avenue for future research is to examine the performance of various groups of individuals in these two different task situations. In general, introverts, younger individuals and labiles exhibit greater overall detection efficiency in vigilance tasks, although even the evidence supporting this generalization is not completely compelling. Although some advances have been made in the theoretical understanding of vigilance performance, and in the maintenance and control of vigilance in practical settings, there is as yet no completely satisfactory explanation of why some people are better able to sustain attention than are others.

Hours of Work
Edited by S. Folkard and T.H. Monk

Chapter 12

Field Studies of Human Inspection: The application of Vigilance Research

Angus Craig

CONTENTS

ABSTRACT

This chapter focuses on field studies of industrial inspection and asks the fundamental questions: (i) Are real operations likely to suffer from the sort of vigilance problems encountered in laboratory studies? (ii) If so, has the laboratory research anything to offer in the way of guiding principles from which operational performance might benefit? An affirmative answer to the first question is followed by a demonstration that the reduction of uncertainty and the elevation of operator alertness are beneficial guidelines for inspection performance levels.

12.1 INTRODUCTION AND OVERVIEW

Chapter 10 reviews theories and laboratory studies on the problems of vigilance. This chapter looks at the role of vigilance in real operations, and attempts to assess the incidence and scope of these problems in real situations. It then proceeds to evaluate the operational relevance and practicability of laboratory findings, and of recommendations for improved efficiency derived from them.

12.2 ON THE NATURE OF VIGILANCE

Vigilance can be regarded as '*a state of readiness to detect and respond to certain specified small changes occurring at random time intervals in the environment*'. (Mackworth, 1957, pp.389-390). As indicated in Chapter 10, this describes various real operations including industrial inspection, process-control monitoring, hospital patient monitoring, radar and sonar operating.

Chapter 10 also indicates that two major performance problems arise during laboratory vigilance: (i) the level of correct detections of the awaited critical event is well below the operator's known capability, and (ii) the level tends to decline with time on task. The problems tend to increase with increased pace of operation, with reduced likelihood of critical event occurrence, and with reduced levels of alertness. Although many of the problems seem to derive from the observer's relative unwillingness, under conditions of uncertainty, to accept perceived evidence as favourable to critical event occurrence, in an important minority of cases the problems are due to reductions in the observer's actual ability, i.e. to deficits in the quality of the perceived evidence.

As a descriptor, the term 'vigilance' applies equally to the laboratory tasks and to the various monitoring tasks encountered in real operations. But whether the problems of efficiency found in the laboratory also arise in real operations is a separate issue, and questions of face validity, regarding the (usually) greater complexity of the real tasks, reduce to elementary empirical questions which can to some degree be answered by laboratory experimentation (see, for example, Craig and Colquhoun, 1977).

Before discussing field applications of vigilance research, it seems appropriate to consider evidence on the incidence and extent of vigilance problems in real operations. This forms the content of the next section.

12.3 INCIDENCE OF VIGILANCE PROBLEMS IN REAL OPERATIONS

The emphasis here is predominantly on industrial inspection. In part, this reflects the relative availability of tractable performance data.

12.3.1 Task duration

The length of time for which continuous attention to the task is demanded is generally regarded as one of the key features of a vigilance task; a duration of 1 hour is quite characteristic of laboratory studies, although there is nothing sacrosanct about it.

Some indication of the duration demanded in inspection tasks is provided by the results of a survey conducted by Megaw (1977). He found a considerable range, from less than ½ h in a quarter of the firms surveyed, to between 2 and 4 h in 40 per cent of the cases. But, of course, the duration expected of the worker may differ quite considerably from the duration he/she actually works. Fox (1977), for example, reports that coin inspectors spend only 14 min out of each 24-min inspection cycle actually examining coins. Belbin (1957b) mentions that in viewing radiographs of light alloy castings, examiners spent no more than 10-15 min on continuous inspection. Nachreiner (1977) reported that the modal period of continuous attention actually paid to various monitoring tasks was of only 5 min duration, and that periods as long as 20 min were rarely observed.

Thus, although typical inspection tasks apparently demand relatively prolonged periods of continuous attention, the actual time spent attending continuously may be relatively short. Real tasks differ in this latter respect from most laboratory situations of vigilance, where the task demands are usually quite rigidly adhered to, so that an hour demanded is, in practice, an hour spent. However, it seems doubtful that the vigilance problems are eradicated merely because operators only attend intermittently to the task in hand (see, for example, Jenkins, 1958). As can be seen in Figure 10.1, the characteristic efficiency problems already exist during the first few minutes of the task. It may even be, as the 'attention theory' reviewed in Chapter 10 implies, that intermittent release from the task is simply one of the ways operators cope with the demands for sustained vigilance (Broadbent, 1958; Jerison *et al.*, 1965).

12.3.2 Signal rate

A second characteristic of a typical vigilance task is that signal events have a relatively infrequent occurrence. In the laboratory, the signal probability is usually held to a moderately low level (frequently of the order of 2-5 per cent of the total event occurrence), but not so low as to preclude the possibility of obtaining reliable estimates of detection rate (see Craig and Colquhoun, 1975). Craig (1984) indicates that in published reports of real inspection tasks, most faults occur with a probability in the range of 1-10 per cent, some are less likely (<1 per cent), while others are quite probable (>50 per cent). In addition to this considerable range in the percentage frequency of occurrence of real signals, there is also a very wide range in the rate of event occurrence over time. For example, Mackworth (1957) pointed out that, in the fastest operation he had observed, lighter flint inspection, inspectors dealt with between 35 000 and 40 000 flints per hour, whereas he had also observed that in the pharmaceutical industry, inspectors of intravenous ampoules typically considered only about 350-400 ampoules per hour. The differences in range between these real rates and those employed in vigilance research would seem merely to be that the latter are somewhat more constrained.

On balance, therefore, considering task duration, signal probability and event rate, there can be little doubt that situations likely to involve problems of vigilance are prevalent in real operations in both the industrial and military spheres.

12.3.3 Performance assessment

Too often it is not possible to determine whether a vigilance problem exists — even though the situation may appear conducive to it — because the requisite performance measures do not exist. For example, in the survey carried out by Megaw (1977), not a single case was reported in which objective performance measurement was carried out. All too frequently, reliance is placed on the supervisor's opinion of how efficiently the job is being done; but his opinion is an unreliable indicator of objective performance (McKenzie, 1958; Mitchell, 1935). Inspection performance can be estimated by post-inspection re-examination of an inspected batch (Drury and Addison, 1973; Mills and Sinclair, 1976), by examining the inspection of a specially prepared batch (Fox, 1975), or by checking detections of inserted known faults which have been marked with a fluorescent dye so that they are subsequently retrievable (Belbin, 1957a). Despite the availability of these techniques, there are insufficient data available to assess properly the incidence of vigilance problems in real situations.

12.3.4 Efficiency problems

The data presented in Table 12.1 are representative of those available, and convince one that considerable problems do exist. In most cases, the operators knew their performance was being assessed, but in fact it is well known that this is likely to result in the acuteness of the efficiency problems being underestimated rather than overestimated (Fraser, 1953; McKenzie, 1958). It should be noted, too, that in a majority of the tasks listed in Table 12.1 the defects or targets are glaringly obvious under alerted conditions, so that there is clear scope for redesigning many of the tasks in order to improve operator efficiency.

It is notable that few studies choose to report on the decrement in performance (final column of Table 12.1). Of the four which do, however, two studies reported a decrement of detection rate, from which one can conclude that a decrement function *may* exist in real operations. Obviously, one cannot assess from these scant data the likelihood of a decrement in real inspection situations, but neither can one dismiss it out of hand (Elliott, 1960; Teichner, 1974). The observation that few studies mention the decrement may well arise from the practical difficulties encountered in assessing real performance over time, and to speculate on other reasons, as some have done (e.g. Smith and Lucaccini, 1969), seems pointless at this stage.

The detection rate achieved by an inspector can be influenced considerably by his standards regarding what constitutes a rejectable fault (McKenzie, 1958). When standards are low, insufficient faults are rejected, while when standards are high, a high detection rate is achieved, but only at the cost of falsely scrapping a high proportion of good products (Sheehan and Drury, 1971). Thus, the percentages of missed signals listed in Table 12.1 could be due to either low

Problems of detection inefficiencies and reports of decrement in a number of real monitoring and inspection tasks

Author	Product of task type	Misses (%)	Decrement
1. Assenheim (1969)	Glass ware (i) foremen	<10	—
	(ii) inspectors	>20	
2. Astley & Fox (1975)	Rubber seals	8	—
3. Belbin (1957a,b)	Ball bearings	37	—
4. Belbin (1963)	Tin cans	42	—
5. Carter (1957), cited in McCornack (1961)	Acoustic tiles	21	—
6. Chapman & Sinclair (1975)	Jam tarts	23	—
	Chicken carcasses	34–44	Yes
7. Drury & Addison (1973)	Glass ware	5–22	—
8. Fox (1975)	Metal fasteners	17	—
	Rubber seals	49	Yes
9. Fox (1977)	Coins (i) before	45.5	—
	(ii) after ergonomic redesign	26	—
10. Fox & Haslegrave (1969)	Screws	30–40	—
11. Gillies (1975)	Glass sheets	9	—
12. Harris (1966)	Electronic equipment	25–80	—
13. Hayes (1950)	Piston rings	36	—
14. Jacobsen (1952)	Solder connections (i) solderless	16	—
	(ii) loosely		—
	soldered	18	—
15. Kelly (1955) cited in McCornack (1961)	TV panels	9	—
16. Rigby & Swain (1968)	Electronic modules (i) complex	7	—
	(ii) simple	1	No
17. Schoonard *et al.* (1973)	Silicon chips	25	No
18. Self & Rhodes (1964)	Side-looking radar	35	—
19. Tiffin & Rogers (1941)	Tin plate (i) Appearance 1	41	—
	(ii) Appearance 2	24	—
	(iii) Appearance 3	65	—
	(iv) Weight	27	—
20. Yerushalmy (1969)	X-rays	20	—

standards or to task difficulty. Although, as already mentioned, most of the tasks listed involve targets or defects which are inherently easy to detect under alerted conditions, it does not necessarily follow that the system as a whole presents an easy task for the operator. Craig (1984) used the familiar d′ measure of discriminability from signal detection theory (Green and Swets, 1966; see also Chapter 10, this volume) to assess the difficulty of a number of real inspection jobs. The d′ measure provides an index of defect discriminability that is independent of operator standards. He found that despite their detection problems, most common operations are moderately easy ($2.5 < d' < 3.5$), but that as with laboratory studies, they encompass the full range, from the prohibitively difficult, as in Assenheim's (1969) study of glass-ware inspectors ($d' < 1.5$), to the exceedingly easy, as in Jacobsen's (1952) report on solder inspection ($d' > 3.5$). Craig (1984) noted in particular that systems in which the individual signals are clearly conspicuous ($d' >> 3.5$) may nevertheless present difficulties for the operator ($d' < 2.5$), because of display and lighting factors. In any case, difficulty level alone is not a reliable guide to detection failures: much depends on the proportion of defects — as Chapter 10 suggests it should.

This section has shown that real operations contain many situations where vigilance problems are likely to arise and that efficiency problems, sometimes of a fairly serious nature, do exist. In addition, the parallels between performances in the laboratory and in industrial situations seem sufficient to suggest that the research effort may have a useful contribution to make towards reducing these problems in the field. This potential contribution provides the content for the next section.

12.4 APPLICATIONS OF RESEARCH FINDINGS

Although the theories about vigilance reviewed in Chapter 10 have not proved conspicuously successful, the laboratory research has nevertheless shown that performance is reliably better when the observer knows what to look for, and where, when and how often it (i.e. the signal) will appear. Collectively, these imply a principle of uncertainty reduction. The question we now examine is whether benefits are gained in application.

12.4.1 Uncertainty reduction

There are two major sources of uncertainty inherent in any task: uncertainty about what constitutes a signal (target/defect) and uncertainty about where the signal will occur. Improved efficiency (reduction in errors of both omission and commission) by specifying the signal in advance (hence ensuring that the operator knows precisely what he is looking for), was amply demonstrated by Gundy (1961) and the benefits are revealingly discussed by McKenzie (1958) in his report on inspector accuracy. Prior specification is also beneficial when applied to tolerance limits, in contexts such as fabric inspection, where deviations from a norm occur (Raphael, 1942); even the accuracy of go-not-go gauging is improved by the provision of tolerance specifications (Lawshe and Tiffin, 1945). Sheehan and Drury (1971) have also demonstrated that when there is more than one kind of signal to be detected, efficiency is improved if advance warning can be given of the particular signal mix to expect.

However, the generally held belief that performance will improve when uncertainty is reduced by providing a reference standard against which events/items can be compared, seems decidedly suspect, and it is doubtful whether much attention is paid to the standard (Baker and O'Hanlon, 1963; Colquhoun and Edwards, 1970a; Drury, 1975); although in the special circumstances where ample time is available and use of the standard actively encouraged (Chaney and Teel, 1967), or where comparison with the standard is the natural strategy imposed by the structure of the task (Parasuraman and Davies, 1977), improvements in efficiency have been observed.

The provision of reference standards can, however, reduce uncertainties about category boundaries in classification tasks, where the examiner's job is to sort or grade material into appropriate classes, rather than merely to detect presence or absence of a signal. For example, Gatherum *et al.* (1959, 1960, 1961) demonstrated that the provision of visual references helped to maintain classification standards in judgements of the quality of meat, improved the consistency between different examiners, and reduced the visual drifts in standards consequent on changes in batch quality (ample time was available to refer to the standards).

Another way of reducing uncertainty, that usually results in improvements in detection efficiency and in the speed of reactions, is to provide additional (redundant) information about items/events in a second sensory modality (e.g. looking *and* listening, instead of just looking). For example, Craig *et al.* (1976) reported a study in which a combined audio-visual presentation yielded a 50 per cent improvement in detections over the visual mode alone. Similar benefits have been claimed when the redundancy is created by employing two or more people to view a single source of information (as opposed to a single individual monitoring multiple sources) (e.g. Konz and Osman, 1977; Yerushalmy *et al.*, 1950), but the advantages have not proved sufficiently reliable across different studies to endorse the practice (Davies and Tune, 1970).

We know that increased signal conspicuity also reduces uncertainty, and there is ample research evidence that such an increase does indeed reduce errors of omission as well as of commission, and improves the speed of performance (Binford and Loeb, 1963; Drury, 1975). Thus, the general rule should be that the more conspicuous the fault, the better, as might be achieved, for example, by improved lighting, or contrast (Astley and Fox, 1975; Faulkner and Murphy, 1975). This directly implies that improvements in processing which merely reduce the severity of defects, without reducing their incidence, are not to be recommended, since they will simply make the operator's task more difficult, degrade his efficiency, and slow him down. Signal conspicuity can also be increased by allowing more time for the examination of each item or event (Drury, 1973), an effect that is simple to engineer, but which can make a very considerable impact on operating costs (Chapman and Sinclair, 1975).

Spatial uncertainty refers to the inevitable absence of specification about where, within the field of view, a signal is likely to appear. Numerous research studies have indicated that when spatial uncertainty exists, vigilance performance is usually degraded, with a reduction in the level of correct detections, and a slowing in the speed of reacting to signals (Nicely and Miller, 1957; Bergum and Lehr, 1963; Adams, 1963). Some contend that these adverse effects are in line with the 'expectancy theory' of vigilance: that detections and latencies are poorest for critical events that arrive where they are least expected on the basis of previous task experience. In one laboratory study (Baker and Harabedian, 1962), the mere introduction of spatial uncertainty reduced detections from 100 to 87 per cent; in another study (Howell *et al.*, 1966), reducing the spatial uncertainty by compressing the display into a smaller area significantly reduced the time taken to react to signals. Similar effects are found in practical situations. For example, Harris (1966) demonstrated that in the inspection of electronic equipment by experienced inspectors, fault detections were inversely related to the number of component parts in which a fault could occur and which therefore had to be examined in each item of equipment. Fox (1977) showed that detections of defective coins were significantly increased by reducing the size of the aperture through which the coins were viewed, and although this tended to lower the total throughput, the improved efficiency of inspection more than compensated in terms of cost-effectiveness. Teel *et al.* (1968) reduced the spatial uncertainty inherent in the photomasters of electronic circuit boards by providing inspectors with a visual aid in the form of an overlay matrix mask. This simple procedure decidely improved detections of one kind of defect (although not of another), and reduced the inspection time; the resultant reduction in scrappage costs was estimated to be in excess of \$10 000 per year.

Uncertainties about what to look for, and where to look for it, may be regarded as related to task difficulty, and, in general, as we have seen, reducing the difficulty increases the efficiency of the operator. There are, in addition, uncertainties about how many to look for, or when to look for them (central to the 'expectancy theory' of vigilance, described in Chapter 10), but it is not clear that the principle of uncertainty reduction applies unequivocally to these.

For example, telling the operator what proportion of the events will be signals (Williges, 1969), or telling him that this proportion will change to a new (and specified) level (Embrey, 1975; Williges, 1973), alters his standards for reporting signals, but does not affect his actual efficiency: errors of omission and of commission shift in opposite directions. In inspection operations, the information (or training) is likely to leave outgoing quality at an unchanged level, and the only real advantage would seem to be that in X-ray examination (or any other situation where detections are at a premium) detection levels might be improved, although at the cost of increased false alarms. But this will only happen if the true signal rate is higher than the operator expects, a circumstance which apparently seldom arises in practice. Indeed, the more usual effect will be that the operator becomes more conservative, with an attendant reduction in detections, as a result of the information. Experienced operators are, in any case, likely to have built up appropriate expectancies about the frequency or proportion of signals in any familiar situation (Bakwin, 1954; Wyatt and Langdon, 1932), and in an unfamiliar or novel context it seems probably that the information to be imparted is simply not available.

The last mentioned comment also applies to temporal cuing: if one knew when the signal was due, the operator could be dispensed with. However, detections may be increased, the reaction time to signals reduced, if temporal uncertainty is reduced by arranging the interval between signals to be more regular (Adams and Boulter, 1964; Baker, 1959; Smith, 1961). Thus, in inspection, where faults tend to occur in bunches, so that some batches contain several while others have none at all, some improvement might be achieved by mixing the material prior to inspection, to create a more uniform distribution of faults over the period of work (Baker, 1964; Wyatt and Langdon, 1932).

The occurrence of a signal is less unexpected when signals are frequent than when they are infrequent. Thus, temporal uncertainty could be reduced by increasing the signal frequency, or the proportion of events which are signals, and as we saw in Chapter 10, this has proved one of the most reliable ways to increase the proportion of signals detected. There is, for example, some evidence that the mere insertion of artificial signals can improve detections of true signals (Garvey *et al.*, 1959), and that adding extra signals can increase the speed of reacting to the original ones (Faulkner, 1962). However, it does seem that the improvement in detections is bought at the price of increased commissive errors, so that the insertion of the artificial signals does not, in fact, improve overall efficiency (Murrell, 1975; Wilkinson, 1964b). Indeed, an examination of data from studies showing an improved detection rate consequent upon an increased signal frequency or signal probability, reveals that the improvement isseldom sufficient to compensate for the increased signal rate; the number of signals remaining undetected is the same or even greater than before, and outgoing quality is the same or even less (Anonymous, 1956; Drury and Addison, 1973).

An example to illustrate this important point is provided in Table 12.2. The data are from the much quoted study by Baddeley and Colquhoun (1969).

Thus, there is no real gain from an increased signal rate — although the practical point has been made by Jerison and Pickett (1963) that the effective signal rate can be increased without the addition of more signals, simply by

TABLE 12.2

Effects of increased proportion of signals on performance: percentage of detections, number of misses and outgoing quality

% signals	Average % detections	Average number missed	Average outgoing quality (% signals)
2	34.3	15.8	1.3
6	34.6	47.1	4.0
18	44.2	120.5	11.1
24	47.1	152.4	14.8
36	51.8	208.2	22.2

instructing monitors to regard the less critical events or items as signals. In general, however, it would seem that reducing uncertainties about signal frequency or about the timing of signal occurrence is of little merit.

One final source of uncertainty remains: uncertainty on the part of the operator as to how well he is performing his job. This can also be reduced by practical means, by feeding back information following a post-inspection audit, or by signalling to the operator his performance in respect of artificial signals. The effects of immediate or delayed feedback are due to motivational as well as instructional influences (Wiener, 1975; Warm, 1977), and are generally beneficial: efficiency is improved (reduction in errors of both omission and commission) in the real situation (e.g. Drury and Addison, 1973; Gillies, 1975) as in the laboratory (Wilkinson, 1964b; Williges and North, 1972), and reactions are generally quicker too (McCormack, 1959). However, since the feedback need not be veridical (Warm *et al.,* 1974; Weidenfeller *et al.*, 1962), there is reason to believe that the facilitative effects are primarily motivational in character, and that the instructional influence is slight (McCormack, 1967; Mackworth, 1970; Warm, 1977). Thus, although it does seem worthwhile to reduce performance uncertainty, the effect may not be due to that reduction *per se.*

12.4.2 Maintenance of interest and alertness

It was noted in the review of vigilance theories in Chapter 10 that McCormack (1962, 1967) invoked the notion of drive level to explain response perseverance in vigilance, in conditions where complete response extinction could be expected. General drive and central motivational state may be regarded as synonymous, and both are equivalent to the notion of tonic arousal which was seen in Chapter 10 to be an important determinant of performance level. It would seem that a second general principle for the benefit of performance is to maintain alert interest in the task.

I have just mentioned that feedback might help to sustain or to increase the operator's motivation. Another effective way of increasing motivation (at least in the short term) is by verbal instruction. For example, Lucaccini *et al.* (1968) showed that detections were significantly better for people who had been instructed that the vigilance task was 'challenging' than for those who had been told it was 'monotonous'. Nachreiner (1977) claimed a similar improvement for subjects who perceived the task as a selection test for a job, rather than as a vigilance experiment. Although false alarm data were not presented in either case, they were reported to be negligible in the earlier study, thereby indicating that a genuine improvement in efficiency had been achieved.

Research has shown that improved detection levels can be attained by verbal encouragement to do better (e.g. Mackworth, 1950), or to be less cautious about reporting signals (Colquhoun, 1967). These manipulations, it now seems, affect the operator's standards of judgement, although they do not appear to influence his overall efficiency (i.e. the improved detections are usually paralleled by increased commission errors). Nevertheless, motivating the operator to detect a greater proportion of signals is clearly advantageous in cases like X-ray examination, where the costs of a miss greatly outweigh those of a false alarm. Unfortunately, artificial manipulation of the pay-off structure (by, for example, financial incentives) is not invariably successful in achieving that end: some results have been encouraging (Davenport, 1968, 1969; Levine, 1966), while others have proved disappointing (Guralnick, 1972; Smith and Barany, 1970; Williges, 1971).

It is, of course, well known that money can be used to motivate greater effort or concentration, although McKenzie (1958) warns that financial incentives can differentially influence judgements and throughput, depending on whether the bonus is applied to the volume of work handled, work passed, or work which has been finally packaged. In addition, in a study reported by Mitten (1952), inspection speed showed only meagre improvement as a result of financial incentives, but increased considerably when the incentive was 'time off' on completion of a weekly quota. Mitten's study demonstrates not only the importance of motivation, but also the need to make a proper investigation of the operator's value system, in order to determine which particular incentive scheme to employ.

Inspection is intrinsically boring and is often of rather low status. As a consequence, in the short term at least, changes which relieve task boredom, or which indicate an interest in or concern for the inspectors, often have a beneficial motivating influence on performance. For example, Fraser (1953) provided experimental evidence that the mere presence of a silent supervisor could elevate detections, an effect which seems to parallel observations in industry, as in Drury and Addison's (1973) study, where the supervisor's presence was necessary to provide information feedback to the inspectors. Chapman and Sinclair (1975) report a similar effect, an increase in inspection speed by inspectors who knew they were being observed.

Where a task is sufficiently complex and interesting in itself, there may be little problem with motivation, and, indeed, Adams and his co-workers (Adams, 1963) suggest that in such cases human operators prove remarkably efficient and reliable. However, where boredom is a problem, the task can be made more interesting by breaking it up into segments and interpolating periods of activity of some other kind. This was demonstrated to improve the accuracy of repetitive vernier gauge setting in an experiment by Saldanha (1957), and has subsequently been shown to benefit performance in the field. For example, Fox (1977) found that batch inspection of coins, with interpolated periods of fetching and loading/unloading the conveyor belt hopper, resulted in a significantly higher percentage of fault detections than was observed with continuous inspection. Rigby and Swain (1975) report a similar improvement when inspection (of X-rays of components in an assembled unit), instead of being continuous, was limited to periods of 30 min, separated by 1 h spent on another job. It is often the case that such job enlargement or enrichment schemes can be applied to a team whose functions rotate at fairly frequent intervals, without reducing the final output level (see, for example, Baker, 1964; Wyatt and Langdon, 1932). Despite Jenkins's (1958) finding that 15-min vigils separated by 10-min rest breaks still showed some decrement, laboratory studies have indicated that the provision of rest pauses of as little as 5-min duration facilitates improved overall detection levels (Colquhoun, 1959; Mackworth, 1950). The effect of a rest break, which appears to relieve boredom, is largely due to the arrest of the decrement, and has led to the recommendation that the break should be given within the first half hour, the period of maximal decrement. This is apparently a fairly common practice in industrial tasks requiring sustained attention (Belbin, 1957b; Bhatia and Murrell, 1969; Hanhart, 1954), and may be one of the reasons why decrements are seldom found or reported.

As mentioned in the discussion of the 'arousal theory' of vigilance, in Chapter 10, one can also stimulate visual monitors to achieve better detection levels by providing them with a programme of background music, the more varied the better (e.g. McGrath, 1963a; Tarriere and Wisner, 1962). The beneficial effects have also been successfully demonstrated in an application to industrial inspection (Fox and Embrey, 1972).

Generally, it would seem that motivating or stimulating the monitor does have a facilitating effect on detections, at least in the short term. What is not yet so clear is whether such changes are lasting, and also whether they reliably improve overall efficiency.

12.5 CONCLUSIONS

Inspection operations, as we have seen, contain many of the features that characterize vigilance laboratory tasks, so that there are no major *prima facie* objections to the application of the vigilance research findings. Unfortunately, vigilance theory has generally proved of little value in prescribing remedies for the efficiency problems encountered in industrial inspection; but then neither has it been conspicuously successful in explaining the vigilance problems encountered in the laboratory. Nevertheless, the research findings that have arisen in the course of numerous theoretical studies conducted across the years, have themselves some degree of applicability, and it is apparent that the parallels that can be drawn between laboratory vigilance and real operations are not limited to the task characteristics alone; they do extend to the results on performance of various manipulations as well.

From this evaluation, two general principles for application have emerged: performance will benefit when (i) task uncertainties are reduced to a minimum, and (ii) an effort is made to keep the operator's interest and alertness at a reasonable level.

These help to fit the task to the man. We should not, of course, lose sight of the other side of the coin, namely the fitting of the man to the task by appropriate selection procedures. But as Roy Davies points out in Chapter 11, our ability to reduce the uncertainties of selection still leaves much to be desired.

The strong general conclusion to be derived from this review is that scepticism about the applicability of vigilance research is largely unfounded. There remains an obvious need for additional data obtained in real operations, and, as Craig (1984) indicates, there is a parallel need for research work that investigates some of the added complexities that are encountered in industrial tasks. But, in general, there seems reason for optimism that the problems of the temporal factors associated with vigilance and inspection can be increasingly brought under control.

Hours of Work
Edited by S. Folkard and T.H. Monk

Chapter 13

Flexitime, Compressed Workweeks and Other Alternative Work Schedules

Donald I. Tepas

CONTENTS

ABSTRACT

'Flexitime' and the 'compressed workweek' are two basic forms of alternative work schedule systems which are aimed at providing workers with more freedom for off-the-job activity scheduling. Flexitime does this by allowing workers to decide when and how long they will work. The compressed workweek increases the length of the workday so the workweek can be shortened, and it retains fixed work starting and stopping times. Although both systems have been in practice for many years and have attracted considerable attention, there is little in the way of quality experimental data to guide future applications. For the present, common sense plus a comprehensive evaluation of many relevant on- and off-the-job variables are the best approach to making decisions. An advance plan for the evaluation of any intervention appears mandatory. The promise of these systems, as a solution to problems evolving from the developing stage of automation, awaits experimental demonstration.

13.1 INTRODUCTION

Alternative work schedules (AWS) are broadly defined as work regimens which differ from the majority practice, said to be the 5-day, 40-hour diurnal workweek. Central definitions of the AWS systems currently practiced in the USA are found in Table 13.1. These systems have been referred to as novel, non-traditional, unusual and/or abnormal work systems. Terminology and practice, of course, vary from country to country, and the bases for these differences are both

TABLE 13.1
Alternative work schedule definitions

SHIFTWORK
Any system of fixed working hours, about 8 hours in length, most of which falls outside the standard day work period (between 0800 and 1700). Examples: night shiftwork, evening shiftwork, rotating shiftwork.

SPLIT SHIFTS
Any system of full-time working hours whereby a person works a given number of hours, is released from work, and returns for additional work the same day. The split is the time between work periods on the same day. Example: 5 days working 1000 to 1400 and 1700 to 2100 each day.

COMPRESSED WORKWEEK
Any system of fixed working hours more than 8 hours in length which results in a workweek of less than 5 full days of work a week. Examples: 4 days at 10 hours per day; 3 days at 12 hours per day.

SHORTENED WORKWEEK
Any full-time work system of starting and stopping hours which amounts to 35 hours or less work per week for full-time workers on a regular and permanent basis. Example: 5 days at 7 hours per day.

PERMANENT PART-TIME/SHARED TIME
Any work system of starting and stopping hours which amounts to less than that required of full-time workers at the same place. This is a regular and permanent system. Examples: two shared time workers fill one full-time job schedule; 1 permanent part-time worker works 25 hours per week on a regular basis.

REQUIRED OVERTIME
Any system of fixed working hours which results in a workweek of more than 40 hours. The overtime is obligatory, non-permanent and performed at higher pay. Examples: 6 days at 8 hours a day; 5 days at 10 hours a day.

FLEXITIME
Flexible work hours whereby starting and stopping hours of work are determined by the individual worker, with a required number of total hours (per day or week) specified by the employer. Usually there is a daily 'core' period when all workers are required to be present.

historical and legal. The perspective of this chapter is the USA. This is a reflection of my own base of knowledge, rather than a desired bias.

The 8-hour workday appears to have its origin in tenth-century England (Langenfelt, 1974). Flexitime, as a formal system, can be traced to an initial German application (Wade, 1974), and the compressed workweek probably began in the USA (Poor, 1970), but its origin is not really clear. Shiftwork practice and law can be traced at least to the times of Julius Caesar (Scherrer, 1981). The formal recognition or implementation of some of these systems may be recent, but it is quite obvious that some form of each of these systems has been in practice for decades or longer. Thus, it is quite inappropriate to consider them as either novel or non-traditional. Given our current state of knowledge, they are unusual or abnormal only in the sense that they are not, individually, the practice of the majority. Even this may be in doubt if one lumps together workers practising all formal and informal alternative work systems. Finally, it is most important to recognize and note that alternative work system practice is shaped and limited by existing local labour laws. One must recognize the culture in which alternative work systems are evolving and realize the real, and in most cases appropriate, restraints which these local regulations present.

13.2 ALTERNATIVE WORK SCHEDULES PRACTICE IN THE USA

In the USA, there has been considerable interest in the media with regard to AWS. Although the use of these systems appears to be growing, little effort has been directed towards making a systematic assessment of the magnitude and range of their applications. As a start, an attempt was made to contact by mail or the telephone every known national US labour organization (Tepas and Tepas,

TABLE 13.2
Alternative work systems practice in labour organizations in the USA

Alternative work schedule	No. of Organizations	Mean no. of members
Shiftwork	81	162 551
Split shifts	21	205 579
Compressed workweek	50	150 737
Shortened workweek	33	254 122
Permanent pt/st	29	266 646
Required overtime	51	119 867
Flexitime	24	248 308
None apply	15	128 397

Note: The membership figures are from the United States Bureau of Labor Statistics 1980 survey files, when available

1982). Responses were provided by 107 labour organizations, giving a 54 per cent response rate. Information concerning industry composition and union membership was obtained directly from the files of the United States Bureau of Labor Statistics, using their unpublished 1980 survey data when available. Table 13.2 presents a tally of the number of organizations reporting use of the AWS systems defined in Table 13.1, and the mean organization membership for each type. A breakdown of the data by industry composition is presented in Table 13.3. Mean membership size is not different for any of the AWS types, but the distribution of AWS type by industry composition is significantly different from what one would expect by chance. Shiftwork, split shifts, shortened workweek, permanent part-time/shared time, and required overtime are all most frequent with non-manufacturing organizations. This is not surprising since this group includes service industries, transportation, mining, utilities and the retail trades. Government organizations show the most flexitime and compressed workweek responses. While more manufacturing organizations favour no AWS type, it is interesting to note that significant percentages do occur for forms other than shiftwork. Manufacturing organizations have been seen by some as the least flexible of all work-scheduling groups, sticking to traditional schedules and approaches to scheduling which are easier with large numbers of workers. These data would seem to suggest that such a view is now a bit dated and that AWS systems may be entering the manufacturing world on a significant scale.

TABLE 13.3
Alternative work system practice by industry composition

Alternative work schedule	Manufacturing		Non-manufacturing		Government	
	No.	%	No.	%	No.	%
Shiftwork	24	27.9	39	45.3	23	26.7
Split shifts	3	14.3	12	57.1	6	28.6
Compressed workweek	12	23.1	19	36.5	21	40.4
Shortened workweek	11	29.7	20	54.1	6	16.2
Permanent pt/st	7	21.9	15	46.9	10	31.2
Required overtime	17	31.5	24	44.4	13	24.1
Flexitime	3	11.5	8	30.8	15	57.7
None apply	1	6.6	10	66.7	4	26.7

Note: The industry composition classification is from the United States Bureau of Labor Statistics 1980 survey files

Perhaps the most revealing data are shown in Table 13.4. In this table are tallied the number of AWS types reported by each organization. A breakdown by industry composition is also presented. Of the respondents reporting an AWS type, 87 per cent report more than one type of AWS. Using the mode as a measure of central tendancy, government organizations report the greatest number of AWS types per organization. Only about 15 per cent of the respondents fell into the 'none apply' category. It should be noted that the actual percentage of respondents in this category is probably even smaller since this group includes a number of respondents who are clearly practising what must be termed AWS, but they do not feel that their schedules fit into any of the categories used.

TABLE 13.4
Number of alternative work schedules types reported for each labour organization by industry composition

No. of Alternatives	Manufacturing	No. of Organizations Non-Manufacturing	Government	All
'None'	1	11	5	16
One	4	6	1	11
Two	9	11	4	21
Three	6	16	7	29
Four	3	6	10	15
Five	5	4	3	8
Six	1	2	3	6
Seven	1	1	0	1
Mode	Two	Three	Four	Three

Note: Some of the labour organizations responding have members working in more than one industry. As a result, some respondents were tallied into the data more than once when the industry composition breakdown was made. Thus, the sum of the industry composition numbers for a given row need not equal the value of 'all' organizations.

13.3 AUTOMATION, FREEDOM AND AWS SYSTEMS

It seems reasonable to conclude from the limited data presented that the spread of AWS is broad, and that it is not limited to workers in any one sector. More importantly, there is every reason to speculate that experience with AWS systems has not significantly inhibited their spread since most of the organizations contacted practice more than one alternative. Given the assumption that many present-day workers are suffering from time-pressure promoted by a fairly constant 40-hour workweek, there is every reason to promote AWS approaches to the 40-hour workweek as a key way to cope with the increasing worker freedom associated with the currently developing automation of industry.

The topic of shiftwork is covered in other chapters in this volume. As can be seen in Table 13.1, the two other AWS types falling within the 40-hour workweek model are flexitime and the compressed workweek. In most cases, these two

AWS types use quite different approaches to increasing worker flexibility. Flexitime allows the worker to vary workday starting and stopping times. The duration of the workweek may remain at 5 days. The compressed workweek retains fixed starting and stopping times for work but increases the length of the workday so that the workweek can be shortened. Thus, the number of consecutive days off may be increased.

Although both approaches can be viewed as simply giving the worker more freedom for off-the-job activity scheduling, they frequently differ in a key dimension: during the workweek, workers on flexitime can be less job-bound than are those on the compressed workweek; that is, flexitime workers can determine when and how long they will work, as well as how they schedule their non-work time. On the other hand, workers on the compressed workweek have virtually no control over when they work or how long for, deferring their freedom to longer blocks of non-work time. Some work systems could be classified as a form of both the compressed workweek and flexitime. So far as can be determined, formal systems of this sort are rare whereas the differences noted are probably representative and common.

The next two sections of this chapter will concentrate on flextime and the compressed workweek. In each case, definitions will be sharpened and a selective review of the literature will be made. The potential advantages and disadvantages will be presented and discussed, followed by comments concerning potential problems and pitfalls. In the final sections of the chapter, some special activities and issues relevant to future developments will be discussed.

13.4 FLEXITIME

13.4.1 Development and Definition

The definition of flexitime contained in Table 13.1 is a very broad one. A broad and general definition of this sort is needed if we are to include all the forms in which this approach has been formally adopted to date. However, it must be recognized that the definition includes many working people who usually are not thought of as being on flexitime. In the USA, 11 per cent of those employed are farmers or self-employed businessmen (Owen, 1979). It seems reasonable to suggest that these are people who, by definition and practice, set their own workhours. If we add to this group pedlars, professors and other poorly-defined groups of workers with considerable freedom to set their own hours, one can argue that a fairly large segment of the population is on informal schedules which might be termed ‘naturally occurring flexitime’. This group of workers has functioned for the most part in a silent flexitime mode for ages, making flexitime neither novel nor new.

As a formal system, flexitime is usually said to have originated in 1967 in Germany with the introduction of a *‘Gleitzeit’* system for 3000 white-collar research and development workers (Wade, 1974). The formal system spread with rapidity throughout the world, taking on a variety of forms. Nollen and Martin (1978) estimate that 6 per cent of US non-governmental employees in organizations with 50 or more employees use flexitime. This percentage is undoubtedly increasing, and is much higher in some European countries (Swart, 1977).

Golembiewski and Proehl (1978) note seven dimensions whereby these various systems differ: (i) band width — the total number of hours between the earliest starting time and the latest finishing time allowed on workdays for the system; (ii) core hours — the placement and length of a period of time within the band width during which all participants must be present; (iii) flexible hours — the total number of hours the worker can make choices about for a given workday; (iv) workweek length — the maximal number of hours the worker can in fact work, for a given week; (v) banking — whether and to what degree the worker can carry forward surplus/deficit hours; (vi) variability freedom — the degree to which the worker can or cannot vary from day to day or week to week without approval; (vii) supervisory role — how approvals are granted and the rights of the employer to override the system when organizational needs require it. A given system can, of course, abolish some of these dimensions. For example, many systems do not allow banking.

13.4.2 Advantages and disadvantages

The preceding section should make it quite clear that formal flexitime systems can and do take a multitude of forms. Obviously this makes it difficult to put forward any firm statements concerning the specific advantages and disadvantages of flexitime. Table 13.5 presents a consensus of factors usually cited as the advantages and disadvantages of a flexitime system. Extended comments concerning these factors can be found in a number of sources dedicated to flexitime issues (Allenspach, 1975; Cohen and Gadon, 1978; Ronen, 1981; Swart, 1977). At first glance, this table may seem cursory and redundant. In practice, it should serve as a simple checklist of the host of variables which should be considered if one is contemplating the installation of a flexitime system or the evaluation of one already in practice.

There is general agreement in the literature that the successful installation of a new flexitime system does require careful planning and discussion at all levels. It would appear that most flexitime systems to date had their origin in management, a reflection of the traditional top-down form of management. With the spreading awareness of flexitime applications, it is probably appropriate to expect that a growing number of efforts will have their origins in requests from non-management personnel. Flexitime may be the chief AWS, other than the shortened workweek, to gain broad union acceptance in the future (Swart, 1977).

Unfortunately, as will be discussed below, the experimental literature provides

TABLE 13.5

Potential advantages – Flexitime
Increased day-to-day flexibility for off-the-job leisure and care activity
A reduction in commuting problems and costs
Improved work times with no loss in base pay
Workforce size can adjust to short-term fluctuations in demand
Less congestion in the work environment
Less fatigued workers
Reduced job dissatisfaction/increased job satisfaction
Increased democracy in the workforce
Recognition and utilization of employee's individual differences
Reductions in tardiness rates
Reductions in absenteeism rates
Reductions in employee turnover
Reductions in on-the-job accidents
Increased production rates
Better opportunities to hire skilled workers in tight labour markets
Potential disadvantages – Flexitime
Decrements in job performance due to off-the-job activity
Increased commuting costs
Overtime pay required by law
Irregularity in workhours produced by short-term changes in demand
Difficulty covering some jobs at all required times
Difficulty in scheduling meetings or training sessions
Poorer communication within the organization
Poorer communication with other organizations
Increases in energy and physical maintenance costs
Increase in buffer stock for assembly-line operations
More sophisticated planning, organization and control
Reduction in quantity or quality of services to the public
Special time-recording or computing services
Additions in supervisory personnel
Extension of health and food service hours

little in the way of concrete expectations. Common sense plus a comprehensive evaluation and discussion of the immediate possible effects of flexitime intervention appear to be the best tactics currently available. The detailed discussion of two of these factors which follows will serve to emphasize the complexity of the issues involved and the degree to which appropriate decisions may in practice be quite dependent upon local issues.

Obviously, flexitime can alleviate commuting problems. With flexibility in selecting work start and stop times, a worker can avoid urban congestion, thereby decreasing travelling time and perhaps reducing energy consumption. It has been suggested that this is a more desirable approach than staggered working hours

(Cohen and Gadon, 1978). On the other hand, a flexitime system can make it difficult to continue an existing car-pooling or van system. Workers using public transport may find their travelling time increases since they no longer take advantage of special rush-hour services such as express systems and more frequent scheduling. In some cases, commuting time may be a moot issue if the place of employment and the residences of workers are always within convenient commuting distance.

Since flexitime systems can provide the worker with some freedom to select actual workhours, one can view them as a positive step towards democracy in the workplace. Democratic systems are frequently viewed as processes whereby communication is increased and improved. On the surface this sounds like a great feature which should improve morale and productivity. Yet, flexible workhours may make it difficult to schedule meetings and training sessions which can also promote communication. Also, unlimited time scheduling in an organization which provides services to others or requires communications restricted by the other organizations can be disastrous. What appears to be a method to improve workplace democracy and communication may in fact result in autocracy, isolation and/or poor service. Thus, decisions concerning whether there should be a core period, or how long it should be, may in fact result in either an increase or a decrease in communications and democratic behaviour. A minimal core period may have a disastrous effect on communications within and outside the organization. A long core period tends to eliminate worker differences in start and stop times, yet may at the same time make democratic meetings and acts more feasible.

13.4.3 Problems and pitfalls

The immediate attraction of flexitime is real and obvious. However, the empirical value of flexitime introduction is not certain. Although there are many ways in which flexitime applications can go wrong, there are few reports in the literature of failure. It is rare to see a concrete report of a situation where a decision was made not to introduce flexitime. On the other hand, there are numerous reports, mainly but not only in the press, which claim large improvements in worker attitudes and productivity. In nearly every case, these reports are deficient and/or appear to contain serious data flaws.

Golembiewski and Proehl (1978) and others have noted the following problems in the studies reported: (i) few studies use comparison (control) groups of any sort; (ii) few studies evaluate the effects of the intervention after a satisfactory period of use; (iii) most studies use only post-intervention measures, making it difficult to determine if any changes from pre-intervention have, in fact, occurred; (iv) studies tend to ignore potential differences associated with job differences; (v) the effects of organized labour are difficult to assess since many of the interventions occur in organizations without unions; (vi) the validity of assessment instruments used is difficult to determine since they tend to be unique to the intervention itself; (vii) concrete productivity data are frequently absent or cited in an abstract manner; (viii) adequate or appropriate statistical methods and controls are usually absent. Thus, despite the nearly unanimous positive tone of the published literature, it is not able to cite a set of firm conclusions.

At the moment, meaningful experimental studies of US flexitime interventions appear to be limited to three studies. Narayanan and Nath (1982), using experimental and control groups of workers, as well as some pre- and post-intervention measures, have reported significant improvement in worker relations and flexibility, but no change in job satisfaction. There was a significant decrease in absenteeism, but no increase, seen subjectively, in workgroup productivity. Unfortunately, the post-intervention measures were limited to a single point 3 months after the introduction of the flexitime system. Thus, although many appropriate statistical and methodological techniques were used, one cannot eliminate the possibility that the results might be attributed to Sleeper or Hawthorne effects (Tepas, 1976).

Schein *et al.* (1977) examined the productivity of clerical workers before and after flexitime introduction using measured work variables. Five groups of workers were studied, 4-month post-intervention measures being compared with data from the previous year. At most, only two groups showed increased productivity. However, no negative effects on measured work productivity were obtained. Again, Sleeper and/or Hawthorne effects may have had a role in the results. This study is of special interest since it did use actual rather than perceived productivity measures.

Golembiewski *et al.* (1974) appear to have conducted the best study to date. It involved two experimental groups and one control group in research and development units. Both pre- and post-intervention measures were made with the final measures being 1 year after the introduction of flexitime. Some long-term attitudinal shifts did occur, and a significant drop in absentieeism as well as support services costs were observed. However, the authors suggest caution in that the results may very well be driven by other dynamics within the organization at the time.

There is not a single experimental study in the literature which allows one to compare directly flexitime effects with those of other AWS types. Thus, even if we choose to conclude that flexitime can have positive effects, we have no way of judging whether these effects outweigh those of other AWS types. Furthermore, each of the existing studies examines short-term, perhaps acute, effects in that no workers were studied after more than a year had passed since flexitime was introduced. Clearly, there is a need for additional research before we can feel comfortable with the notion that flexitime can be a good thing. Given the complexity and interacting nature of the factors involved, it is prudent to state that flexitime introductions require careful analysis and planning as well as a systematic evaluation of any interventions made.

13.5 THE COMPRESSED WORKWEEK

13.5.1 Development and definition

As with flexitime, the definition of the Compressed Workweek contained in Table 13.1 is a very broad one. If we add to the definition the specification that the workweek totals around 40 hours, the compressed workweek appears to have a fairly recent origin. There are two major forms of the compressed workweek: 4 days of 10 hours each, and 3 days of 12 hours each. In the USA, Nollen (1979) estimates that about 2 per cent of the labour force uses compressed workweek systems. It should be noted that compressed workweeks are, by definition, contrary to the standing traditional fight of labour for an 8-hour day (Langenfelt, 1974). Although without success, most of the recent efforts of organized labour in the USA have been aimed at reducing the workday below the 8-hour level (Levitan and Belous, 1977). As a result, it does seem reasonable to infer that most of the existing compressed workweek systems are in worker groups which do not have national union representation.

Although popular impressions prevail that the compressed workweek is a very new development, it appears that formal compressed workweek systems have been in operation for around 40 years (Poor, 1970; Northrup *et al.*, 1979), with the rate of introduction increasing since 1970 (Wheeler *et al.*, 1972). To put this in historical perspective, permanent part-time/shared time (see Table 13.1) was practised in the USA prior to the legal acts which defined the standard workweek as 40 hours (Best, 1981). The 10- and 12-hour workdays were standard prior to this legislation (Wheeler *et al.*, 1972). Thus, it would seem logical to argue that the combination of a longer workday and work-sharing in a very literal sense resulted in compressed workweek systems more than 50 years ago. They just didn't call them that! In any case, compressed workweeks are not new, and their origin is not clear.

As with flexitime, the basic compressed workweek systems may differ on a number of dimensions: (i) consecutive workdays — for either 10- or 12-hour workday, the number of consecutive workdays may vary; (ii) consecutive non-workdays — for either the 10- or 12-hour workday, the number of consecutive days off may vary; (iii) workday variability — whether the number of consecutive workdays is constant or not; (iv) non-workday variability — whether the number of consecutive non-workdays is constant or not; (v) workday length — the length of the workday and whether it varies with the preceding dimensions; (vi) shiftwork — the time of day for the workday and whether it varies. A given system can, of course, abolish some of these dimensions. For example, many systems do not involve shiftwork.

13.5.2 Advantages and disadvantages

The preceding section should not be taken to suggest that formal compressed workweeks as a rule take a multitude of forms. Data suggests that among organizations on the compressed workweek, over 70 per cent use 4 days and a 40-hour or less workweek (Wheeler *et al.*, 1972). Comments concerning this AWS system can be a little more specific than those about flexitime. Table 13.6 presents a consensus of the factors usually cited as the advantages and disadvantages of a compressed workweek system. Extended comments concerning these factors can be found in a number of sources (Cohen and Gadon, 1978; Wade, 1974; Poor, 1970; Wheeler *et al.*, 1972). Again, this table should serve as a checklist or guide to the host of variables which should be considered if

TABLE 13.6

Potential advantages – the compressed workweek

Increased possibility for multi-day off-the-job leisure and care activity
A reduction in commuting problems and costs
Fewer workdays with no loss of pay
A regular, steady workweek
Ease in covering all jobs at the required times
More time for scheduling meetings or training sessions
Increased opportunity for communication within the organization

Increased opportunity for communication with other organizations
Decreases in start-up and/or warm-up expenses
Fewer supervisory personnel may be needed
More efficient stock flow for assembly-line operations
Less night work
Increased production rates
Improvement in the quantity or quality of services to the public
Better opportunities to hire skilled workers in tight labour markets

Potential disadvantages – the compressed workweek

Decrements in job performance due to 'moonlighting'
Increased commuting costs
Overtime pay required by law
More fatigued workers
Little recognition of employee's individual differences
Increases in tardiness rates
Increases in absenteeism rates
Increases in employee turnover
Increases in on-the-job and off-the-job accidents
Decreases in production rates
Increased exposure to toxic substances and/or physical hazards
Scheduling problems if the organization operations are longer than the workweek
Difficulty in scheduling child care and family life during the workweek
Contrary to traditional objectives of labour unions
Increased energy and physical maintenance costs

one is contemplating use of a compressed workweek system or the evaluation of one that is already in practice.

Although data suggest that size of organization is not related to success in adopting the compressed workweek (Wheeler *et al.*, 1972), this may very well be an artifact. One analysis (Nollen, 1979) suggests that many compressed workweek organizations are small businesses operating only 4 days per week. Another review (Northrup *et al.*, 1979) suggests that compressed workweeks are popular in larger, continuous-process shiftwork organizations. They may very well both be correct. However, the advantages and disadvantages of the compressed workweek for such diverse groups are quite different. For example, small work groups tend not to be unionized, whereas large organizations do. As with flexitime, most compressed workweek applications appear to have an origin in management, and the compressed workweek has even been heralded in some publications as a 'management innovation' (Wheeler *et al.*, 1972). Few leaders of organized labour would view this as a step in the right direction, and their fears would be supported by the comments of Northrup *et al.* (1979) which suggest wage revisions and a reduction in the workforce as likely outcomes. The small business would, of course, welcome such prospects.

Once again, common sense and planning are required when considering the potential impact of many of these factors. Commuting, for example, may benefit from the compressed workweek in that there is a reduction in the number of trips to and from work, and periods of urban congestion can be avoided. This can save energy and cut down travelling time. On the other hand, those using public transport will almost certainly face increases in travelling time since they are forced to travel when services are poorer. For most items in this table, one must either plan an individual case evaluation, or be prepared to track down immediate effects. Solid facts, gathered with appropriate control and evaluation methods, are not for the most part available.

Clearly, fatigue is an issue, but the proponents of the compressed workweek tend to devalue this factor. Although Colquhoun *et al.* (1969) and others have studied individuals in laboratory situations resembling the compressed workweek, Volle *et al.* (1979) have reported one of the few experimental studies of workers with actual compressed workweek experience. This study included both experimental and control groups, but the results are limited since they only examined changes during the workweek and subsequent week recovery. The differences between groups were quite modest. Noting the severe limitations of their study, the authors concluded that there is little in their data to suggest that fatigue is a serious problem.

13.5.3 Problems and pitfalls

Exposure to night work results in chronic sleep deprivation (Tepas, 1982) and other problems. Assuming that extended work shifts cause a transient form of fatigue, it follows that the combined effect of compressed workweek acute fatigue and nightwork chronic fatigue may be quite severe. This would argue against having nightworkers on the compressed workweek. However, if having a compressed workweek on the dayshift allows an organization to eliminate some nightwork, the overall benefits for the workforce may be positive. Additionally, there is a wealth of evidence from 'time on task' studies which suggests that even an 8-hour day is too long, especially when the worker is performing a scanning task in a situation where the frequency of a deviant event is quite low (see Chapter 12).

Extending the duration of the workday raises a crucial factor, in view of the nature of many existing compressed workweek installations in the petroleum and chemical industries. Most countries have regulatory standards for exposure to chemical substances and physical agents in the work environment. In the USA these standards are administered by the Occupational Safety and Health Administration and in many cases the standard is a time-weighted average exposure limit, assuming that the normal day is an 8-hour one. A number of authors have noted this problem and the need for establishing an acceptable mode for adjusting these standards to 10- and 12-hour exposure limits (Brief and Scala, 1975; Hickey and Reist, 1977, 1979). Given current models and knowledge, it is possible to generate at least six different adjusted limits for some substances (Reist and Hickey, 1982)!

As noted earlier, one of the attractive features of the compressed workweek is the fact that the worker has longer periods of free time. This increases the likelihood of 'moonlighting', i.e. having a second job. If a worker is already suffering from acute and perhaps chronic fatigue, moonlighting will exacerbate it. Hickey and Reist (1979) express concern that this may make evaluations concerning chemical exposure difficult. Since moonlighting is perhaps impossible to control and difficult to monitor, one has another potential pitfall for the compressed workweek. At the very least, this discussion highlights the importance of educating individual workers concerning potential fatigue and exposure problems to ensure that they are able to consider more fully the hazards of moonlighting while on the compressed workweek. Once again, worker cooperation and participation are necessary parts of a successful AWS system.

13.6 THE MAGNIFICENT TRIAL?

In 1978 the US government enacted Public Law 95-390 which allowed government employees to adopt flexitime and compressed workweek systems during a 3-year trial period. Among other things, the law required evaluation of the applications by the Office of Personnel Management, followed by recommendations to the President and Congress. The final results of this project are not as yet available, and although the *Alternative Work Schedules Experimental Program: Interim Report to the President and the Congress* (1981) is written, it is not widely available. It suggests a trial of these two AWS systems which may be very helpful in the future. This is a 'magnificent trial', if one only considers the magnitude of the effort. Whether the empirical data to be produced by this trial deserve such a label remains to be seen.

Participants in this effort include 1554 government organizations employing approximately 325 000 workers. Most of the organizations appear to have had no prior AWS experience. Four forms of evaluation were attempted, with many being limited to selected groups: (i) narrative reports and statistical profiles; (ii) longitudinal reports from selected organizations; (iii) on-site data collection from selected organizations; (iv) a study of the energy impact on transportation and operating costs. Preliminary results suggest the following: for the majority of the organizations, there was no reported change in the efficiency of operations; a modest reduction in commuting costs and an increase in mass transit use occurred; there was an increase in the number of hours organizations were available to serve the public; there was satisfaction with, and a wish to retain, the AWS plans on the part of both workers and supervisors. Overall, 79 per cent of the organizations judged the project a success.

At a point roughly 2 years after the project began, only 85 of the more than 1500 organizations notified the investigators of plans to terminate their AWS system. Of these, 75 per cent were organizations using compressed workweek systems. On the surface, it would appear that this magnificent AWS trial is a positive vote in favour of flexitime with perhaps a reserved or qualified vote for the compressed workweek. Further conclusions must wait for the final report, however.

13.7 COMPUTER-ASSISTED TIME-SCHEDULING (CAT)

In a small business, scheduling workers is not usually a difficult or time-consuming task and it can be handled in an informal manner. As the size of the organization increases, scheduling difficulty increases. This is especially true when one considers time demands of service, continuous-process, and assembly-line situations in which shiftwork or some other AWS system is practised. The traditional approach to the scheduling problem is a manual one. The responsible individual(s) sits down, usually with paper and pencil, and works out a schedule. This is frequently a very time-consuming task which can result in costly errors.

Another problem which organizations face as size increases is keeping a firm track of the number of hours worked by hourly workers. The traditional approach to this is the time-clock (recording clock). Time-clocks date back to the 1800s (Wright, 1968), work in a reliable manner and can be quite efficient in their modern form. They are also a source of considerable time-pressure, which is counter to many of the objectives of flexitime. As Golembiewski *et al.* (1974) note, flexitime claims to enhance a worker's freedom, but the use of a time-clock is an objective reminder to all that the worker is, in the end, not to be trusted! This problem in time-accounting was recognized early in flexitime applications, and a variety of methods and automatic devices have been developed in attempts to overcome it (Ronen, 1981).

Difficulties in scheduling workers and in accounting for their time have frequently been used as arguments against the introduction of flexitime in service, shiftwork, continuous-process and assembly operations. Manual scheduling is more time-consuming and complex. New time-accounting equipment may be required. When assembly operations are involved, stock inventory may have to be increased. Finally, additional supervisory staff may be required. Very similar arguments are raised with regard to the compressed workweek, where irregular workweek length, rather than irregular workday length, is the issue. In practice, there are examples where all of these objections have been overcome. These factors, in combination, have undoubtedly restricted the spread of flexitime and compressed workweek systems. In sum, fears concerning cost of implementation have kept many organizations from giving these systems a trial. Also, poor planning has probably led some organizations to abandon their trial efforts.

'Computer-assisted time-scheduling' (CAT) is a way to overcome these unnecessary liabilities. Computers can be used to schedule workers and record their actual worktime. In the USA this innovation has been used successfully for the scheduling of hospital personnel for at least 20 years (Young *et al.*, 1981). CAT appears to work well, and significant savings in scheduling time and flexibility have been reported (Warner, 1976; Morrish and O'Connor, 1970). In general, existing batch-processing computer systems are used, with off-line production of future staff schedules. As a rule, schedules for several weeks of work are computed a number of weeks before their use. In some cases, the CAT program includes inputs from workers with regard to personal aversions and preferences. These applications include some very large organizations.

One can envisage a CAT system in the not-too-distant future which resembles the computer-driven reservation services now commonly used by airlines and many other present-day service organizations. Given a system with appropriate controls and restraints, workers may be able to phone a CAT to add flexibility to their time-pressured lives. It may save employers from costly errors caused by fatigued workers, by providing workers with a cost-free way of deferring their work when they are not in the best of condition. Such a system would allow workers to make inquiries about their current schedule, as well as enter requests for changes in it. Workers with complementary schedule requests or needs might be matched up so they could substitute for each other. The system could monitor and control the complex matrix of legal, health and organizational requirements to ensure that all these restrictions are met at all times. It might also be used to record work time for direct input into various cost-accounting systems. Personal supervision of requests might be minimal and the workers and supervisors might enjoy the added benefit of being able to make requests in a fairly anonymous manner. This might very well spill over into improved workplace communications, since most issues about workhours may be dealt with by CAT rather than by immediate supervisors. Above all, it should reduce time-pressure, since the result would be less job-bound workers.

13.8 SUMMARY AND DISCUSSION

AWS systems are quite common. They are not new. Flexitime and the compressed workweek are AWS approaches aimed mainly at providing the worker with more time flexibility rather than less working time. Many claims are made for the merits of these two approaches. Unfortunately, there is little in the way of sound empirical data to support these claims. The most that can be said for flexitime is that, given proper and adequate planning, there is little evidence to indicate that it does any harm. For compressed workweek systems, the picture is not as positive. Excessive fatigue and extended exposure to dangerous agents may be harmful to both worker and production. When combined with nightwork, these negative features may have amplified effects. On the positive side, daytime compressed workweeks may reduce the number of workers required for nightwork.

As automation progresses and spreads, it is reasonable to suggest that the role of the worker will change. The very nature of the automation process itself will mean more flexibility for the worker on the job. A more flexible and varied approach to job hours is probably one way in which on-the-job performance at machine-watching tasks may be improved. A product of the automation age, the computer may very well be an important tool in making it possible to add flexitime and/or compressed workweek systems to service, continous-process and assembly tasks frequently viewed as being out of the reach of these methods. Interesting initial efforts have been taken in this direction. As these efforts continue to evolve, more empirical research is needed to ensure that automated work scheduling does not perpetuate errors of the past or introduce new and even worse problems.

Just as it is possible to introduce flexitime and compressed workweek systems that seem to work, it is also easy to fail. Unfortunately, apparent success draws public attention whereas failures vanish without notice. Everyone agrees that smooth applications require extensive planning before their implementation. Those involved in planning must employ evaluation programmes. Planning should include the collection of pre-intervention base-line data, the selection and study of appropriate control groups, and long-term plans for post-intervention data collection and analysis. Post-intervention evaluation should include efforts to measure short-term acute effects as well as long-term chronic effects.

A key dimension is major involvement in the decision and evaluation process on the part of individuals at all levels within the organization, and an effort to ensure that unbiased decisions and evaluations are made. Participation by workers and their representatives is essential. Outside participation in the evaluation process is warranted to ensure objectivity and accuracy. As the automation stage develops and worker flexibility evolves, dramatic changes in legal and institutionalized regulations may be required. Needed changes will not occur if they appear to violate the hard-won and well-deserved established rights of labour. Empirical data of quality are needed to guide the decision process accurately.

In the end, the complexity of these situations must be stressed, and the fact that every potential AWS intervention is unique. Direct comparisons of the effects of various AWS systems are absent from the experimental literature. Superior solutions to complex problems demand that all AWS system alternatives be considered, not just the current fad. One needs more than just a set of recommendations with regard to a single AWS. One needs recommendations for each of the alternatives so that the most appropriate match is made for each situation. The question is not 'will flexitime work?' but rather, 'which AWS will work best for this situation?'.

Chapter 14

Introduction to the Problems of Shiftwork

Kazutaka Kogi

CONTENTS

ABSTRACT

This chapter introduces the reader to the general problems associated with shiftwork. It describes the development of shiftwork in industrialized countries, and its recent spread to developing countries. The disturbances of normal circadian rhythms are discussed and related to the type of shift system, and in particular to the incidence of nightshifts. Finally, the main ways in which the problems of shiftwork may be reduced are considered. These include the judicious choice of shift systems, and the encouraging of shiftworkers to develop appropriate coping strategies.

14.1 DAILY LIFE OF SHIFTWORKERS

14.1 The nature of shiftwork

Shiftwork today spreads over a wide range of industries. It is introduced where work is necessary at night or in the early morning, and takes the form of multiple 'shifts', or manning of a workplace by two or more teams of employees that work at different times of day. The total period of time covered can be either continuous for 24 hours, or discontinuous for less than 24 hours a day. As a result of working unusual hours, many shiftworkers complain of fatigue, sleep disturbances and social hardships. This appears to be largely due to the fact that their circadian rhythms cannot immediately adjust to the 'phase-shift' of their schedule (Aschoff, 1978a). To understand these complaints fully, however, we have to consider these short-term disturbances, and the more chronic effects leading to physical disorders (Chapter 16) and the disruption of social life (Chapter 17). Shiftworkers are typically engaged in it for many years, and fit their daily life routines in with it. Effects of shiftworking are thus far-reaching compared to those of a casual night vigil.

Shiftwork may be defined as a system of working in which a regular change of one group of workers for another takes place on the same type of job and in the same workplace. From the point of view of manning different shifts, shiftwork is thus an organizational problem. However, this type of definition fails to take account of how each worker actually works from day to day. The practical problems encountered by an individual worker are obviously related to how he or she goes from one shift to another. Thus to understand the impact of shiftwork on an individual, we need to examine the manner of swapping from one shift to another for each individual worker. In contrast, from an organizational point of view, the reasons for adopting shiftwork are important. They form the basis for determining how many hours are worked a day and how shifts are arranged. These reasons may be very complex, since shiftwork may be implemented for technological, economic, social and other reasons, and all these reasons may be interdependent. As a result, various forms of shift system have emerged. This makes it difficult to establish widely acceptable forms of shiftwork. In addition, more recently the economic reasons for shiftwork have become more and more predominant, resulting in an increase in irregular shift systems.

From the shiftworkers' point of view, the extra effort needed to adjust themselves to their unusual work–rest schedules is important. In spite of the large diversity of shift systems, there are many similarities between the problems encountered by an individual. These include keeping alert at work, securing sleeping time and scheduling free-time activities. Coping strategies may develop throughout the working life and are sometimes effective enough to modify the results of circadian rhythm disruptions. Indeed, recent studies have paid increasing attention to long-term effects, psychosocial factors and social support. Let us take an example of daily activities of an individual two-shift worker in a print shop (Sakai *et al.*, 1982). In Figure 14.1, solid lines show nighttime sleep and dotted lines daytime sleep. This is a two-shift system with three teams, a period of two consecutive 10-h nightshifts occurring after two days off and two dayshifts. Note that daytime sleeps around these nightshifts are very different from normal night sleeps and are often split into two. Mealtimes also become irregular around the nightshift period, as do defecation times. Apart from travelling to and from the print shop, free-time periods outside the home are very limited on workdays as well as immediately before or after nightshifts. After

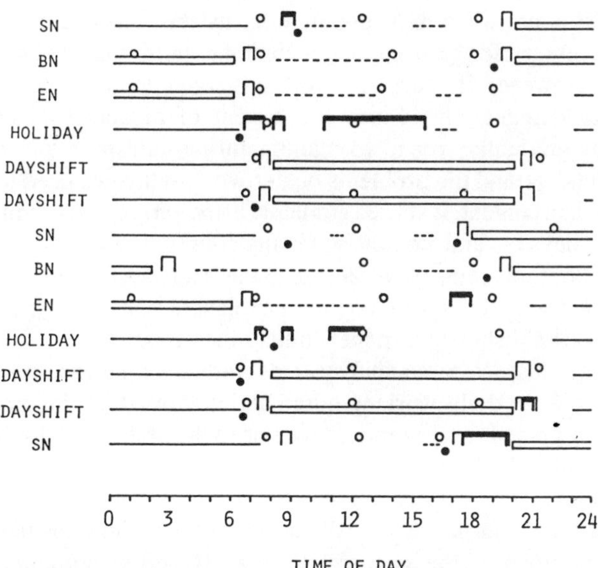

Figure 14.1 An example of records of daily activities for a two-shift worker in a print shop
work; —— night sleep; - - - - daytime sleep;
o meal; • defecation; travelling;
free time outside home
SN day of starting the first nightshift
BN day between two nightshifts
EN day of ending the last nightshift

repeating such routines for many years, workers at the print shop complained of sleep deficit, chronic fatigue, gastroenteric disorders and disrupted family and social life.

Thus it would seem that the extra efforts required of each shiftworker extend over the complete shift cycle period, and perhaps to the whole of their occupational career. These extra efforts may be classified as 'short-term', e.g. sleep strategy, alertness efforts, mealtime arrangements and free-time allocation and 'long-term' e.g. securing restful conditions, coping with health disorders, cooperating with family members, long-term adaptation to shiftworking and professional career-making.

These are the unique problems of shiftworkers. Organizational aspects of shiftwork need to be assessed in relation to these problems at their multiple levels. The problems of shiftwork are, in effect, the 'problems of shiftworkers'.

14.1.2 The development of shiftwork

Occupational activity at night, or in the early morning hours, is by no means a modern phenomenon. From early times, there have been workers whose jobs kept them awake at hours when most people were asleep. The extension of working hours was necessary for gatekeepers, watchmen, herdsmen, policemen, sailors and soldiers. However, modern shiftwork has some unique aspects not seen in these traditional night jobs. Since the advent of modern industrial society, nightwork has gradually spread to manufacturing industries and many public services. To understand the problems of shiftwork today, we need to look at this spread in its social context. It started gradually in the early days of industrialization. Long working days became common in many countries, and were soon followed by the use of different teams of workers, e.g. the 'relay system'. By the nineteenth century, two 12-hour shifts were common in blast furnaces, forges, rolling mills, metallurgical establishments, paper mills and glass works. In continuous manufacturing industries, three-shift systems gradually replaced two-shift systems while restrictions on daily working hours and nightwork in the employment of children, young persons and women, gave rise to the practice of double day shifts in textile and other industries.

These developments resulted in the extension of shiftwork to various sections of industry where it was not technically necessary, and the special technical and economic conditions of the post-World War II period promoted this trend. Shiftwork is now found widely in food-processing, textile, printing, machinery and other manufacturing industries. Increasing urbanization has also affected the development of shiftwork through its requirement for continuous and semi-continuous operation of wide-ranging public and private services. These include postal services, telecommunications, broadcasting, transport, power supply, health services, security and entertainment. This increasing dependence on shiftwork has been universal in recent years. According to recent figures for industrialized countries, approximately 15–30 percent of industrial workers may be said to be engaged in shiftwork. This spread has followed economic expansion, growing into the 1950s, levelling off in the 1960s and accelerating again from around 1970 (ILO, 1978).

The reasons for the development of shiftwork are similar in different countries, although the emphasis may depend on the characteristics of different economic climates. *Technological* requirements have been foremost in necessitating the adoption of shiftwork. Many automated machines are operated continuously for economic reasons even when automation does not actually require continuous operation, and this often leads to multiple shifts (Maurice, 1975). Indeed, the *economic* advantages of shiftwork have gained in importance over recent years. Extending working hours to abnormal hours of work has increased the utilization of capital, and thus profit margins. This profitability results from the rapid depreciation of expensive equipment (often linked with a reduction of tax burdens), increased competitiveness due to reduced overall costs per unit of production, and increased flexibility in meeting rapid changes in production or temporarily increased demand. The availability of skilled manpower, and the additional costs, limit the extent of such advantages, although recently employers using sophisticated electronics or computer-aided machines have started introducing shiftworking.

Another reason for introducing shiftwork is the need to extend the availability of various *services*. This is often related to technological and economic reasons, and is enhanced by accelerated urbanization. Continuous or semi-continuous operation is required in communication services, public transport, power generation, health services and security. Radio and television stations, motor car service stations, entertainment centres and restaurants also often require shiftwork. Three-shift systems are increasingly used for computer centres in insurance offices, banks and local authorities. *Social and macroeconomic* factors have also played a significant role. The reduction in normal hours of work has undoubtedly resulted in the adoption of shiftwork, while a widely accepted macroeconomic advantage of shiftwork is that its adoption may reduce unemployment.

It has been shown (Kogi, 1976) that the percentages of two- and three-shift workers vary considerably across different sectors, reflecting differences in the underlying reasons for adopting shiftwork. Industries, such as paper and chemical, that require predominantly continuous operation, have a higher percentage of three-shift workers, and a relatively small proportion of two-shift workers. In contrast, those industries adopting shiftwork for economic reasons, such as the textile industry, have a high percentage of two-shift workers and few three-shift workers. Other industries, such as mining and petroleum, fall in between these two extremes, while yet others, such as transport and communication, are characterized by high rates of irregular night duties. The growth of shiftwork is thus governed by various factors, and there is a continuing trend of introducing various forms of shiftwork into sectors where daywork was previously the rule. Clearly, this trend should be reassessed in view of the reduced quality of the working life of shiftworkers and the overall social costs.

14.1.3 The spread to developing countries

The rapid industrialization taking place in many developing countries is associated with an increase in the use of shiftwork for economic reasons and as a means of increasing employment (Kabaj, 1968; Betancourt and Clague, 1976). However, this is giving rise to concern over the impact on local economy, and on the health and social life of the workers, especially where it is extensively applied for purely economic reasons, e.g. in the textile industry (Shri Ram Centre for Human Relations, 1970; Kogi, 1977; Khaleque and Rahman, 1982).

Statistics on the incidence of shiftwork are, as yet, not usually available in developing countries. The types of shift system, and problems arising from them, seem to vary considerably with the requirements of national legislation and local customs. However, it is well known that, for example, in the textile industry almost all modern plants employ shiftwork (Textiles Committee, 1978). In industrialized countries, double day shifts excluding nightwork are in the most common in textile mills, but in developing countries the use of three-shift systems is widespread in textile mills. It would appear that nightwork has been 'exported' to developing countries from industrialized countries, often for purely economic reasons. In developing countries, in contrast to most industrialized countries, legislation often allows women to work at night or makes exceptions for women working in industry. It is also noteworthy that the working and welfare conditions of shiftworkers in developing countries are often alarming, to say nothing of their low wages. Many shiftworkers work six to seven successive nightshifts with high levels of heat and noise, and have to sleep in unhygienic and congested rooms. Many of them suffer from sleep disturbances and physical complaints (Wongphanich *et al.*, 1982). Poor water and food supplies, commuting problems (including rape at night), poor dormitory and housing conditions, and conflicts arising from religious and cultural customs add to their hardship.

An interesting argument in support of the spread of shiftwork in these countries, which are mainly in the tropical zone, is that the cool nightshifts are favoured by the workers themselves. However, the daytime heat in which these workers have to sleep has also to be taken into account, and shiftworking textile workers in tropical climates have high rates of sleep disturbances (Khaleque and Rahman, 1982; Wongphanich *et al.*, 1982) due to heat, noise and insects. These hardships apply to shiftworkers on both fixed and rotating shifts, and constitute a real problem (Khaleque and Rahman, 1982).

One of the few sets of data available concerning the extent of shiftwork in manufacturing industries in a developing country is from Singapore (Ong and Hong, 1982). Although Singapore is highly industrialized compared to many other developing countries, the report indicates that rapid industrialization is associated with a spread of shift systems. In Singapore in 1980, 74 out of 419 firms (18 percent) had adopted a shift system. The proportion of firms with shiftwork varied according to the type of industry, but was significant in most groups. Of the total 43 000 workers employed in these 419 firms, 16 000 or 37 per cent were on shiftwork. The great majority (67 per cent) were in machinery and equipment, wood products, textile and food-processing industries, apparently for primarily economic reasons. Among the shiftworkers, 63 per cent were on two-shift rotation, 6 per cent on permanent second shiftwork in two-shift systems, 18 per cent on three-shift rotation and 12 per cent on permanent nightwork.

Reports on shiftwork in developing countries indicate that, in selecting workers, enterprises do not seem to apply any criteria other than those imposed by legislation, such as the exclusion of young persons or women (Dumont, 1982; Fischer, 1982). Few, if any, measures are taken to prevent the problems associated with shiftwork, and any examinations conducted are the same as those for dayworkers. In practice, many of these shiftworkers are subjected to particularly long hours of work, often in the form of two 12-hour shifts, or the frequent doubling of two 8-hour shifts (Dumont, 1982). Low wages, high levels of unemployment and underemployment, poor housing conditions, and the generally poor availability of social services are also relevant factors. Clearly, it is necessary, when examining the problems of shiftworkers, to take account of the social context. Shiftwork conditions are affected by the social and cultural status of the society in which it is undertaken. This is particularly important when considering the improvement of shift systems, and the social support necessary for alleviating the difficulties of shiftworkers.

14.1.4 Characteristics of 'shift-lag'

The recent growing concern over the problems of shiftwork contrasts with the fact that it has been practised for so many years. However, the difficulties met by nightworkers and shiftworkers in their daily life have long been neglected. Indeed, it was once believed that the hardship of these workers could be tolerated, and that they could eventually adapt to it. The real gravity of their complaints and difficulties has only emerged as a result of recent studies on human circadian rhythms, and on the unique problems of shiftworkers (Saito, 1954; Menzel, 1962; Kogi, 1971; Rutenfranz *et al.*, 1976). Two decades ago, some texts claimed that nightshifters could adapt to the reversal of work–rest schedules after a few days. However, it is now known that circadian rhythms cannot be completely reversed, even if nightwork is continued for weeks without any 'rest' days (Van Loon, 1963; Knauth *et al.*, 1981). In addition, social conditions have greatly changed in recent times, such that shiftworkers are exposed to conflicting social events and are affected by a generally urbanized and stressful lifestyle. Their jobs have also changed to ones in which they have to maintain their level of vigilance and this is only achieved at some cost. They suffer from performance decrement at night, sleep problems and physical and mental disorders to a greater extent than in former times (Rutenfranz *et al.*, 1977; Shift Work Committee, 1979).

In this respect, a comparison between 'jet-lag' (Chapter 21) and the shiftworkers' problems is of interest. For several days after a quick inversion of the sleep–wakefulness cycle, we suffer from disturbed sleep, reduced work capacity and feeling unwell. This effect is typically seen after a jet flight to a place with a time difference of several hours, and has become known as 'jet-lag'. Similar symptoms appear when working on nightshifts. However, while the jet-lag symptoms disappear after a week or so, the nightshifters' symptoms persist for as long as the night-work/day-sleep schedule continues. This has been attributed to the incomplete reversal of the circadian rhythm of nightworkers due to conflicting social stimulations and awareness of clock time (Rutenfranz *et al.*, 1977). While jet-lag has attracted publicity due to the quick change of many people's sleep–wakefulness schedules made possible by jet planes, 'shift-lag' has become recognized due to a rapidly increasing number of people affected by it.

The increasing publicity given to shiftwork issues is also related to recent concern for the health and well-being of shiftworkers. It is only in the last two decades that gastrointestinal diseases, and in particular gastric or duodenal ulcers, have been reported to occur more frequently among nightshift workers and former shiftworkers than among dayworkers (Aanonsen, 1964; Taylor *et al.*, 1972; Angersbach *et al.*, 1980). The relationship of other illnesses to shiftwork is also being considered (see Chapter 16). Shiftworkers complain more frequently than dayworkers of respiratory and motor organ disorders, suggesting that other illnesses may also be increased if other aggravating factors come together. One of the most recent findings is that cellular immunological functions of lymphocytes in peripheral blood show a circadian variation, and that they are lowered at night among shiftworkers (Nakano *et al.*, 1982). If shiftwork affects the general defence mechanisms of the human body, it may well lead to higher morbidity for certain diseases. Further, there is an increasing number of reports on sleep-disruption and related social hardships when nightshifts are worked (Wedderburn, 1967; Rutenfranz *et al.*, 1977; Koller *et al.*, 1978; Colquhoun, 1981) although until recently these non-clinical difficulties had not been assessed sufficiently (Kogi, 1981a; Rutenfranz *et al.*, 1981a).

It is thus understandable that shift-lag is becoming an increasing concern. We need to assess the complex effects of shift-lag on various forms of shift schedule and under different social conditions. Further, this assessment needs to take account not only of the lag that arises from the disruption of circadian rhythms, but also of the fact that the degree of such disruption, and its adverse effects, depends on how the shift-lag difficulties are met and overcome (Colquhoun, 1981).

14.2 THE DIVERSITY OF SHIFT SYSTEMS

14.2.1 Shiftwork versus normal daywork

Shift systems are very diverse. Surveys conducted in different countries indicate that hundreds of types of shift schedule can be found in almost any country. Even if we classify these types into several basic patterns, the distribution still varies considerably across sectors and countries. Any description of a shift system must start by showing how it is distinguished from 'normal daywork'. For example, dividing shift systems simply into two-shift, three-shift and other systems does not tell us much, since two-shift systems can comprise those without nightwork as well as those with nightwork, the latter being more akin in some respects to three-shift systems.

Normal daywork is carried out during the day and usually involves two spells of duty separated by a lunch break. A shift system may include daywork, but also has one or more 'shifts' worked outside these normal daywork hours. These shifts may be shorter than, longer than, or of the same duration as normal daywork hours, and indeed may overlap with them. The crucial aspect appears to be whether any shift that extends to abnormal hours requires the workers to 'phase-shift' their sleep–wakefulness cycle from that for normal daywork, and if so, to what extent. Thus the question of whether a morning shift starting at 0500 h, or an evening shift ending at 2200 h, should be considered as normal daywork can only be answered on the basis of evidence concerning circadian activity phases such as sleep, meal-taking, etc.

Typically, it appears that it is more difficult to phase-shift sleep than it is to phase-shift work. Thus, any shift hours that result in a phase-shift of the sleep period may create problems for the shiftworker, whereas a minor extension of day duty hours towards the evening need not necessarily hamper the sleep period and is usually more or less tolerable. For this reason, discussion will concentrate on nightshifts, early morning shifts and evening shifts that extend until about midnight. Weekends and between-shift intervals are also important since they determine the degree of recovery from the phase-shift. Thus, four basic features of a shift system are important (Kogi, 1971; Rutenfranz *et al.*, 1977; Knauth *et al.*, 1979): (i) whether any shift extends into hours that would normally be spent asleep (i.e. if on daywork); (ii) whether the shifts are worked throughout the week, or with daily intervals and/or a free weekend; (iii) the number of shifts that the daily operation hours are divided into (two, three or four shifts, etc.); and (iv) whether the crews of different shifts rotate or work permanently on a particular shift.

Most shift systems can be classified according to these four features (see Figure 14.2). Shift systems are first categorized according to whether or not they rotate,

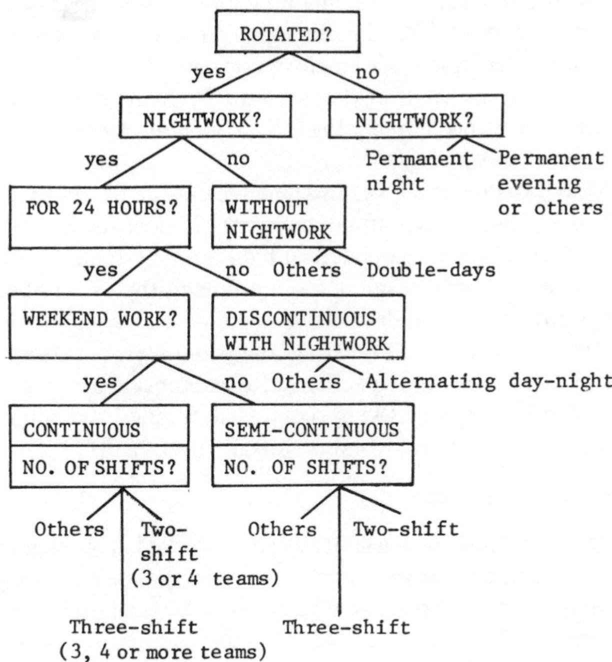

Figure 14.2 Classification of different types of shift systems by key features

and then into two groups, those without nightwork and those involving nightwork. The former usually take the form of double day shifts without weekend work. The latter are either manned for less than 24 hours a day (discontinuous systems) or continuously for 24 hours a day (whole-day systems). A typical discontinuous system involving nightwork is one in which day and night shifts are alternated, but with operations suspended for a few hours between them, and during the weekend. Whole-day systems can be further subdivided into continuous systems, worked 7 days a week, and semi-continuous systems that do not involve weekend work. Both continuous and semi-continuous systems usually have three shifts, although occasionally they have only two and, in some certain cases, four. Any of these types of shift system can be permanent shift systems, in which each crew works a fixed shift, or rotated, in which each crew will rotate from one shift to another. Finally, it should be noted that mixed or hybrid systems are not uncommon. Thus, for example, the night hours may be covered by a permanent nightshift, and the day hours by a rotating double day shift.

The proportions of different types of shift systems vary between countries and between sectors. However, in general, the most common types of system are: double days; alternating days and nights; semi-continuous (mostly three-shift); continuous (either two- or three-shift); permanent night; and irregular. In a relatively industrialized country of today, about 10–20 per cent of shiftworkers are to be found on double day systems that spread over the day and evening. About a quarter to one third are engaged on two-shift systems involving nightwork, while the remainder are employed on some form of three-shift system, permanent nightwork or an irregular system. Permanent nightwork is more common in some countries, notably the USA (Sergean, 1971; ILO, 1978; Shift Work Committee, 1979).

Although this classification gives us some idea of the extent of deviation of a shiftworker's daily life from normal daywork, it does not allow a detailed comparison of the problems associated with different systems. Thus, although a double day system is likely to result in fewer problems than a continuous or semi-continuous system, it is more difficult to make a valid comparison between a continuous system and an alternating days-and-nights system. For such comparisons we need to be more specific and to examine factors such as nightshift frequency or sleep deficiency. This requires a detailed examination of shift schedules and data concerning workers' reactions to them.

14.2.2 Types of shift pattern

In order to understand fully how a shift system is worked, a number of key pieces of information need to be known, namely: the starting time and stopping time of shifts; the number of days of operation per week; the standard hours of work per week; the number of teams or crews; whether each team works only on a particular shift or on different shifts; the number of holidays per week or per rotation cycle; the number of consecutive days on the same shift (e.g. nightshift)

TABLE 14.1
Examples of different 5-day-week shift systems

System	A/B	Notation
Permanent night	5/2	3 3 3 3 3 - - (or $\bar{3}$ $\bar{3}$ $\bar{3}$ $\bar{3}$ $\bar{3}$ - -)
Double days	10/4	1 1 1 1 1 - - 2 2 2 2 2 - -
Alternating days and nights	10/4	1 1 1 1 1 - - 3 3 3 3 3 - -
Semi-continuous three-shift	15/6	1 1 1 1 1 - - 2 2 2 2 2 - - 3 3 3 3 3 - - (or 1 1 1 1 1 - - 3 3 3 3 3 - - 2 2 2 2 2 - -)

Note: The values of A and B represent the total number of work and off days respectively in a complete cycle of the shift system. 1 = dayshift; 2 = evening shift; 3 = nightshift; $\bar{3}$ = half-day night shift; - = day off.

and whether this is a fixed or variable number; and the schedule of working the assigned shifts and having days off for an individual worker.

If the system is a permanent type, or a weekly rotation type with weekend holidays, then it is fairly easy to identify the schedule. For example, using a fairly straightforward notation, it is possible to represent different types as in Table 14.1. There are, of course, modifications to each of these types, especially depending on the starting/stopping times of shifts, holidays and the order of shift changes. If, however, the system is of a continuous type, there is a far greater variety of possible systems. This is largely due to the fact that the number of teams may be more than the number of shifts, and that the cycle length may vary considerably. Some typical examples are given in Table 14.2, although there are, of course, many other possible schedules. In practice, systems are found that involve the same shift being worked for up to 7 successive days. The position of days off can vary, as can the order of different shifts, as shown in Table 14.2. The 'continental rota' is rather strange but is found in many plants since it allows double days off and has a cycle period of exactly 4 weeks.

The values of A and B in Tables 14.1 and 14.2 (i.e. the number of work and rest days respectively in a complete cycle) give the relation of workdays to days off which is an important feature of any shift system (Knauth *et al.*, 1979). They also give the length of the complete cycle (A+B), and can be used to calculate two more important features of shift systems. One is the total number of days off per year, calculated as 365 x B/(A+B), and the other is the 'weekday-relevant cycle', i.e. the number of days that need to be worked before a given shift (e.g. the first nightshift) recurs on a given day of the week (e.g. Monday). This value is (A+B) x 7 (if (A+B) is not divisible by 7) or simply (A+B) (if the sum of A and B is divisible by 7).

TABLE 14.2
Examples of different continuous shift systems

System	A/B	Notation
Two-shift in three teams	4/2	$\bar{1}$ $\bar{1}$ $\bar{3}$ $\bar{3}$ - -
"	6/3	$\bar{1}$ $\bar{1}$ $\bar{1}$ - $\bar{3}$ $\bar{3}$ $\bar{3}$ - -
Two-shift in four teams	2/2	$\bar{1}$ $\bar{3}$ - -
"	4/4	$\bar{1}$ $\bar{1}$ $\bar{3}$ $\bar{3}$ - - - -
Three-shift in three teams	9/0	1 1 1 3 3 3 2 2 2
"	8/1	1 1 $\bar{1}$ 2 2 $\bar{3}$ 3 3 -
"	11/1	1 1 1 $\bar{1}$ 2 2 2 $\bar{3}$ 3 3 3 -
Three-shift in Four teams	6/2	1 1 2 2 3 3 - - (known as 'metropolitan rota')
"	9/3	1 1 1 - 2 2 2 - 3 3 3 -
	or	1 1 2 2 3 3 - - 1 3 2 -
"	12/4	1 1 1 1 2 2 2 2 - - 3 3 3 3 - -
	or	1 1 2 2 2 3 3 - - 2 1 1 3 - - 3
"	15/5	1 1 1 1 1 - - 2 2 2 2 2 - 3 3 3 3 3 - -
"	21/7	1 1 2 2 3 3 3 - - 1 1 2 2 2 3 3 - - 1 1 1 2 2 3 3 - - - (known as 2-2-3 system or 'continental rota')

Note: Notation as in Table 14.1 $\bar{1}$ = half-day day shift

The number of days off per year is an important feature that can be compared with that for dayworkers. If it is less than the 104 plus special holidays enjoyed by a dayworker on a 5-day workweek, for example, the system would need to assign additional holidays. Similar calculations can be made for the average number of hours per week, and it is often the case that shiftworkers get additional days off, or have to work additional days, in order to equate the average hours per week with those of dayworkers. The weekday-relevant cycle is also important since it determines when, if ever, an individual shiftworker's days off coincide with the weekend, and, if so, how often.

Typically, a four-team/three-shift system involves 42 work-hours per week for any individual worker and thus, assuming an average workweek of 40 hours or less, requires additional holidays.

14.2.3 The incidence of nightshifts

There are some shift patterns that seem to have significantly more adverse influences on the workers than others, notably those that deviate considerably from normal daywork in terms of the frequency and density of nightshifts. Figure 14.3 shows the distribution of the frequency of nightshifts per month in different sectors in Japan (Natsuhara and Shimizu, 1982). In production, about half the workers worked a nightshift six to nine times a month, while nearly a third worked ten nightshifts, and 11 per cent worked fourteen or more. A similar pattern emerged for transport workers, with 40 per cent working ten or more nightshifts per month. People in medical and welfare services were split between those

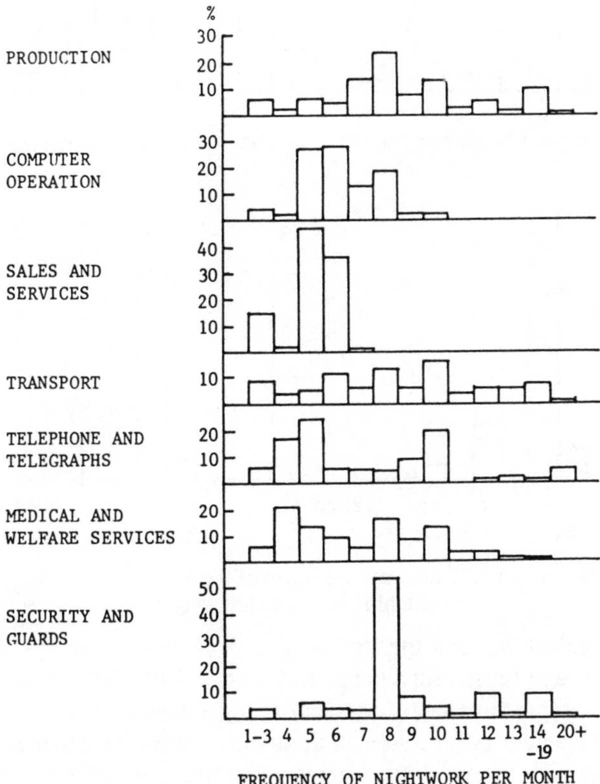

Figure 14.3 Distribution of the frequency per month of nightwork duties in a survey in Japan (1981)

working at night only a few times per month and those doing so around eight times or more. Most computer operators, and sales and services workers, worked nightshifts rather less frequently. Since the monthly frequency of nightshifts for a four-team/three-shift system should be six to seven, many of the shiftworkers appear to have been rather heavily loaded with nightwork.

Equally crucial for nightworkers is the number of consecutive nightshifts involved in their system. The more consecutive nightshifts worked, the greater will be the accumulated sleep deficit and hence adverse effects on health (see Chapters 15 and 16). Figure 14.4 summarizes the distribution of the number of

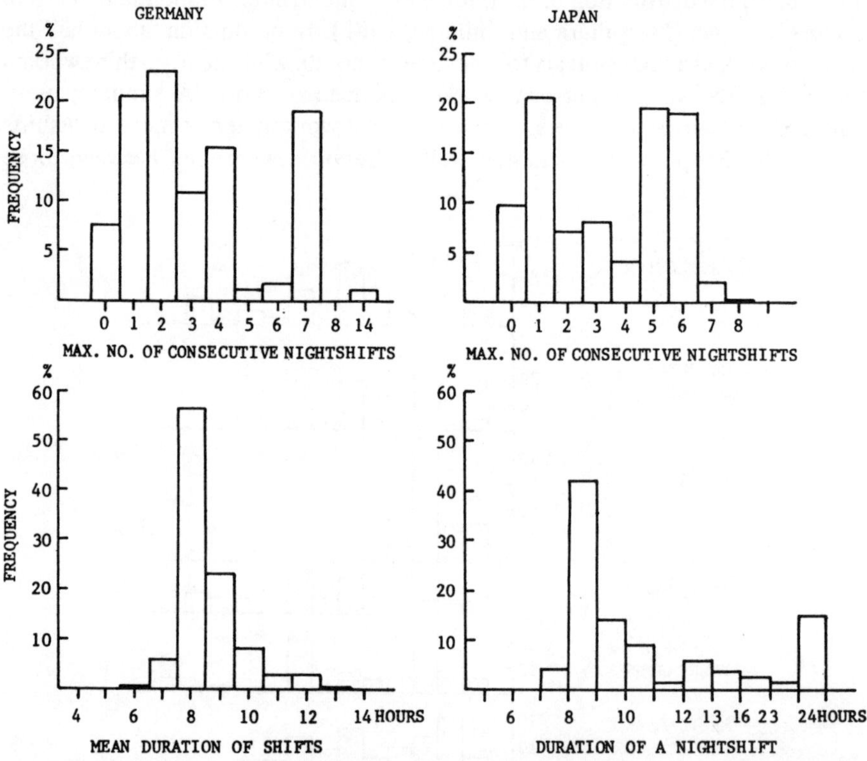

Figure 14.4 Distribution in Germany and Japan of the maximum number of consecutive nightshifts and the shift length

consecutive nightshifts, and the shift length, from recent surveys conducted in West Germany and Japan (Knauth and Rutenfranz, 1982; Shift Work Committee, 1979). The maximum number of consecutive nightshifts ranged form one to seven or more, with a tendency for a smaller number of consecutive nightshifts than six or seven, but with many shift systems retaining a relatively long period of nightshifts (see section 14.2.4). As for shift length, a clear peak can be seen at 8 hours, but there are a number of systems with much longer nightshifts. When one considers the distribution of the maximum number of consecutive nightshifts over different Japanese shift systems, a sharp contrast can be drawn between weekly rotated systems and continuous ones. Four-team/three-shift systems, now common in process industries, typically rotate swiftly, while weekly rotating shift systems clearly involve a rather longer period of consecutive night shifts (Shift Work Committee, 1979).

14.2.4 Recent trends in shift patterns

There have been drastic changes in shift systems in the post-World War II period. An important impetus for this has been the reduction in working hours, which has typically reduced the number of days worked per week in the case of systems without weekend work, and increased the number of teams in the case of continous systems. This latter change has been mainly from 'three-team/three-shift' to 'four-team/three-shift' systems, and more recently to systems involving five or even more teams. There has also been a trend towards reducing the number of consecutive nightshifts worked from six or seven to five or less, and sometimes even to three or less.

The spread of shiftwork, for economic reasons, has resulted in some new forms of discontinuous systems, such as weekly rotated alternating days and nights in mechanical and other industries, and three-shift systems for less than 24 hours in computer services, etc. There has also been a trend towards irregular rotation in the services sector to meet changing demands, and a spread of two- and three-shift systems involving six or seven consecutive night shifts in developing countries. This latter trend is contrary to that in most industrialized nations and probably reflects differences in economic pressures.

One irony is that although most current shift systems could be greatly improved, there is considerable inertia and a tendency to stick to the ongoing system. Since both production and business operations and the workers' daily routines are well adjusted to the existing shift schedule, changing it requires considerable effort. As a result, various minor modifications are often introduced to meet additional needs without changing the basic pattern. Frequent overtime and double shifts are worked, sometimes to 'cover' for an absent co-worker, and this often gives rise to extra problems for the workers concerned.

In general, there is a clear trend in shift patterns towards swift rotation, and thus fewer consecutive nightshifts. Although this is true for continuous systems, it is apparently precluded for weekly rotation of discontinuous or semi-continuous systems. This general trend coincides with a recommendation of many shift researchers. This recommendation is based on the finding that shift-lag does not disappear even if many consecutive nightshifts are worked, and thus a swift return to the normal sleep–wakefulness rhythm is seen as desirable in order to prevent the accumulation of sleep deficit and minimize the effects of shift-lag.

Another trend is for systems with a reduced frequency of night shifts compared to that of day and evening shifts. This helps to ease the burden of the shiftworkers, although it requires a reduced amount of nighttime work. Many irregular shift systems in telecommunication, hospitals and public services also have fewer nightshifts than dayshifts. Such systems, as well as three-shift systems with five or more crews, will undoubtedly become more popular in the future as the concern over the problems of nightwork increases.

14.3 PROSPECTS FOR SHIFTWORK

14.3.1 The shiftworkers' problems

The major problems that shiftworkers have in coping with shiftwork schedules are dealt with in the following chapters. They range from effects on circadian rhythms, work performance, sleep and health, to those on family and social life and professional career. Field studies of shiftwork have used varied methods depending on the main aims of the research, but there is little doubt that the selection of methods has been guided by the actual consequences of shiftwork. It is noteworthy that these consequences are similar in most shiftworking situations (Kogi, 1981a; Rutenfranz, 1982; Rutenfranz *et al.*, 1977; Rutenfranz, Knauth and Angersbach, 1981). This led Rutenfranz, Knauth and Angersbach (1981) to develop the so-called 'stress-strain' model of shiftwork problems. In this model stress is seen as resulting from the worker's exposure to a phase-shifting of his work–sleep schedules in relation to the normal circadian rhythms of physiological and psychological functions. The resultant strain, which is modified by various intervening variables, may express itself in complaints, lowering of well-being and possible adverse health effects (see also Chapter 16).

The degree of strain experienced by an individual worker depends on the intervening variables. The more important of these are housing conditions (especially sleeping conditions), family status (age of children, acceptance of shiftwork by the family), personality and differences in physiological adaptability. Thus, the extent of initial phase-shift stress and its modification by these intervening factors determines whether an individual shiftworker is able to cope with his work schedule or whether he is disturbed to such a degree that his well-being is reduced, or actual diseases occur.

In practice, it seems unlikely that the shiftworker passively accepts this stress, but rather that he tries actively to counteract the stress by, for example, trying to sleep in advance before a nightshift, or having a long sleep after it. Although such efforts are by no means entirely effective, they are made quite deliberately. The most prominent effort made by shiftworkers involves the sleep–wakefulness rhythm. Many studies have revealed that the basic circadian rhythm persists over the whole shiftwork period. Desynchronization of rhythms occurs during the nightshift period, and this reflects the persistence of natural rhythms (see Chapters 2 and 15). Shiftworkers therefore try to fit in with these persisting

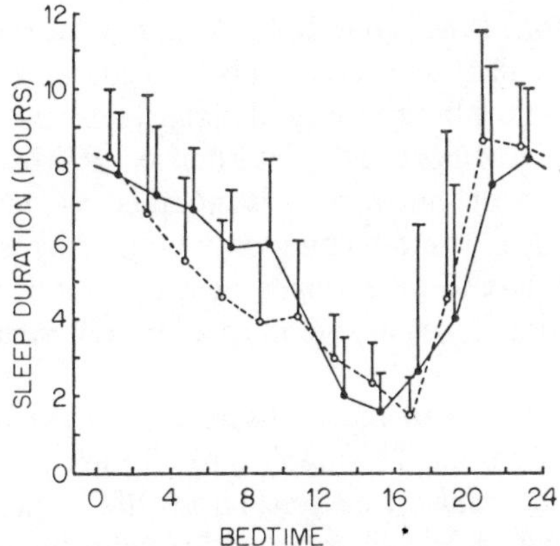

Figure 14.5 Mean and standard deviation of sleep length of German and Japanese shiftworkers as a function of the time of sleep onset

●——● German workers in radio and television stations and airport cargo handling (2332 cases, Knauth and Rutenfranz, 1981)

0---0 Japanese workers in print shops, computer centres and train driving (3240 cases, Institute for Science of Labour 1983)

rhythms rather than to resist them. Sleep timing and duration thus depend on the type of shift system, and on many systems a deficit accumulates (Lille, 1967; Knauth *et al.*, 1980). This is illustrated in Figure 14.5, which shows the duration of sleep as a function of the time of sleep onset for German and Japanese workers based on diary records (Knauth and Rutenfranz, 1981; Kogi, 1983). Daytime sleeps are forced to be short, while evening sleeps may be long or short depending on their precise timing. In order to secure as long a sleeping time as possible during a nightshift period, the workers need to have split sleep during the daytime and to add some sleep in the evening where possible. After the period of night duty, they could have a long night sleep by going to bed early.

Efforts to secure adequate rest are also reflected in the social behaviour of shiftworkers. A recent study of print shop workers and computer operators in Japan indicated that social activity was restricted before, between and after the nightshifts. On the day leading up to the first nightshift, some workers went out in the morning, but usually came home by midday to rest. Between two nightshifts, the sleeping time was about 5–7 hours, but they remained at home for most of the rest of the day, only a few spending a short time at places within walking distance. On the day following the last nightshift, all but one went home quickly.

Another interesting coping strategy is the use of a nighttime nap. Many shiftworkers in Japan are found to have a formal or informal nap of a few hours during a nightshift. A recent survey of nighttime naps (Kogi, 1981b) indicated that more than 40 per cent of two- and three-shift workers took a night nap, usually of 2–3 hours' duration. About one third of nurses also took one. Such a nap can be very effective and yields sleep similar to the initial stages of a normal sleep (Matsumoto *et al.*, 1982; Naitoh, 1982) and reduces post-nightshift fatigue (Kogi, 1981b). These nighttime naps can be considered as short 'anchor sleeps' which are taken during the time of normal night sleeps and help maintain normal physiological rhythms (Minors and Waterhouse, 1981b).

The sleeping strategy of shiftworkers is modified by individual differences. A short late afternoon sleep is more commonly utilized by 'split-sleepers' than by 'lump-sleepers' who tend to take longer sleeps at a time (Sakai *et al.*, 1982). 'Morning' and 'Evening' types also tend to adopt different sleep strategies (see Chapters 3 and 18).

The problems of shiftworkers must thus be understood in terms of the limits of their active coping strategies. This applies to all their problems, such as sleep, performance and safety, health, free time, family life, social activities and career. For example, although error probability is known to increase during the night hours (Bjerner *et al.*, 1948), this need not necessarily imply that accidents will also increase. Shiftworkers may be able to adopt coping strategies to combat any reduced capacity and their success will be reflected in the accident statistics. However, accidents do occur frequently in night drivers and certain industrial workers, and it clearly is important to support nightworkers in counteracting their reduced work capacity. For this reason, 4-hour nightshifts have been proposed for certain critical work situations, such as at nuclear power stations, where public safety is at stake (Andlauer *et al.*, 1982). Similarly supportive views are necessary in all the other aspects.

14.3.2 The shiftworker/shiftwork interface

Can shiftworkers continue to work shifts for a long period of time? Should young or elderly people refrain from shiftwork? Should women be protected from nightwork? Or is it possible and necessary to stop the spread of shiftwork? All these questions seem acute. In view of its adverse effects on the well-being and health of workers, shiftwork needs to be controlled. How we control it should be determined by the extent to which we can support shiftworkers' coping strategies for reducing the detrimental effects. If we can support shiftworkers' efforts, and improve their shift schedules and living conditions, they may be able to continue on a swiftly rotating system for a long period. However, if the schedules are stressful, and only poor social support is available, then we must start by trying to improve their schedules and by inhibiting the spread of shiftwork.

To promote this dynamic viewpoint, we need to understand the nature of the shiftworker/shiftwork interface. This should enable us to assess the problems and to determine where support is needed. In general, shiftworkers start to prepare themselves a few days before the beginning of a period of unusual shift hours, such as nightshifts. Whenever possible, they sleep for longer the night before, try to spare more time for sleep and recuperation between nightshifts, and sleep for longer after the period of nightwork. This sleep strategy is linked with efforts to

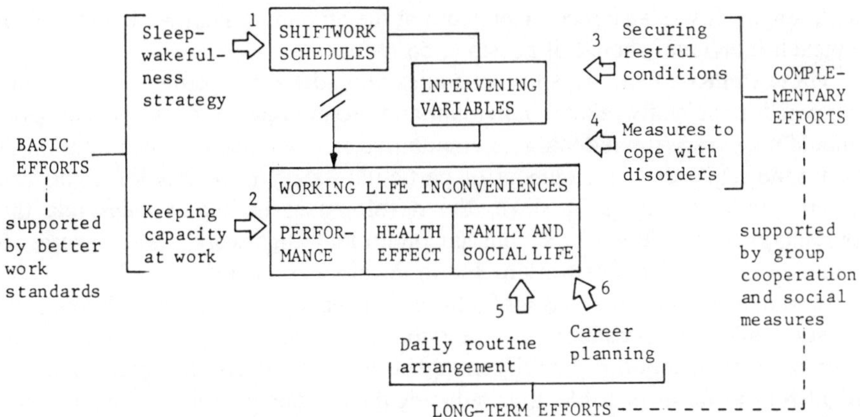

Figure 14.6 Basic (1,2), complementary (3,4) and long-term (5,6) efforts made by shiftworkers in coping with the shiftworking load. Improvements must encompass all these areas and support these efforts

keep alert at work, to secure rest and health, and to maintain the standard of their family and social life.

These efforts are summarized in Figure 14.6. The basic efforts are towards establishing a reasonable sleep–wakefulness strategy. These are complemented by additional efforts to offset physical or health disorders. Further, long-term efforts are made to minimize the lowering of family and social life standards. The long-term adjustments of shiftworkers depends on these efforts, but seldom results in adverse effects being fully offset. Folkard *et al.* (1978) suggested that differences in the rate of reentrainment may reflect differences in the degree to which workers scheduled their lives towards nightwork, while the initial habituation, as indicated by the recovery of body weight in girls, to a new shift system seems to occur within 3 to 4 months (Sakamoto and Matsui, 1972). Long-term habituation may, however, take several years (Depta, 1973). It is therefore important to determine the aspects of short-term and long-term efforts that need supporting in each group of shiftworkers (Thierry *et al.*, 1975; Tepas, Walsh and Armstrong, 1981).

In recent discussions concerning the improvement of shiftworking conditions, two main recommendations emerged (Kogi *et al.*, 1982). The first was to try to improve shift-scheduling itself, rather than to compensate for the disadvantages of shiftworkers by additional pay. The second was to support and develop measures for protecting shiftworkers from these disadvantages.

With regard to shift schedules, it was suggested that where practicable a shift system should (i) have few nights in succession, (ii) have a short cycle period with regular rotas, (iii) include some free weekends with at least 2 full days off, (iv) give adequate intervals between shifts, and (v) be flexible about shift change times and shift length. It was also recommended that the amount of nightwork undertaken by each individual should, if possible, be reduced.

These improvements to shift schedules should be complemented by broad support for the shiftworkers' individual and group coping efforts. This support should encourage the reduction of cumulative sleep deficiency, the inclusion of nighttime naps, the development of particular safety measures for nightwork where public safety is at stake, the development of health measures, the protection of female workers from 'unconditional' nightwork, and measures to enhance the standards of working life in developing countries.

In sum, there are many reasons for the continued use of shiftwork. Although we must not allow its spread for purely economic reasons, it would be unrealistic to propose its total abolition. Priority should be given to reducing the total amount of nightwork as far as possible, thus reducing the frequency of nightshifts for each individual worker. At the same time, we should study the coping strategies of shiftworkers and try to support them, especially in relation to their sleep, safety, free time, health, social life and career.

Hours of Work
Edited by S. Folkard and T.H. Monk

Chapter 15

Adjustment of Physiological Circadian Rhythms and the Sleep–Wake Cycle to Shiftwork

Torbjorn Akerstedt

CONTENTS

ABSTRACT

Shiftwork, when it includes nightwork, will be in conflict with the circadian system of the body. This chapter will attempt to summarize what is known about the effects of this conflict in terms of the adjustment of circadian rhythms and the implications for well-being.

15.1 INTRODUCTION

The major characteristic of shiftwork is that it displaces the sleep–wake pattern. This displacement will affect, and be affected by, the circadian organization of man's physiology and psychology. The purpose of this chapter is to summarize what is known about these effects and their practical implications. This is done first by describing the adjustment of circadian rhythms and the sleep–wake cycle, and then by discussing which factors influence this process, what its relation is to well-being, and finally, what implications it has for work-scheduling.

15.2 ADJUSTMENT OF CIRCADIAN RHYTHMS

15.2.1 Phase-shifts in the laboratory

One of the first major long-term laboratory experiments of sleep–wake inversion was carried out by Colquhoun *et al.* (1968b). These authors found that over twelve consecutive nightshifts (without social isolation) the oral temperature rhythm flattened, but never completely inverted, i.e. adjustment was only partial.

In a similar vein, Knauth *et al.* (1978) recorded the rectal temperature of four subjects continuously over a period of 21 consecutive nightshifts (2200–0600 h). During the first 24-hour period the only adjustment was a slight increase during the new (night) work hours (Figure 15.1). Over the subsequent days this increase continued, as did a corresponding decrease during the new (day) sleep hours; the curve, as a whole, was flattening out. Somewhere between the seventh and fourteenth shifts, new stable levels were reached, and the cosinor estimated peak had changed by approximately 8 hours. Even so, by the twenty-first shift, night and day curves were still not quite identical, and the subsequent reentrainment to daywork was very fast.

Both of these observations indicate that the adjustment to nightwork had not been complete. Interestingly, it was observed that *sleep* was a more important adjustment agent than *working.* Actually, in Figure 15.1 it is possible to identify three temporal segments that behave differently: the forenoon (sleep) during which the most pronounced change (decrease) occurs, the night (work) during which a smaller, but clear, change (increase) occurs; and the afternoon-evening (leisure) during which very little change occurs and where the peak essentially remains at about 2100 h.

In a similar study, but with a 12-hour shift of sleep, Weitzman and Kripke (1981) demonstrated that considerable change had taken place the first week but that three weeks were still insufficient for regaining the original curve shape at the new expected phase. As was found in the Knauth *et al.* (1978) study, the amplitude was strongly reduced and the return to diurnality rapid. The adjustment process was described as a gradual growth of a new peak and a gradual decline of the old one.

Wever, (1979c), who studied 6-hour shifts under conditions of total isolation from external synchronizers, found that the estimated phase had made 83 per cent of the shift in slightly less than a week. Interestingly, a phase advance (earlier bedtime) was followed by a more rapid phase adjustment than was a phase delay, although the amplitude was sharply reduced and the curve shape distorted.

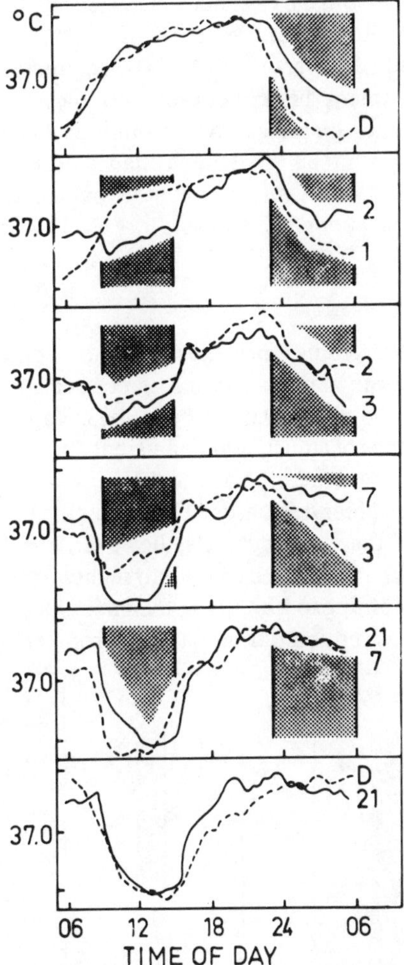

Figure 15.1 Rectal temperature pattern at different stages of adjustment to 21 days of experimental nightwork in the laboratory (D = daywork). Stippled area indicates night sleep during daywork and day sleep during nightwork. The lowest panel compares the pattern of the 21st day with that of the expected curve derived from delaying the daywork curve 9.5 hours. The temperature scale indicates 37±0.5°C. N=4. From Knauth *et al.* (1978)

Other variables than body temperature have been less systematically studied. Weitzman and Kripke (1981), however, showed that in spite of rhythm adjustment beginning early, neither urine volume, potassium, 17-OHCS, sodium, nor creatinine exhibited circadian rhythms which had shifted 180° by the end of the 3-week nightshift experiment described above. As with body temperature, amplitudes were reduced and curve shapes distorted. Results along similar lines have been obtained by others, e.g. Perkoff *et al.* (1959), Krieger *et al.* (1969), Elliott *et al.* (1972) and Chevrier (1973, 1974). A common trait across studies is that the speed of adjustment differs between variables.

In conclusion, laboratory studies give the impression that rhythms start to adjust after the first nightshift and that much change occurs during the first week. It does not seem possible, however, to conclude that a complete inversion takes place within the periods studied (3 weeks).

15.2.2 Nightwork

The results from early studies of adjustment to nightwork range between disturbed diurnal patterns and indications of perfect adjustment (e.g. Jaeger, 1881; Benedict, 1904; Toulouse and Pieron, 1907). Van Loon (1963), in one of the first systematic studies of adjustment, found that during 13 weeks of nightwork the temperature rhythm was merely flattened (Figure 15.2), i.e. night values had increased and morning values decreased. This flattening process appeared afresh each week. In one of the three subjects, however, the flattening/adjustment became more rapid with increased exposure to nightwork (thus indicating 'long-term adjustment'). According to Van Loon, the major factor preventing complete adjustment was the interruption during days off from work.

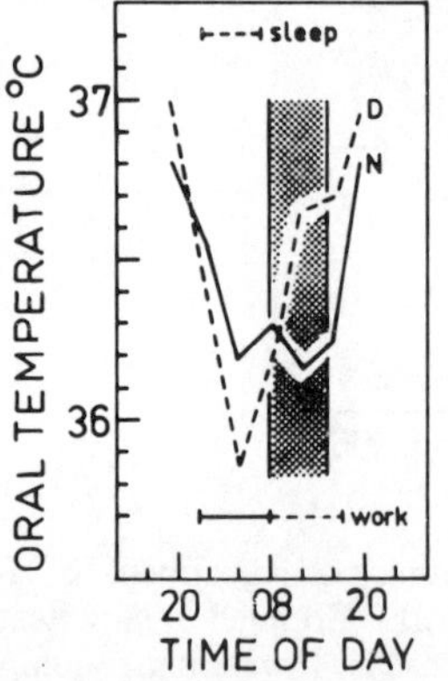

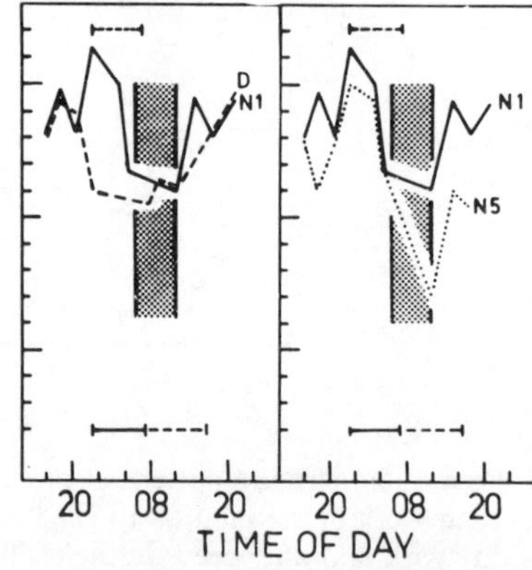

Figure 15.2 Left: Mean oral temperature during day (D) and night (N) work periods. Day sleep during the nightwork period is indicated by the stippled area whereas night sleep during the daywork period is indicated by the broken line at the top. At the bottom is indicated the hours of night (—) and day (- - -) work. N=3. From Van Loon (1963) Right: Oral temperature in permanent nightworkers during days off (D), the first (N1) and the fifth (N5) nightshift. N=6. From Dahlgren (1981c)

In a study of more experienced nightworkers (printers) we found a flattened temperature rhythm with no further adjustment across the 6-day working week (Patkai *et al.*, 1977). The peak was located in the (early) nightwork hours but the decrease thereafter was very steep. Dahlgren (1981a) later extended this study and found that the curve had a nocturnal orientation also during the days off (Figure 15.2). As a contrast, Folkard *et al.* (1978) did not find any pronounced nocturnal orientation in night nurses, although some adjustment did occur, particularly among those who worked full-time.

In respect to other physiological parameters, Patkai *et al.* (1977) found that both adrenaline and noradrenaline showed a nocturnal orientation in permanent nightworkers. Conroy *et al.* (1970a, 1970b) found a good adjustment of 11-OHCS and potassium in nightworking printers, but not of sodium and water, which both reached high levels during the day sleep period. Finally, Migeon *et al.* (1956) found no adjustment of 17-OHCS in night nurses and night watchmen.

15.2.3 Alternating work hours

Somewhere between permanent nightwork and rotating three-shift work one finds schedules that require an alternation between night and day shifts. We have studied one such group (typesetters) working 6 nightshifts, 2 dayshifts, followed by 4 days off (Akerstedt, Patkai and Dahlgren, 1977). Figure 15.3 demonstrates that by the first nightshift some adjustment of the oral temperature rhythms had already taken place, and by the seventh there was a clear peak during the night hours. Yet, the sharp fall during the second half of the work period shows that the pattern was not yet inverted.

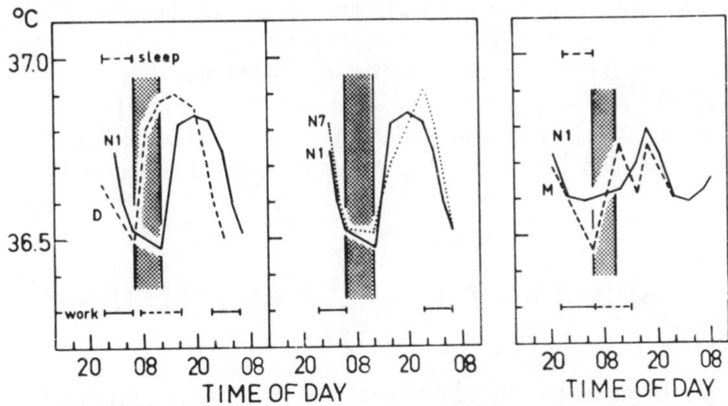

Figure 15.3 Left: Oral temperature during day and night work in experienced shiftworkers. N=13. From Akerstedt, Patkai and Dahlgren, (1977)
Right: Oral temperature during the first morning and night shifts in rapidly rotating, experienced shiftworkers. N=15. See Figure 15.2 for further explanations. From Dahlgren (1981a)

Knauth *et al.* (1981) have carried out the most extensive studies of rotating three-shift workers. Visual analysis of the temperature rhythm of 133 workers demonstrated that nightwork values increased over successive shifts and that day sleep values decreased. Cosinor analysis yielded a significant reduction of amplitude but no change in phase estimates. Similar moderate amounts of adjustment have been demonstrated (without curve fitting) by, for example, Colquhoun and Edwards (1970b), Meers (1975), Smith (1979) and Vokac and Rodahl (1975). More rapid adjustment has been demonstrated by Chaumont *et al.* (1979) and Vieux *et al.* (1979), although based on cosinor-estimated phase-shifts.

With rapidly rotating three-shift work (1–2 nights in succession) the adjustment of the temperature rhythm is usually only marginal (Smith, 1979; Vokac *et al.*, 1981; Dahlgren, 1981b). This is also the case with individuals on irregular work hours (Kolmodin-Hedman and Swensson, 1975). Laboratory studies have yielded very similar conclusions (Kleitman and Jackson, 1950b; Knauth *et al.*, 1978; Vokac *et al.*, 1981).

Other variables appear to behave in a very similar way to body temperature, e.g. adrenocortical steroids, catecholamines, electrolytes, heart rate and others (Kojima and Niiyama, 1965; Lobban and Tredre, 1966; Conroy *et al.*, 1970a; Daleva *et al.*, 1972; Tooraen, 1972; Kolmodin-Hedman and Swensson, 1975; Vokac and Rodahl, 1975; Akerstedt, Patkai and Dahlgren, 1977; Lille *et al.*, 1981; Vrancianu *et al.*, 1982). One exception is the extensive series of studies by Reinberg and his associates. As with body temperature, these studies indicate a more rapid (cosinor-estimated) phase adjustment for all variables (e.g. Chaumont *et al.*, 1979). Of particular interest is the observation that the rate of circadian phase adjustment differs between variables, i.e. the displacement of the sleep–wake pattern causes a transient internal dissociation.

Circadian rhythms, then, are distorted by nightwork, only begin to adjust during the run of duty, and do not seem to adjust completely even during permanent nightwork. Different variables adjust at different speeds and the adjustment period is therefore characterized by internal temporal disorder.

15.3 ADJUSTMENT OF SLEEP AND WAKEFULNESS

15.3.1 Sleep

Compared to circadian rhythms, there is less detailed information on the adjustment of sleep to shiftwork. Most survey studies, however, have found sleep disturbances to be a major complaint of shiftworkers (e.g. Graf *et al.*, 1958; Thiis-Evensen, 1958; Menzel, 1962; Aanonsen, 1964; Andersen, 1970). EEG studies of sleep in rotating shift workers have shown fairly consistent results, whether recorded in the laboratory (Ehrenstein *et al.*, 1970; Foret and Benoit, 1974, 1978a; Matsumoto, 1978; Dahlgren, 1981c) or in the natural sleep environment (Foret and Lantin, 1972; Torsvall *et al.*, 1981; Tilley *et al.*, 1981). Day sleep is 1–4 hours shorter than night sleep. The shortening is primarily taken out of stage 2 sleep ('basic' sleep) and stage REM sleep (dream sleep). Stages 3 and 4 ('deep' sleep) do not seem to be affected. Furthermore, sleep latency is usually shorter and stage REM, often but not always, appears earlier. In our own study (Torsvall *et al.*, 1981), we also found that noradrenaline and water excretion were significantly higher during day sleep.

Rather little is known about the adjustment process of sleep. Foret and Benoit (1978b), however, found that neither the total sleep length, nor the amount of stages 3 and 4, recovered significantly over four consecutive nightshifts (all were strongly reduced on the initial day sleep). Apparently, though, the initially disturbed temporal distribution of sleep stages did tend to recover its usual pattern. Dahlgren (1981c) found that on the first nightshift sleep length was reduced to 4.5 hours (from 6.0 hours), but increased again over six consecutive nightshifts to reach a level of 5.7 hours. Also, the amount of stage 2 and REM increased as the amount of waking decreased. The temporal distribution of stages 3 and 4 and REM, however, seems to have gradually increased in deviation from the usual nightshift pattern.

Just as *permanent* nightworkers show the most circadian rhythm adjustment, so also do they seem to sleep more like dayworkers, although sleep lengths are somewhat shorter (Lille, 1967; Kripke *et al.*, 1971; Bryden and Holdstock, 1973; Tepas, Walsh and Armstrong, 1981; Dahlgren, 1981c). The Dahlgren study followed the adjustment process and even recorded (night) sleep during days off. This showed that the first day sleep was reduced by 1.1 h and actually decreased a further 0.8 h over the six nightshifts. Very few other changes were found.

Experimental phase-shifts in the laboratory seem to produce fewer changes of sleep than might be expected from shiftwork results obtained in the field (Weitzman *et al.*, 1970; Berger *et al.*, 1971; Knauth and Rutenfranz, 1972a; Knauth, Landau *et al.*, 1980; Hume, 1980; Webb and Agnew, 1978). Part of the discrepancy could be due to age, since day sleep difficulties increase with age (Foret *et al.*, 1981; Akerstedt and Torsvall, 1981a), and the laboratory studies have been carried out with the traditional young student subjects. Part of the discrepancy may also be due to the fact that the shiftworker gets out of bed as soon as he wakes up, while the laboratory subject usually has a fixed time allotted for staying in bed. As has been demonstrated by Feinberg *et al.*, (1980) and Nakagawa (1980), remaining in bed after the 'final' awakening will invite a resumption of sleep, although that sleep will be frequently interrupted. Interestingly, Weitzman *et al.* (1970) found that, after 4 hours of day sleep, intervening wakefulness started to increase at a fairly high rate. In addition, two recent studies of *ad lib* day sleep show a sleep length of 4–5 hours (Benoit *et al.*, 1980; Akerstedt and Gillberg, 1981).

Sleep, then, is obviously shortened and distorted by shiftwork, and particularly by the nightshift. Some adjustment does occur but it is insufficient both in rotating shift workers and, apparently, in permanent nightworkers. Whether or not this may be compensated for by naps or sleep at other times is not known.

15.3.2 Wakefulness/fatigue

Several questionnaire studies have demonstrated a reduced wakefulness in shiftworkers as compared to dayworkers (Wyatt and Marriott, 1953; Thiis-Evensen, 1958; Dirken, 1966; Andersen, 1970). An increased fatigue, primarily in connection with the nightshift, may also be deduced from the occurrence of compensatory sleep episodes during more suitable shifts or during days off (Tune, 1969a; Akerstedt and Torsvall, 1978), and from reports of dozing off (Prokop and Prokop, 1955; Kogi and Ohta, 1975).

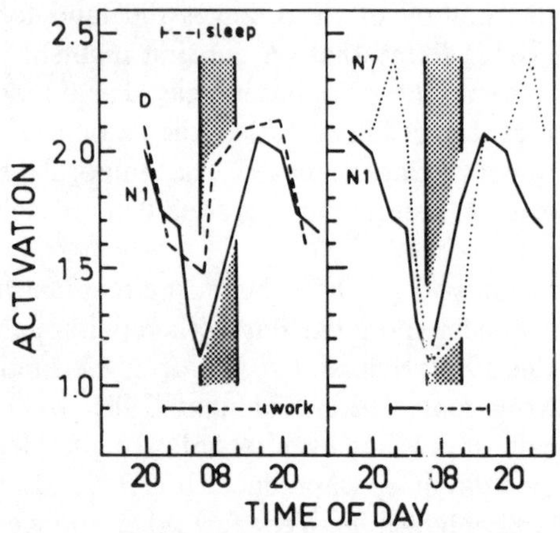

Figure 15.4 Self-rated activation during day (D) and night (N) work in experienced shiftworkers. N=13. From Akerstedt, Patkai and Dahlgren, (1977)

More detailed studies, having frequent measurements of wakefulness, are rare and most concern self-ratings. In one study of adjustment to temporary nightwork, mean alertness was reduced and no change in curve shape took place over the 3 weeks of nightwork (Akerstedt, 1977). Figure 15.4 demonstrates that self-rated 'activation' tended to drift towards a night peak over seven consecutive nightshifts in a group of experienced shiftworkers who were alternating between day and night work (Akerstedt, Froberg, Levi, Torsvall and Zamore, 1977). Froberg, Karlsson and Levi (1972) found a persistent day-oriented fatigue pattern in rotating three-shift workers but a significant reduction of nightshift fatigue over the seven shifts. Dahlgren (1981a) found reduced mean activation and no adjustment in *rapidly* rotating three-shift workers. Chaumont *et al.* (1979) did find a (cosinor) phase adjustment effect in ratings of 'vigor' in rotating three-shift workers but this was also associated with a reduction in mean level. In the permanent night nurses of the Folkard *et al.* (1978) study, alertness ratings remained day-oriented except for a slight blunting of the steep fall in alertness during the nightshift. In contrast, in another group of nightworkers activation ratings were found to have a nocturnal orientation even on the *first* nightshift and did not change over the subsequent five shifts (Patkai *et al.*, 1977; Dahlgren, 1981a).

In summary, shiftwork will reduce feelings of wakefulness or alertness; and the circadian rhythm of alertness will adjust in a way similar to that of body temperature, i.e. rather slowly.

15.4 FACTORS AFFECTING ADJUSTMENT

An important issue in considering the adjustment to shiftwork is the question of which factors bring it about and, equally important, which factors prevent it. Factors to be considered in this context are the exposure to shiftwork, the environmental synchronizers, and how the adjustment process is analyzed. Individual factors in adjustment are discussed in Chapter 18.

15.4.1 Amount of exposure

The preceding sections clearly confirm the common-sense notion that (short-term) adjustment to nightwork will increase with the number of consecutive nightshifts worked, although never, it seems, to the point of perfect inversion. Rapid rotation will cause very marginal adjustment. Probably, part-time nightwork is a form of rapid rotation since a diurnal (day-oriented) life will characterize 5 out of every 7 days. Thus, 'commitment' to nightwork is low in such groups. The reverse appears to hold for permanent, full-time nightworkers in traditional nightwork occupations, such as newspaper printers, for example. Here a nocturnal orientation may be found to carry over to the days off, reducing the weekend interruption in adjustment (see Patkai *et al.*, 1977).

Compared to the influence of the length of the nocturnal sequence (i.e. run of nightshifts), the length of nightwork experience seems less important. Neither Folkard *et al.* (1978) nor Knauth *et al.* (1981) observed any such 'long-term' adjustment. Van Loon (1963) did claim that one of his three subjects increased his speed of adjustment and Dahlgren (1981a) did find that after 3 years of rotating shiftwork the flattening occurred earlier in the week. It is not clear, however, whether this was due to a permanent adjustment, i.e. one that included days off. The data cited, together with the increased subjective nightshift difficulties which have been found to be associated with increasing age and experience (Akerstedt and Torsvall, 1981, 1981b; Foret *et al.*, 1981), do not speak strongly for experience as a major factor in adjustment. The issue, however, can only be answered definitively through a longitudinal study.

15.4.2 Type of synchronizer

Even if the amount of nightwork is a major factor of adjustment, it is not clear which synchronizers are the most important. Laboratory studies of entrainment have not been conclusive. Thus, the pattern of the sleep–wake cycle is seen as important by, for example, Webb and Agnew (1974b) and Minors and Waterhouse (1981c); the pattern of the social environment is emphasized by Aschoff *et al.* (1971); and the lighting pattern is favoured by Czeisler *et al.* (1981). The relative importance to the shiftworker of these factors is impossible to determine. Clearly, a forced alternation of the sleep–wake pattern is a major synchronizing agent, but synchronization of social factors appears to speed up adjustment to time-zone shifts (Klein and Wegmann, 1974), and make adjustment to nightwork possible in isolated arctic mining communities (Lobban, 1963). The presence of natural light/dark alteration in Klein and Wegmann's study and the absence of it in Lobban's, may also have contributed to the observed results. More important, however, is the conclusion that the major synchronizers have to work in concert, if perfect adjustment is to be obtained. Normally, only rapid time-zone crossings offer such optimal conditions for adjustment to occur (see Chapter 21).

15.4.3 Methods of analysis

Apart from the effects of exposure, the amount of adjustment observed will depend on how it is defined and analyzed. Thus, the phase that is estimated using the usual curve fit ('cosinor') methods will differ from that defined by the absolute peak, if the data deviate from sinusoidality and/or symmetry. Furthermore, the most frequently used parameter, the phase estimate, will be more unreliable and less important as a curve characteristic as the curve becomes flattened and distorted. Unfortunately, flattening and distortion are precisely the characteristics of adjustment of a circadian rhythm to a major phase-shift. A more suitable alternative might thus involve a closer adherence to the analysis of raw data, perhaps using the amount of deviation from baseline shape as a criterion for adjustment (see Mills *et al.*, 1978a; Weitzman and Kripke, 1981).

A related problem is that of the direct effects which external factors will exert on the overt rhythm, thus masking (see Aschoff, 1960) the behaviour of the underlying central oscillator. Sleeping and waking are important as such factors (Mills *et al.*, 1978a) and it appears that part of the observed 'adjustment' of shiftworkers is actually only a 'masking' effect. An application of 24 hours of constant conditions (see Mills *et al.*, 1978b) during adjustment might help to clarify this issue.

A third point worth observing is that the phase-shift in shiftwork also includes a change from the 'work–leisure–sleep' sequence of activities to that of 'work–sleep–leisure'. Since sleep appears immediately after work in the latter case, a normal progression towards the trough is not possible if the peak is to appear during work hours. Thus, one might suspect that the only way to obtain a perfect adjustment to the nightshift would be to locate leisure time in the morning and postpone sleep to around noon. For most people, however, this would be socially unacceptable.

15.5 RHYTHMICITY AND WELL-BEING

A peculiar observation in applied research on physiological circadian rhythmicity is that intensive efforts are made to describe in detail the *circadian* consequences of changes in synchronizers without much evidence of their *practical importance.* This is particularly true in discussing the long-term health consequences of disturbed rhythmicity, although possible connections are frequently suggested (see Aschoff, 1967; Smolensky, 1981; Moore-Ede and Sulzman, 1981).

However, somewhat more is known about short-term consequences, especially in relation to sleeping and waking. Thus, there exists a well-established circadian propensity to sleep. When sleep is experimentally postponed to different times of day, the evening bedtimes are the ones most conducive to sleep (yielding 8–11 hours), whereas morning-to-noon bedtimes are the ones most hostile (yielding 4–5 hours) (Akerstedt and Gillberg, 1981). Afternoon and night bedtimes fall in between. The sleep loss is usually taken mainly out of stages 2 and REM, whereas deep sleep (stages 3 and 4) is largely unaffected. Similar results, but without connection with the time of day, have been demonstrated during desynchronization in association with long-term temporal isolation (Zulley, 1979; Czeisler *et al.*, 1980). The results thus indicate that the time when shiftworkers usually go to bed after nightwork is the time of day most unsuitable for it.

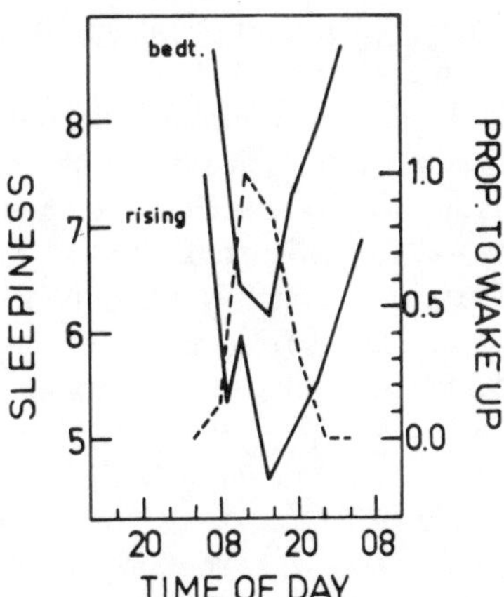

Figure 15.5 Self-rated sleepiness at bedtime and rising, in connection with sleep at different times of day. Broken line indicates the propensity of wake up (proportion of subjects who wake up within 6 hours of a given bedtime). N=6. From Akerstedt and Gillberg (1981)

The circadian propensity to sleep has been tentatively associated with the body temperature rhythm, such that high or rising levels of body temperature interfere with sleep and low or falling levels facilitate it (Czeisler *et al.*, 1980; Zulley *et al.*, 1981; Gillberg and Akerstedt, 1982). Recently, it has been shown that a similar relation holds for adrenaline and urine excretion and an opposite one for melatonin excretion and self-rated sleepiness (Akerstedt and Gillberg, 1982). Even if all four factors could theoretically influence sleep–wake regulation, the self-rated sleepiness factor has the most apparent face value. Figure 15.5 demonstrates that sleepiness during continuous waking coincides both with the propensity to maintain sleep and also with sleepiness immediately after awakening (Akerstedt and Gillberg, 1981). This suggests that the alertness rhythm continues its progress during sleep, and may well be involved in spontaneous sleep termination.

It should be pointed out that *sleep loss* also contributes to sleep regulation. Since it is normally very difficult to sleep in the morning after a full night's sleep, the fact that it is possible to sleep at all during the morning after a phase-shift is most likely due to the prior sleep loss involved. This leads to the conclusion that the amount and structure of sleep depends on the combined effects of circadian rhythmicity and sleep loss. To this may, in some cases, be added the effects of disturbances (e.g. traffic noise) from the environment, as has been demonstrated by Knauth *et al.*, (1980).

Wakefulness/fatigue will also be regulated both by circadian rhythmicity and by sleep loss. This is particularly evident during prolonged sleep deprivation, when the mean level of the sleepiness rhythm increases day by day (Froberg *et al.*, 1975a, 1975b; Akerstedt *et al.*, 1982). This has also been demonstrated in experimental phase-shifts using the multiple sleep latency test (Akerstedt and Gillberg, 1982). Thus, one must assume that the reports of fatigue in shiftworkers are due at least partly to the accumulation of a sleep deficit.

As with the propensity to sleep, self-rated wakefulness/fatigue has been associated with the rhythmicity of the body temperature, adrenaline and melatonin (Froberg *et al.*, 1975a; Akerstedt *et al.*, 1982). Even if conclusive evidence could be found for such a link, it would only be a partial relation, since none of these physiological variables respond to sleep loss the way wakefulness does. The same argument may be applied to their relation to sleep propensity (see Gillberg and Akerstedt, 1981b).

Some further information that is relevant to shiftwork may be obtained from Wever's (1979a, pp. 245–255) analyses of subjects during (forced) desynchronization. When the sleep–wake rhythm was 180° out of phase with the temperature rhythm the amplitude of the latter was strongly reduced, sleep was shortened, daytime performance was reduced and daytime fatigue increased. In-phase rhythms had the opposite consequences.

Curiously, *overall* mean performance levels were increased (and amplitudes strongly reduced) when the rhythms ran counterphased. This may have been due to the fact that fatigue during the 'night' (awakenings from sleep) was unusually low. It also appears that performance and alertness during the 'day' were lower than usual. Both of these consequences are obviously undesirable for the shiftworker.

The above results indicate that in-phase rhythms with large amplitudes are desirable. This is also the conclusion of Andlauer and Reinberg (1979) who found a large, non-adjusting amplitude to be associated with a greater 'tolerance' to shiftwork. This ties in with the fact that, when adjustment to shiftwork does occur, it is slow and seldom gets beyond the transitory phase of temporal disorder. The evidence is circumstantial, however, and there is an urgent need for carefully executed longitudinal studies of these issues.

15.6 IMPLICATIONS FOR SHIFT SCHEDULES

The above conclusions suggest that since adjustment to phase-shifts apparently has negative consequences and is slow, one should prefer a rapid rotation between shifts where little, if any, adjustment occurs. Since the opposing phases of circadian rhythms and the sleep–wake pattern are associated with disturbed sleep and wakefulness, this should be compensated for by an immediate recovery period without nightwork. In some work settings a short sleep at midnight might be useful since this, apparently, prevents adjustment to the nightshift (Minors and Waterhouse, 1981b, 1981c). Days off should be distributed to offset the negative consequences of difficult shifts, and *not* accumulated by compressing the workweek (Dahlgren, 1981b). Three reservations have to be made, however, about the advantages of rapid rotation. First, performance for many tasks on the nightshift will *always* be at the trough, i.e. low, even if a sleep deficit, like that which occurs in slow rotation, has not had time to accumulate (but see Chapters 4 and 19). This is of special importance in occupations demanding high alertness and may possibly, as has been suggested by Andlauer *et al.* (1982), be dealt with by shortening the nightshift. Second, there is no knowledge about the long-term consequences of rapid rotation, namely the frequent phase conflicts, resultant sleep disturbance and fatigue. Third, rapid rotation might cause difficulties in relation to family and social life, the consequences of which are largely unknown. For a further discussion of the systematic selection of shift rotas, see Knauth *et al.* (1979).

15.7 CONCLUSIONS

The main conclusion of this chapter is that circadian rhythms and the sleep–wake pattern never adjust completely to rotating shiftwork or irregular work hours. The adjustment is better but not perfect in permanent nightwork. The short-term consequences of this temporal disorder are fatigue, disturbed sleep and general malaise. The long-term consequences are unknown. The evidence today seems, with some reservations, to indicate that a *rapid* alternation between shifts is to be preferred.

Hours of Work
Edited by S. Folkard and T.H. Monk

Chapter 16

Occupational Health Measures for Nightworkers and Shiftworkers

Joseph Rutenfranz, Manfred Haider and Margit Koller

CONTENTS

ABSTRACT

This chapter reviews the evidence relating to the potential health problems of shiftworkers. It suggests that these problems are most likely to occur with shift systems that involve nightwork, and proposes a four-stage model of the development of such problems. It is argued that people with certain diseases should, if possible, be excluded from nightwork, and that individual differences may be important in determining general tolerance to shiftwork. Finally, some possible preventive health measures are proposed.

16.1 INTRODUCTION

The health of shiftworkers has been a concern of occupational medicine since World War I, while in the last 10 years there has been worldwide discussion as to whether certain diseases are actually caused by shiftwork. These discussions have focused on the question of whether such diseases should be considered as occupational diseases, or as job-related diseases. In contrast to occupational diseases, job-related diseases cannot usually be defined by simple cause–effect relationships. They are usually multifaceted in origin, having risk factors that are not only related to work, but also to the individual person and his lifestyle (Rutenfranz, 1983).

In describing these occupational health problems the so-called 'stress and strain' concept may be of value. Colquhoun and Rutenfranz (1980) used this concept for defining the nightwork condition as follows:

> The objective stress resulting from the disruptions of physiological rhythms by shiftwork, and from the slow rate of re-entrainment of these rhythms to the changed wake/sleep cycle, induce a state of subjective strain in the shiftworker that can potentially affect his working efficiency, his physical and psychological health and well-being, and his family and social life.

Thus, the magnitude of the effects observed in any individual will be influenced by a number of 'intervening variables' acting separately, or in combination. These variables include (i) particular characteristics of the shiftworker such as his age, personality, rhythmic 'type' and physiological adaptability; (ii) factors relating to the actual job in which he is engaged, such as the physical or mental load of the task, the length of the shift, the type of shift system in operation, and the environmental conditions at the workplace; and (iii) his social and domestic circumstances such as marital state, number of children, housing conditions and community 'status'.

Because of the number and complexity of these intervening variables, it is not surprising that people vary widely in their tolerance of what is essentially an unnatural way of life. Identification of the factors which are most influential in determining successful adjustment to shiftwork is, therefore, of great importance not only to the individual and his family, but also to all organizations employing shiftworkers, and to the community at large. It is these intervening variables that explain why the same stress of nightwork may for one particular individual be a normal (or even a chosen) way of life, while for another it may be a potential risk or even the main cause of a job-related disease.

16.2 EFFECTS OF SHIFTWORK ON WELL-BEING AND DISEASE

16.2.1 Health-relevant aspects of shiftwork

It may be generally assumed that work at irregular times is disagreeable to the majority of human beings. Shiftwork has this in common with all other forms of work which differ from our average expectations of working conditions. Despite this, it cannot be denied that shiftwork is expressly sought after by a small proportion of the working population because they believe that only with this kind of organization of their work can they realize certain expectations or enjoy certain hobbies. (The best-known examples of this are the farmers shiftworking in the chemical industry in Germany, and the fishermen shiftworking in the paper industry in Norway.) According to Harrington's (1978) findings, it would appear that 20–30 per cent of all workers offered shiftwork decline it, approximately 10 per cent see certain advantages in it, and the rest simply tolerate it.

It is also the case that working at unusual times of day disturbs the order of our social life, and, at least partially, the order of our biological functions as well. This does not, however, mean that in every case it entails danger to health. If the various forms of shiftwork are considered in relation to the problems of biological rhythms, it would appear that all forms of shiftwork, including nightwork, deserve special attention from the point of view of occupational medicine (Rutenfranz *et al.*, 1976; Rutenfranz and Knauth, 1982). Irregular forms of shiftwork, 'continuous' shiftwork and 'permanent' nightwork should be examined particularly closely, because of their special psychosocial problems. No noticeable influence on health may, however, be expected from forms of shiftwork that exclude nightshifts.

In considering the health effects of shiftwork, one tends to forget that shiftwork, as a special time-oriented organization of work, is superimposed upon the most varied of activities. Thus, when discussing the possible harmful effects of this work organization, it is necessary to distinguish them from the stresses, and potential for harm, of the work itself (i.e. the so-called 'confounding factors' of epidemiology; MacMahon and Pugh, 1970). On the other hand, stresses which might otherwise lie within the range of harmlessness (Hacker and Macher, 1977), such as work in hot climatic conditions or with health-endangering substances (within permissible limits), work with noise, etc., may lead to health-endangering situations when they are in conjunction with nightwork. Nevertheless, in all cases of reduced health associated with shiftwork, it is advisable to distinguish between a lowering of well-being and a disease proper.

16.2.2 Lowering of well-being

The lowering of well-being in shiftworkers appears to result mainly from the disturbance of their sleeping and eating habits. Although the need for sleep varies considerably across individuals, and with age, the normal amount is considerably longer than that which can be achieved with nightwork. A number of investigations (e.g. Menzel, 1962; Knauth *et al.*, 1980) have shown that whereas the average sleeping time amounts to 7.5 hours before a morning shift, and 8.5 hours after an afternoon shift, it only reaches 4–6 hours on the day after a nightshift. This shortening of sleeping time is brought about by the transference of sleep to an unfavourable time of day in relation to the worker's circadian rhythms, and by the disturbance of day sleeps by noise. Children and traffic are usually mentioned as the most important sources of the latter (Knauth and Rutenfranz, 1972a, 1972b). In view of this, one would expect the frequency of sleep disturbance to be determined by the type of shift system, and indeed it appears that shiftwork which does not include nightshifts, and normal daywork, do not lead to sleep disturbance to any significant degree, while shiftwork which includes nightshifts, and continuous nightwork, do result in sleep problems (Rutenfranz *et al.*, 1981).

Similarly, the available literature (Rutenfranz, Knauth and Angersbach, 1981) indicates that shiftworkers doing either some nightshifts, or continuous nightwork, clearly suffer from more disturbances of eating habits than dayworkers or shiftworkers who do not work at night. These disturbances of appetite during nightwork are probably caused by the temporal structuring of work, the sequencing of meals and the disruption of sleep. One reason for this seems to be that shiftworkers try to keep to their normal eating habits through their changing work periods, and even on the days between nightshifts. This behaviour interferes radically with their need for sleep. In other words, there is no inversion of eating habits during nightwork; and indeed a lower frequency of meal-taking can be observed during periods of nightshifts (Cervinka *et al.*, 1984).

Such irregularities in food intake can, as experience shows, lead to digestive disorders and gastrointestinal complaints. Although the reasons for this complex of symptoms are surely manifold, complaints concerning the gastrointestinal system are often named as a predominant symptom in shiftworkers. On the basis of our own investigations, and those published by other authors dealing with a total of 8060 persons, we have assembled the findings for various forms of shiftwork (Rutenfranz, Knauth and Angersbach, 1981). One striking factor in these findings is the wide overlap, allowing no clear differentiation in gastrointestinal symptomology between the various types of work schedule. This is especially noticeable for dayworkers and shiftworkers without nightwork. It is conspicuous that (especially in the studies from Scandinavia) even dayworkers show a high percentage of gastrointestinal complaints. If one compares the groups investigated in a single study there are only non-significant differences between shiftworkers doing nightshift and dayworkers. In contrast, it appears that it is *former* shiftworkers (i.e. those who have left shiftwork) who show the greatest frequency of complaints. A similar finding emerges for the small group of shiftworkers on continuous nightwork. Finally, gastrointestinal complaints were strikingly rare in studies where experienced occupational physicians had, for a number of years, been making special medical examinations on beginners, and subsequent follow-up tests.

16.2.3 Dangers to health

The disturbance discussed above suggested that not all forms of shiftwork will be equally problematic with respect to health, but, rather, that it is mainly those forms of shiftwork which include nightwork that result in special risks. In these cases, shiftwork may become a health risk factor if the unavoidable disturbances which result from changes in biological rhythms are augmented by other personal or situational factors at home or at the working place (Rutenfranz, 1976). Such transgressions of the adaptability limits of the human organism should show up in an excessive mortality rate or in an increased frequency of disease.

Unfortunately, studies of mortality in shiftworkers have been very rare. In an unusually careful study, Taylor and Pocock (1972) compared mortality rates in a sample of 8603 shiftworkers and dayworkers from ten factories over a 13-year period, with 1578 deaths occurring. They found no difference in the mortality rates of shiftworkers and dayworkers. However, shiftworkers who had given up shiftwork prematurely did show a higher mortality rate (standard mortality ratio: 118.9 against 101.5). An excessive mortality due to neoplasms was found among shiftworkers, and due to pulmonary complaints among the dayworkers. While it is not possible to draw any strong conclusions from this single study, it seems that there is a clear need for further studies of this type.

In view of the high incidence of disturbed appetite and gastric complaints in shiftworkers discussed above, it seems probable and plausible that the gastrointestinal system may be at risk if other aggravating factors accrue. However, the findings for ulcer incidence compiled from the literature (Rutenfranz, Knauth and Angersbach, 1981) indicate that there is a wide overlap in the incidence of ulcers among shiftworkers and non-shiftworkers. Gastric and duodenal ulcers are not monocausal diseases. Reviewing the role of stress in peptic ulcer disease, Wolf *et al.* (1979) concluded that there are several factors which may predict increased likelihood of developing duodenal ulcer, and none of these factors was job-related. This suggests that nightwork may only be a minor risk factor in predicting increased likelihood of developing duodenal ulcers.

Similarly, with regard to other illnesses, a significant hypermorbidity caused by shiftwork seems unlikely. To date, investigations of cardiovascular diseases, neurological disturbances and psychiatric illnesses have been made, and, as a recent review indicates (Harrington, 1978), no effects of shiftwork have been demonstrated on these aspects of health.

16.2.4 The development of health problems

Since the effects of shiftwork on well-being and health are chronic, it is important to analyse these effects in relation to both age and the duration of exposure to work. In some studies (Akerstedt, Fröberg, Levi, Torsvall and Zamore, 1977; Koller *et al.*, 1978; Kundi *et al.*, 1979a, 1979b; Haider *et al.*, 1981) it has been demonstrated that the worsening in health with increasing age is more pronounced in nightshift workers than in dayworkers. Moreover, the relationship between health state and variables such as family life, social activities, work strain, job satisfaction, attitude towards shiftwork, sleep quality, etc., is not constant, but differs between shiftworkers and dayworkers (Kundi *et al.*, 1981). On the basis of this one might assume that both the process of adaptation to shiftwork, and the possible deterioration of such adaptation, follow a certain temporal pattern. The interaction between health and these intervening variables seems to develop through four phases: an 'adaptation phase', a 'sensitization phase', an 'accumulation phase' and, finally, a 'manifestation phase'.

Within the first 5 years of shiftwork, novelty effects have to be overcome and adaptation and habituation have to be gained with regard to the workplace, work environment, work tasks and colleagues, as well as to shift-dependent rhythm alterations. Furthermore, the family situation (marriage, babies, children, need for own flat or house, etc.) and social situations (limitation of personal and social freedom) alter markedly. It seems clear that the quality of sleep, family life and social activities, together with work strain, have the strongest influence on health and well-being during this *'adaptation phase'* (Kundi *et al.*, 1979a, 1979b; Koller, in press).

From the fifth to twentieth year of shiftwork, the life circumstances of a shiftworker can be described as a cumulated need for, and pressure to achieve, improved family conditions (children in school, house-building, financial problems) and working conditions (engagement in work for promotion and for financial improvement). According to the level of success in these areas, and to the success in developing coping strategies, attitudes towards shiftwork change. Thus, in this *'sensitization phase'* attitudes towards shiftwork, and satisfaction with both shiftwork and family and social life, play an important role in the incidence of health and well-being problems.

From about the twentieth year of shiftwork onwards, family, living, financial and social situations seem to remain roughly constant, or to improve. However, risky behaviour seems to develop, environmental hazards accumulate, and the ageing factor plays an increasing role. Thus, in this period, called the *'accumulation phase',* risk factors and sleep quality show the strongest relationship to health state.

At the end of the 'accumulation phase', and in the following *'manifestation phase'* (40+ years in shiftwork), the gastrointestinal disorders and diseases (chronic gastritis, gastric and duodenal ulcer) reach their highest frequency in shiftworking populations.

16.2.5 Open questions

The question as to whether health is damaged by shiftwork has not, as yet, been satisfactorily answered. So far, our discussions have concentrated on gastrointestinal diseases; the possibility that shiftwork has a co-responsibility for other illnesses is only considered by a few authors (e.g. Carpentier and Cazamian, 1977). The investigations published so far reveal the following deficiencies: (i) the diagnosis of diseases is based on very different kinds of evidence (questionnaires on subjective health, medical history, X-ray, endoscopy); and (ii) only cross-sectional studies have been made, and very often no control group has been included. With regard to the latter point, it is clearly very difficult to answer the health question by cross-sectional studies, since shiftworkers represent a self-selected group. As in epidemiology, retrospective (or better still, prospective) cohort studies as well as case-studies, are necessary.

One of the first studies to have used one of these techniques in shiftwork (Angersbach *et al.*, 1980) supports the assertion that the health data of shiftworkers can only be evaluated in relation to time. Thus, it was found that the process of self-selection continued for at least 10 years. The group of workers who for health reasons changed from shiftwork to daywork proved to be of special importance. The true reasons for the withdrawal of shiftworkers from shiftwork can only be determined by a follow-up of the losses through prospective cohort studies of all workers. Such work-intensive studies are especially necessary today.

16.3 SPECIAL HEALTH MEASURES FOR NIGHTWORKERS

16.3.1 Individual differences

It is apparent that workers react to shiftwork in very different ways despite relatively constant conditions. This fact can only be explained by individual and/or situational differences. If such individual differences can be identified, and shown to be of importance for adaptation to shiftwork, it may be possible to use them as criteria for selection.

People with certain diseases suffer from shiftwork more than others, and thus certain groups should, if possible, be excluded from shiftwork (Collier, 1943; Rutenfranz, 1971). These include people with a history of digestive tract disorders since shiftwork produces special psychosomatic problems and involves unusual mealtimes, both of which may affect gastric functions (Andersen, 1958; Collier, 1943; Dervillée and Lazarini, 1958; Menzel, 1962; Thiis-Evensen, 1958). Diabetes and thyrotoxicosis suffers should also be excluded, as regular food intake and correct therapeutic timing can be difficult to maintain under shiftwork conditions (Cook, 1954). In view of the disturbed sleep of shiftworkers, narcoleptics and those suffering from chronic sleep disturbances (allegedly caused by, e.g. traffic noise etc) may have particular problems, while epileptics should be excluded since reduced sleep increases the incidence of fits (Cook, 1954).

Disturbed sleep may also cause problems for people with severe mental derangements, and in particular depression, since this disease often starts with sleep disturbances which result in disruption of the sleep–wakefulness cycle and other circadian rhythms (Tölle, 1981). Finally, there is some evidence suggesting that it may be wise to exclude patients with heart diseases exhibiting a significant reduction of physical performance capacity, active and extensive tuberculosis patients, alcoholics and other drug addicts, and people with marked hemeralopia, or visual impairment that is too severe for effective compensation to be possible. Illumination of many parts of factories is normally reduced at night and thus this latter group may have an especially high risk of accidents.

In addition to these negative health criteria, various parameters of circadian rhythms have been discussed as possible physiological yardsticks for the prediction of adaptability to shiftwork (see also Chapter 18). Breithaupt *et al.* (1978) used the circadian phase position, and concluded that in evening types (as defined by Ostberg, 1973a) the normal maximum and minimum body temperature appear later than in morning types. Evening types also show fewer sleeping problems and better adjustment to shiftwork than morning types. In contrast, Reinberg *et al.* (1978, 1979) and Andlauer and Reinberg (1979) used the circadian rhythm amplitude as a measure of individual capacity to adjust to shiftwork. They combined the observation of Aschoff, that subjects with a greater amplitude of circadian rhythms will adapt to time changes more slowly, with that of Andlauer (1971), that subjects with a greater amplitude tolerate nightwork better. Reinberg *et al.* concluded from these observations, and from their own experience, that in general it may be better to use swiftly rotating shift systems. They found that a smaller amplitude of body temperature on normal days increased the probability of some adjustment of this circadian rhythm to shiftwork, but that complete adjustment did not occur within a reasonable span of night duty.

Individual differences in adjustment to shiftwork have also been linked to differences in personality. Most of these studies have taken the time needed for the re-entrainment of physiological functions — usually body temperature — as a measure of the capacity to adjust to shiftwork. Thus, Blake (1971) found 'small but significant differences in certain aspects of the mean body temperature rhythms of introverts and extraverts', while Colquhoun and Folkard (1978) were able to show that 'neurotic extraverts exhibited the greatest degree of adjustment' as far as the trend of body temperature during nightshift was concerned. Preferred activity habits were considered by Ostberg (1973a) who drew a distinction between 'morningness' and 'eveningness', and stated that 'the morning type of subject had the most pronounced difficulty in adapting to night work'. Patkai (1971b) found 'a significant relationship between morningness and introversion, and eveningness and extraversion' so that it is possible that both factors may have a common basis. Nachreiner (1975) used these personality variables in order to classify attitudes towards shiftwork among groups of shiftworkers. He found that 'if a shiftworker is rather introverted and tends to be emotionally unstable, the probability that he feels uncomfortable with shiftwork and would like to get out of it is fairly high'.

Unfortunately, all this evidence is based on cross-sectional studies, and to date little attempt has been made to make any predictions about the capacity to adapt to nightwork. Folkard *et al.* (1979) recently developed a predictive test of adjustment to shiftwork which is based on the hypotheses referred to above, while Nachreiner (1975) has formulated a test of attitude to shiftwork using these hypotheses. Validation of these tests, however, will only be possible in prospective cohort studies that have yet to be conducted.

Since none of these positive criteria has so far been validated in prospective studies, they are of rather limited value to the occupational health practitioner for the selection of nightworkers. Nevertheless, they are of great importance for shiftwork research. Nor have the negative criteria for the selection of nightworkers yet been validated in prospective epidemiological studies. However, they are based on the experience of occupational medicine practitioners in fairly well-controlled case studies (Loskant, 1970; Aanonsen, 1964). These indicate that the selection of nightworkers using such negative criteria leads to a reduction in both the number of nightworkers complaining of a lowering of well-being, and the incidence of job-related diseases.

16.3.2 Situational differences

Living conditions are of special importance in determining adjustment to shiftwork. As Knauth and Rutenfranz (1972b), Knauth *et al.* (1975), and Rutenfranz *et al.*, (1974) have shown, approximately 60–80 per cent of shiftworkers complain that their sleep is disturbed by noise on the day after a nightshift, the most frequent sources of noise mentioned being traffic and children. Both these kinds of noise have been shown to disrupt sleep (Griefahn *et al.*, 1976; Knauth and Rutenfranz, 1972a, 1975; Williams, 1973). It is therefore hardly surprising that people with unfavourable living conditions (i.e. those with badly sound-insulated bedrooms, near roads carrying a lot of traffic, and with small children in the family) should complain more often about a lowering of well-being, and about health problems, than people in more favourable living conditions (Küpper *et al.*, 1980). So far, only Angersbach (1980) has investigated the value of living conditions as a predictor of good or bad adaptability to nightwork in a retrospective cohort study; prospective cohort studies are also needed here.

A situational factor which has received hardly any attention is the family's acceptance of shiftwork. If a shiftworker's family cannot accept shiftwork, this is likely to have a deleterious effect on his well-being.

16.4 POSSIBLE PREVENTIVE HEALTH MEASURES

16.4.1 Time-contingency

In order to prevent adaptation disturbances and adverse health effects one should try to introduce counteracting measures in good time. According to the phases in the development of possible health problems described above, one might propose that during the 'adaptation phase' a primarily advisory function should be observed. This would include giving information about the effects of disturbed rhythms, developing a sleep regimen in conjunction with the workers, and discussing problems of eating habits during nightshifts, etc. Then, during the 'sensitization phase', medical care should be improved and groups should be established for physical training, training in relaxation techniques, and for weight reduction, etc. Information should be given concerning the adverse effects of stimulating substances, drug and alcohol abuse, etc. Subsequently, during the 'accumulation phase' preventive cures should be provided for obese people, smokers, and people with high alcohol intake, etc. Additional free days should be given for rehabilitation measures in order to prevent serious health hazards. Finally, during the 'manifestation phase' additional free weeks should be included in the work schedule for rehabilitative measures; i.e. for cures in existing rehabilitation centres for gastrointestinal, cardiovascular, lumboischialgic, and neurovegetative disorders.

16.4.2 Regular health checks

According to Taylor (1968), standard medical examinations before starting work have only a limited predictive value for sickness-absence. Loskant and Knauth (1976) have therefore proposed that shiftworkers should be subjected to a second health examination not later than 1 year after starting shiftwork in order to assess their degree of adaptation to it. A special German study group, that included experienced occupational health practitioners as well as scientific experts in the fields of circadian rhythms and shiftwork research, proposed the following measures (Herrmann, 1982): (i) All persons working 6 hours on a regular shift system, or at least 5 hours on an irregular shift system, during the hours from 2200 to 0600 h, should have regular health checks; (ii) the recruiting medical examination should exclude people from nightwork on the basis of the negative health criteria discussed above; (iii) there should be a second health check not later than 12 months after starting nightwork, and regular health checks at least every 2 years for those under 25, every 5 years for those between 25 and 50, every 2-3 years for those between 50 and 60, and every 1-2 years for those above 60. These regular health checks could use the same negative criteria as used at the first medical examination, but would have to disregard temporary changes in health status or living conditions.

16.4.3 Other preventive measures

Other preventive health measures include the possibility of giving the shiftworker a regular chance to live under normal conditions with respect to circadian rhythms. Certain large German plants have recently begun to offer regular preventive treatment of this kind for 2 to 3 weeks, to shiftworkers over 50 years old, at 2-3 year intervals, in specialized hospitals (Kurkliniken). This treatment provides the worker with a chance to normalize his circadian rhythms by following a regular sleep–wake routine with normal mealtimes. Physiotherapeutic measures and a general health check are also available. On a lesser scale, shiftworkers (especially those following 'continuous' shiftwork systems) in many branches of industry have been awarded additional free days as a result of recent labour disputes. The medical basis for this is that the workers now have more 'normal' days to allow the circadian system to return to day orientation. However, the efficiency of these measures for improving health has yet to be demonstrated epidemiologically.

Since gastrointestinal complaints are very common in shiftworkers, it seems reasonable to propose that the provision of regular meals at night might reduce health problems. Debry and Bleyer (1972) were able to show that disturbances of appetite did not lead to a lessening of calorie intake, but had more to do with a dislike of having to eat, at unusual times, food that is often cold and has to be taken outside the normal social environment. The idea of offering a hot meal, that can be eaten in a near normal social situation, not later than 0100 h, seems to be a health measure that has not yet been taken up very often, even in large factories (Hohmann-Beck, 1981).

In addition, any measure that may improve the sleep of shiftworkers is obviously important. In modern conditions, work consists more and more of observing machinery rather than controlling it. Thus, it might be better to allow formalized short naps at work, rather than force people to struggle for hours to avoid falling asleep. As Kogi (1981b) has shown, many plants in Japan have such (more or less) legalized sleeping allowances during nightwork. Andlauer *et al.* (1982) have proposed legalized sleeping hours in all industries where public safety is at stake.

16.4.4 Nightshift-scheduling

There are many reasons for the existence of shiftwork (e.g. technological, economic and social), and so it is unreasonable to propose its total abolition. However, nightwork in particular should be reduced to the lowest possible level (Knauth *et al.*, 1983). In our experience, shiftwork is very often organized in such a way that day and night shifts are equally manned simply because in constructing shift systems the easiest solution is to have the same number of workers on each shift. This, however, often leads to a situation where work has to be 'found' for nightworkers that could equally easily be done on either the morning or the afternoon shift. One of the duties of occupational health doctors should therefore be to encourage management, trade unions and workers to offer suggestions for reducing the amount of nightwork in their particular industry, thus reducing the frequency of nightshifts for an individual worker. This appears to be a potentially important health measure for nightworkers, but it may not always be acceptable at first, since it may result in a reduction of the special nightshift allowance.

However, in the long term, such measures might be of great benefit to the workers' health and social life.

The responsibility for the construction of shift schedules should not be restricted to trade unions, management and workers. It has been demonstrated (Knauth *et al.*, 1979) how the introduction of physiological criteria for the construction of shift schedules could be used to minimize the health problems of shiftworkers.

16.5 CONCLUSIONS

In conclusion, occupational health measures for nightworkers and shiftworkers should include actions designed to reduce the complaints of the workers, in order to prevent a lowering of well-being, and the occurrence of job-related diseases. Such measures should not be restricted to those normally used in occupational health practice, but should include activities outside the workplace such as bringing pressure to bear for the improvement of housing conditions, and counselling workers on the organization of their social life in relation to their shift systems, using physiological criteria.

Hours of Work
Edited by S. Folkard and T.H. Monk

Chapter 17

Social Problems of Shiftwork

James Walker

CONTENTS

ABSTRACT

The displacement of the shiftworker in time and space results in domestic inconvenience for the individual and spouse, and for other members of the family. Shiftwork may also affect family relationships. Participation in institutional life may be impaired and social contacts impoverished. Countervailing advantages include the opportunity to pursue hobbies and interests in daylight hours and the availability of facilities open during weekdays. People's characteristics and circumstances are too diverse for generalizations to be made, although it can be concluded that at present the social disadvantages of shiftwork are greater than the advantages.

17.1 INTRODUCTION

Work on the biological aspects of shiftwork has been underpinned by a theoretical background in chronobiology which goes some way to account for the quantity and quality of work in this area. Research on the social problems of shiftwork has on the whole not been based on any theoretical background and it tends to be sparse, but there are some ways of thinking about the effects of shiftwork on social and domestic life which are helpful.

There has been extensive collection of time budgets by diary-keeping methods which record the activities of people throughout the 24 hours, and where the activities take place (Bullock *et al.*, 1974; Shapcott and Steadman, 1978). Time budgets show a pattern of activity which follows the circadian rhythms, superimposed on which are weekly and seasonal cycles. The time budgets are grouped into the type of activity people undertake, e.g. work, leisure, sleep. In modern society the daily patterns of activity are highly routinized according to the role occupied — e.g. worker, housewife, schoolchild — with the result that the picture which emerges shows the pattern of a community's activity. This can be used for planning purposes. It is clear that shiftworkers will have distinctive time budgets which will prevent them from engaging in activities at the same time as normal dayworkers. Up to the present, time budget studies on shiftworkers have been concerned mainly with sleep patterns (Knauth and Rutenfranz, 1981), but recent work (Rutenfranz, Knauth, Kupper, Romahn and Ernst, 1981) has extended time budget studies on shiftworkers to record how their time for social activities is distributed. It is possible to carry out such studies as superimposing the time budgets of schoolchildren on those of their fathers to find out the opportunity the parents have to discharge their parental roles.

It is not sufficient to chart the distribution of activities in time, for shiftworking also results in a displacement in space. Carlstein *et al.* (1978) wrote, 'In this development space should be treated as an equal to time rather than a competitor or methodologically obstructing factor. Just as geographers would profit by not treating the world as if it were temporally flat and void of temporal organization and structure, many sociologists and economists should by the same token include the spatial structure of society and habitat.'

Time-geographers have been concerned with time–space analysis. Lee (1978) has applied the theories of the Lund School in Sweden to rotating three-shift work, taking into account such variables as the 'paths' in time–space the shiftworkers follow, the 'constraints' under which their activities are carried out and the 'stations' where they are performed. It lies outside the scope of this chapter to pursue the analysis further, but it may be a fruitful way of examining the effects of shiftwork on social and family life.

There is a need for caution because of the extreme complexity of shift arrangements and their effects. First, there are different types of shift system, two-shift, three-shift, continuous and discontinuous with a break at the weekend, and fixed shifts — e.g. permanent nightwork — each one of which can be arranged in a variety of ways. The arrangements have distinctive effects on the shiftworkers' lives and the lives of their families. Second, shiftworkers themselves vary in sex, age, marital status, composition of family, etc., all of which interact with shiftwork hours. For instance, the social activities of the young unmarried are quite different from those of their elders. Third, there are cultural differences in response to shiftwork both among shiftworkers and non-shiftworkers. The attitude towards shiftwork and the status of shiftworkers may be quite different in a 'steel town', where shiftworking is the norm, from in a residential suburb of a city where shiftwork is the exception. One must try to take into account these complexities.

Another concept which is useful in thinking about the social and domestic consequences of shiftwork is 'social time' and the value which is attached to different times of the day and days of the week. Obviously not all times have equal value. Blakelock (1960) writes about time as a commodity with exchange value or liquidity. Free time in the morning may have little exchange value for there may be few leisure activities which the shiftworker cares to follow, so shiftworkers may sleep during the morning free time in excess of physiological need. On the other hand, the social value of time in the evening, and especially the weekend, is high. The social value of time and the inconveniences of working unsocial hours are recognized in shiftwork premia payments. In the United Kingdom there are great variations in these (Sergean, 1971), but Wedderburn (1981) has tabulated the common extra payments for time of day and day of week as follows: Monday to Friday (0600 to 2000) — 100 per cent; Monday to Friday (2000 to 0600) — 120 per cent; Saturday (0600 to 2000) — 150 per cent; Sunday (0600 to 2000) — 200 per cent; Sunday (2000 to 0600 Monday) — 240 per cent.

Wedderburn went on to obtain the subjective value of different hours of the week from matched groups of dayworkers and shiftworkers. The results indicated that Saturday evening was rated the highest value for time off work. Evenings were valued higher than time off during the day, and weekends higher than weekdays. On the whole, shiftworkers valued the same times off work as dayworkers and there appeared to have been little adjustment in the subjective value of time off work at unusual hours, although the possibility of stereotyped assessment of social time value was discussed.

Another viewpoint is the flexibility of activities in respect of their timing (Blakelock, 1960; Vroom, 1964). Some activities such as gardening or walking can be carried out at nearly any time of day and are temporally flexible activities; there is a limited amount of flexibility in mealtimes, while other activities such as watching a television programme or a football match have no temporal flexibility. A second concept used by Vroom is the *discordance* of a work schedule for a given activity which is defined as 'the amount of overlap between the work schedule and the time pattern for that activity'. An afternoon shift deprives a young person of social activities in the evening, but it allows a golfer to play a round in the morning. It is the variation in people's interests, in the degree to which these are temporally flexible, and the extent to which particular shift arrangements aid or hinder the following of an interest, which accounts for some of the individual differences in response to shiftwork. It is also possible to cultivate interests which are congruent with shiftwork schedules, such as outdoor activities during the day, including outings with the shiftworker's wife and young children.

A further concept which is useful in thinking about shiftwork is marginality. Shiftwork, and particularly nightwork, is often spoken of as unnatural; shiftworkers may become relatively isolated and find it difficult to become active members of organizations. Shiftwork itself may not be held in high esteem outside geographical areas where shiftwork is commonplace, and shiftworkers may suffer in social status. As Brown (1975) remarks about shiftwork, 'even if it does provide the opportunity for a middle class consumption pattern, it denies the worker some of the social prestige normally associated with such consumption'. Shiftworkers may not be fully integrated in the communities in which they live and work; they themselves may feel this and other members of the community may not regard them as fully part of it. The shiftworker may be considered in some sense a 'marginal man'. The concept may become clearer by analogy with the health professions where those who deliver unorthodox care — the osteopath, the chiropractor — work on the margins and are not necessarily accepted by the orthodox health care professions, nor by the community in which they work.

Finally, it is very useful to consider the roles that people fill and test whether the shiftworker is at a disadvantage (or advantage) compared to the dayworker. Every person has a variety of roles. At home the shiftworker is spouse and parent; there are role obligations to the family of origin and that of the spouse, and other relatives may make demands on the individual. Outside the home there are roles in relation to friends, clubs, political parties, churches, etc. The work role is largely defined by a person's occupation — e.g. fitter, turner, computer operator, foreman — but it is also defined in part by whether the individual is a shiftworker. It is readily seen that shiftwork can interfere with the functioning of these roles. The shiftworker on nightwork will not be able to provide companionship, protection or emotional support or fulfil the sexual role in relation to the spouse when he is at work in the evening and at night. It may be difficult to keep up with friends, for they find the free time of the shiftworker unpredictable, and they may not be able to include him in social activities. Even if it is possible for him to join organizations, membership may be qualitatively affected through his being unable to hold office or attend regularly. Some activities may be impossible, like pursuing further education courses.

All the social effects of shiftwork which have been discussed so far can and do occur. What is less well understood is their prevalence. Further, what is not well documented is the interaction between the physical effects of shiftwork and the effects on social and domestic life. If the shiftworker on nights has circadian rhythms out of phase, has difficulty in sleeping and feels below par, it can be hypothesized that damage to social and domestic life will result. Irritability is said to be a characteristic of the shiftworker (Brown, 1959). If working a sequence of afternoon shifts and nightshifts is a boring period when there is little opportunity for social life, then the physical effects of shiftwork may seem heightened.

17.2 EFFECTS OF SHIFTWORK ON DOMESTIC LIFE

One of the most thorough examinations of domestic life and shiftwork has been by Mott *et al.* (1965). They considered the roles of the shiftworker and his wife. The role behaviour of the husband included companionship, assistance with the housework, providing diversion and relaxation, protection of wife from harm, understanding, decision-making and support. Shiftworkers were asked whether it was easier or harder to perform these roles on shiftwork than on daywork. On the whole they reported that they were less able to fulfil the aspects of family life on shiftwork, except for assisting with the housework which was easier on shifts. Similar results were found when the shiftworker was asked about his parental role; he claimed to be less able than on daywork to provide companionship for the children, to teach skills or control and discipline, and to maintain close family relationships. Diekmann *et al.* (1982) refer to research which shows that the school careers of shiftworkers' children are negatively affected, although the National Child Development Study in England, which has followed the progress of 16 000 children since their birth in 1958, showed that whatever effects shiftwork may have on the family it did not impair the school performance or emotional adjustment of the shiftworkers' children (Lambert and Hart, 1976). These results are not clear-cut, as is often the case in this area, and there are problems in drawing matched samples of shiftworkers and dayworkers (Maasen, 1978). When shiftworkers indicate an adverse attitude by expressing a wish to change onto another shift their family difficulties seem greater.

Another study which has quantified the effects of two-shift and three-shift working is reported by Nilsson (1981), and the results are shown in Table 17.1. The fact that two-shift working was associated with more interference with family life than three-shift work is perhaps surprising, but two shifts usually means being at the workplace during the late afternoon and evening when so much of family life takes place.

TABLE 17.1
The proportion of two- and three-shift workers who experience difficulties in their family relations and activities

Interference with	**% of shift workers**	
	2-shift	**3-shift**
Relations with children	51	38
Relations with husband/wife	45	35
Leisure time activities with family	42	35
Discussing family issues	22	6

Mott *et al.* (1965) went on to examine the effects of shiftwork on marital happiness and family integration, and the evidence of strain and friction in the family. They concluded that shiftwork has a 'two-step' effect upon the family.

> First of all, the conflict between the hours of work and the times usually given over to certain role behaviour seems to result in reports of difficulty and interference with valued activities. Secondly, there seems to be a cumulative effect of these various interferences with role performance leading to some reduction in marital happiness and an even greater reduction in the ability to co-ordinate family activities and to minimize strain and friction among family members.

Perhaps most seriously, the studies show that the interference with family roles interacts with mental health as expressed by self-esteem, anxiety and conflict pressure. It has sometimes been alleged that shiftwork breaks up family life and leads to divorce, but evidence for this has not so far been forthcoming.

Another way of looking at the effects of shiftwork on domestic life is to consider the burden on the shiftworker's spouse. Brown (1959), on the basis of interviews with shiftworkers and their wives, has classified the disadvantages of the husband's nightwork to the wife as follows: interference with the daily work in the house because the husband is asleep or in the way; wife nervous at night; wife lonely in the evening; strain of keeping the children quiet; wife cannot go out in the evening; problem of feeding the husband; irritable husband.

The problems of the housewife were centred on having her husband at home during the times when she normally carried out her household duties. Thus, she had to postpone her housework if her husband was asleep and prevent the children from making a noise. Such difficulties are increased in poor housing conditions and in large families. Maurice (1975) quotes continental studies which showed (i) rest was difficult for the husband in 55 per cent of cases where the family had two rooms, 41 per cent of cases in homes of three rooms, 27 per cent in homes of four rooms and only 7.6 per cent of cases where the family had five rooms; (ii) similarly, disturbances to rest increased from 24 per cent in families with one child to 40 per cent in families with two children and 50 per cent in those with five.

Nervousness and loneliness in the evening and at night, experienced by shiftworkers' wives when they are alone in the house, are very real disadvantages to family life. It was found by de la Mare and Walker (1968) that one of the most important reasons why a group of telegraphists on dayshift declined to work at nights was their wives' dislike of being left alone during the evening and at night.

A further difficulty for the wife is providing her husband with meals which are appetizing to him. Shiftworkers often do not want a main meal after a nightshift, nor when they wake up from their daytime sleep, nor before they go on the nightshift, which led one of Brown's housewives to remark that every meal she prepared seemed like a breakfast. The times of shiftworkers' meals may also be inconvenient for their wives although the husband after a nightshift or a morning shift may make an effort to eat his main meal with the family in the evening. With the afternoon shift it is impossible for the shiftworker to have his meals at the same time as his family.

The wives of shiftworkers interviewed by Brown noted some advantages arising out of the husbands' nightwork which centred round free time during the day. They were help at home when she is at work; help with the children (e.g. on Mondays), help at home (especially on Mondays), more leisure time together.

The weekend is the time when most social activities occur. In small towns and in the country, social life may be largely centred round Saturday afternoon and evening and Sunday. Banks (1956, 1960) provides interesting evidence or how husbands and wives value their time off at the weekends. She interviewed a group of steelworkers and their wives after a change from discontinuous shiftwork with free weekends to a three-shift continuous system, with days off on different days of the week. The wives made few complaints about changes in their domestic routine but they resented the loss of the weekend when they usually enjoyed social activities with their husbands. The husbands' free time during the week did not compensate, and some of the wives had to stay at home to prepare midday meals for schoolchildren. For women who worked, the weekend was the only opportunity to enjoy free time during the day with other members of the family and to go out with them. Disappointment went further than this, and there seemed to be a feeling that there was a 'proper' time for leisure. The husbands shared the views of their wives and made such comments as 'We like to go out at the weekend. If you are at home on washing day you can't do much, can you?'

Legislation in a number of countries such as Belgium, Holland and West Germany designates Sunday as the rest day (with exceptions). The ILO conventions suggests that the rest day should coincide with the established traditions and customs of the country or district. In Western society this will normally mean Sunday is the rest day. One consideration is that the Sunday break should preserve religious observance as well as family and social life. Women and young persons are protected from working at certain times at the weekend. As has been illustrated, shiftwork premia are high at the weekend and highest on Sunday. Trade unions press for these payments, partly as compensation to staff for working unsocial hours, but also to discourage employers from adopting weekend working by penalizing them for doing so. The preservation of the weekend for rest and leisure is well institutionalized, but shiftworking prevents compliance with established practice.

Shiftworkers' domestic problems cannot be seen in isolation from social trends affecting the family. The breaking up of the extended family in industrial society which results in a withdrawal of support will affect the shiftworker's family — as does the trend for married women to pursue a career. The increasing tendency for husbands and wives to follow joint rather than segregated roles (Young and Wilmott, 1973) in the small nuclear family results in the husbands and wives sharing the major activities of the household. Husbands take on tasks which are traditionally 'women's work' such as shopping and bed-making, and they share in the rearing of the children. Leisure interests may be pursued together, the husband taking his family with him on recreational or social outings. The trend towards joint roles was very noticeable, and increasing, among the families surveyed by Young and Wilmott. They argued that the symmetrical pattern of family life which results is prevented by shiftwork. 'Fathers are forced to work when other members of their family are at leisure and to take their leisure when other members are at work. The life of the family can hardly be enhanced, even though the motive is to enhance the means for its support.' On the other hand, the working wife looks to the support of her husband in domestic tasks and shiftworkers may be better able to provide the assistance than dayworkers. Rutenfranz, Knauth and

Angersbach (1981) in a pilot study in the services sector, where hours of work can be very irregular, show that the wives of shiftworkers often go to great lengths to adapt to their husbands' hours to the extent, for instance, of sharing breakfast before the early shift at 0400 or 0500 h. Time budget studies and interviews indicated that there was a very considerable burden on the shiftworkers' wives, and family life was difficult with children, or if the wife worked. Maasen (1978), working in the chemical industry in Belgium, showed that there was indeed a burden on wives, but that they did little to adapt; the shiftworker, and his wife with children, seemed to lead relatively independent lives. The issues of shiftwork and family life are not simple, and cultural differences must play a large part in the varying conclusions of research workers. It is encouraging that the research groups under Professor Nachreiner at Oldenburg and Professor Rutenfranz at Dortmund are turning their attention to a systematic analysis of the social and domestic problems of shiftwork.

17.3 EFFECTS OF SHIFTWORK ON SOCIAL LIFE

A number of studies have been carried out on the social effects of shiftwork, sometimes in connection with a larger study and sometimes when a change in the nature of the organization takes place, such as a move to automated plant. Examples include studies of printers (Lipsett, Trow and Coleman, 1956), oil refinery workers (Blakelock, 1960), power station workers (Mann and Hoffman, 1960), steelworkers (Banks, 1960; Chadwick-Jones, 1969; Wedderburn, 1975) and railwaymen (Salaman, 1974). Two more general studies are by Brown (1959) and Mott *et al.* (1965), and descriptive reviews of the social and sociological implications of shiftwork are by Brown (1975), Maurice (1975), Carpentier and Cazamian (1977) and Bunnage (1979). The extent to which unsocial hours affect the social life of a shiftworker is difficult to determine as it varies according to local circumstances such as the nature of the shift system, the location of the work, or the length of time worked on shifts. After an analysis of the social effects of different shift systems on steelworkers, Wedderburn writes, 'the sheer variety of individuals' preferences and habits in their social lives defies reduction to a few generalisations'. Nevertheless, at a very general level the pattern of what can happen to the social life of shiftworkers is becoming clear. It may be divided into (i) organizational membership and institutional activities, (ii) contacts with friends and relatives, and (iii) solitary or near solitary activities.

Membership of organizations and participation in institutionalized activities follow the pattern which would be expected from working unusual hours and the use made of social time. Shiftworkers are less likely than dayworkers to be members of organizations or to be office holders once they have joined. There is some doubt about whether they as frequently attend meetings of those organizations of which they are members. Thus, shiftworkers are less likely to be active in a political party, civic group, parent–teacher association, etc., or in organizations devoted to recreation and leisure. Participation in these activities has sometimes been regarded as an indication of the vitality of a society (Mott *et al.*, 1965) or of its integration (Brown, 1975) and there is cause for concern if a section of the population is prevented from taking part in organizational life.

If the notion of institutional activity is extended to access to commercial facilities such as shops, banks and cinemas, or to welfare facilities such as doctor's surgery, clinic or dentist, then the shiftworker is at an advantage compared to the dayworker, particularly the dayworker on overtime. The shiftworker can readily find the opportunity to cash a cheque or visit the hairdresser in the time off during the day, although these activities can scarcely be called social. The shiftworker may accompany his wife when shopping or shop for her if she works.

The results of studies about contact with friends and relatives are more equivocal. Some studies mentioned have shown that shiftworkers have fewer friends than dayworkers or that friends are concentrated among other shiftworkers. The shiftworker may not be able to attend meetings with friends and his whereabouts may seem unpredictable to them. On the other hand, shiftworkers do have friends; meeting with them need not take place at fixed or regular times and the occurrences may be planned or they may be informal and spontaneous. Similarly, shiftworkers do not seem to be at much of a disadvantage in keeping in touch with relatives, although the shiftworker may be absent at work on family anniversaries, or public holidays which are family centred times. Visiting relatives is a flexible activity and arrangements can be made to visit during the shiftworker's off duty time. Shiftwork seems to have a limited effect on informal social life.

With respect to hobbies and activities of a solitary or near solitary nature, and particularly those which are pursued during the day, the shiftworker is at an advantage compared to the dayworker. When questioned, shiftworkers often say they garden, engage in major 'do it yourself' projects, tinker with the car, walk or fish. One study has shown that dayworkers engage in the same number of these activities but are unable to pursue them as intensively as the shiftworker.

Double jobbing, or 'moonlighting', is the practice of holding more than one paid occupation, with the second job usually being a subsidiary part-time activity. Double jobbing is believed to be prevalent among shiftworkers, when it may generally be considered as an extension of the active hobbies which they pursue. In a study of second jobs in Cardiff, Alden (1976) showed that the second job is typically of about 10 hours per week, often in a service industry. Examples of second jobs are gardening and small-holding, window-cleaning, home repairs and decorating, or working as taxi driver or part-time bar person. Other work is seasonal such as fruit-picking or jobs during the holiday season in certain areas. The people involved in double jobbing are amongst the most energetic in the community as nearly a third of them in Alden's sample also worked an average of 8 hours overtime in their main jobs.

The extent of double jobbing among shiftworkers is difficult to determine for the remuneration can form part of the 'black economy' and be associated with tax evasion. Wedderburn (1975) found 16 per cent of steelworkers on three-shift work engaged in a secondary job. In America, Mott *et al.* (1965) found that 11 per cent of workers on day, 19 per cent on afternoon shifts, 23 per cent on nightshifts and 10 per cent on rotating shifts had second jobs. The two fixed shifts, permanent afternoons and permanent nights, which allowed for regular free time during the day, led to more double jobbing. The rotating shift workers were no more likely to have second jobs than dayworkers. A study in France (Maurice and Monteil, cited by Maurice, 1975) produced contradictory results. They found that 12 per cent of permanent shift, 14 per cent of rotating two-shift, 27 per cent of discontinuous three-shift and 33 per cent of continuous shift workers held second jobs. So that it was the three-shift rotating workers who were most likely to hold a second job. It is probably unprofitable to refer to exact figures since the opportunities to engage in second jobs will vary widely, but the practice does seem to be extensive among shiftworkers.

Double jobbing has its social and economic critics, and is not legal in all EEC countries. Managers may disapprove of second job holding on the grounds that it may interfere with performance on the main job by inducing undue fatigue or through weakening motivation because the second job attracts the interest of the job holder. Another source of criticism is economic: that second job holders diminish the amount of work available and in times of high unemployment prevent others from gaining employment. There is no doubt that double jobbing leads to rumours and exaggeration. Most managers can point to the case of a shiftworker who holds down a second job. Fellow workers may display envious curiosity. On the other hand, it is possible to take the view that the bulk of double jobbing is in the nature of remunerative hobbies pursued for a few hours each week, sometimes in the open air, which may provide a beneficial contrast to the full-time occupation.

The social and domestic difficulties of shiftworkers are partly dependent on (i) the shiftworker's personal characteristics, (ii) the shift rota worked, and (iii) the kind of community the shiftworker lives in. The results of surveys have shown that shiftworkers are more common in some demographic groups than others. As increased earnings are the primary reward of shiftwork, and the reason why many workers say they are on shifts, it might be expected that those with the greatest needs would be attracted to shiftwork. An opportunity to examine the hypothesis was provided by the income tax code numbers which were allocated by the Inland Revenue in the United Kingdom. These at the status level of factory work were good indicators of domestic financial responsibilities. Income tax code numbers indicated primarily the number of an individual's dependants (this is no longer the case), but also took into account allowances on the interest of a house mortgage and other allowances.

Walker and De la Mare (1971) selected groups of men, permanent nightshift and dayshift workers, in three organizations. The workers were then divided into income tax code groups to correspond to single men, married, married with two children and married with three or more children. The results in Table 17.2 show the numbers of men on nightshift and dayshift in the different groups. It is seen that there are fewer single men and married men with no children on the nightshift than on the dayshift, but a greater number of men with four or more dependants on the nightshift.

TABLE 17.2
Number of men in different tax code groups on dayshift and nightshift

ITC groups	Number of dependants					
	0	1	2	3	4 or more	Total
Dayshift	125	187	124	84	55	575
Nightshift	86	148	117	100	128	579

Similar results were found by Fishwick and Harling (1974) in studies of the British motor car industry and a Belgian plant. They carried the analysis a stage further. The amount of domestic responsibilities in a population is related to age, and it is not possible to say which factor identifies differences between shiftworkers and dayworkers. The investigators selected a group of men with common tax codes and examined what relationship there was between shiftwork and age. It was found that there was a greater proportion of shiftworkers in their late 20s, 30s and early 40s. The dayworkers tended to be disporportionately represented by the young and the old. The investigators selected a group of men in the same age group and examined the relationship between tax code and shiftwork. The results illustrated in Table 17.2 held. Thus, both age and domestic responsibilities are independently related to shiftwork.

It is interesting to speculate why shiftworkers, compared to dayworkers, should show particular characteristics of age and family responsibilities. So far as the latter is concerned the influence of financial rewards may be paramount. When a family is in the phase of expansion and children are growing up, maintenance of a standard of living is of vital concern. The age relationship seems to be due to other causes and the young and older men may avoid shiftwork for different reasons. It might be speculated that the young value their leisure at the normal times, whilst the older men may avoid shiftwork because they find it physically stressful.

Different types of shift systems have different effects on social life as do the individual shifts. On three-shift work, the morning shift is generally most popular because it allows the shiftworker to lead a normal social and domestic life. The shift usually starts early in the morning and the worker should retire early the night before in order to be fresh for work, but in practice a sleep 'debt' is frequently built up. The afternoon shift is often the most unpopular shift because it precludes normal social life. Free time is in the morning which may not have a high 'social value'. The shift is particularly disliked by young single people because it interferes with their evening activities, although older people may welcome the opportunity for rest. The nightshift also interferes with social activity but there is some opportunity for social life in the early evening. The time at home after a nightshift may be affected by the physical disadvantages of nightwork, including the difficulty of sleeping, as has been discussed elsewhere. Each shift also has its different effects on the organization of domestic routines and family relations.

The acceptability of shift systems varies for social reasons. The double day shift, although there is not the stress of nightwork, makes social life difficult because afternoon shifts are worked for half the time. However, the weekends are free, as they are on the discontinuous three-shift system. The continuous three-shift system, as well as involving nightwork, also has the disadvantage that only the occasional weekend is free. But the most stressful system is the alternating day and night shift which is usually organized by working a week or a fortnight on days followed by a week or a fortnight on nights. This system is common in the United Kingdom but not elsewhere. In spite of the physical stress and social disadvantages of the alternating day and night shifts, employers cling to the system because of its administrative flexibility, and workers tolerate it because of the high remuneration.

The way the shift rotas are arranged also has considerable effects on the opportunity to engage in social life. The traditional arrangement on three-shift work has been to work for about 1 week on one shift, e.g. the morning shift, enjoy a rest break, and then change to the next shift. The 2 weeks on the afternoon and night shifts is largely a period of social inactivity. There has been, in recent years, a widespread working of rapidly rotating shifts where two or three shifts are worked in a row and then a change is made to the next shift so that all three shifts are worked in a week. Walker (1966) and Wedderburn (1967) have shown that these swiftly rotating rotas are highly acceptable for they enable some normal social life to be followed every week. However, there is no consistency in shiftworker's preferences and the 'blocking' of working time on shiftwork has also become popular (Tejmar, 1976). One way of doing this is to work 12-hour shifts for a period and alternate between day and night. Depending on the number of 12-hour shifts worked in a row, a block of disposable time is available. Tejmar writes, 'a large German chemical company has made excellent records, with a 12–24–12 hour schedule in some of its work-shops where continuous observation is needed, leaving the operators free to take up to 10 days leave at one time every quarter of the year, in addition to the leave prescribed by law'.

With the reduction of hours of work there are many ways of arranging shift rotas to accommodate social needs. McEwan Young (1980) has documented a case of small groups of workers in a chemical plant planning their own shift arrangements to suit their own needs. The opportunity for shiftworkers to exercise some control over the arrangement of their working time is likely to increase (Walker, 1978) following the practice of flexible working hours for dayworkers. It may lessen the burden of shiftwork on social and domestic life, and lead to feelings of freedom, although care needs to be taken that the choices do not lead to arrangements which are socially acceptable but physiologically stressful.

The type of community the shiftworker lives in may partly determine the social acceptability of shiftwork. Sociologists have described occupational communities, which are characterized by a special relationship between work and non-work life. The one almost becomes an extension of the other so that friendships are formed with fellow workers, social activity is in the company of workmates and conversation is often about work. Unusual hours may be one of the features of the occupational community, although they are not a necessary condition. Other features include hard physical work, which is possibly dangerous, a strongly unionized workforce, or rules which have to be observed outside the working environment, as with policemen. Proximity in the same location is common but again not a necessary condition. Descriptive accounts have been given of printers, fishermen, steelworkers, miners, policemen, jazz musicians and railwaymen.

Lipsett, Trow and Coleman (1962) describe an occupational community of printers in the USA. The printers were highly unionized and controlled recruitment to their trade and into the workplace; they were considered to be an elite with a craft interest which bound them together; most printers were on nightwork for at least part of their careers which reduced the opportunity to associate with non-printers. 'It habituates him [the printer] to occupation-linked leisure activities and releases him from the pressure of regular family life.' The printers had an extensive network of social and sports clubs, and welfare and benevolent institutions, which led to frequent interaction between printers in their time off duty. Salaman (1974) studied a small occupational community of railwaymen in Cambridge. They interacted socially mainly with each other, and 47 per cent of them said they had four or more workmates as friends. The irregular hours of work was one reason why workmates were friendly with each other rather than with members of the wider community. It seems probable that the traditional occupational communities centred round mines, steelworks, harbours or railway stations are breaking down. Technological change has meant that undertakings have increased in size, and urban planning has ensured that the locations of workplace and home are separated. Chadwick-Jones (1969) studied the break up of occupational communities which formerly were centred around the small tinplate hand-rolling mills in South Wales. The mills were situated in the same villages or townships in which the workers lived. They walked to and from work together and the work itself was arduous and dangerous. The small works were then abandoned for a large automated plant set at some distance from where the workers lived. They changed from a discontinuous three-shift system to continuous three-shifts. The occupational community tended to disintegrate as it was impossible to maintain the former level of social interaction.

17.4 WOMEN ON SHIFTWORK

Women have traditionally worked double day shift but they have been prevented from working at night by legislation. This is usually based on the International Labour Organization's conventions designed to protect women and young persons. Many countries have ratified the conventions but this is not the case in the United Kingdom because it is possible to obtain exemption orders from the protective legislation, and the number of these for women on nightwork has been increasing in recent years. This is one reason why there has been a growing interest in research on women engaged in shiftwork. Another reason has been the concern of the Equal Opportunities Commission which feels that protective legislation confined to women denies them opportunities, including the higher earnings on shiftwork, and changes in legislation are required. Whatever the legislation, there will always be some industries, such as the health services, where women will be employed at night.

The scanty evidence suggests that there is 'no general physiological or medical contradiction for women's night work' (Carpentier and Cazamian, 1977), but examination of the social and domestic consequences of nightwork on women presents a different picture. Charles and Brown (1981; Brown and Charles, 1982) studied the social and domestic effects of shiftwork on women, including a few nightworkers. It was striking that the shift hours which were compatible with child-rearing, such as permanent nightshift or twilight shifts, attracted a large number of women with young children. Brown concluded that the constraints of child care responsibilities coupled with financial need were two of the determinants in the women's choice of shift system worked. Gadbois (1981) reports similar results with nursing auxiliaries. Older women with children, but who are less qualified than the other staff, tended to work on fixed nightshifts which appeared to be due to the greater compatibility of fixed hours of work with the special needs of mothers of young children. In the Paris area rotating shifts were introduced for young nurses, and fixed nightshifts were maintained for nursing auxiliaries who were mothers. To say that fixed nightshifts for mothers is compatible with their child-rearing responsibilities ignores the 'costs'. Gadbois shows that married women nightworkers with children slept in the daytime 1 hour 20 minutes less than unmarried women. This was associated with getting the children off to school and doing housework before the mother went to bed. She was also more likely to interrupt her sleep in the middle of the day than the single woman. Gadbois writes, 'for women night workers with family responsibilities accomplishment of off-the-job tasks takes priority over daytime sleep'. Brown and Charles (1982) comment on the constant tiredness experienced by women shiftworkers and the interference which resulted with family relationships and social life.

Mention has been made of the movement towards joint family roles of husband and wife, but this has not proceeded far. Bunnage (1981) quotes the results from a Danish welfare survey which showed that although men spend some time on household tasks daily, and male shiftworkers spend more time working with their wives in the home than dayworkers, the division of labour still results in the bulk of the home tasks being done by the wife. The women shiftworkers may have an even heavier domestic workload than women on normal daywork, and it is clear that the shiftworkers have a double burden. Brown and Charles (1982) reached the same conclusion and write that women's nightworking 'takes place *without* any fundamental transformation of the sexual division of labour and at considerable cost to the women themselves'.

17.5 CONCLUSION

After a thorough review of the literature, Bunnage (1981) concluded that 'shift work interferes with the social and family life of shift workers more than it facilitates them', and from this there is no reason to dissent. Shiftworkers cite disturbance to social life with disturbance to sleep as the two most frequent adverse affects. There has been a large increase in the number of people working unsocial hours, which has sometimes been called the 'colonization of time'. The trend is unlikely to cease, but at the same time there has been a reduction in the hours individuals work. There is the probability that this trend will also continue and developed countries are on the threshold of a further substantial decline in hours worked. This permits shiftworkers to rearrange working hours and obtain large blocks of free time. What people do in this time and how it affects social and domestic life awaits research, but the outlook for shiftworkers is a lightening of the burden on them and their families.

Chapter 18

Individual Differences in Shiftwork Adjustment

Timothy H. Monk and Simon Folkard

CONTENTS

ABSTRACT

This chapter provides a summary of the various individual-difference measures, such as age, sex and personality, which can be used in an attempt to predict which people would find it hard, and which would find it easy, to cope with shiftwork. Each variable is considered in terms of the triad of factors (circadian rhythms, sleep and social/domestic adjustment) that govern shiftwork adjustment. Some of the less obvious variables, such as commitment to shiftwork and rhythm amplitude, are also discussed.

18.1 INTRODUCTION

From the individual's point of view, shiftwork involves having to work when you should be asleep, and having to sleep when you should be awake. Sadly, there is a significant proportion of the shiftworking population who find one or both of these almost impossible to live with, and whose lives are, as a consequence, made miserable. Clearly, if one could predict who these individuals were going to be, then they could be counselled against taking up shiftwork before they became engaged in it, and financially committed to it, thus sparing themselves considerable hardship. The question of which individuals will find it hard to cope with shiftwork and which will find it easy is thus of more than academic interest.

To the shiftworker himself, a main preoccupation of life becomes that of ensuring that he gets enough sleep. Recent surveys have shown that shiftworkers regard sleep as their prime problem (Rutenfranz *et al.*, 1977), and that they get an average of 7 hours less sleep per week than their dayworking counterparts (Bjerner and Swensson, 1953). It should be borne in mind, however, that sleep is merely one of a triad of factors that have to be 'just right' if one is to cope successfully with shiftwork. The other two factors in the triad are circadian rhythm adaptation and social and domestic adjustment. A failure in any one of the triad can effectively wreck a shiftworker's ability to cope with the situation. Thus, for example, a shiftworker's circadian rhythms might be well adjusted and his sleep hygiene good, but if these are won at the cost of rapidly deteriorating relationships with his wife and family, he would still be likely to seek a change to daywork.

Clearly, it is no use simply documenting differences in shiftwork adjustment between one individual and the next without any unifying classification. Thus, this chapter will be structured in terms of a variety of dimensions on which people differ, and by which one can divide people into groups. These groups can then be compared in their ability to cope with shiftwork, expressing the comparison in terms of the triad of factors mentioned above.

18.2 GENERAL FACTORS

18.2.1 Age

As the shiftworker progresses into his 50s, one might intuitively expect that, with regard to coping with shiftwork, things would start to get easier. His income would probably be increasing with seniority, bringing the opportunity of better housing; his family is likely to have grown up and left home, leaving fewer domestic responsibilities (and less noise!); his sleep need will have naturally decreased with age; and he is likely to have had several decades of experience in mastering the art of coping with shiftwork. Paradoxically, this is exactly what does *not* happen. Instead, as the shiftworker enters his 50s things start to get dramatically worse, rather than better. The question of why this should happen is one of the most crucial of shiftwork research, since it bears on the whole question of whether or not shiftwork is 'harmful'.

There is now fairly good evidence for a 'certain age' in the late 40s or early 50s at which, for some, shiftwork suddenly becomes intolerable (Akerstedt and Torsvall, 1981a). Alain Reinberg, one of the 'fathers' of shiftwork research, nicely characterizes it as the time of life at which glasses become needed for reading. The analogy is a good one, for the change is a combination of a gradual deterioration in ability, punctuated by an irrevocable admission of defeat.

It is possible to consider ageing effects within the framework of four possible contributory factors: (i) cumulative adverse shiftwork effects (since age is usually associated with experience); (ii) general weakening of the worker's health and ability to cope with stressors; (iii) flattening of circadian rhythms; and (iv) tendency towards sleep fragility and/or 'morningness' (see later section).

Clearly, the first factor is the most disturbing, since it suggests that prolonged experience of shiftwork may indeed be harmful. Foret *et al.* (1981) sought to separate out the usually confounded effects of age and experience in relation to sleep hygiene in a sample of about 750 shiftworkers in an oil refinery. As expected, older (over 40 years) shiftworkers reported poorer sleep and greater use of sleeping pills than their younger colleagues. More importantly, Foret *et al.* showed that *even within a particular age group,* the longer the experience with shiftwork, the poorer the sleep hygiene. Thus, experience with shiftwork does have an effect on sleep quality and sleeping pill use which is *not* simply a function of the increased age of the worker. Fortunately, Foret *et al.* were also able to demonstrate that this did not carry over to vacations, and that the deterioration was thus unlikely to be irreversible.

The second factor in the classification is in terms of the general weakening in health, and intolerance to change which characterizes the passing of the years. This is an aspect of shiftwork that regards it as a stressor, which, although not necessarily harmful *per se*, has the potential for exacerbating any new or existing problems for the shiftworker. Thus the problems themselves (poor health, family troubles, etc.) might not usually be insurmountable, but when combined with shiftwork they can interact to produce a situation which is intolerable (Monk and Folkard, 1983). Problems associated with the changes that come with age clearly fit into this category, and the 'stressor' explanation is thus certainly a plausible one.

The gradual flattening of circadian rhythms that occurs with increased age has now been well-documented in a number of studies (e.g. Weitzman *et al.*, 1982). As is discussed below, there is held to be a relationship between small rhythm amplitude and phase lability which can lead to difficulties in coping with shiftwork (Reinberg *et al.*, 1980). Thus, this too must be considered as a contributory factor.

Finally, and perhaps most importantly, there is the general deterioration in 'sleeping performance' that is characteristic of increased age. This deterioration is characterized by a rise in the number of wakenings during sleep, and a reduction in the total number of hours slept (Weitzman *et al.*, 1982). It can also be characterized by a change in phase, such that the individual tends to be more of a 'morning' than an 'evening' type (see below). Since sleep (particularly morning sleep) is so important to the shiftworker, it seems very likely that this general sleep fragility might, in conjunction with the other three factors mentioned above, be sufficient to outweigh any of the positive aspects of decreased sleep *need*.

In conclusion, the problem of ageing in shiftwork is not due to a single underlying factor. Rather, it would appear to be a complex interaction of many different factors, tending to affect the circadian rhythm and sleep components of the triad. It is only the social and domestic factors which seem to improve with increased age. Sadly, with regard to coping with shiftwork, the related factor of experience appears to weigh in as a negative attribute, rather than a positive one.

18.2.2 Sex differences

As Gadbois (1981) has pointed out, nightwork for women was forbidden by an international convention in 1948, and in theory at least is still outlawed in many countries. The main exception to this is, of course, provided by the nursing profession which involves many thousands of women in nightwork. Also, there has recently been a trend, largely stemming from antidiscriminatory ideas and legislation, for women to become more involved in nightwork and shiftwork. However, the fact remains that the vast majority of non-nursing shiftworkers are male, and that most studies of shiftworkers have been studies of *male* shiftworkers. Perhaps as a consequence of this, there is remarkably little published evidence for any difference between the sexes in ability to cope with shiftwork.

One obvious question that arises in considering the female shiftworker is whether there is a problem of menstrual dysrhythmia. Female airline personnel who are subject to repeated transmeridianal flights often complain of this problem, and it might also be expected to follow from the rapid changes in schedule required by shiftwork. Incidental evidence on the question is provided by Tasto and Colligan (1978) who, as part of a large-scale shiftwork survey, obtained menstrual cycle information from two groups of female shiftworkers. Unfortunately, though, the results appeared contradictory, with the nurses showing a very different pattern of results from those of the food processors, and both sets achieving statistical reliability. Thus, although there was some evidence for increased menstrual dysrhythmia in rotating shiftworkers, the evidence was by no means conclusive.

Gadbois (1981) concluded that it is probably best to regard any differences between men and women in ability to cope with shiftwork as springing primarily from social and domestic pressures rather than from any inherent differences in biology. Unlike her male counterpart, the female shiftworker is very often expected to perform extensive household management duties when she returns home from work. Any differences that there are in biological terms are likely, in the present Western culture at least, to be so swamped by the domestic factors that they become irrelevant.

18.2.3 Personality

There are reliable differences in circadian rhythm characterstics between one personality type and another (see Chapter 3). One might thus expect that differences might also exist in the rate with which such rhythms re-entrain to the new schedules required by shiftwork. Colquhoun and Folkard (1978) confirmed this to be true, with the slight difference in phase between (normally diurnal) neurotic introverts and neurotic extraverts being associated with quite a dramatic difference in rate of phase adjustment to both jet-lag and shiftwork situations. Thus, neurotic extraverts showed better phase adjustment than neurotic introverts, and in situations where phase adjustment is to be encouraged (i.e. slowly rotating or permanent shifts) they might thus be expected to cope more easily with shiftwork.

Looking at the problem from a different perspective, Nachreiner (1975) found that people who scored high on the 'neurotic' scale also tended to be the ones who complained most about shiftwork and were more likely to transfer to daywork. This finding raises the question of whether an inability to cope well with shiftwork 'causes' personality changes (as measured by the standard tests) or whether it is an underlying personality trait which leads to poor adjustment to shiftwork. Evidence that causality cannot be wholly ruled out is provided by Meers *et al.*'s (1978) longitudinal study of shiftworkers in a Belgian wire mill. This study revealed that exposure to shiftwork resulted in a change in personality (or, rather, in the responses to personality test questions) towards the neurotic end of the scale. It is thus a distinct possibility that 'shiftwork makes you neurotic'.

Combining the two sets of research results, we are left with the conclusion that stable extraverts are likely to be the ones who are most able to cope with shiftwork, and neurotic introverts the ones who are least able. This difference would appear to exist primarily in the 'circadian rhythm' and 'social and domestic' components of the triad, rather than in the sleep component. However, the usual caveats about the situation, the individual and the shiftwork system still apply. What is really needed in order to answer the question more definitively is a large-scale longitudinal study in which a cohort of new shiftworkers can be followed throughout their shiftworking careers.

18.2.4 Level of commitment

This category is rather different from those of age, sex and personality. However, it does represent a meaningful division between shiftworkers, and is one of the most powerful effects to be discussed in this chapter. Indeed, certain of the more recognized individual differences (e.g. sex) can be viewed as being primarily mediated by differences in level of commitment.

By 'level of commitment' we mean the degree to which the shiftworker is willing or able to structure his or her life around the need to work at unusual hours. The most obvious indicant of a lack of commitment is the practice of 'moonlighting' (or perhaps more accurately in the shiftworker's case, 'daylighting') in which the shiftworker holds down a second job during his time off. Thus, for example, a fireman might have a window-cleaning business during the day, or a night nurse fill in with 'relief nursing' during her time off. Almost by definition, *any* moonlighting will involve shiftwork within either the primary or the secondary job, and is thus likely to result in shiftwork coping problems.

A lack of commitment to shiftwork may also result from other causes. As mentioned above, in the case of female shiftworkers, extensive household and child care functions are often expected of the worker during her time off, and thus severely limit the time available for recreation and sleep. An illustration of this is provided by a study of full-time (4 nights per week) and part-time (2 nights per week) night nurses carried out by Folkard *et al.* (1978). Few (36 per cent) of the full-timers had children living with them at home compared to the part-timers (96 per cent), and there was anecdotal evidence that some of the part-timers might have additionally been 'moonlighting' during the day. The study took place over the first 2 nights of a run of duty following some time off. From the sleep records of the two groups shown in Figure 18.1, it is clear that the full-timers were able to make more of a commitment to nightwork than the part-timers in their ability to

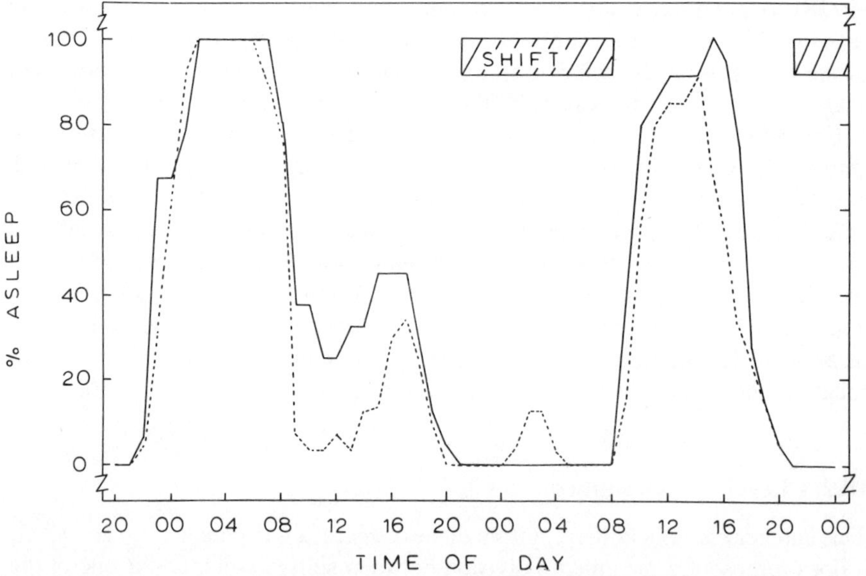

Figure 18.1 The percentage of full-time (solid line) and part-time (dotted line) night nurses asleep before, during and after the first of a period of successive nightshifts

'sleep-in' later in the morning, to take afternoon naps prior to coming on shift, and to sleep between two shifts. Indeed, some of the part-timers remained so diurnal in their orientation that they even took brief naps during their 'lunch' hour, in the middle of the nightshift.

This difference in commitment between the groups was reflected in equivalent differences in the adjustment of physiological circadian rhythms (oral temperature, urinary electrolyte secretion). There were also differences between the groups in feelings of malaise and alertness halfway through the nightshift. Thus, in terms of the triad of factors, the lack of commitment was reflected in poorer adjustment in both sleep hygiene and circadian rhythms which was probably a consequence of social and domestic pressures.

18.3 CIRCADIAN RHYTHM PARAMETERS

There has been considerable interest shown in the idea that individual differences in the ability to adjust to shiftwork might be related to differences in the various parameters of an individual's 'normal' circadian rhythms. Most of this research has concentrated on individual differences in phase (see Chapter 3), although recently authors have also considered the amplitude and stability/lability of circadian rhythms. In some cases these individual differences in the parameters of circadian rhythms have been measured objectively, but this requires considerable effort on behalf of both the shiftworkers and researchers. Nor is it clear that such an objective assessment would ever prove feasible for counselling and/or selection purposes. In view of this, other researchers have developed subjective questionnaire techniques for assessing individual differences in circadian rhythm parameters, the most notable being the morningness/eveningness questionnaire that attempts to distinguish between individuals with an early or late phase, respectively.

Before considering the research results from the studies in this area, it is worth commenting on two fundamental problems that affect most, if not all, of the results obtained from these studies. The first problem is a methodological one that is particularly important in the case of studies that have objectively assessed the individual shiftworker's 'normal' circadian parameters. This assessment clearly needs to be based on 'normal days' when the shiftworker is fully entrained to a nychthemeral routine. Unfortunately, the nature of most shift systems is such that days of this type seldom, if ever, occur outside the annual holiday period (a time when most shiftworkers would be unwilling to take the necessary recordings). Thus, researchers have been forced to base their estimates of an individual shiftworker's circadian parameters on data collected when his rhythm may have been adjusting to or from his shift system. The estimated parameters will thus confound individual differences in the 'normal' rhythm with those in the degree of the disruption or adjustment of it. This confounding may also affect the way in which an individual shiftworker completes a subjective questionnaire on his circadian parameters.

The second problem is conceptual in nature and concerns the direction of causality between individual differences in circadian parameters and adjustment to shiftwork. If individual differences in circadian parameters are ever to be used to *predict* differences in adjustment, then it has to be shown that they *cause* them.

All the studies in this area have been cross-sectional in nature, and it is thus possible that long-term differences in adjustment to shiftwork have resulted in any differences found in 'normal' circadian parameters. The only solution to this problem appears to be the use of longitudinal studies in this area, of the sort pioneered by Meers *et al.* (1978) for personality. Experimental studies of shiftwork that examine individual differences in the adjustment of the circadian rhythms of non-shiftworkers avoid this problem, but beg the question as to whether such short-term adjustment bears any relationship to the long-term ability to cope with shiftwork.

18.3.1 Phase differences

Most studies of the relationship between phase differences and adjustment have used the subjective questionnaire approach originated by Oquist (1970) and subsequently developed by Patkai (1971a, 1971b) and Ostberg (1973b; see also Horne and Ostberg, 1976, for an English-language version). This approach involves the use of a pencil and paper questionnaire about daily habits and preferences to divide people into 'morning types', 'intermediate types' and 'evening types'. It is often characterized as a division of people into 'morning larks' or 'night owls'. On the whole, it would appear that evening types are better able to cope with shiftwork than morning types. Thus, for example, morning types are the ones more likely to want to transfer to daywork (Akerstedt and Torsvall, 1981b). There are two ways in which morningness can be considered to take effect, corresponding to the 'circadian rhythm' and 'sleep' components of our initial triad.

There is believed to be a link between 'morningness' and natural ('free running') endogenous circadian period. Thus, it is thought that if they were to be isolated from all time cues, morning types would show a circadian rhythmicity of shorter period than that of evening types (see Chapter 3). However, the evidence for this relationship is far from conclusive (Folkard and Monk, 1981). If such a link were to exist, though, the advantage to evening types would be clear, particularly in forward-rotating (morning–afternoon–night) shift systems, where a series of phase delays (stretchings of the circadian rhythm) are required (Folkard and Monk, 1981).

The other way in which morningness effects can be regarded is solely in terms of the sleep component; in particular, sleep during the morning and early afternoon. Characteristically, the shiftworker fills his time in the order *work–sleep–recreation,* as compared to the order *work–recreation–sleep* which is typical of the dayworker. This means that the shiftworker on evening and night shifts is usually trying to get his sleep during the morning. Indeed, one can predict that the sooner the shiftworker wakes during the late morning or early afternoon, the greater will be his sleep debt. Thus, the problem with the morning type is that (almost by definition) he feels that at his most alert and wakeful during the morning, as compared to the evening type, whose ideal is to 'sleep-in' until lunchtime. So the morning-type's predispositions, whilst commendable for a diurnal '9–5' worker, can be disastrous for an evening- or night-working shiftworker (Hildebrandt and Stratman, 1979).

18.3.2 Rhythm amplitude

Recently, a considerable body of research — due mainly to Reinberg and his associates (see Reinberg *et al.*, 1980) — has been stimulated by Aschoff,'s (1978b) suggestion that if a rhythm's amplitude is comparatively small, it will adjust more rapidly to a change in schedule. This notion is very plausible, since one of the first stages in circadian rhythm re-entrainment (particularly for the shiftworker) is one of dramatic decreases in amplitude. The particular thesis that Reinberg *et al.* (1980) have put forward is that a person's circadian rhythm amplitude can be used as an indicant of the speed with which his circadian rhythms will adjust to a new schedule: i.e. how easily he can 'reset' his 'circadian clock', and thus how well he will be able to cope with shiftwork. In a series of experiments, Reinberg *et al.* have supported this thesis by finding significant negative correlations in shiftworkers between rhythm amplitude and amount of phase-shift.

Reinberg *et al.*'s subjects were on a comparatively rapid (3–4 day) shift rotation schedule, and for them rapid phase adjustment led to problems (i.e. those with the fastest phase adjustment suffered the worst malaise, etc.). However, for permanent nightworkers, rapid phase adjustment may be positively beneficial to workers' well-being on the nightshift (see, for example, Folkard *et al.*, 1978), while Colquhoun (1979) failed to find any relationship between rhythm amplitude and speed of adjustment to 'jet-lag' (see Chapter 21). Thus, although the rhythm amplitude thesis is potentially a most useful one for determining rate of phase adjustment, there is a clear need for further research (i) to examine its generality to different types of shift system, and (ii) to determine whether fast adjustment of circadian rhythms is indeed desirable.

18.3.3 Circadian type

Although traditional 'morningness' questionnaires (e.g. Horne and Ostberg, 1976) have met with some success, they have recently been criticized by a number of authors (e.g. Wendt, 1977; Torsvall and Akerstedt, 1980) on the grounds that they are not 'pure' measures of morningness, but rather confound two or more factors. Several 'purer' scales of morningness have been developed and have been successfully used by their authors (e.g. Torsvall and Akerstedt, 1980; Moog, 1981), although none has yet gained the widespread usage enjoyed by that of Horne and Ostberg.

A rather different approach was adopted by Folkard *et al.* (1979) who attempted to devise a more general 'circadian type questionnaire' (CTQ) with separate scales relating to the phase, amplitude and stability of circadian rhythms. The original purpose-built questionnaire was given to about 50 night nurses whose circadian rhythm adjustment was measured in a variety of physiological (oral temperature, urinary electrolytes) and psychological variables (Folkard *et al.*, 1979). Factor analysis of the questionnaire results yielded three main factors. The first of these concerned the rigidity or flexibility of sleeping and other daily habits, enabling a division to be made between rigid sleepers (R_s types) and flexible sleepers (F_s types). It seems probable that this factor relates to the stability or lability of an individual's circadian rhythms. The second factor concerned the ease with which individuals could overcome drowsiness when they had to, dividing people into vigorous (V) and languid (L) types, and may be related to rhythm amplitude. The third factor was one of morningness and thus presumably relates to phase.

In their initial study, Folkard *et al.* found that, in general, F_s types showed better circadian adjustment that R_s types, and V types better adjustment than L types. Additionally, R_s types complained of more disturbance of their day sleep by noise than did F_s types. Thus, in both 'circadian rhythm' and 'sleep' components of our triad, these two scales of the CTQ were able to predict which subjects might be less able to cope with shiftwork. Subsequent unpublished studies, including those by Costa *et al.*, Frese *et al.* and Vidacek (some of which are reviewed by Folkard *et al.*, 1982; see also Costa and Gaffuri, 1983), have also found these scales to relate to differences in the social and subjective health problems of shiftworkers. In none of these studies, however, was the morningness scale of the CTQ found to relate to any measure of adjustment. While this failure could simply reflect a poor scale of morningness, it could alternatively imply that the success met with by the more traditional morningness scales is due to their confounding of different factors. It may be that it is not morningness or phase *per se* that is important, but other circadian parameters that have been confounded with phase in these questionnaires. Some support for this contention can be derived from the recent finding that R_s scores from the CTQ correlate better with general measures of adjustment to shiftwork than do Horne and Ostberg's morningness scores (Vidacek, personal communication). Whatever the case, it would appear that this general approach is a fruitful one, and that future studies could profitably include this questionnaire as well as the more traditional ones.

18.4 CONCLUSIONS

In a chapter such as this it is very tempting to end with a list of broad generalizations of the form 'Xs will cope better with shiftwork than Ys'. However, although it is possible to make some generalizations (e.g. morning types and neurotic introverts are more likely to have problems), one cannot ignore all of the caveats and qualifications that make such generalizations so risky. The major of these is the question of whether circadian phase adjustment is desirable, or to be avoided. The answer to that question depends not only upon the type of shift system being worked, but also on the nature of the tasks being performed (Folkard and Monk, 1979), and the number of days off that are available for recovery (Rutenfranz *et al.*, 1977).

It thus seems unlikely that we will ever reach a position where we can distinguish between people who are suited and those who are not suited to shiftwork in general. An individual may be able to cope extremely well with one form of shiftwork, but not at all with another. The way ahead would appear to demand an integrated approach that takes account of both differences between individuals *and* differences between shift systems.

Hours of Work
Edited by S. Folkard and T.H. Monk

Chapter 19

Shiftwork and Performance

Timothy H. Monk and Simon Folkard

CONTENTS

ABSTRACT

This chapter discusses the various factors that govern a shiftworker's performance. Although the prime emphasis is on either circadian performance rhythms and their adjustment or sleep deprivation effects, it is recognized that the process is a multifaceted and interactive one. Other factors, associated with the constraints of the job, and the situation and needs of the worker, are also discussed. The area is thus viewed in the context of the various factors discussed in the three preceding chapters.

19.1 INTRODUCTION

At about 0400 h on Wednesday, 28th March 1979, a series of events occurred in a quiet control room which brought the topic of this chapter into sharp focus in news media around the world. The 'Three Mile Island Incident' occurred because of human error, and the humans involved were weekly rotating shiftworkers, halfway through their nightshift (Ehret, 1981). The errors involved may have jeopardized the safety not only of the shiftworkers themselves, but also of thousands of people in surrounding communities. This incident thus accelerated the growing awareness that the study of shiftworkers' performance is not merely a quibbling discussion about a few percentage points of worker productivity or vague notions of subjective health. It is, potentially, a vital issue affecting the public safety, and considerable amounts of money.

Assessing the extent to which shiftwork affects the worker's productivity and safety is one of the most complex problems facing shiftwork researchers. This complexity stems not only from the influence of task demands on both time-of-day effects in performance efficiency and the oscillatory control underlying them (Chapter 4), but also from the influence of sleep deprivation effects (Chapter 6), subjective and objective health effects (Chapter 16), motivation effects (which will be influenced by social and family problems — Chapter 17), and the effects of interindividual differences on both normal rhythm parameters (Chapter 3), and the rate at which such parameters readjust to a change in routine (Chapter 18).

Although it represents something of an oversimplification, the conceptual model of Folkard and Monk (1979), which is illustrated in Figure 19.1, represents a useful framework in which to consider these effects. Essentially, the model reinforces the point that the 'on-shift' performance of the shiftworker is the product of many different factors, some interacting directly, others having their effect through changes in the adjustment process.

The three major inputs to the system are task demands (i.e. the levels of vigilance, physical and cognitive work required of the individual), the particular shift system used (very different effects spring from fixed (permanent) shifts than from rotating schedules, for example), and interindividual differences (including the worker's personality, age, health, sleep needs and behaviour patterns). These factors will then serve to affect the adjustment process in performance function (circadian performance rhythms), affective state (circadian rhythms in subjective vigilance and well-being), and physiological functions (sleep being the most crucial, but also the circadian rhythms in temperature and neuroendocrine function). The interaction of those adjustment effects will then influence the worker's on-shift performance, both directly and through indirect effects on his subjective health and well-being. Thus, one cannot simply assert that a nightshift performance will be poor because the worker is then 'at a low ebb'. That assertion may be quite wrong for some tasks, and certainly is remiss in leaving out the sleep deprivation, health and motivational effects that can often outweigh the strictly circadian ones.

Despite the undoubted importance of the social, domestic and subjective health factors governing a shiftworker's performance, much of the research in this area has adopted a strictly circadian point of view. Most studies have been concerned primarily with circadian performance rhythms and their adjustment rates, or the effects on performance of partial sleep deprivation. The neglect of the other factors (including those related to interindividual differences) stems from the major difficulties that arise when one tries to study them using the usual

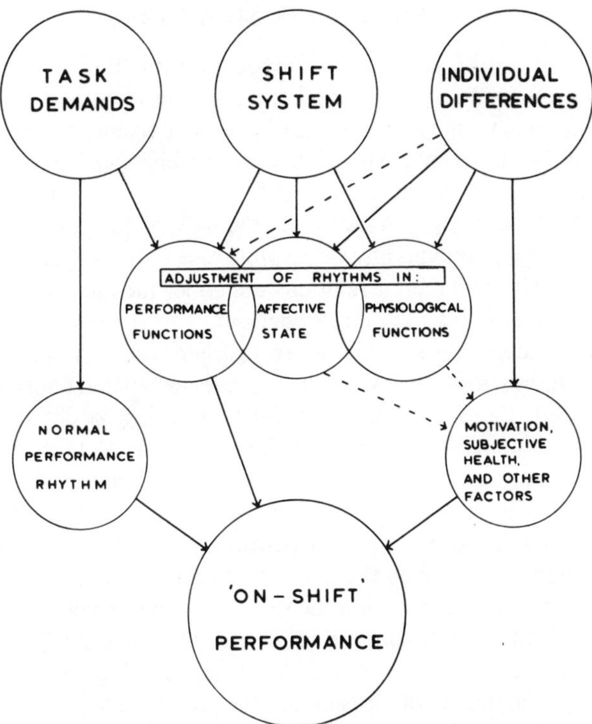

Figure 19.1 A conceptual model of the factors affecting 'on-shift' performance. Solid lines represent known influences, and dashed lines probable ones. From Folkard and Monk (1979)

laboratory and field techniques. By their very nature, laboratory shiftwork studies are concerned with only a few subjects (thus ruling out interindividual comparisons), and cannot be concerned with factors such as the need to run a household, do the shopping and have a reasonable social life. Conversely, field studies are heavily constrained by the limits of situation. Thus, the workers can only devote relatively little time to performance tests, and the more satisfactory 'real task' performance measures are very often either a group average, or confounded by factors such as production line speed and machine maintenance. Also, there are often methodological problems involved in deciding which shiftworkers are the most socially and/or domestically disadvantaged.

In reading this chapter, one should thus bear in mind that circadian and sleep deprivation effects are but a small part of the interaction of factors serving to influence a shiftworker's performance. The factors discussed in Chapters 16, 17 and 18 may have as much impact on the problem of 'Shiftwork and Performance' as those discussed in the present one.

19.2 REAL TASK MEASURES

As any worthy industrial psychologist or sociologist will testify, it is incredibly difficult to gain entry into a factory or other working environment for the purposes of objective scientific inquiry. Usually, the management will only let the researcher in if they have an axe to grind regarding changes in procedures and/or production quotas, and the unions will only let the researcher in if they have a grievance or a claim pending. Most often, the lack of acceptance by one or the other of these groups precludes any worthwhile research being done. If everything *is* running smoothly, and labour relations are good, then a 'don't rock the boat' attitude will often still keep the researcher out.

As a consequence, there are very few researchers who have been able to carry out good field studies of shiftwork. Moreover, even when that considerable hurdle has been jumped, there are major problems in trying to determine intershift differences in 'real task' performance. The most important of these is the difference in working environments. Not only lighting levels, but also supervision levels, group morale, and distractions can all be very different indeed between nightshifts and dayshifts. Also, poorer performance can occur on the nightshift simply because there is nobody there to repair broken machines (Meers, 1975). Not only the work environment, but the work itself may be quite different on the nightshift. Very often particular parts of the job are actually saved for the nightshift, either because the process demands it (preparing things for shipment in the morning), or to make life easier for the nightworkers (e.g. long-running computer jobs held back in order to be run at night). Even in continuous-process operations, complicated development work may intrude during the day, but not at night.

Despite all these problems and complications, there are a few studies that have been able to obtain relatively continuous 24-hour 'real task' data, and indeed these studies show a remarkable similarity in time-of-day function (Figure 19.2).

The six studies can be divided into three that actually measure the speed (Browne, 1949; Wojtczak-Jaroszowa and Pawlowska-Skyba, 1967) or accuracy (Bjerner and Swensson, 1953) with which the primary task is done, and three that measure the consequences of lapses in attention or vigilance (Prokop and Prokop, 1955; Hildebrandt *et al.*, 1974; Folkard *et al.*, 1978). All six are in agreement in showing performance to be worse during the night hours, although in three of them there is also evidence of a pronounced post-lunch dip of almost equivalent magnitude. Thus, it would seem reasonable to assert that, in general, nightshift performance is inferior to dayshift performance. However, as we have been careful to point out, there are a number of different ways in which nightshift performance can be degraded, not all of them directly circadian. Additionally, it is possible that differences in motivation level can differentially affect time-of-day functions. Khaleque and Verhaegen (1981) showed this in a comparison of cigar-making speeds between morning and afternoon shifts; significantly time-of-day

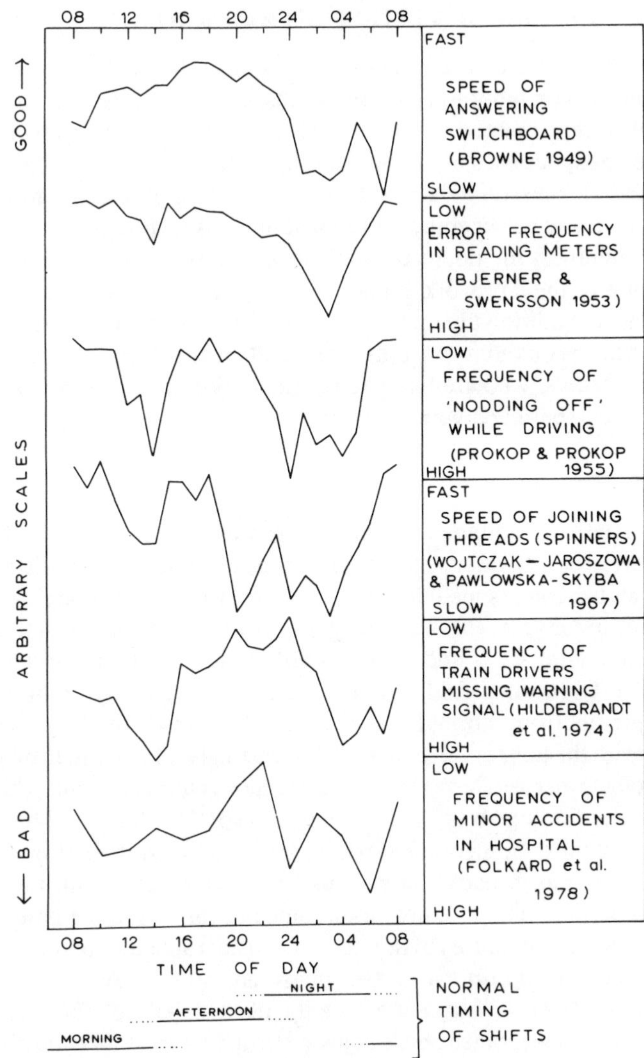

Figure 19.2 Variations in 'real job' measures over the 24-h period. From Folkard and Monk (1979)

differences only appeared in highly stressed workers who were making considerable efforts to gain extra piecework bonuses. Thus, it is possible that circadian effects can only 'show through' when workers are under pressure. In the absence of such pressure, nightworkers may be able to equate dayshift and nightshift performances because both are considerably suboptimal.

19.3 SIMULATED SHIFTWORK STUDIES

Because of the multitude of problems that occur in the field, many researchers have concentrated on laboratory shiftwork studies. In addition to avoiding all the problems of access mentioned above, the study can be made much 'cleaner' avoiding the idiosyncrasies of most actual shift rotas, and the irregularities due to vacations and sickness. There are, however, considerable costs to be paid in terms of realism and applicability. The most obvious factors that are ignored are those stemming from the domestic and social situations of the worker, and the chronic nature of the shiftwork experience with its propensity for a build-up of negative effects. Additionally, there is a tendency to use student volunteers in the laboratory, who may exhibit very different circadian and sleep need characteristics from actual workers, who are likely to be older (Weitzman *et al.*, 1982) and to have had more experience with shiftwork.

19.3.1 Circadian studies

During the 1960s, Colquhoun and his associates at Cambridge performed an extensive series of laboratory experiments that were designed to determine the optimum watchkeeping schedules for naval personnel. These are described in greater detail in Chapter 20. Various patterns of watchkeeping schedule were considered, including 4-, 8- and 12-hour spells of duty (Colquhoun *et al.*, 1968a, 1968b, 1969). The tasks considered were usually of a relatively simple nature. As one would predict from 'normal' day studies (Chapter 4), these tasks showed a parallelism with the temperature rhythm. Interestingly, this parallelism persisted, even during the process of entrainment to the new routine, a result which was in line with earlier findings by Kleitman and Jackson (1950a,b), who used fairly similar types of task. In theoretical terms, this reinforced the notion of a single performance rhythm, broadly parallel to, and predictable from, the circadian temperature rhythm. The practical importance of this result stemmed from the findings that the temperature rhythm took a considerable number of days on the new routine even to *approach* perfect phase adjustment. As we have seen in Chapter 15, at least 12 days are usually needed before, for example, the temperature rhythm becomes phase adjusted to nightwork. Since the night part of the circadian cycle in both temperature and (simple repetitive) task performance is lower than the 'day' part, the slow rates of phase adjustment provide an obvious explanation for the impaired nightshift performance observed in 'real task' measures (Figure 19.2). These findings have been used to support the view that stable hours of work (i.e. fixed shift systems) are preferable, since they allow phase adjustment of the circadian system, and thus (theoretically, at least) nightshift performance that is as good as that on the dayshift (Wilkinson and Edwards, 1968).

Although the parallelism between circadian temperature and performance rhythms can be quite striking (Chapter 4), it must be remembered that the relationship between the two is probably *not* directly causal. Thus, Moses *et al.* (1978) showed that when time of day was held constant, and temperature and performance levels were compared in a 40-hour napping study, no significant correlations emerged. Moreover, recent studies, using a broad spectrum of performance tests, have revealed different rates of phase adjustment for different tasks. In the mid-1970s, Hughes and Folkard (1976) gave subjects both simple repetitive tasks (simple serial search, manual dexterity) and more complex cognitive ones (mathematical additions, verbal reasoning). Six subjects in an isolated community inverted their routine, and the degree of phase adjustment was measured on the ninth and tenth consecutive nights. Urine flow temperature was used as a marker rhythm. As can be seen in Figure 19.3, there were marked differences between the tasks, with the more cognitive ones showing greater phase adjustment than either the body temperature rhythm or the simple repetitive tasks.

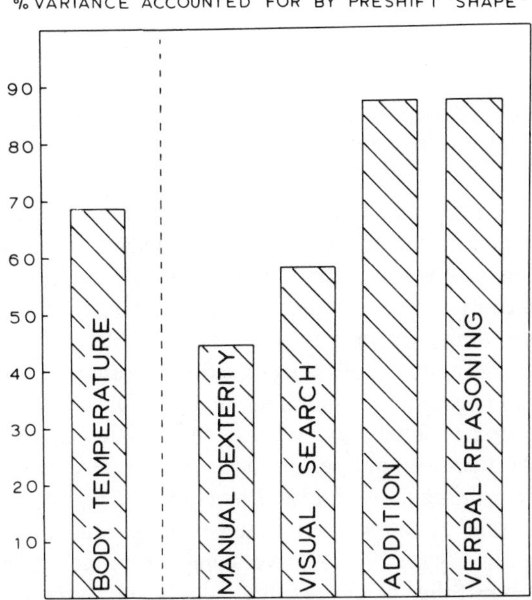

Figure 19.3 The degree of adjustment of performance and temperature rhythms at the end of a 10-day period of successive nightshifts. After Hughes and Folkard (1976)

This result was confirmed in a laboratory study of 21 consecutive nightshifts by Monk *et al.* (1978). Two subjects performed low- and high-memory load versions of a performance test every 4 hours, around the clock. Figure 19.4 illustrates the average phase adjustment curves of the two measures, plotted together with that for the rectal temperature rhythm. Again, the more complex task showed the faster phase adjustment.

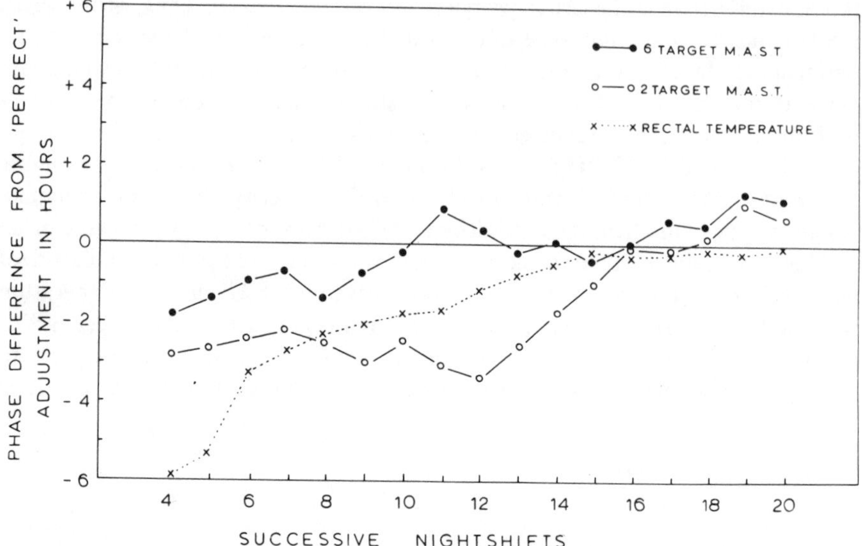

Figure 19.4 The phase adjustment of the circadian rhythms in the performance of high (6-target) and low (2-target) memory-loaded tasks, and in rectal temperature. After Monk *et al.* (1978)

These results (together with later ones regarding underlying oscillator control — see Chapter 4) indicate that the picture is very much more complicated than the simple 'parallelism with temperature' argument would suggest.

Because of the complexities detailed above, it may be that for some tasks the permanent or fixed shift system is in fact less desirable than the more rapidly rotating one. Thus, for more cognitive tasks, a diurnal orientation of the circadian system may actually *benefit* nightshift performance. This rather counterintuitive prediction was tested in a laboratory study by Folkard *et al.* (1976). Low-, medium- and high-memory load performance tests were given to two subjects working a rapidly rotating (2 mornings, 2 evenings, 2 nights, 2 days off) shift system. The resultant circadian performance curves and rectal temperature rhythm are plotted in Figure 19.5. By averaging across a complete cycle of the shift system, around the clock readings could be obtained without the contamination of sudden awakening effects. The shift rotation was sufficiently rapid for the subjects to retain a diurnal orientation, with the tempature rhythm showing a peak at about 1600 and a trough at about 0900. The simple version of the test (top panel) paralleled that trend very closely, but as the complexity increased the parallelism broke down, until for the complex version (bottom panel) best performance was in the early hours of the morning, and *worst* performance in the late afternoon. Thus, for the complex version of the task, performance was significanty better on the nightshift than on neither of the other shifts, and the prediction was verified.

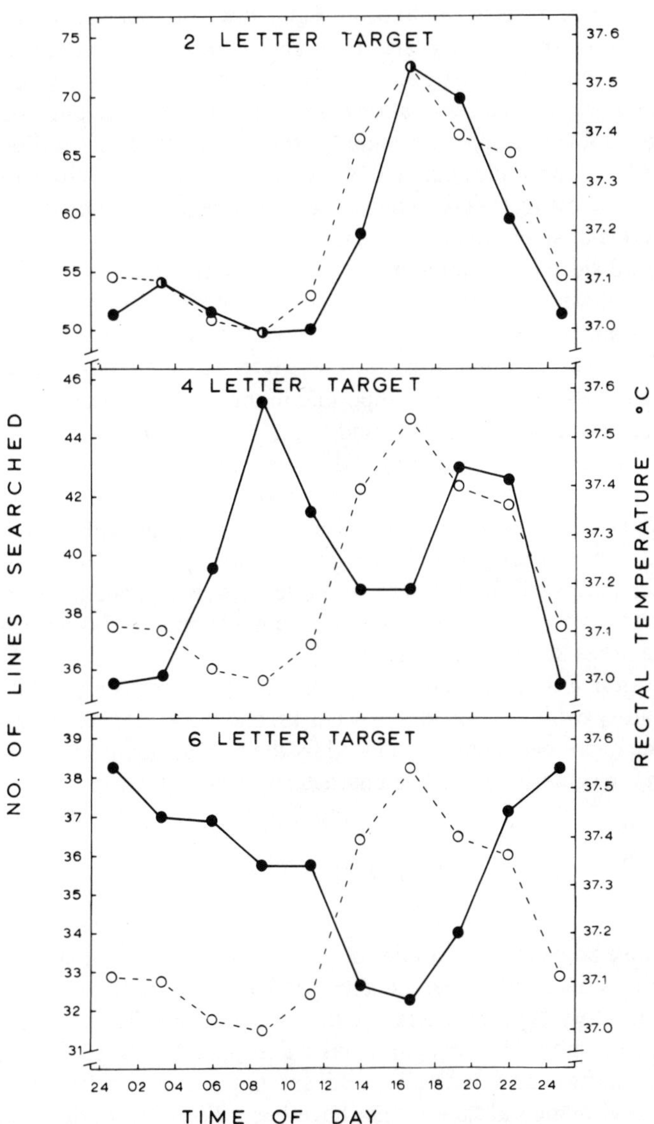

Figure 19.5 The circadian rhythm in low (2-target), medium (4-target) and high (6-target) memory-loaded performance (●——●), and in rectal temperature (0- - -0). After Folkard *et al.* (1976)

19.3.2 Sleep deprivation studies

To the shiftworker himself, sleep (or rather, the lack of it) is *the* major problem, and many shiftworkers would assert that if only their sleep problem could be cured, then everything else would be all right. It would thus seem reasonable to assume that many detrimental effects in shiftworker performance will accrue simply from a build-up of partial sleep deprivation. Chapters 5 and 6 provide extensive reviews of sleep deprivation effects on performance, and those reviews will not be duplicated here. Essentially, they indicate that sleep deprivation effects tend to be more pronounced in boring tasks, and those that are machine paced. Very interesting tasks can motivate the worker sufficiently that even quite dramatic levels of sleep deprivation can be overcome. Moreover, as one would expect, partial sleep deprivation effects are less robust than those of total sleep deprivation, with some authors finding no significant performance decrements (e.g. Rutenfranz *et al.*, 1972), although Wilkinson *et al.* (1966) did find decrements in vigilance performance when sleep was limited to 3 hours or less.

Other sleep-related factors are important in this respect. In a series of studies, Taub and his associates (e.g. Taub and Berger, 1976; Taub, 1978) have shown that small changes (under 3 hours) and general irregularities in the sleep–wake routine can produce significant decrements in performance efficiency. Also, both in shiftwork (Folkard *et al.*, 1984) and in jet-lag (Snyder, 1983) the intriguing possibility has been raised that performance failure can occur through something akin to 'sleep paralysis'. In this state, the sufferer is awake, but unable to move or speak for some minutes. Clearly, such a phenomenon must be borne in mind when considering areas such as pilot error.

In conclusion, although sleep deprivation effects are not totally robust, there is good laboratory evidence that for boring tasks, and those that are machine paced, performance decrements can be induced by the partial sleep deprivation and/or sleep-timing irregularities that are characteristic of shiftwork.

19.4 INTERPOLATED TASK STUDIES

A compromise between field studies of actual real task performance and totally artificial laboratory studies, can be achieved by asking shiftworkers to perform artificial laboratory-type tasks either at their workplace or immediately before or after coming on shift. This technique has the major advantage of using subjects who are real shiftworkers, with all the advantages in terms of demographics and social and environmental factors that have been discussed earlier, without the disadvantages of pooling and/or contamination that are characteristic of real task measures.

The disadvantages of the technique stem from the artifical nature of the tasks, which is obvious to the subjects and may bias their performance, either in a negative way (if they perceive the interpolated task to be trivial and irrelevant) or in a positive way (if they perceive it to be a contest in which much more effort is extended than in the primary job). In either case, the data is contaminated, and may not be a true measure of the shiftworkers' performance.

19.4.1 Circadian studies

An example of an interpolated task study is provided by Wojtczak-Jaroszowa *et al.* (1978), who administered three very brief (1-minute) performance tests to ten shiftworkers on rotating morning, afternoon and night shifts. The tests measured manual dexterity, and simple and complex serial search performance, and were given just before the start of the shift, and again after 4 and 8 hours of work. All three tests showed the nightshift to have the worst performance. For the manual dexterity and simple serial search tasks, the morning and afternoon shift performance levels were roughly comparable, but for the more complex serial search task the morning shift was clearly the better of the two. All three shifts showed 'within session' declines that were equivalent in magnitude to the circadian effects.

Costa *et al.* (1979) performed a similar interpolated task study on 18 weekly rotating nurses, giving a battery of tests including simple auditory reaction time, digit–symbol substitution and manual tracking. Testing was only once per shift, at about the middle. Although Costa *et al.* found the nightshift to be associated with the worst feelings of tiredness and perceived exertion, no significant differences were found in the performance measures. This may have been due to the fact that testing was carried out at the end of a run of duty, when adjustment effects would be maximal. There were, however, non-significant trends towards a nightshift inferiority.

Interpolated task studies were conducted by the present authors in order to test the laboratory prediction that for some tasks (in particular, those involving an immediate memory load), performance might actually be better on the nightshift than on the day or evening shifts. In the first (Monk and Folkard, 1978; Folkard and Monk, 1980), immediate and (28-day) delayed memory for a training film was tested following presentation at either 2030 h (prior to the nightshift) or 0400 h (in the middle of the nightshift). The 50 subjects were night nurses on either their first or their second night of a run of duty. To factor out phase adjustment effects, the subjects were divided into those who remained day-oriented ('unadjusted') and those who showed some adjustment (a flattening) in terms of the body temperature rhythm. As predicted by the laboratory studies, in the unadjusted subjects immediate recall was better following presentation at 0400 h than at 2030 h. Moreover, the theory-based prediction that the reverse would be true for delayed retention was also validated (see Chapter 4).

The second study (Monk and Embrey, 1981) was concerned with six process controllers working at a large automated chemical plant. The subjects were studied for one complete cycle (1 month) of their rapidly rotating 12 h shift system. Every 2 hours while on shift the subjects were asked to take their temperature, rate their alertness, and perform high- and low-memory load versions of a serial search task. Examination of the circadian temperature and subjective alertness rhythms confirmed that the subjects remained day-oriented, with a temperature peak at 2000 and a trough at 0600. As predicted by the laboratory studies, there was a significant negative correlation between the two versions of the task, with the more memory- loaded version showing better performance on the nightshift (1900–0700), than on the dayshift (0700–1900). This finding was, moreover, shown to generalize to the actual job the subjects were doing. For the month of the study, the computer that the process controllers used to control the plant was set to record automatically every human error that the process control program detected. The subjects' task was a complex cognitive one, requiring the input of device codes, temperatures and pressures, and the laboratory (and interpolated task) prediction was thus that performance would be better on the nightshift than during the day. As we can see from Figure 19.6, the prediction was validated, even when differences in usage rates between day and night were accounted for.

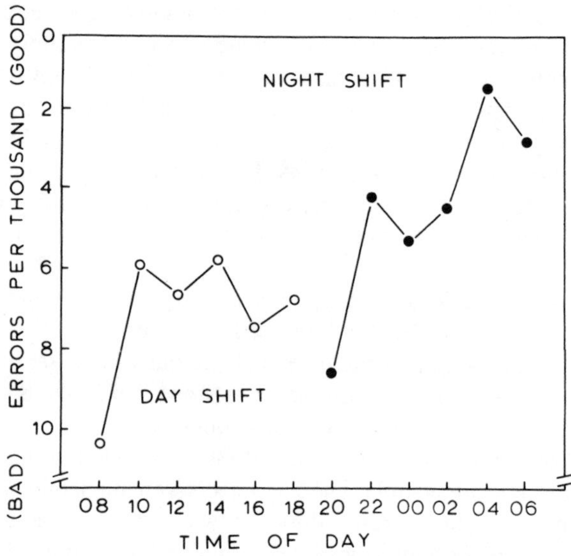

Figure 19.6 The trend in error rates over the day (0—0) and night (●—●) shifts, plotted on an inverted scale. After Monk and Embrey (1981)

19.4.2 Sleep deprivation studies

Although all studies of shiftworker performance must have circadian rhythms as a major area of interest, some studies have tended to focus on the sleep deprivation aspects, rather than the more strictly circadian ones. One of these is the 'work–sleep study' carried out by Tepas and his associates (Tepas *et al.*, 1981a,b). This comprehensive study brought actual shiftworkers into the sleep laboratory for polysomnography and performance testing while they continued to work, commuting from the laboratory rather than from home. Tepas *et al.* used a vigilance task presented just prior to bedtime, and a machine paced additions test at bedtime and upon awakening. The subjects comprised ten nightworkers, ten dayworkers and ten (slowly) rotating shiftworkers who were working days or evening shifts at the time of being recorded. Nightshift workers were the group that performed worst on all three performance tests (there being no reliable differences between the other two groups). The performance differences were not accompanied by any equivalent differences in body temperature, but *were* correlated with the polysomnographic data in a way that was typical of a subject undergoing chronic partial sleep deprivation.

Rather than bringing shiftworkers into the laboratory for polysomnography and performance assessment, Tilley *et al.* (1982) took the tests out to the field. Twelve shiftworkers were studied for one complete cycle of their weekly rotating shift system. The results were very similar to those found by Tepas *et al.*, with day sleeps appearing to be disrupted and of shorter duration than night sleeps. As one would predict from circadian considerations, reaction speeds (both simple and multiple choice) were slower on the nightshift. However, there was also strong evidence for a night-to-night deterioration in performance, which the authors interpreted in terms of a build-up of partial sleep deprivation. They concluded that rapid rotation of shifts, with shorter runs of night duty, might be more conducive to better sleep and performance.

In conclusion, these two thorough studies of shiftworker performance confirm (for the tasks they used) a nightshift inferiority, and also emphasize the importance of cumulative partial sleep deprivation effects in governing shiftworker performance.

19.5 ENVIRONMENTAL FACTORS

While this chapter has tended to concentrate upon effects stemming from the individual worker's interaction with the shift system, there are environmental aspects which will, for some jobs, have a considerable impact on his ability to perform. The most obvious is the absence of daylight on the nightshift. This is clearly of direct importance to truck, bus and train drivers, but can also be important in industrial settings which often rely in part on windows and skylights for ambient lighting. Moreover, it has recently become clear that the high lighting levels only achieved by daylight are necessary for the suppression of melatonin — a hormone shown to be important to the circadian system and a potential link to certain types of depression (Wehr and Goodwin, 1981).

A less obvious environmental factor is ambient temperature. In certain climates and for certain jobs (e.g. steelwork), the nightshift can be the *least* fatiguing, simply because it is the coolest (Oginski *et al.*, 1976). Ambient temperature can also affect the ability of the nightworker to sleep on a hot summer day (if air-conditioning is beyond his means), thus introducing a further seasonal influence on shiftworker performance. Such influences, like those of other stressors such as noise and fumes, must be regarded as an integral part of the shiftworker performance question.

19.6 CONCLUSIONS

From the above discussion, it is clear that there are many different ways that shiftworker performance can be improved. Unfortunately, it is also clear that there is no simple solution, and that the countermeasures proposed must take into account many different factors associated with the job and its constraints, and with the worker and his situation and needs. Thus, for example, one cannot even begin to advise on the optimum form of shift system without a knowledge of the task to be performed. However, the elimination of some of the grosser violations of the circadian biological system can lead to an improvement in morale and performance as Czeisler *et al.* (1982) have shown in a recent intervention study. Although it is generally agreed that weekly rotating by phase advance — i.e. mornings, nights, evenings — is a particularly *bad* shift system for shiftworker performance, to suggest the *best* form of shift system requires considerably more knowledge about the situation as a whole.

Hours of Work
Edited by S. Folkard and T.H. Monk

Chapter 20

Scheduling Watches at Sea

W. Peter Colquhoun and Simon Folkard

CONTENTS

ABSTRACT

The problem of scheduling watches for ships' crews at sea is closely bound up with the adjustment of circadian rhythms to unusual work–rest routines. Traditional 'fixed hours' watchkeeping systems with short watches inevitably result in split sleep. 'Rotating' systems maximize between-watch variations in performance efficiency, and on long voyages may lead to rhythm disintegration. Alternative systems have been devised for warships, but these may not be applicable to the civilian situation. A programme of research is proposed that takes account of factors such as jet-lag, the increasingly cognitive nature of the watchkeeper's task, and known individual differences in adaptability to shifted sleep–wake cycles.

20.1 INTRODUCTION

The problems of shiftwork, or 'watchkeeping', at sea are in some ways very different from those encountered ashore. Whereas a land-based shiftworker will usually travel home after each shift, the seafarer is confined to his place of work, i.e. his ship, for the duration of a voyage. Many personnel on board have no rest days or weekends off for this period. In addition, opportunities for social activities during a voyage are relatively limited compared to those ashore. These factors, together with the specific functions of the vessel concerned, have resulted in a considerable variety of watchkeeping routines, many of which are quite different from normal shiftworking rotas.

This chapter will consider the results of studies relevant to work-scheduling on both merchant and military vessels, in particular those undertaking prolonged transoceanic voyages. Such voyages are typically characterized by prolonged periods of relative inactivity while other conditions remain more or less constant. This situation is epitomized on nuclear submarines and, indeed, much of the research in this area has been concerned with the work–rest schedules on submersible vessels. Unfortunately, some of these schedules, as in all warships, differ fundamentally from those found in the merchant marine, and this complicates consideration of the optimal form of scheduling.

20.2 WATCHKEEPING SCHEDULES

On a voyage a ship has to function 'around the clock', necessitating at least some of its personnel being on duty at all times. Normally in both merchant vessels and warships the watchkeeping personnel are divided into three crews. Thus, the primary hours of duty of any given individual crew member amount to 8 out of 24, although both officers and ratings may have additional duties such as recordkeeping and management, or cleaning and maintenance.

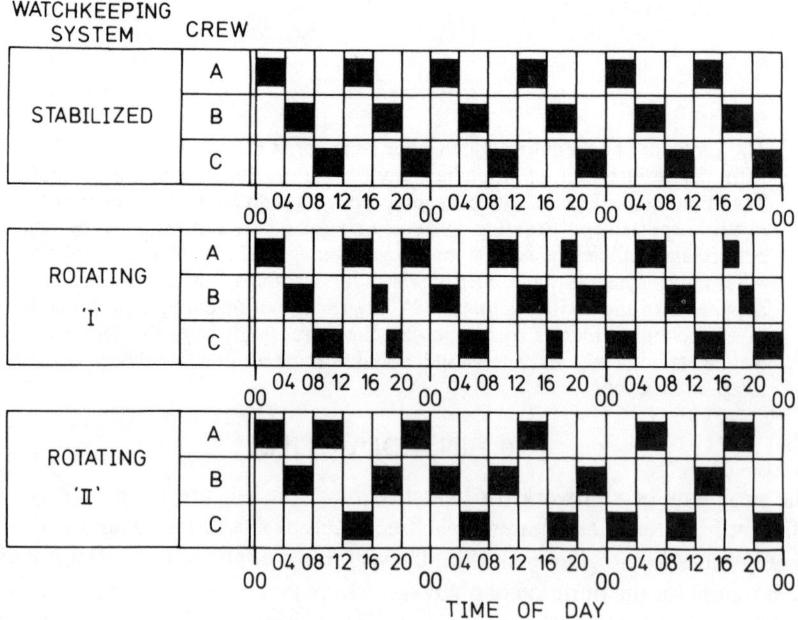

Figure 20.1 Examples of three-crew watchkeeping systems. The shaded areas represent the times 'on-watch'

Watchkeeping crews traditionally work for spells of a maximum length of 4 hours at a time, the 24 hours being divided into six watches based on midnight. These watches are commonly referred to as the 'middle' (0000–0400), 'morning' (0400–0800), 'forenoon' (0800–1200), 'afternoon' (1200–1600), 'dog(s)' (1600–2000) and 'first' (2000–0000). Most merchant mariners, and officers on warships, are assigned to a particular pair of these watches with two watches 'off' between duty spells. Such assignment results in the hours of duty being stabilized on a particular 4 hours on, 8 hours off schedule for any given individual, and in the merchant marine the assignment is often based on seniority. However, for a substantial proportion of a warship's crew, the 4-hour watches are not stabilized in this way, but, rather, change each day on a cyclical or 'rotating' basis. The two commonest rotating watchkeeping systems are illustrated in Figure 20.1, together with the stabilized 4 on, 8 off system.

The essential feature of the two rotating systems is that the sequence of work and rest periods repeats every 3 days. Both systems allow one full 'normal' night's sleep in three, and share out the 'unsocial' watch times among the three crews. System I is found on the warships of many countries, while System II is one of several employed by the British Royal Navy, where it is known as the 'West Country' routine. All three systems illustrated in Figure 20.1 have different variants, and are subject to minor modifications such as the staggering of change-over times to ensure continuity, or to fall in with meal and 'cleaning' times which normally remain fixed.

20.3 STUDIES OF THE THREE-CREW SYSTEMS

These three-crew systems, and certain alternatives to them, have been the subject of various seagoing and/or 'land-based simulation studies'. Unfortunately, the situational difference between sea and land has been found to affect some of the results, most probably because of the relative lack of social isolation of the individuals taking part in the land-based simulations.

20.3.1 Stablilized systems

Two seagoing studies have examined 4 on, 8 off systems in submariners, and have concentrated on their sleep–wake cycles and body temperature rhythms (Kleitman, 1949; Utterback and Ludwig, 1949). Both studies found that most individuals tended to take a sleep during *both* their 8-hour off-duty periods in each 24-hour span, since they were unable to obtain sufficient sleep during either one of them. Kleitman (1949) also observed that they rated these sleeps as poorer in quality than those obtained ashore. The bimodality of the sleep–wake cycle was paralleled by a similar bimodality in the temperature rhythm, such that body temperature was higher during the two periods when the individuals were awake, and lower during the two sleeps (see Figure 20.2).

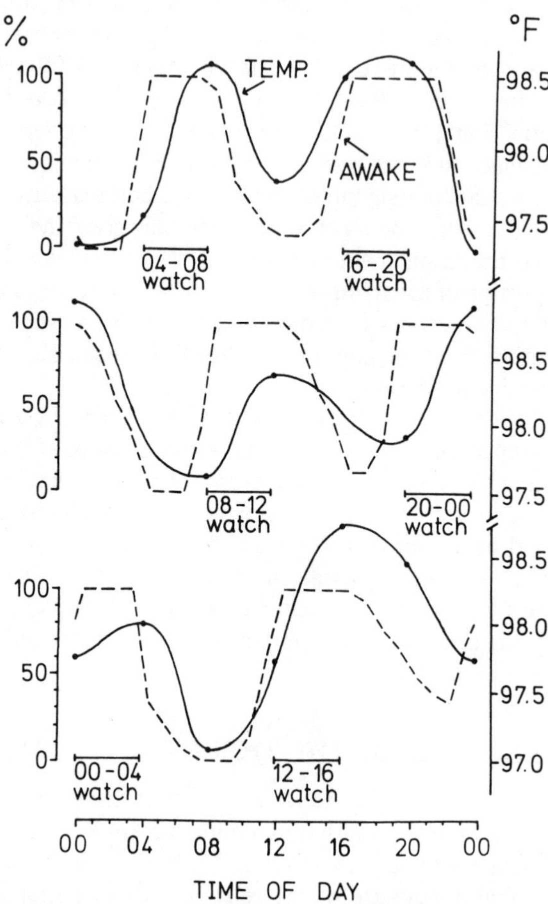

Figure 20.2 Hourly percentages of wakefulness, and mean body temperature curves, of one man from each crew (section) in the stabilized system. Data based on nine full 24-h periods during a 2-week submarine patrol. Redrawn from Kleitman (1949) by permission of the National Research Council

In contrast, the two shore-based simulation studies that have been conducted on this stabilized system have failed to show any bimodality of the temperature rhythm (Kleitman and Jackson, 1950a, 1950b; Colquhoun *et al.*, 1968a). It seems probable that this was due to the fact that the majority of the sleep was taken in a single episode, and that this was possible in view of the somewhat different conditions pertaining ashore. These shore-based studies also examined performance efficiency, including a measure of reaction time (RT). Both studies found variations in RT to follow the body temperature rhythm, although only in the study of Colquhoun *et al.* was the latter found to adjust to the 0000–0400,

1200–1600 schedule. The reason for the divergence between the results of these two studies is unclear (but see Colquhoun, 1971, for a possible explanation).

20.3.2 Rotating systems

The timing of sleep on rotating systems obviously differs on successive days. However, when averaged over a number of individuals and cycles, the distribution of sleep is less bimodal than that obtained on stabilized systems. Nevertheless, considerably greater variability than normal is found in both the number of hours elapsing between successive sleeps, and the number of hours of uninterrupted sleep obtained (Naitoh, 1982). Thus, sleep still tends to be 'fragmented', although the total amount of sleep obtained is usually similar to that ashore (Colquhoun *et al.*, 1978).

Typically, the amplitude of the body temperature rhythm has been found to reduce over the course of a voyage or simulated voyage (Colquhoun *et al.*, 1968a, 1978; Kleitman and Jackson, 1950b), and indeed there is some evidence that the temperature rhythm of submariners may even free run (Colquhoun *et al.*, 1978). An exception to this reduction in amplitude of the temperature rhythm was found by Rutenfranz *et al.* (1972) in cadets who were required to study from 0700 to

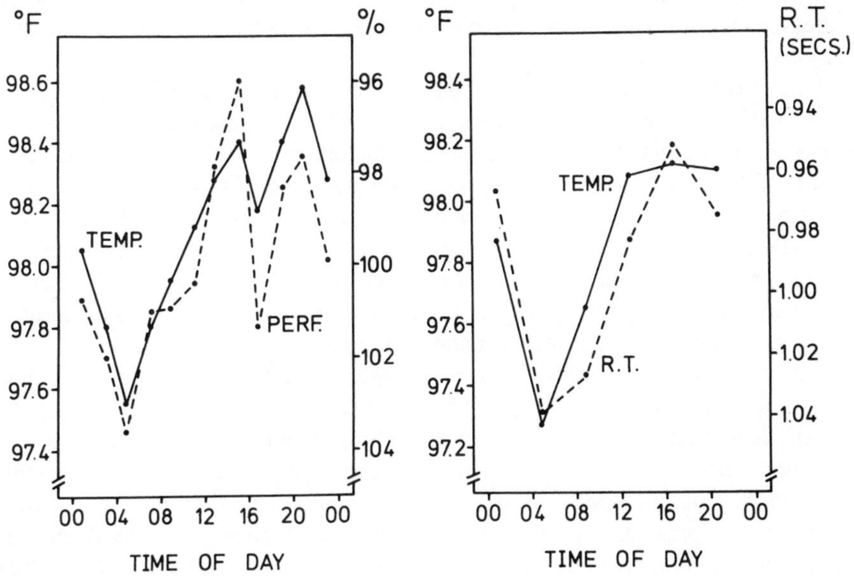

Figure 20.3 Variations in the mean levels of body temperature and performance in rotating watch systems. Left: The performance score is the group mean time to name 600 colours, expressed as a percentage of the total group mean score. Data from Kleitman and Jackson (1950b). Right: The performance score is reaction time to detected signals in a vigilance task. Data from Colquhoun *et al.* (1968a)

1700 each day *as well as* following a rotating System I (Figure 20.1). This resulted in considerably reduced sleep that was largely limited to relatively normal hours, and it seems probable that this was responsible for their maintaining normal temperature rhythms. Again, the available evidence suggests that performance levels follow the body temperature rhythm fairly closely in rotating systems (see Figure 20.3) (Kleitman and Jackson, 1950b; Colquhoun *et al.*, 1968a; Rutenfranz *et al.*, 1972; Dega *et al.*, 1976), implying that efficiency is likely to be lower on certain night watches than on certain day watches.

20.3.3 Alternative three-crew systems

Several authors have devised and studied alternative three-crew systems with a view to reducing the disruption of the sleep–wake cycle and the circadian rhythms in body temperature and performance. Kleitman (1949) devised a stabilized three-crew system (the 'close' routine) in which each crew works two 3-hour and one 2-hour watch per 24 hours and has an uninterrupted off-duty spell of at least 10 hours. There have been three studies of this type of system, and their results suggest that it may be superior to the traditional 4 on, 8 off stabilized system in a variety of ways (Utterback and Ludwig, 1949; Kleitman and Jackson, 1950a; Caille and Bassano, 1977). However, in common with other stabilized systems, it suffers from the drawback that the crew whose main sleep is taken during the day may have problems in adjusting.

This drawback also holds for the 'industrial' routines proposed by Colquhoun *et al.* (1968b). These authors questioned the need for the continuation of short watches, in view of the considerable change that has occurred over the years in the nature of the seafarer's job. They proposed the adoption of a stabilized 8 on, 16 off system. In a shore-based simulation study of a 'night' watch (2200–0600) that might be involved in this type of system, they failed to find complete adjustment of the temperature rhythm. However, there was a considerable degree of flattening of the rhythm over the course of twelve watches, and a concomitant disappearance of the on-watch decline in performance efficiency.

Other authors have studied work–rest schedules that are not based on a unit of 24 hours, or a submultiple thereof. These 'non 24-hour' routines are, in practice, usually based on an 18-hour 'day', although there is no theoretical reason why this should be the case. These studies have been limited to the 6 on, 12 off system used on American nuclear submarines. The results from these studies agree in showing an approximately 18-hour sleep–wake cycle (Beare *et al.*, 1981; Naitoh *et al.*, 1983) and there is also a tendency for the total amount of sleep to reduce (Schaeffer *et al.*, 1979). Indications of 18-hour rhythms in temperature and other physiological variables were also seen (Schaeffer *et al.*, 1979; Naitoh *et al.*, 1983), although since an 18-hour period is outside the range of entrainment of the temperature rhythm, it seems probable that these findings reflect a masking effect of the sleep–wake cycle (see Chapter 2). Indeed, Naitoh *et al.* (1983) considered the evidence for this 18-hour rhythm to be relatively weak; these authors also found a 25-hour component in the temperatures of some of their subjects, which suggested that the rhythm may have been free-running.

Finally, it is worth noting that stern-loading 'freezer' trawlers employ a 12 on, 6 off shift system for their 'line workers' that must *impose* split sleeps. Unfortunately, no studies appear to have been made of this system.

20.4 TWO-CREW SYSTEMS

If there are insufficient qualified personnel to man a three-crew system, or if the available manpower needs to be temporarily increased (e.g. because of an alert on a warship), then a two-crew system may be used. These systems are usually stabilized, and require each crew to work 12 hours in each 24. The schedules used range from 4 on, 4 off through to 12 on, 12 off, with the most common being 6 on, 6 off.

Not surprisingly, the available evidence indicates that a 6 on, 6 off (or 7 on, 5 off, 5 on, 7 off) routine results in split sleeps (Vokac *et al.*, 1979, 1980; Wilkinson and Edwards, 1968). There is also evidence that the temperature rhythm reduces in amplitude over a spell on this type of system, and that the resultant 'flattening' of the curve over the night watch is accompanied by a partial adaptation of performance trends (Wilkinson, 1971). A similar flattening of the temperature curve, and partial adaptation in performance, was observed by Colquhoun *et al.* (1969) in the 'night' crew of a 12 on, 12 off system. This system has the advantage of avoiding split sleeps, and hence bimodality of the temperature rhythm, but requires the provision of meal and/or rest breaks. It is thus more similar to the industrial shiftwork routines described in earlier chapters.

Only two studies of the 4 on, 4 off system appear to have been conducted. One of these simulated a short-lived (12-hour) alert in which subjects were required to perform a task of continuous simulated sonar monitoring during the watches (Colquhoun *et al.*, 1975). Performance on this task was found to show a greater decrease between the two night watches investigated (2000–0000, and 0400–0800) and less of an increase between the two day watches (0800–1200, and 1600–2000) than would be expected on the basis of normal circadian variation. However, it is unclear to what extent this was due to fatigue arising from the sustained attention demanded by the task, as opposed to the effects of the 4 on, 4 off system itself. Nor is it possible, from this study, to assess the likelihood of long-term adjustment to the system.

Such adjustment can be examined in the results of the second study (Alluisi *et al.*, 1963), which simulated a prolonged (30-day) flight in an advanced aerospace vehicle. The circadian rhythm in body temperature showed only a slight reduction in amplitude, and a small phase delay, over the course of the study. However, while performance paralleled temperature for the first 5 days of the study, this relationship was disrupted for the last 10 days (Wilkinson, 1982), with the rhythm in performance showing a greater phase delay than that in temperature. It seems probable that this dissociation of the temperature and performance rhythms occurred because of the relatively isolated conditions under which the study was run (see Chapter 2). The results may thus only be applicable to submarine voyages.

20.5 CONCLUSIONS

The vast majority of studies in this area have been concerned with watchkeeping schedules on warships, notably submarines. Few attempts have been made to examine the appropriateness of traditional watchkeeping systems, and in particular the common 4 on, 8 off system, for today's merchant marine vessels. There is a clear need for research aimed at improving the arrangement of working hours on these ships, and the results discussed above offer some suggestions as to the types of schedule that might profitably be studied.

Perhaps the main finding is that stabilized systems appear to be preferable to rotating short watch systems that result in fragmented sleep and disrupted rhythms. The only advantage of these latter systems is that they avoid unfairness in the allocation of 'unsocial' hours, but it is unclear how important this is in the context of a prolonged voyage where the whole crew is, in any case, relatively isolated. Indeed, it seems probable that this isolation is responsible for the differences in the results obtained from seagoing and simulated studies of stabilized systems. The results of the latter studies must be considered to be of limited applicability, although they have been able to demonstrate the persistence of the relationship between temperature and performance. This relationship has been confirmed in a seagoing study of a rotating system (Rutenfranz *et al.*, 1972) and must thus be considered to have at least some generality.

A problem that has received little attention, and clearly deserves further study, is that of individual differences. In a reanalysis of the results From Colquhoun *et al.*'s (1968b) study, Colquhoun and Condon (1981) were able to demonstrate that the considerable differences in the degree to which subjects adjusted to a night watch (2200–0600) were related to the personality dimension of extraversion. Future studies might profitably explore this relationship further, as well as examining other dimensions of personality. They should also extend the range of performance tests to include more mentally taxing tasks that better reflect the increasingly cognitive nature of the seafarer's job. Performance on such tasks is now known to show a rather different relationship to body temperature to that found for simple tasks (Folkard *et al.*, 1976), and to adjust rather faster to altered sleep–wake schedules (Hughes and Folkard, 1976; Folkard and Monk, 1979).

In sum, it would appear that little is known about the effects of the stabilized systems currently used on merchant vessels. Future studies in this area need to pay greater attention to the type of task used; where possible, they should attempt to obtain 'real job' measures of efficiency. They also need to examine as many subjects as possible to enable the personality correlates of individual differences to be investigated. All of the various types of voyage undertaken should be covered, including those that cross time-zones. The practice of flying out crew members to join ships at distant ports (see Buckley *et al.*, 1973) also needs to be studied in view of the 'jet-lag' problem associated with it (see Chapter 21). Finally, the merits of alternative systems need to be assessed. This would require, in each case, changing not only the work–rest schedule of the mariners, but also the whole of the rest of their normal routine, including the timing of meals and leisure activities. Only thus would it be possible to ensure that the assessment made was a truly valid one.

Hours of Work
Edited by S. Folkard and T.H. Monk

Chapter 21

Jet-lag and Aircrew Scheduling

Hans M. Wegmann and Karl E. Klein

CONTENTS

ABSTRACT

Hours of aircrew duty interfere with the human circadian system more frequently than work hours in other industrial areas. Basically, interference arises from two different sources: irregular work–rest schedules, and jet-lag through rapid time-zone transitions. The underlying determinants of jet-lag are explained and the disruptive effects are described. Particular emphasis is placed on the 24-hour rhythm of performance, and problems for the pilot population are discussed.

21.1 INTRODUCTION

The hours of work in commercial aviation interfere with the human circadian system more frequently than in other industrial fields. Conflicts arise in two ways which can be conveniently characterized as 'shifted work' and 'shifted time'. These two sources of interference have in common a disparity between the internal 'body time' and the external time of the environment.

The term 'shifted work' refers to the fact that airline pilots and flight attendants must perform duty at abnormal times of the habitual 24-hour cycle, e.g. during night flights or extended duty periods. This situation is predominantly associated with long-distance operations, where duty may start at any time of the day or night. However, it also occurs with short-haul routes where, although the timing of services is closer to those of business and commerce, flight duty hours are usually extended on either side of the normally accepted times of work. The problems arising from this type of conflict are not specific to air operations but are associated with shiftwork in general (see Chapters 14–19). In certain instances they may also become significant for the flight passenger travelling on business who may be required to perform at a high level, and make important decisions, after an overnight flight without sufficient time for rest and recovery.

The second type of conflict, 'shifted time', arises after flights in an eastward or westward direction, involving rapid time-zone transitions with major shifts in environmental time. The resulting effects are specific to the field of aviation since high aircraft speeds facilitate the traversing of several time-zones within a few hours; this cannot be achieved by surface transportation systems. The human body is suddenly transferred into a time-zone completely out of alignment with its biological processes. The typical consequences for the organism have been variously named 'desynchronosis', 'transmeridian dyschronism' and 'jet-lag syndrome'. However, this terminology may be misleading, since it implies some kind of illness rather than a state of transitory cyclic adjustment while, as yet, there is no evidence that illness is directly involved. Thus, purely descriptive terms, such as 'desynchronization', 'dysrhythmia' or simply 'jet-lag' may be more appropriate. On the other hand, there is no doubt that various symptoms of impaired well-being are experienced, and marked impairments in performance efficiency are frequently observed, even if only subjectively.

21.2 DETERMINANTS OF JET-LAG

In order to understand the causes of jet-lag it is necessary to examine the underlying physical and biological determinants. Basically there are three determinants of jet-lag: the environmental timing system, high aircraft cruising speeds, and circadian rhythmicity.

The environmental timing system is based on the periodic variation of light and darkness. Because of the Earth's rotation, daylight travels from one meridian to the next every 4 minutes, thus covering 15 meridians in 1 hour (Figure 21.1). The globe is divided into 24 time-zones, each of which is equivalent to 15 meridians (in reality, boundaries of time-zones do not strictly coincide with the lines of meridians, but frequently follow national or natural borders). On eastbound flights, the day shortens and the clock has to be set ahead by as many hours as time-zones have been traversed. In contrast, after westbound flights the clock has to be set back and the day is extended. Eastward flights are associated with an 'advance shift', westward flights with a 'delay shift' of local time. In this context, it is notable that there are more international air routes following these directions than going north or south. This state of affairs appears to have developed because most of the major centres of industry and commerce are located at similar latitudes, i.e. in Europe, Japan and the USA.

Cruising speed is another determinant of jet-lag. Travelling that results in

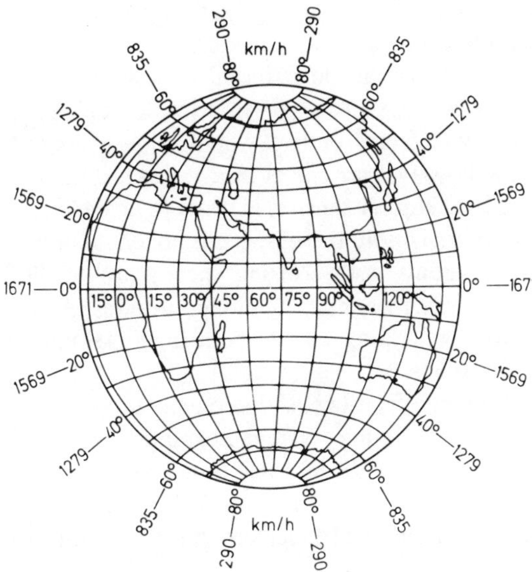

Figure 21.1 Globe with meridians equivalent to 1-h time difference or one time-zone. Numbers beside latitude degrees represent rotation speed of the Earth's surface

zeitgeber shifts of not more than 60–90 minutes per day, e.g. by ship, lies within the normal human 'range of entrainment' (Aschoff, 1978b, 1978c) and thus complete adjustment can be achieved during the voyage (see Chapter 2). As cruising speed increases beyond this range, the internal timing system lags further and further behind the changing environmental time. In fact, it has been demonstrated that the speed of jet-propelled aircraft is such that, on arrival after an 8-hour flight across six time-zones, the circadian system is still synchronized to preflight time, and adjustment to the new local time does not commence before onset of the first sleep period (Klein and Wegmann, 1980a, 1980b). This suggests that even higher speeds, such as achieved by supersonic flight, will not enhance the degree of jet-lag, since it is already maximal with subsonic flying speeds. The adverse effects of rapid time-zone transitions are not only associated with the high speed of today's aircraft. Many years before the advent of widespread commercial jet travel, Wiley Post, the first pilot to fly around the world, reported on attempts to reduce the impact of these effects during his global flight in a piston-engine powered plane (Post and Gatty, 1931). It was probably not so much the speed of modern aircraft which led to the term 'jet-lag', but more the broad public awareness of the problem which only evolved with the development of faster jet planes. Since their introduction, increasing numbers of people have been transported on routes over increasing distances. Estimates indicate that several hundred million people per year travel by air on transmeridian routes (Moore-Ede *et al.*, 1982).

In Figure 21.1, values are given indicating the speed of the Earth's rotation at different latitudes. They may also be considered to reflect the speed of daylight proceeding around the world at the different regions. For air travel, they thus indicate the groundspeed that is necessary to 'pace the sun' on westward flights, or to 'compress time' by a factor of two when going eastward. As a practical example, they show how fast air travel in a westward direction must be if an aircraft leaves, say, Frankfurt at sunrise, in order to arrive at, say, San Francisco at sunrise or even earlier. This air travel speed is no longer impracticable. Normal passenger aircraft of today, with cruising speeds around 900 kilometres per hour, fulfil these conditions when flying along latitudes above 50 degrees. The supersonic Concorde, with a speed of about 2000 kilometres per hour, can achieve this at all latitudes.

The third determinant of jet-lag is 'biological time', i.e. that reflected by circadian rhythms. This timing system regulates internal body time and coordinates internal events with external time cues (zeitgebers) such as the environmental light–dark cycle. Time-zone flights are associated with sudden phase-shifts of the synchronizing timegivers in the environment, thus causing a

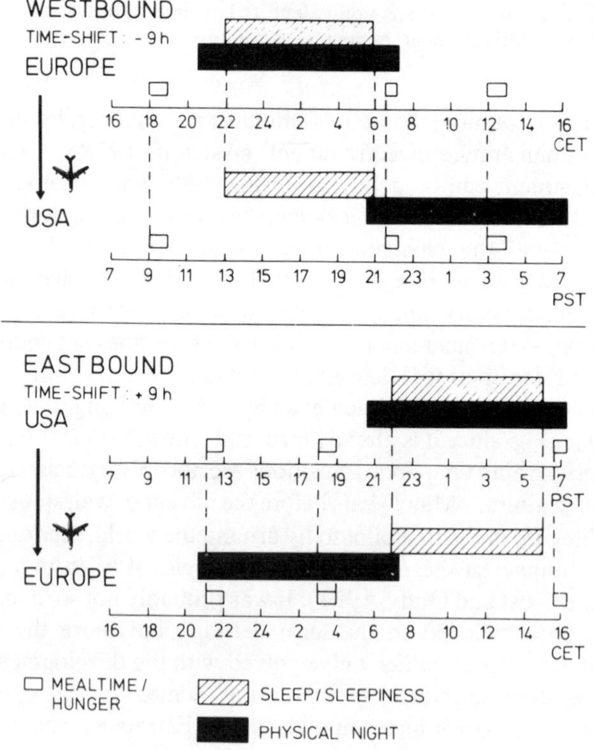

Figure 21.2 Schematic illustration of jet-lag effects upon sleep and meal timing

disparity between internal body time and the external environmental time. The biological system is unable to adjust immediately to the new local time. Rather, it shows some 'inertia' in adjusting, and it can take several days or even weeks before complete synchrony is regained. It is this inability of the endogenous rhythm to adjust immediately to an abrupt shift in the external timing system which causes jet-lag, a transitory desynchronization between body and environment.

As a consequence of this disparity, a high percentage of individuals suffer impairment of well-being. This is associated with a disturbance of vegetative functions such as hunger, wakefulness, sleepiness and bowel movements, which are normally dependent on the time of day. Due to the persistence of the internal timing system, they occur at unusual and inconvenient hours on the new local time. A schematic illustration of these effects with respect to sleep and meal timing is shown in Figure 21.2. As an example, transmeridian flights were chosen which cross nine time-zones, i.e. as on Atlantic routes between Central Europe and the US west coast. Complete adjustment to local time is assumed before departure. After arrival in the new time-zone, sleepiness is experienced when the surrounding population is most active, and people feel hungry during the early or late night. As a countermeasure against jet-lag, aircrews are sometimes advised to stay on their home-base time as far as possible. However, as this figure indicates, this could be very difficult. For adequate sleep to occur, bedrooms would be required that were well shielded from light and noise. In addition, lunch or supper would have to be served during late night hours. There are few places in the world where these provisions are available, and their installation in other places would involve an airline in unreasonably high extra costs.

The similarity between the consequences of jet-lag and those of shiftwork is obvious. Both situations result in a disruption of the habitual synchrony between internal and external timing systems. However, there is also a distinct difference between them. After time-zone flights, all synchronizing inputs from the environment (physical and social) are phase-shifted. However, the changes in the work–rest cycle resulting from shiftwork give rise to the opposite effect. Here the internal body time is shifted, but the physical and social surroundings remain unchanged. Thus shiftwork results in a state of almost permanently conflicting time cues, and entrainment during shiftwork is therefore accomplished more slowly and less completely than resynchronization after time-zone flights.

21.3 AIRCREW-SCHEDULING

In many cases, aircrews on long-distance routes are not only confronted with time-zone changes, but also with shiftwork. However, in contrast to most shift systems in industrial situations, flight duty schedules typically involve considerable irregularity of rest and activity patterns. Thus, the disruption of the circadian system may become very complex; jet-lag is only one component.

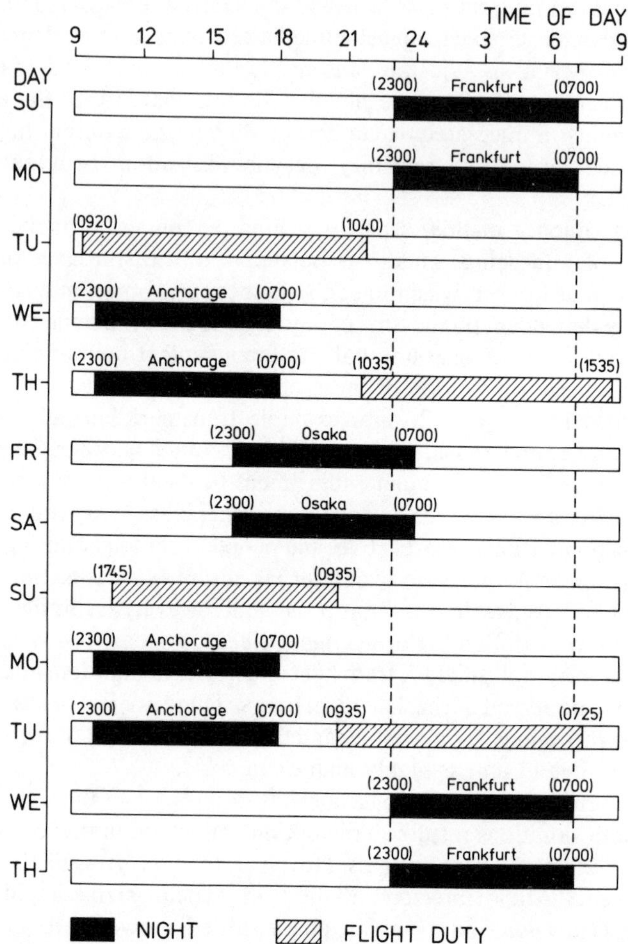

Figure 21.3 Airline flight duty schedule for the polar route between Germany and Japan. As compared with Frankfurt, local time is shifted by -11 h in Anchorage and by +7 h in Osaka. Figures in parentheses indicate the beginning and end of a period in local time

To give a practical example, Figure 21.3 presents a relatively clear and simple flight duty pattern actually scheduled for the polar route between Frankfurt and Osaka. The schedule comprises four sections of flight duty, the first commencing on Tuesday at 0920 and the last ending a week later at 0725 also on Tuesday. There are three stopovers scheduled: one on the outgoing flight and one on the return flight, both in Anchorage, and one at the destination in Osaka. Assuming that sleeps are always taken between 2300 and 0700 local time, their timing relative to Frankfurt time is –11 and +7 hours respectively. In relation to their time position within the 24-hour cycle, there are two distinctly different types of flight duty periods that are almost exactly 12 hours apart.

However, which is the day and which is the night flight? According to Frankfurt time, the two duty periods on the left-hand side of the figure would be day flights, while the two on the right-hand side would be considered night flights. If Anchorage time is taken as the reference, the situation would be just the reverse. If the duty periods are related to the pilot's biological time, the situation becomes even more complicated since, due to the various stopovers in different time-zones, the internal system will be permanently shifting. En route, it will never achieve synchronization with local time because the time differences are too large, and the stopovers too short. Estimates of average shift rates (Wegmann and Klein, 1982) suggest a phase delay of 5.5 hours at departure from Anchorage to Osaka, and a further delay of 7.5 hours when leaving Japan on the return flight. This implies a difference of 5.5 or 4 hours from the respective local time. A phase advance of 1 hour can be expected when the aircrew departs from Anchorage for the last flight sector. Thus, on arrival at home base, the circadian system would be out of phase to local time by 12 hours. These figures should be treated with some caution. They are not based on actual measurements en route, but are derived from experimental studies of non-pilot populations (Wegmann and Klein, 1973). They do not take account of individual differences — which may be considerable (see Chapter 18) — nor do they take into consideration certain strategies that may possibly be acquired by experienced aircrews to cope better with jet-lag effects. On the other hand, there is considerable evidence that these extrapolations offer a reasonable estimate with sufficient precision and operational significance.

It must be emphasized that the flight duty pattern presented here is not an especially complex one. There are many airlines operating around the world which employ much more complex schedules, with many more days away from the home base and many more transit stops in different time-zones. Crews assigned to these routes frequently have to cope with extremely irregular work–rest patterns, and their circadian system may be continuously in de-adaptation/re-adaptation mode (Mohler, 1976; Nicholson, 1972; Moore-Ede *et al.*, 1982).

In view of the potential risk that excessively demanding duty patterns impose on flight safety, there has been general agreement on the necessity to prescribe limits for minimum rest requirements and maximum permissible duty time. National and international regulations have been established whose purpose is to ensure that aircrews are not unduly fatigued, and to force airline operators and their economic interests to comply with safety requirements. The regulations of several countries have been compared and discussed in detail in a recent paper (Wegmann, Conrad and Klein, 1983). One surprising finding is that only three out of nine sets of regulations take account of circadian rhythm disruption resulting from time-zone transitions, or from night and irregular duty hours. This omission probably stems from the lack of scientific data when the regulations were established, rather than from general ignorance.

21.4 DISRUPTIVE EFFECTS OF TRANSMERIDIAN FLIGHTS

Rapid time-zone transitions affect not only physiological functions, but also the rhythms of behaviour and performance. Disruptive effects are manifest in changes in one, several or all of the parameters defining the regular oscillation of the biological system, i.e. by phase displacements and/or by alterations of the level and range of oscillation (Klein and Wegmann, 1980a). For aircrews, this interference with performance rhythms may be of major operational significance.

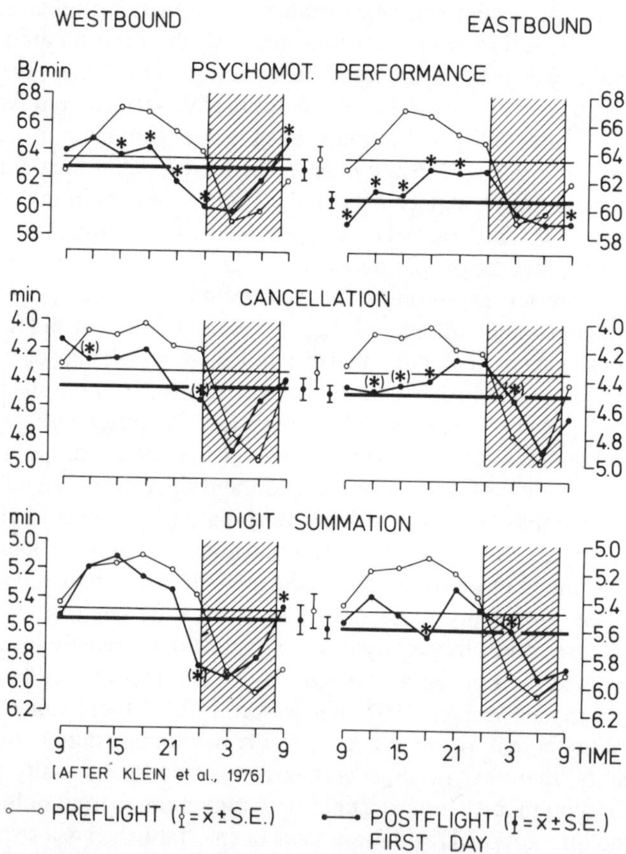

Figure 21.4 Desynchronization of circadian rhythm in three performance tests on the first day after arrival. Curves represent average values of a group of eight subjects after westward and eastward flights traversing six time-zones. (Asterisks indicate significant differences from preflight control values)

The acute effects of jet-lag upon the circadian rhythm in performance are shown in Figure 21.4. These curves represent the average values of eight subjects for three performance tests after transmeridian flights involving the transition of six time-zones. In relation to the 'normal' preflight fluctuations, the curves on the first day after arrival show typical disruptive effects. The most striking of these is the phase displacement to earlier hours after the westward flight, and to later hours after the eastward flight. In addition, there is a reduction in amplitude, and a decrease in the 24-hour mean levels. At specific times of day, these differences between the normal and desynchronized rhythms are statistically reliable. They are more pronounced after the eastbound flight. The deficits in psychomotor performance are of particular interest in view of their obvious implications for pilot performance. At certain times of the postflight day this type of performance is 8–10 per cent lower than on the preflight day. This impairment is comparable to that resulting from the effects of a blood-alcohol concentration of 0.05 per cent, on the same performance test (Klein *et al.*, 1972).

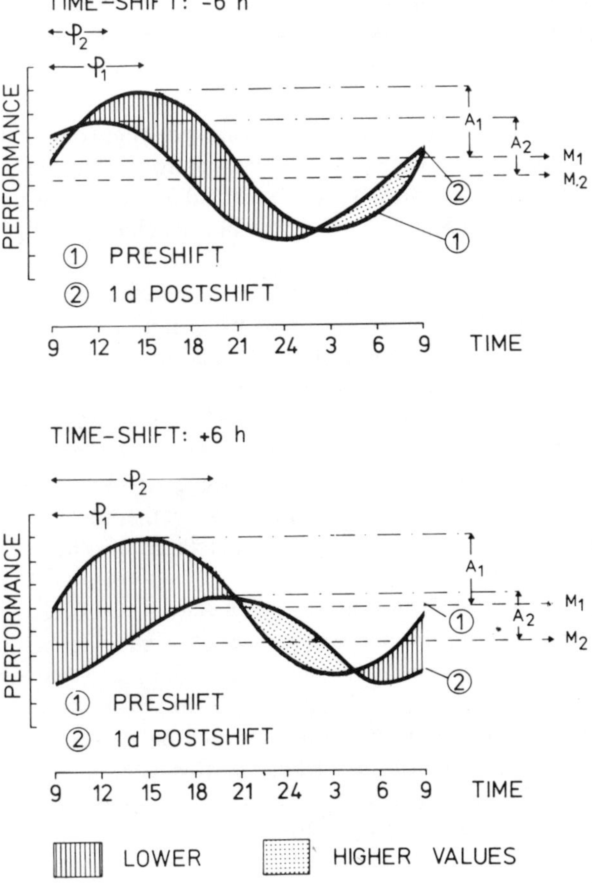

Figure 21.5 Schematic illustration of typically observed changes in circadian performance rhythms on the first day after transmeridian flights resulting in time differences of 6 h

The disruptive effects of transmeridian flights on performance have been confirmed in several subsequent experiments (Klein *et al.*, 1976). The consistency of the results allows us to represent them schematically in Figure 21.5. Desynchronization causes phase displacements in the appropriate direction, necessarily resulting in lower performance levels at certain points in the 24-hour day. Phase delay and advance can be demonstrated by differences in acrophases ($\varphi_1 - \varphi_2$) between the preflight and postflight rhythms. Additional effects include decrease in amplitude ($A_1 - A_2$) and a diminution of the 24-hour means ($M_1 - M_2$). These latter alterations evidently magnify the decrements caused by the phase differences alone. Although both postflight curves exhibit some adjustment on the first day in the new time-zone, the resynchronization after the 6-hour phase advance is less complete, and results in more pronounced performance deficits, than after the 6-hour delay. Decreased performance generally occurs mainly during the afternoon and early night hours after a westbound flight, but during the morning and early afternoon after travelling eastwards. These deficits can be demonstrated up to 5 days after arrival, but are not usually statistically significant after the third postflight day. Although there is little doubt that circadian oscillation in mental performance can be overcome by high motivation and extra effort, it seems reasonable to conclude that during these periods it will be more difficult, if not impossible, to achieve preflight performance levels.

Despite the emphasis on performance *decrements* resulting from rapid transmeridian transitions, there are times when performance may actually be *better* as compared with the completely adjusted rhythm. These times occur at sections of the 24-hour cycle when performance is usually low for someone who is living in the time-zone of arrival. Thus, US residents, for instance, who arrive in Europe, may perform better at night than European residents. These benefits are, of course, transient, and their implication for everyday life is questionable. However, there has been some discussion as to whether they could be utilized in military situations, and it also seems possible that they may have implications for flight duty scheduling.

Finally, it has been shown that not all of the observed changes in rhythm parameters are necessarily a consequence of time-zone displacements. In particular, changes in the amplitude and the 24-hour mean may also be affected by other factors related to air travel, such as flight stress, sleep deprivation and fatigue. There is some evidence that desynchronization is not necessarily associated with a lowering of the 24-hour performance mean, implying that a change in overall performance level is not a compulsory result of rhythm disruption (Klein and Wegmann, 1980b).

21.5 INTERNAL DISSOCIATION

During the transition from the preflight to the postflight steady state, different circadian rhythms show different rates of adjustment to the new local times. This is true for both physiological and performance functions. This difference in the speed of resynchronization causes 'internal dissociation' (Wever, 1979a), i.e. abnormal phase relationships between various rhythms. For example, the circadian rhythm in urinary catecholamine excretion adjusts more rapidly than does that in body temperature, while the rhythm in urinary corticosteroids resynchronizes more slowly than either of these (Wegmann and Klein, 1973). Performance rhythms also adjust at different rates, depending on the nature of the task (Klein *et al.*, 1972; see also Chapter 19). Internal dissociation is of a transitory, dynamic nature, in contrast to the steady state nature of the internal desynchronization sometimes observed in free-running subjects isolated from all external zeitgebers (Wever, 1979a).

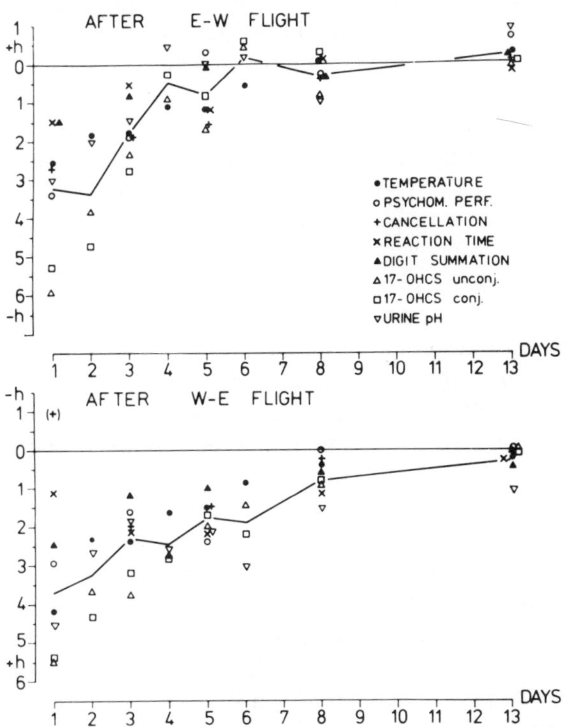

Figure 21.6 Acrophases of various circadian body functions in a group of eight subjects after flights in west-bound and east-bound directions over six time-zones and depending on days after arrival. Solid lines represent mean values of acrophases obtained from the different variables. Sources: Wegmann and Klein (1982); Wegmann, Klein, Conrad and Esser (1983)

Figure 21.6 presents the average acrophases of the circadian rhythm in various physiological, biochemical and performance variables, as related to the normally synchronized state, after westward and eastward flights. It is based on the results of an experiment involving eight subjects. A negative sign on the vertical axis indicates an earlier, and a positive sign a later, occurrence of the circadian maxima compared to normal. All tests were performed every 3 hours, day and night. In order to avoid an acumulative sleep loss, the more time-consuming performance tests were conducted only every other day. The graph clearly indicates that the various functions do not resynchronize immediately, but need some time to adjust completely. During this adjustment the various rhythms do not maintain a fixed temporal relationship among themselves. Rather they show distinctly different rates of resynchronization. The magnitude and duration of this internal dissociation appear to depend on the flight direction. Changes in the phase relationship between different functions are more pronounced, and their normalization occurs more slowly, after eastwards flights than after westward ones. This 'directional asymmetry' (Aschoff, 1973; Graeber, 1982) between phase advance and phase delay shifts has been observed in several flight experiments for several different variables (though not for all variables).

In attempting to explain this directional asymmetry phenomenon, several factors have been studied. Most of them have been excluded as possible causes of the observed differences in resynchronization rate. Neither the time of flight (whether a day or a night flight) nor the relative flight direction (whether outgoing or homegoing) have a major influence on the adjustment speed (Klein and Wegmann, 1980a; Wegmann and Klein, 1973). At the present time, the findings from different laboratories are still somewhat controversial (Graeber, 1982). In particular, the results of jet-lag simulations in bunkers indicate faster resynchronization rates after phase advances than after phase delays (Wever, 1980a). Wever has also pointed out that oscillatory theory predicts faster resynchronization after eastward flights. The reasons for this discrepancy between simulated and real flights have been discussed in detail by Graeber (1982).

The implications of internal dissociation are, as yet, poorly understood (see also Chapters 14–16). It has generally been thought that a disturbance of the temporal harmony among various circadian rhythms might result in harmful effects on performance and efficiency. However, there is some evidence that this is not generally true (Wegmann and Klein, 1973). Apart from the phase adjustment which takes at least five postflight days (if six or more time-zones are traversed), the 24-hour mean performance level usually exhibits a consistent decrement only on the first day after arrival. This suggests that internal dissociation does not lead to impairment of performance *per se*. This view is supported by recent results from isolated subjects under free-running conditions who exhibited improved performance and mood at the point at which their rhythms became internally desynchronized (Wever, 1982).

It is still an open question whether internal dissociation, when frequently repeated, has harmful chronic effects, a problem of particular relevance for aircrews who perform flight duty on transmeridian routes over lifetime spans of perhaps 20 or more years. One approach to the investigation of this problem is to compare the health statistics of pilot populations working predominantly on cross time-zone routes with those employed on non-transmeridian flights, such as north–south routes. Progress in tackling the problem in this way has been disappointing for a variety of reasons. One is that it is almost impossible to find populations with the clearcut distinction required for statistical analyses. Another is the difficulty in obtaining sufficiently large numbers of pilots living under comparable conditions. A third reason may be a lack of support from employers, possibly because of the commercial impact that the outcome of such studies might have (Wegmann and Klein, 1981).

Another approach to the investigation of chronic effects of internal dissociation can be seen in animal experiments in which the lighting regimen can be artificially shifted over longer periods of time (Aschoff *et al.*, 1975; Halberg *et al.*, 1975; Pittendrigh and Minis, 1972). However, the results from studies on insects and mice are equivocal, at least with respect to the more serious prediction of a decreased lifespan (Brown, 1982; Finger, 1982). In fact, some organisms actually appear to live longer under continuously repeated phase-shifts of the light–dark cycle. Various explanations of this effect have been suggested based on the age at which time displacements were introduced, the pattern of shifting, or an inhibition of maturing processes. Thus, to date, animal studies have not proved very helpful in shedding light on the implications of chronic dissociation.

Like those of normal shiftworkers (Chapter 16), questionnaire studies of aircrews reveal a high incidence of sleep problems, nervous disturbances and gastrointestinal complaints (Cameron, 1971; Lavernhe, 1970). However, objective health reports do not implicate psychosomatic diseases as a major factor for grounding, nor do they deviate significantly from those of the general population. Nor do these questionnaire results reveal sickness trends that can be attributed to irregular working patterns. These findings conflict to some extent with those for industrial shiftworkers (Chapter 16), but it must be remembered that aircrew populations are carefully preselected and receive intensive medical supervision.

21.6 CONCLUSIONS

Jet-lag is an inevitable consequence of rapid time-zone transitions. It is caused by a desynchronization between the circadian and the environmental timing systems. It not only affects physiological functions, but also the rhythms in behaviour and performance. Disruptive effects are evidenced as phase displacements and/or as alterations of the level and range of oscillation in the circadian rhythms. Phase displacements necessarily result in performance deficits at certain points of the 24-hour day, and can be observed for several postflight days. In contrast, the 24-hour mean performance level usually exhibits a consistent decrement on only the first day after arrival. There is some evidence that this is not a compulsory effect of rhythm disruption, but may also result from other factors, such as flight stress, sleep deprivation and fatigue. The results from several field studies suggest a directional asymmetry: in general, the disruptive effects are more pronounced and longer lasting after eastward than after westward flights.

During the transition from the preflight to the postflight steady state, internal dissociation occurs, i.e. different body functions show different rates of adjustment to the new local time. Thus, the various rhythms are unable to maintain their normal fixed temporal relationship. Again, the magnitude and duration of these disturbances appear to depend on the flight direction. The implications of such internal dissociation are as yet poorly understood, especially with regard to its potential risk for the aircrews' performance and health.

Hours of Work
Edited by S. Folkard and T.H. Monk

References and Author Index

(The numbers in parentheses at the end of each reference indicate the pages where the references are cited.)

Aanonsen, A. (1964) *Shift Work and Health.* Oslo, Universitetsforlaget. (172, 190, 207)

Abplanalp, J.M.; Donnelly, A.G. and Rose, R. (197) Psychoendocrinology of the menstrual cycle: I. Enjoyment of daily activities and moods. *Psychosomatic Medicine,* **41,** 587-604. (89, 90)

Abplanalp, J.M. Livingston, L., Rose, R.M., and Sandwich, D. (1977) Cortisol and growth hormone responses to psychological stress during the menstrual cycle. *Psychosomatic Medicine,* **39,** 158-177. (94)

Abplanalp, J.M., Rose, R., Donnelly, B.A., and Livingston-Vaughan, L. (1979) Psychoendocrinology of the menstrual cycle: II. The relationship between enjoyment of activities, moods and reproductive hormones. *Psychosomatic Medicine,* **41,** 605-615. (90, 92)

Adam, M.N. (1983) Time of day effects in memory for text. Unpublished D. Phil. thesis, University of Sussex. (49)

Adams, J.A. (1955) A source of decrement in psychomotor performance. *Journal of Experimental Psychology,* **49,** 390-394. (109)

Adams, J.A. (1963) *Experimental Studies of Human Vigilance.* United States Air Force ESD Technical Documentary Report, No. 63-320. (140, 144)

Adams, J.A. and Boulter, L.R. (1964) Spatial and temporal uncertainty as determinants of vigilance performance. *Journal of Experimental Psychology,* **67,** 127-131. (141)

Adams, J.A., Humes, J.M. and Stenson, H.H. (1962) Monitoring of complex visual displays: III. Effects of repeated sessions on human vigilance. *Human Factors,* **4,** 149-157. (111)

Agnew, H.W. and Webb, W.B. (1973) The influence of time course variables on REM sleep. *Bulletin of the Psychonomic Society,* **3,** 131-133. (63)

Åkerstedt, T. (1977) Inversion of the sleep wakefulness pattern: Effects on circadian variations in psychophysiological activation. *Ergonomics,* **20,** 459-474. (192)

Åkerstedt, T. and Fröberg, J.E. (1976a) Individual differences in circadian patterns of catecholamine excretion, body temperature, performance, and subjective arousal. *Biological Psychology,* **4,** 277-292. (33)

Åkerstedt, T. and Fröberg, J. (1976b) Shift work and health — interdisciplinary aspect. In P.G. Rentos and R.D. Shepard (eds.), *Shift Work and Health,* Washington, US Dept of Health, Education and Welfare, pp. 179-197. (35)

Åkerstedt, T. and Fröberg, J. (1977) Psychophysiological circadian rhythms in women during 72h of sleep deprivation. *Waking and Sleeping.* **1,** 387-394. (68)

Åkerstedt, T., Fröberg, J. Levi, L., Torsvall, L. and Zamore, K. (1977) *Shift Work and Well-being.* Report No. 63 of Laboratory of Clinical Stress Research, Karolinska Institute, Stockholm. (192, 203)
Åkerstedt, T. and Gillberg, M. (1979) Effects of sleep deprivation on memory and sleep latencies in connection with repeated awakenings from sleep. *Psychophysiology,* **16,** 49-52. (83)
Åkerstedt, T. and Gillberg, M. (1981) The circadian variation of experimentally displaced sleep. *Sleep,* **4,** 159-169. (63, 191, 195, 196)
Åkerstedt, T., Gillberg, M. and Wetterberg, L. (1982) The circadian covariation of fatigue and urinary melatonin. *Biological Psychiatry,* **17,** 547-554. (196)
Åkerstedt, T., Patkai, P. and Dahlgren, K. (1977) Field studies of shift work: II. Temporal patterns in psychophysiological activation in workers alternating between night and day work. *Ergonomics,* **20,** 621-631. (189, 190, 192)
Åkerstedt, T., Palmblad, J., de la Torre, B., Marana, M. and Gillberg, M. (1980) Adrenocortical and gonadal steroids during sleep deprivation. *Sleep, 3,* 23-30. (58)
Åkerstedt, T. and Torsvall, L. (1978) Experimental changes in shift schedules — their effects on well-being. *Ergonomics,* **21,** 849-856. (192, 193)
Åkerstedt, T. and Torsvall, L. (1981a) Age, sleep and adjustment to shift work. In W.P. Koella (ed.), *Sleep 1980,* Basle, Karger, pp. 190-194. (34, 191, 228)
Åkerstedt, T. and Torsvall, L. (1981b) Shift work. Shift-dependent well-being and individual differences. *Ergonomics,* **24,** 265-273. (193)
Åkerstedt, T., Torsvall, L. and Gillberg, M. (1981) Napping and irregular work hours. *Sleep Research,* **10,** 132. (78, 82, 234)
Alden, J. (1976) The extent and nature of double jobbing in Great Britain. Unpublished Report, University of Wales Institute of Science and Technology, Cardiff. (219)
Allenspach, H. (1975) *Flexible Working Hours.* Geneva, International Labour Office. (153)
Alluisi, E.A., Chiles, W.D., Hall, T.J. and Hawkes, G.R. (1963) *Human Group Performance during Confinement.* USAF AMRL Technical Documentary Report No. 63-67, (AD 426 661). (259)
Alternative Work Schedules Experimental Program: Interim report to the President and the Congress (1981) Washington, DC, United States Office of Personnel Management.
Altmann, M., Knowles, E. and Bull, H.D. (1941) A psychosomatic study of the sex cycle in women. *Psychosomatic Medicine,* **3,** 199-225. (93)
Andersen, J.E. (1958) The main results of the Danish medico-psychosocial investigation of shiftworkers. *Proceedings of the XII International Congress on Occupational Health,* Helsinki vol. III, pp. 135-136. (205)
Andersen, J.E. (1970) *Three-Shift-Work. A Socio-Medical Investigation,* vol. 42. Copenhagen, Socialforskningsinstitutet. (190, 192)
Andersen, R.P., Halcomb, C.G., Gordon, W. and Oxolins, D.A. (1974) Measurement of attention distractability in LD children. *Academic Therapy,* **9,** 261-266. (129)
Andlauer, P. (1971) Differentes modalites du travail en equipes alternantes. *Archives des Maladies Professionelles de Medecine du Travail et de Securite Sociale,* **32,** 393-395. (206)
Andlauer, P. and Reinberg, A. (1979) Amplitude of the oral temperature circadian rhythm and tolerance to shift work. *Chronobiologia,* **6,** suppl. 1, 67-76. (197, 206)
Andlauer, P., Rutenfranz, J., Kogi, K., Thierry, H., Vieux, N. and Duverneuil, G. (1982) Organization of night shifts in industries where public safety is at stake. *International Archives of Occupational and Environmental Health,* **49,** 353-355. (182, 197, 209)
Angersbach, D. (1980) Epidemiologische Untersuchungen uber langfristige gesundheitliche Auswirkungen von Nacht- und Schichtarbeit. Dissertation, Münster. (207)

Angersbach, D. Knauth, P., Loskant, H., Karvonen, M.J., Undeutsch, K. and Rutenfranz, J. (1980) A retrospective cohort study comparing complaints and diseases in day and shift workers. *International Archives of Occupational and Environmental Health,* **45**, 127-140. (172, 205)

Angiboust, R. and Gouars, M. (1972) Tentative d'evaluation de l'efficacite operationelle du personnel de l'aeronautique militaire au cours de veilles nocturnes. In W.P. Colquhoun (ed.), *Aspects of Human Efficiency: Diurnal Rhythm and Loss of Sleep,* London, English Universities Press. pp. 151-170. (82, 83)

Anonymous (1956) Vigilance — the nature of alertness and the problem of its maintenance during long spells of work. *Nature,* **178**, 1375-1377. (141)

Antrobus, J.S., Coleman, R. and Singer, J.L. (1967) Signal-detection performance by subjects differing in predisposition to day-dreaming. *Journal of Consulting Psychology,* **31**, 487-491. (128)

Aschoff, J. (1960) Exogenous and Endogenous components in circadian rhythms. *Cold Spring Harbor Symposium on Quantitative Biology,* **25**, 11-28. (194)

Aschoff, J. (1965) The phase-angle difference in circadian periodicity. In J. Aschoff (ed.), *Circadian Clocks,* Amsterdam, North-Holland, pp. 262-276. (30)

Aschoff, J. (1967) Adaptive cycles: Their significance for defining environmental hazards. *International Journal of Biometerology,* **11**, 255-278. (98, 195)

Aschoff, J. (1973) Internal dissociation and desynchronization of circadian systems. In *XXI International Congress of Aviation and Space Medicine, Munchen,* p. 255. (274)

Aschoff, J. (1978a) Features of circadian rhythm relevant for the design of shift schedules. *Ergonomics,* **21**, 739-754. (166)

Aschoff, J. (1978b) Problems of re-entrainment of circadian rhythms: Asymmetry effect, dissociation and partition. In J. Assenmacher and D.S. Farner (eds.), *Environmental Endocrinology,* Berlin and Heidelberg, New York, Springer Verlag, pp. 185-195. (235, 265)

Aschoff, J. (1978c) Circadian rhythms within and outside their ranges of entrainment. In J. Assenmacher and D.S. Farner (eds.), *Environmental Endocrinology,* Berlin, Heidelberg and New York, Springer Verlag, pp. 172-181. (265)

Aschoff, J. Fatranska, M., Giedke, H., Doerr, P., Stamm, D. and Wisser, H. (1971) Human circadian rhythms in continuous darkness: Entrainment by social cues. *Science,* **171**, 213-215. (194)

Aschoff, J., Hoffman, K., Pohl, H. and Wever, R. (1975) Re-entrainment of circadian rhythms after phase shifts of the zeitgeber, *Chronobiologia,* **2**, 23-78. (275)

Aserinsky, E. (1969) The maximal capacity for sleep: Rapid eye movement density as an index of sleep satiety. *Biological Psychiatry,* **1**, 147-159. (62)

Aserinsky, E. (1973) Relationship of REM density to the prior accumulation of sleep and wakefulness. *Psychophysiology,* **10**, 545-558. (62)

Assenheim, G. (1969) Etude d'un systeme au travers d'un centre privilegie: un poste de controle en cristallerie. *Le Travail Humain,* **32**, 1-12. (137, 138)

Astley, R.W. and Fox, J.G. (1975) The analysis of an inspection task in the rubber industry. In C.G. Drury and J.G. Fox (eds.), *Human Reliability in Quality Control,* London, Taylor and Francis, pp. 253–272. (137, 139)

Baddeley, A.D. and Colquhoun, W.P. (1969) Signal probability and vigilance: A reappraisal of the signal-rate effect. *British Journal of Psychology,* **60**, 169-178. (141)

Baddeley, A.D., Hatter, J.E., Scott, D. and Snashall, A. (1970) Memory and time of day. *Quarterly Journal of Experimental Psychology,* **22**, 605-609. (43, 44)

Baddeley, A.D. and Hitch, G. (1974) Working memory. In G.A. Bower (ed.), *The Psychology of Learning and Motivation: Advances in Research and Theory,* vol. 8, New York, Academic Press. (46, 49)

Bakan, P. (1959) Extroversion–Intraversion and improvement in an auditory vigilance task. *British Journal of Psychology,* **50,** 325-332. (131)
Baker, C.H. (1959) Attention to visual displays during a vigilance task: II. Maintaining the level of vigilance. *British Journal of Psychology,* **50,** 30-36. (113, 141)
Baker, C.H. (1960) Observing behavior in a vigilance task. *Science,* **132,** 674-675. (117)
Baker, C.H. (1963a) Further toward a theory of vigilance. In D.N. Buckner and J.J. McGrath (eds.), *Vigilance: A Symposium,* New York, McGraw-Hill, pp. 127-154. (113, 124)
Baker, C.H. (1963b) Consistency of performance in two visual vigilance tasks. In D.N. Buckner and J.J. McGrath (eds.), *Vigilance: A Symposium,* New York, McGraw-Hill. (124)
Baker, C.H. (1964) *Industrial Inspection Considered as a Vigilance Task.* Los Angeles, Human Factors Research Inc. (141, 144)
Baker, C.H. and Harabedian, A. (1962) *A Study of Target Detection by Sonar Operators.* Report no. 206–16. Los Angeles, Human Factors Research Inc. (140)
Baker, C.H. and O'Hanlon, J. (1963) *The Use of Reference Signals in a Visual Vigilance Task. I. Reference Signals Continuously Displayed. Report no. 750–1.* Los Angeles, Human Factors Research Inc. (139)
Bakwin, H. (1954) Pseudoxia pediatricia. *New England Journal of Medicine,* **232,** 691-697. (141)
Banks, O. (1956) Continuous shift work: The attitude of wives. *Occupational Psychology,* **30,** 69-84. (216)
Banks, O. (1960) *The Attitudes of Steel Workers to Technical Change.* Liverpool University Press. (216, 218)
Beare, A.N., Bondi, K.R., Biersner, R.J. and Naitoh, P. (1981) Work and rest on nuclear submarines. *Ergonomics,* **24,** 593-610. (258)
Beaumont, P.J.U., Richards, D.H. and Gelder, M.G. (1975) A study of minor psychiatric and physical symptoms during the menstrual cycle. *British Journal of Psychiatry,* **126,** 431-434. (90)
Belbin, R.M. (1957a) New fields for quality control. British Management Review. (136, 137)
Belbin, R.M. (1957b) Compensating rest allowances. Work Study and Industrial Engineering. (135, 137, 144)
Belbin, R.M. (1963) Inspection and human efficiency. *Ergonomics for Industry,* **4,** 13. DSIR & Warren Springs Laboratory. (137)
Bell, B., Christie, M.J. and Venables, P.H. (1975) Psychophysiology of the menstrual cycle. In P.H. Venables and M.J. Christie (eds.), *Research in Psychophysiology,* London, Wiley, pp. 181-207. (93)
Benedek, T. and Rubenstein, B. (1942) *The Sexual Cycle in Women: The Relation Between Ovarian Function and Psychodynamic Processes.* Washington, DC, National Research Council. (90, 92, 93)
Benedetti, L.H. and Loeb, M. (1972) A comparison of auditory monitoring performance in blind subjects with that of sighted subjects in light and dark. *Perception and Psychophysics,* **11,** 10-16. (124)
Benedict, F.G. (1904) Studies in body temperature. *American Journal of Physiology,* **11,** 145-169. (188)
Benoit, O., Foret, J., Bouard, G., Merle, B., Landau, J. and Marc, M.E. (1980) Habitual sleep length and patterns of recovery after 24 hour and 36 hour sleep deprivation. *Electroencephalography and Clinical Neurophysiology,* **50,** 477-485. (61, 64, 191)
Berger, T.J., Walker, J.W., Scott, T.D., Magnusson, L.J. and Pollack, S.L. (1971) Diurnal and nocturnal sleep stage patterns following sleep deprivation. *Psychonomic Science,* **23,** 273-275. (61, 191)

Bergum, B.O. and Lehr, D.J. (1963) *Vigilance Performance as a Function of Task and Environmental Variables.* US Army Air Defense Human Research Unit, Research Report no. 11. (140)

Bertelson, A.D. (1979) Effects of napping and bedrest on performance and mood. PhD dissertation. Ohio State University. (79, 80, 81)

Bertelson, P. and Joffe, R. (1963) Blockings in prolonged serial responding. *Ergonomics,* **6**, 2, 109-116. (116)

Best, F. (1981) *Work Sharing: Issues, Policy Options and Prospects.* Kalamazoo, Mich., W.E. Upjohn Institute for Employment Research. (157)

Betancourt, R. and Clague, C. (1976) Multiple shifts and the employment problems in developing countries. *International Labour Review,* **114**, 187-196. (169)

Bhatia, N. and Murrell, K.F.H. (1969) An industrial experiment in organized rest pauses. *Human Factors,* **11**, *2*, 167-174. (144)

Bicknell, A. (1970) Aging, arousal and vigilance. Unpublished PhD thesis, Texas Tech. University. (130)

Bills, A.G. (1931) Blocking: A new principle of mental fatigue. *American Journal of Psychology,* **43**, 230-245. (116)

Binford, J.R. and Loeb, M. (1963) Monitoring readily detected auditory signals and detection of obscure visual signals. *Perceptual and Motor Skills,* **17**, 735-745. (139)

Binford, J.R. and Loeb, M. (1966) Changes within and over repeated sessions in criterion and effective sensitivity in an auditory vigilance task. *Journal of Experimental Psychology,* **72**, 339-345. (119, 120)

Bjerner, B., Holm, A. and Swensson, A. (1948) Om natt och skiftarbete. *Statens Offentliga Utredningar (Stockholm),* **51**, 87-159. (182)

Bjerner, B. and Swensson, A. (1953) Shiftwork and rhythm. *Acta Medica Scandinavica* (Supplement 278), 102-107. (228, 242, 243)

Blake, M.J.F. (1967) Time of day effects on performance in a range of tasks. *Psychonomic Science,* **9**, 345-350. (40, 41, 47, 49, 105)

Blake, M.J.F. (1971) Temperament and time of day. In W.P. Colquhoun (ed.), *Biological Rhythms and Human Performance,* London and New York, Academic Press, pp. 109-148. (41, 42, 49, 206)

Blakelock, E. (1960) A new look at the new leisure. *Administrative Science Quarterly,* **4**, **4**, 446-467.(213, 218)

Boakes, R.A. (1973) Response decrements produced by extinction and by response — independent reinforcement. *Journal of the Experimental Analysis of Behavior,* **19**, 293-302. (111)

Borbely, A. (1981) Sleep regulation: Circadian rhythms and homeostasis. In D. Ganten and D. Pfaff (eds.), *Sleep and the Autonomous Nervous System,* Berlin, Springer, pp. 83-104.

Borbely, A.A., Baumann, F., Brandeis, D., Strauch, I. and Lehmann, D. (1981) Sleep deprivation: Effect on sleep stages and EEG power density in man. *Electroencephalography and Clinical Neurophysiology,* **51**, 483-493. (61)

Boulter, L.R. and Adams, J.A. (1963) Vigilance decrement, the expectancy hypothesis, and intersignal interval. *Canadian Journal of Psychology,* **17**, 201-209. (113)

Bowden, D.M., Kripke, D.F. and Wyborney, U.G. (1978) Ultradian rhythms in waking behavior of rhesus monkeys. *Physiology and Behavior,* **21**, 929-933. (104)

Breithaupt, H., Hildebrandt, G., Dohre, D., Josch, R., Sieber, U. and Werner, M. (1978) Tolerance to shift of sleep, as related to the individual's circadian phase position. *Ergonomics,* **21**, 767-774. (206)

Breithaupt, H., Hildebrandt, G. and Werner, M. (1981) Circadian type questionnaire and objective circadian characteristics. In A. Reinberg, N. Vieux and P. Andlauer (eds.), *Night and Shift Work: Biological and Social Aspects,* Oxford, Pergamon Press, pp. 435-440. (33)

Brief, R.S. and Scala, R.A. (1975) Occupational exposure limits for novel work schedules. *American Industrial Hygiene Association Journal.* **36,** 467-469. (160)

Broadbent, D.E. (1953) Classical conditioning and human watchkeeping. *Psychological Review,* **60,** 331-339. (111)

Broadbent, D.E. (1958) *Perception and Communication.* London, Pergamon. (115, 127, 135)

Broadbent, D.E. (1963a) Some recent research from the Applied Psychology Research Unit, Cambridge. In D.N. Buckner and J.J. McGrath (eds.), *Vigilance: A Symposium,* New York, McGraw-Hill, pp. 72-82. (114)

Broadbent, D.E. (1963b) Possibilities and difficulties in the concept of arousal. In D.N. Buckner and J.J. McGrath (eds.), *Vigilance: A Symposium,* New York, McGraw-Hill, pp. 184-192. (117)

Broadbent, D.E. (1971) *Decision and Stress.* London, Academic Press. (115)

Broadbent, D.E. and Gregory, M. (1963a) Vigilance considered as a statistical decision. *British Journal of Psychology,* **54,** 309-323. (125)

Broadbent, D.E. and Gregory, M. (1963b) Division of attention and the decision theory of signal detection. *Proceedings of the Royal Society,* Series B, **13,** 221-231. (128)

Brodan, V., Vostechovsky, M., Kuhn, M. and Cepelak, J. (1969) Changes of mental and physical performance in sleep deprived healthy volunteers. *Activitas Nervosa Superior,* **11,** 175-181. (57)

Brown, D. (1975) Shiftwork: A survey of the sociological implications of studies of male shift workers. *Journal of Occupational Psychology,* **48,** 231-240. (213, 218, 219)

Brown, D. and Charles, N. (1982) *Women and Shiftwork: Some Evidence from Britain.* Dublin, European Foundation for the Improvement of Living and Working Conditions. (224, 225)

Brown, F.M. (1982) Rhythmicity as an energing variable for psychology. In F.M. Brown and R.C. Graeber (eds.), *Rhythmic Aspects of Behavior,* Hillsdale, NJ, and London, Lawrence Erlbaum Associates, pp. 3-38. (275)

Brown, H.G. (1959) *Some Effects of Shiftwork on Social and Domestic Life.* Yorkshire Bulletin of Economic and Social Research, Occasional Paper no. 2, Hull. (214, 216, 218)

Browne, R.C. (1949) The day and night performance of teleprinter switch board operators. *Occupational Psychology,* **23,** 121-126. (242, 243)

Bryden, G. and Holdstock, T.L. (1973) Effects of night duty on sleep patterns of nurses. *Psychophysiology,* **10,** 36-42. (191)

Buckley, C., Conroy, R.T.W.L. and Lindsay, G.C. (1973) Time zone transitions and master mariners. *Journal of the Irish Colleges of Physicians and Surgeons,* **2,** 109-112. (261)

Buckner, D.N. (1963) An individual difference approach to explaining vigilance performance. In D.N. Buckner and J.J. McGrath (eds.), *Vigilance: A Symposium,* New York, McGraw-Hill. (124)

Buckner, D.N., Harabedian, A. and McGrath, J.J. (1960) *A Study of Individual Differences in Vigilance Performance.* Los Angeles, Human Factors Research Inc. Technical Report no. 2. (108, 124)

Buckner, D.N., Harabedian, A. and McGrath, J.J. (1966) Individual differences in vigilance performance. *Journal of Engineering Psychology,* **5,** 69-85. (124, 131)

Buckner, D.N. and McGrath, J.J. (1963) A comparison of performance on single and dual mode vigilance tasks. In D.N. McGrath and J.J. Buckner (eds.), *Vigilance: A Symposium,* New York, McGraw-Hill. (124)

Bullock, N., Dickens, P., Shapcott, M. and Steadman, P. (1974) Time budgets and models of urban activity patterns. *Social Trends,* **5,** 45-63. London, HMSO. (211)

Bunnage, D. (1981) Study on the consequences of shift work on social and family life. In *The Effects of Shiftwork on Health, Social and Family Life.* Dublin, European Foundation for the Improvement of Living and Working Conditions. (225)

Bush, I.E. (1962) Chemical and biological factors in the activity of adrenocortical steroids. *Pharmacological Reviews,* **14,** 317-428. (57)

Cahoon, R.L. (1970) Vigilance performance under hypoxia. *Journal of Applied Psychology,* **54,** 479-483. (129, 131)

Caille, E.J. and Bassano, J.L. (1977) Biorhythm and watch rhythms: hemeral watch rhythm and anhemeral watch rhythm in simulated permanent duty. In R.R. Mackie (ed.), *Vigilance: Theory, Operational Performance and Physiological Correlates,* New York, Plenum Press, pp. 461-509. (258)

Cameron, C. (1971) Questionnaire study of fatigue in civil aircrew. In B. McGann (ed.), *Psychological Aspects of Transmeridian Flying,* Dublin, Institute of Psychology. (275)

Canestrari, R.E. (1962) The effects of aging on vigilance performance. Paper presented to a meeting of the Gerontological Society, Miami, Florida. (130)

Carlstein, T., Parkes, D. and Thrift, N. (1978) *Timing Space and Spacing Time.* London, Edward Arnold. (212)

Carpentier J. and Cazamian, P. (1977) *Night Work: Its Effects on the Health and Welfare of the Worker.* Geneva, International Labour Office. (204, 218, 223)

Carr, G.D. (1969) Introversion–extraversion and vigilance performance. Unpublished PhD thesis, Tufts University. (126, 128)

Carskadon, M.A. and Dement, W.C. (1975) Sleep studies on a 90-minute day. *Electroencephalography and Clinical Neurophysiology,* **39,** 145-155. (84)

Carskadon, M.A. and Dement, W.C. (1977) Sleepiness and sleep state on a 90-min schedule. *Psychophysiology,* **14,** 127-133. (84)

Carskadon, M.A. and Dement, W.C. (1979) Effects of total sleep loss on sleep tendency. *Perceptual and Motor Skills,* **48,** 495-506. (105)

Carter, C.W. (1957) Quality control of visual characteristics. ASQC convention transactions, 623-634. (137)

Cervinka, R., Koller, M., Haider, M. and Kundi, M. 1984 Shift related nutrition problems. *Proceedings of the International Research Workshop on Psychological Approaches to Night and Shift Work,* Edinburgh, 1982. (202)

Cervinka, R., Kundi, M., Koller, M. and Arnhof, J. (1984) Ernährungsverhalten und Schichtarbeit. *Z. Arb. wiss.* **38/1(10 NF),** 30-35

Chadwick-Jones, J.K. (1969) *Automation and Behaviour.* London, Wiley. (218, 223)

Chaney, F.B. and Teel, K.S. (1967) Improving human performance through training and visual aids. *Journal of Applied Psychology,* **51,** 311-315. (139)

Chapman, D.E. and Sinclair, M.A. (1975) Ergonomics in inspection tasks in the food industry. In C.G. Drury and J.G. Fox (eds.), *Human Reliability in Quality Control,* London, Taylor & Francis, pp. 231-251. (137, 140, 141)

Charles, N. and Brown, D. (1981) Women, shiftwork and the sexual division of labour. *Sociological Review,* **9,** 685-704. (224)

Chaumont, A.J., Laporte, A., Nicolai, A. and Reinberg, A. (1979) Adjustment of shift workers to a weekly rotation. *Chronobiologia,* **6,** suppl. 1, 27-36. (190, 192)

Chevrier, J.P. (1973) Etude experimentale des variations physiologiques du sodium at du potassium urinaires, liee au decalage horaire. *Comptes Rendus des Seances de la Societe de Biologie et des ses Filiales (Paris),* **167,** 2014-2018. (188)

Chevrier, J.P. (1974) Etude experimentale des variations physiologiques des 17-hydroxycorticosteroides urinaires liees au decalage horaire. *Comptes Rendus des Seances de la Societe de Biologie et des ses Filiales (Paris),* **168,** 910-914. (188)

Christie, M.J. and McBrearty, E.M.T. (1979) Psychophysical investigations of post lunch state in male and female subjects. *Ergonomics,* **22,** 307-323. (34, 42)

Claridge, G.S. (1960) The excitation-inhibition balance in neurotics. In H.J. Eysenck (ed.), *Experiments in Personality, vol. 2.* London, Routledge & Kegan Paul. (127)

Cloudsley-Thompson, J.L. (1980) *Biological Clocks, Their Functions in Nature.* London, Weidenfeld & Nicolson. (13)

Clugston, G.A. and Garlick, P.J. (1982) The response of protein and energy metabolism to food intake in lean and obese man. *Human Nutrition: Clinical Nutrition.* **36C,** 57-70. (56)

Cohen, A.R. and Gadon, H. (1978) *Alternative Working Schedules: Integrating Individual and Organizational Needs.* Reading, Mass., Addison-Wesley. (153, 155, 158)

Coles, M.G.H. and Gale, A. (1971) Physiological reactivity as a predictor of performance in a vigilance task. *Psychophysiology,* **8,** 594-599. (129)

Coles, M.G.H., Gale, M.A. and Kline, P. (1971) Personality and habituation of the orienting reaction: Tonic and response measures of electrodermal activity. *Psychophysiology,* **8,** 54-63. (128)

Collier, H.E. (1943) *Outlines of Industrial Medical Practice.* London, Edward Arnold. (205)

Colquhoun, W.P. (1959) The effect of a short rest pause on inspection efficiency. *Ergonomics,* **2,** 367-372. (111, 131, 144)

Colquhoun, W.P. (1960) Temperament, inspection efficiency and time of day. *Ergonomics,* **3,** 377-378. (114)

Colquhoun, W.P. (1961) The effect of unwanted signals on performance in a vigilant task. *Ergonomics,* **4,** 41-52. (112, 125)

Colquhoun, W.P. (1962) Effects of hyoscine and meclozine on vigilance and short-term memory. *British Journal of Industrial Medicine,* **19,** 287-296. (125, 131)

Colquhoun, W.P. (1967) Sonar target detection as a decision process. *Journal of Applied Psychology,* **51,** 187-190. (143)

Colquhoun, W.P. (1971) Circadian variation in mental efficiency. In W.P. Colquhoun (ed.), *Biological Rhythms and Human Performance,* London, Academic Press, pp. 39-107. (40, 41, 47, 81, 257)

Colquhoun, W.P. (1975) Evaluation of auditory, visual and dual-mode displays for prolonged sonar monitoring in repeated sessions. *Human Factors,* **17,** 425-437. (125)

Colquhoun, W.P. (1979) Phase shift in temperature rhythm after transmeridian flight, as related to pre-flight phase angle. *International Archives of Occupational and Environmental Health.* **42,** 149-157. (35, 235)

Colquhoun, W.P. (1981) Shift work discussion and conclusion. In L.C. Johnson, D.I. Tepas, W.P. Colquhoun and M.J. Colligan (eds.), *Biological Rhythms, Sleep and Shift Work,* New York, Spectrum Publications, pp. 607-613. (172)

Colquhoun, W.P. and Baddeley, A.D. (1964) Role of pretest expectancy in vigilance decrement. *Journal of Experimental Psychology,* **68,** 156-160. (112)

Colquhoun, W.P. and Baddeley, A.D. (1967) Influence of signal probability during pretraining on vigilance decrement. *Journal of Experimental Psychology,* **73,** 153-155. (111, 112)

Colquhoun, W.P., Blake, M.J.F. and Edwards, R.S. (1968a) Experimental studies of shift work I: A comparison of 'rotating' and 'stabilized' 4-hour systems. *Ergonomics,* **11,** 437-453. (40, 115, 244, 256, 257, 258)

Colquhoun, W.P., Blake, M.J.F. and Edwards, R.S. (1968b) Experimental studies of shift work II: Stabilized 8-hour shift system. *Ergonomics,* **11,** 527-546. (115, 186, 244, 258, 260)

Colquhoun, W.P., Blake, M.J.F. and Edwards, R.S. (1969) Experimental studies of shift work III: Stabilized 12-hour shift system. *Ergonomics,* **12,** 865-882. (159, 244, 259)

Colquhoun, W.P. and Condon, R. (1981) Introversion-Extraversion and the adjustment of the body-temperature rhythm to night work. In A. Reinberg, N. Vieux and P. Andlauer (eds.), *Shift Work: Biological and Social Aspects,* Oxford, Pergamon Press, pp. 449-455. (260)

Colquhoun, W.P. and Edwards, R.S. (1970a) Practice effects on a visual vigilance task with and without search. *Human Factors,* **12,** 537-545. (139)

Colquhoun, W.P. and Edwards, R.S. (1970b) Circadian rhythms of body temperature in shift work at a coal face. *British Journal of Industrial Medicine,* **27,** 266-272. (190)

Colquhoun, W.P. and Folkard, S. (1978) Personality differences in body-temperature rhythm, and their relation to its adjustment to night work. *Ergonomics,* **21,** 811-817. (206, 231)

Colquhoun, W.P., Hamilton, P. and Edwards, R.S. (1975) Effects of circadian rhythm, sleep deprivation and fatigue on performance during the night hours. In P. Colquhoun, S. Folkard, P. Knauth and J. Rutenfranz (eds.), *Experimental Studies of Shiftwork* (Forschungsberichte des Landes Nordrhein-Westfalen Report no. 2513), Opladen, Westdeutscher Verlag, pp. 20-28. (259)

Colquhoun, W.P., Paine, M.W.P.H. and Fort, A. (1978) Circadian rhythm of body temperature during prolonged undersea voyages. *Aviation, Space and Environmental Medicine,* **49,** 671-678. (257)

Colquhoun, W.P. and Rutenfranz, J. (eds.), (1980) *Studies of Shiftwork.* London, Taylor & Francis. (200)

Conroy, R.T.W.L., Elliott, A.L. and Mills, J.N. (1970a) Circadian rhythms in plasma concentration of 11-hydroxycorticosteroids in men working on night shift and in permanent night workers. *British Journal of Industrial Medicine,* **27,** 170-174. (189, 190)

Conroy, R.T.W.L., Elliott, A.L. and Mills, J.N. (1970b) Circadian excretory rhythms in night workers. *British Journal of Industrial Medicine,* **27,** 356-363. (189)

Cook, F.O. (1954) *Shift Work.* London, Institute of Personnel Management, Management House. (205)

Copes, K. and Rosentsweig, J. (1972) The effects of sleep deprivation upon motor performance of ninth-grade students. *Journal of Sports Medicine and Physical Fitness,* **12,** 47-53. (71)

Corcoran, D.W.J. (1965) Personality and the inverted-U relation. *British Journal of Psychology,* **56,** 267-273. (114)

Costa, G. and Gaffuri, E. (1983) Circadian rhythms, behaviour characteristics and tolerance to shiftwork (Abstract). *Chronobiologia,* **10,** 395. (236)

Costa, G., Gaffuri, E., Perfranceschi, G. and Tansella, M. (1979) Re-entrainment of diurnal variation of psychological and physiological performance at the end of a slowly rotated shift system in hospital workers. *International Archives of Occupational Health,* **44,** 165-175. (249)

Craig, A. (1978) Is the vigilance decrement simply a response adjustment towards probability matching? *Human Factors,* **20,** 441-446. (119)

Craig, A. (1979) Vigilance for two kinds of signal with unequal probabilities of occurrence. *Human Factors,* **21,** 647-653. (119)

Craig, A. (1980) Effect of prior knowledge of signal probabilities on vigilance performance at a two-signal task. *Human Factors,* **22,** 361-371. (119, 120)

Craig, A. (1981) Monitoring for one kind of signal in the presence of another; the effects of signal mix on detectability. *Human Factors,* **23,** 191-197. (111)

Craig, A. (1984) Human engineering: The control of vigilance. In J.S. Warm (ed.), *Sustained Attention in Human Performance,* Chichester, Wiley pp. 247-291. (135, 138, 145)

Craig, A., Baer, K. and Diekmann, A. (1981) The effects of lunch on sensory-perceptual functioning in man. *International Archives of Occupational and Environmental Health,* **49**, 105-114. (115)

Craig, A. and Colquhoun, W.P. (1975) Vigilance: A review. In C.G. Drury and J.G. Fox (eds.), *Human Reliability in Quality Control,* London, Taylor & Francis, pp. 71-88. (135)

Craig, A. and Colquhoun, W.P. (1977) Vigilance effects in complex inspection. In R.R. Mackie (ed.), *Vigilance: Theory, Operational Performance and Physiological Correlates,* New York, Plenum Press, pp. 239-262. (111, 134)

Craig, A., Colquhoun, W.P. and Corcoran, D.W.J. (1976) Combining evidence presented simultaneously to the eye and the ear: A comparison of some predictive models. *Perception and Psychophysics,* **19**, *6,* 473-484. (139)

Craig, A., Wilkinson, R.T. and Colquhoun, W.P. (1981) Diurnal variation in vigilance efficiency. *Ergonomics,* **24**, 641-651. (42)

Craik, F.I.M. (1969) Applications of signal detection theory to studies of aging. In A.T. Welford and J.E. Birren (eds.), *Decision Making and Age,* Basle, Karger. (130)

Craik, F.I.M. and Blakstein, K.R. (1975) Psychophysiology and human memory. In P.H. Venables and M.J. Christie (eds.), *Research in Psychophysiology,* London, Wiley, pp. 389-417. (44)

Crider, A. and Augenbraun, C.B. (1975) Auditory vigilance correlates of electrodermal response habituation speed. *Psychophysiology,* **12**, 36-40. (129)

Crider, A. and Lunn, R. (1971) Electrodermal lability as a personality dimension. *Journal of Experimental Research in Personality,* **5**, 145-150. (128)

Czeisler, C.A., Moore-Ede, M.C. and Coleman, R.M. (1982) Rotating shift work schedules that disrupt sleep are improved by applying circadian principles. *Science,* **217**, 460-463. (252)

Czeisler, C.A., Richardson, G.S., Zimmerman, J.C., Moore-Ede, M.C. and Weitzman, E.D. (1981) Entrainment of human circadian rhythms by light-dark cycles: A reassessment. *Photochemistry and Photobiology,* **34**, 239-247. (194)

Czeisler, C.A., Weitzman, E.D., Moore-Ede, M.C., Zimmerman, J.C. and Knauer, R.S. (1980) Human sleep: Its duration and organization depend on its circadian phase. *Science,* **210**, 1264-1267. (195)

Dahlgren, K. (1981a) Long-term adjustment of circadian rhythms to a rotating shift work schedule. *Scandinavian Journal of Work Environment and Health,* **7**, 141-151. (189, 192, 193)

Dahlgren, K. (1981b) Adjustment of circadian rhythms to rapidly rotating shift work — a field study of two shift systems. In A. Reinberg, N. Vieux and P. Andlauer (eds.), *Advances in the Biosciences,* vol. 30: *Night and Shift Work: Biological and Social Aspects,* London, Pergamon Press, pp. 357-364. (190, 197)

Dahlgren, K. (1981c) Adjustment of circadian rhythms and EEG sleep functions to day and night sleep among permanent night workers and rotating shift workers. *Psychophysiology,* **18**, 381-391. (188, 190, 191)

Daleva, M., Hadjiolova, I., Tsaneva, N. and Taidovski, G. (1972) Physiological changes in operators during shift work. *Studia Laboris et Salutis,* **11**, 26-32. (190)

Dalton, K. (1968) Menstruation and examination. *Lancet,* 2, 1386-1388. (94)

Dardano, J.F. (1962) Relationship of intermittent noise, intersignal interval and skin conductance to vigilance behaviour. *Journal of Applied Psychology,* **46**, 106-114. (113)

Davenport, W.G. (1968) Auditory vigilance: The effects of costs and values on signals. *Australian Journal of Psychology,* **20,** 213-218. (143)

Davenport, W.G. (1969) Vigilance for simultaneous auditory and cutaneous signals. *Canadian Journal of Psychology,* **23,** 93-100. (143)

Davies, A.D.M. and Davies, D.R. (1975) The effects of noise and time of day upon age differences in performance at two checking tasks. *Ergonomics,* **18,** 321-336. (130)

Davies, D.R. (1968) Age difference in paced inspection tasks. In G.A. Talland (ed.), *Human Aging and Behaviour,* New York, Academic Press. (130)

Davies, D.R. (1983) Attention, arousal and effort. In A. Gale and J. Edwards (eds.), *Physiological correlates of human behaviour,* vol. II, London, Academic Press. (128)

Davies, D.R., Hockey, G.R.J. and Taylor, A. (1969) Varied auditory stimulation, temperament differences and vigilance performance. *British Journal of Psychology,* **60,** *4,* 453-457. (114)

Davies, D.R., Jones, D.M. and Taylor, A. (1983) Selective and sustained attention tasks: Individual and group difference. In R. Parasuraman and D.R. Davies (eds.), *Varieties of Attention,* New York, Academic Press. (130)

Davies, D.R., Lang, L. and Shackleton, V.J. (1973) The effects of music and task difficulty on performance at a visual vigilance task. *British Journal of Psychology,* **64,** 383-389. (114, 125)

Davies, D.R. and Parasuraman, R. (1982) *The Psychology of Vigilance.* London, Academic Press. (109, 126, 130)

Davies, D.R., Shackleton, V.J. and Parasuraman, R. (1983) Monotony and boredom. In G.R.J. Hockey (ed.), *Stress and Fatigue in Human Performance,* Chichester, Wiley (128)

Davies, D.R. and Tune, G.S. (1970) *Human Vigilance Performance.* London, Staples. (131, 139)

Deaton, M., Tobias, J.S. and Wilkinson, R.T. (1971) The effects of sleep deprivation on signal detection parameters. *Quarterly Journal of Experimental Psychology,* **23,** 449-451. (125)

Debry, G. and Bleyer, R. (1972) Influence du rhythme des trois-huit sur l'alimentation des travailleurs. In G. Debry and R. Bleyer (eds.), *Alimentation et travail,* Paris, Masson, pp. 153-177. (209)

Deese, J. (1955) Some problems in the theory of vigilance. *Psychological Review,* **62,** 359-368. (112, 113, 114)

Dega, K., Dolmierski, R. and Klajman, S. (1976) Untersuchungen des Rhythmus der psycho-physiologischen Leistungsfahigkeit beim Schiffspersonal. In G. Hildebrandt (ed.), *Biologische Rhythmen und Arbeit.* Vienna and New York, Springer Verlag, pp. 109-115. (258)

De la Mare, G. and Walker, J. (1968) Factors influencing the choice of shift rotation. *Occupational Psychology,* **42,** 1-21. (216)

Delgado-Garcia, J.M., Grau, C., DeFeudis, P., Del Pozo, F., Jienez, J.M. and Delgado, J.M.R. (1976) Ultradian rhythms in the mobility and behavior of rhesus monkeys. *Experimental Brain Research,* **25,** 79-91. (104)

De Marchi, G.W. and Tong, J.E. (1972) Menstrual, diurnal and activation effects on the resolution of temporally paired flashes. *Psychophysiology,* **9,** 362-367. (93)

Depta, E. (1973) The four-shifts work system and sick absence. *Zdrowie Publiszne (Warszawa),* **84,** 821-823. (183)

Dervillee, P. and Lazarini, H.J. (1958) Considerations sur le travail par roulement et ses repercussions sur la sante. *Proceedings of the XII International Congress on Occupational Health,* Helsinki, 1-6. 7. 57, vol. III, pp. 128-130. (205)

Diamond, M., Diamond, A.L. and Mast, M. (1972) Visual sensitivity and sexual arousal levels during the menstrual cycle. *Journal of Nervous and Mental Disease,* **155,** 170-176. (94)

Diekmann, A., Baer, K., Ernst, G. and Nachreiner, F. (1982) The influence of shiftwork of the father on the school career of the children (Abstract). *20th International Congress of Applied Psychology,* International Association of Applied Psychology. (215)

Dinges, D.F., Orne, E.C., Evans, F.J. and Orne, M.T. (1981a) Performance after naps in sleep-conducive and alerting environments. In L.C. Johnson, D.I. Tepas, WP. Colquhoun and M.J. Colligan (eds), *Biological Rhythms, Sleep and Shift Work,* New York, Spectrum Publications, pp. 539-552. (81, 84)

Dinges, D.F., Orne, M.T., Orne, E.C. and Evans, F.J. (1981b) Behavioral patterns in habitual nappers. *Sleep Research,* **10,** 136. (79)

Dirken, J.M. (1966) Industrial shift work: Decrease in well-being and specific effects. *Ergonomics,* **9,** 115-124. (192)

Donnell, J., Lubin, A., Naitoh, P. and Johnson, L. (1969) Relative recuperative value of sleep stages after total sleep deprivation: a progress report. *Psychology,* **6,** 239-240. (71)

Drury, C.G. (1973) The effect of speed of working on industrial inspection accuracy. *Applied Ergonomics,* **4,** 2-7. (140)

Drury, C.G. (1975) Human decision making in quality control. In C.G. Drury and J.G. Fox (eds), *Human Reliability in Quality Control,* London, Taylor & Francis, pp. 45-53. (139)

Drury, C.G. and Addison, J.L. (1973) An industrial study of the effects of feedback and fault density on occupational performance. *Ergonomics,* **16,** *2,* 159-169. (136, 137, 141, 142, 143)

Dumont, C. (1982) Conditions of work and life of shift workers in industry in developing countries. Proceedings of the 6th International Symposium on Night and Shift Work. *Journal of Human Ergology,* **11,** Suppl. (170)

Ehrenstein, W., Muller-Limmroth, W., Schaffler, K. and Thebaud, C. (1970) Polygraphische Schlafuntersuchungen des Tagschlafs nach einer Nachtschicht und des Nachtschlafs nach einer Tagschicht an 8 Krankenschwestern. *Pflugers Archiv,* **319,** 121. (190)

Ehret, C.F. (1981) New approaches to chronohygiene for the shift worker in the nuclear power industry. In A. Reinberg, N. Vieux and P. Andlauer (eds), *Night and Shift Work: Biological and Social Aspects,* Oxford, Pergamon Press. pp. 263-270. (239)

Elliott, A., Mills, J.N., Minors, D.S. and Waterhouse, J.M. (1972) The effect of real and simulated time-zone shifts upon the circadian rhythms of body temperature, plasma 11-hydroxycorticosteroids and renal excretion in human subjects. *Journal of Physiology,* **221,** 227-257. (188)

Elliott, E. (1960) Perception and alertness. *Ergonomics,* **3,** 357-369. (125, 136)

Embrey, D.E. (1975) Training the inspector's sensitivity and response strategy. In C.G. Drury and J.G. Fox (eds), *Human Reliability in Quality Control,* London, Taylor & Francis, pp. 123-131. (140)

Englander-Golden, P., Chang, H.S., Whitmore, M.R. and Dienstbier, R.A. (1980) Female sexual arousal and the menstrual cycle. *Journal of Human Stress,* **6,** 42-48. (91, 92)

Englander-Golden, P., Willis, K.A. and Dienstbier, R.A. (1977) Stability of perceived tension as a function of the menstrual cycle. *Journal of Human Stress,* **3,** 14-21. (90)

Evans, F.J. (1967) Field dependence and the Maudsley Personality Inventory. *Perceptual and Motor Skills,* **24,** 526. (128)

Evans, F.J. Cook, M.P., Cohen, H.D., Orne, E.C. and Orne, M.T. (1977) Appetitive and replacement naps: EEG and behaviour. *Science,* **197,** 687-689. (63)

Evans, F.J. and Orne, M.T. (1975) Recovery from fatigue. Final report on contract no. DADA 17–71–C–1120. Washington, US Army Medical Research and Development Command. (78, 79)

Eysenck, H.J. (1957) *The Dynamics of Anxiety and Hysteria.* New York, Praeger. (127)

Eysenck, M.W. and Folkard, S. (1980) Personality, time of day, and caffeine: Some theoretical and conceptual problems in Revelle et al. *Journal of Experimental Psychology: General,* **109,** 32-41. (34)

Faulkner, T.W. (1962) Variability of performance in a vigilance task. *Journal of Applied Psychology,* **46,** 325-328. (141)

Faulkner, T.W. and Murphy, T.J. (1975) Lighting for difficult visual tasks. In C.G. Drury and J.G. Fox (eds), *Human Reliability in Quality Control,* London, Taylor & Francis, pp. 133-147. (139)

Feinberg, I., Fein, G. and Floyd, T.C. (1980) EEG patterns during and following extended sleep in young adults. *Electroencephalography and Clinical Neurophysiology,* **50,** 467-476. (62, 191)

Finger, F.W. (1982) Effects of atypical illumination schedules. In F.M. Brown and R.C. Graeber (eds), *Rhythmic Aspects of Behavior,* Hillsdale, and London, Lawrence Erlbaum Associates, pp. 345-361. (275)

Fischer, F.M. (1982) Working conditions of the shiftworkers of the metropolitan area Sao Paulo, Brazil. Proceedings of the 6th International Symposium on Night and Shift Work. *Journal of Human Ergology,* **11,** Suppl. (170)

Fisher, L.B. (1968) The diurnal mitotic rhythm in the human epidermis. *British Journal of Dermatology,* **80,** 75-80. (56)

Fishwick, F. and Harling, G.J. (1974) *Shift Working in the Motor Industry.* London, National Economic Development Office. (221)

Fisk, A.D. and Schneider, W. (1981) Control and automatic processing during tasks requiring sustained attention: A new approach to vigilance. *Human Factors,* **23,** 737-750. (119)

Fleishman, E.A. (1972) On the relation between abilities, learning and human performance. *American Psychologist,* **27,** 1017-1032. (118)

Folkard, S. (1975a) Diurnal variation in logical reasoning. *British Journal of Psychology,* **66,** 1-8. (46, 47, 49, 51)

Folkard, S. (1975b) The nature of diurnal variations in performance and their implications for shift work studies. In P. Colquhoun, S. Folkard, P. Knauth and J. Rutenfranz (eds), *Experimental Studies of Shiftwork,* Opladen, Westdeutscher Verlag, pp. 113-122. (49)

Folkard, S. (1980) A note on 'Time of day effects in school children's immediate and delayed retention of meaningful material' – the influence of the importance of the information tested. *British Journal of Psychology,* **71,** 95-97. (49)

Folkard, S. (1982) Circadian rhythms and human memory. In F.M. Brown and R.C. Graeber (eds), *Rhythmic Aspects of Behaviour,* Hillsdale, and London, Lawrence Erlbaum Associates, pp. 241-272. (44, 48)

Folkard, S. (1983) Diurnal variation. In G.R.J. Hockey (ed.), *Stress and Fatigue in Human Performance,* Chichester, Wiley, pp. 245-272. (41, 47)

Folkard, S., Condon, R. and Herbert, M. (1984) Night shift paralysis. *Experientia* (in press). (248)

Folkard, S., Knauth, P., Monk, T.H. and Rutenfranz, J. (1976) The effect of memory load on the circadian variation in performance efficiency under a rapidly rotating shift system. *Ergonomics,* **19,** 479-488. (47, 246, 247, 260)

Folkard, S. and Monk, T.H. (1979) Shiftwork and Performance. *Human Factors,* **21,** 483-492. (237, 240, 241, 243, 260)

Folkard, S. and Monk, T.H. (1980) Circadian rhythms in human memory. *British Journal of Psychology,* **71,** 295-307. (32, 42, 43, 44, 45, 249)

Folkard, S. and Monk, T.H. (1981) Individual differences in the circadian response to a weekly rotating shift system. In A. Reinberg, N. Vieux and P. Andlauer (eds), *Night and Shift Work: Biological and Social Aspects,* Oxford, Pergamon Press. pp. 367-374. (234)

Folkard, S. and Monk, T.H. (1983) Chronopsychology: Circadian rhythms and human performance. In *Physiological Correlates of Human Behaviour,* vol. 2: *Attention and Performance,* London, Academic Press, pp. 57-78. (38)

Folkard, S., Monk, T.H., Bradbury, R. and Rosenthall, J. (1977) Time of day effects in school children's immediate and delayed recall of meaningful material. *British Journal of Psychology,* **68,** 45-50. (44, 45)

Folkard, S., Monk, T.H., Lewis, E.K. and Whelpton, C.P. (1982) *Individual Differences and Adjustment to Shiftwork.* Shanklin, Co. Dublin, European Foundation for the Improvement of Living and Working Conditions. (236)

Folkard, S., Monk, T.H. and Lobban, M.C. (1978) Short and long-term adjustment of circadian rhythms in 'permanent' night nurses. *Ergonomics,* **21,** 785-799. (183, 189, 192, 193, 232, 235, 242)

Folkard, S., Monk, T.H. and Lobban, M.C. (1979) Towards a predictive test of adjustment to shift work. *Ergonomics,* **22,** 79-91. (206, 236)

Folkard, S., Wever, R.A. and Wildgruber, C.M. (1983) Multioscillatory control of circadian rhythms in human performance. *Nature,* **305,** 223-226. (51)

Foret, J. and Benoit, O. (1974) Structure du sommeil chez des travailleurs à horaires alternants. *Electroencephalography and Clinical Neurophysiology,* **37,** 337-344. (190)

Foret, J. and Benoit, O. (1978a) Etude du sommeil chez des travailleurs à horaires alternants: Adaptation et recuperation dans le cas de rotation rapide de poste (3–4 jours). *European Journal of Applied Physiology,* **38,** 71-82. (190)

Foret, J. and Benoit, O. (1978b) Shift work: The level of adjustment to schedule reversal assessed by a sleep study. *Waking and Sleeping,* **2,** 107-112. (191)

Foret, J. and Benoit, O. (1979) Sleep recordings of shift workers adhering to a three to four-day rotation. *Chronobiologia,* **6,** suppl. 1, 45-53.

Foret, J., Benoit, O & Royant-Parola, S. (1982). Sleep schedules and peak times of oral temperature and alertness in morning and evening 'types'. *Ergonomics,* **25,** 821-827. (30)

Foret, J., Bensimon, G., Benoit, O. and Vieux, N. (1981) Quality of sleep as a function of age and shift work. In A. Reinberg, N. Vieux and P. Andlauer, (eds), *Night and Shift Work: Biological and Social Aspects,* Oxford, Pergamon Press, pp. 149-154. (191, 193, 229)

Foret, J. and Lantin, G. (1972) The sleep of train drivers: An example of the effects of irregular work schedules on sleep. In W.P. Colquhoun (ed.), *Aspects of Human Efficiency,* London, English Universities Press, pp. 273-282. (190)

Fort, A. and Mills, J.N. (1976) Der Einfluß der Tageszeit und des vorhergehenden Schlaf-Wach-Musters auf die Leistungsfahigkeit unmittelbar nach dem Aufstehen. In G. Hildebrandt (ed.), *Biologische Rhythmen und Arbeit,* Springer Verlag, Heidelberg. (40)

Fox, J.G. (1975) Vigilance and arousal: A key to maintaining inspectors' performance. In C.G. Drury and J.G. Fox (eds), *Human Reliability in Quality Control,* London, Taylor & Francis, pp. 89-96. (114, 136, 137)

Fox, J.G. (1977) Quality control of coins. In E.S. Weiner and H.G. Maille (eds), *Case Studies in Ergonomics Practice* vol. 1, *Human Factors in Work, Design Production,* London, Taylor & Francis, pp. 101-130. (135, 137, 140, 144)

Fox, J.G. and Embrey, D.E. (1972) Music: An aid to productivity. *Applied Ergonomics,* **3**, 202-205. (144)

Fox, J.G. and Haslegrave, C.M. (1969) Industrial inspection efficiency and the probability of a defect occurring. *Ergonomics,* **12**, 713-721. (137)

Francescioni, R.P., Stokes, J.W., Banderet, L.E. and Kowal, D.M. (1978) Sustained operations and sleep deprivation: Effects on indices of stress. *Aviation, Space and Environmental Medicine.* **49**, 1271-1274. (57)

Fraser, D.C. (1953) The relation of an environmental variable to performance in a prolonged visual task. *Quarterly Journal of Experimental Psychology,* **5**, 31-32. (136, 143)

Friedman, S. and Fisher, C. (1967) On the presence of rhythmic, diurnal, oral instinctual drive cycle in man: A preliminary report. *Journal of the American Psychoanalytic Association,* **15**, 317-345. (99)

Friedman, J., Globus, G., Huntley, A., Mullaney, D., Naitoh, P. and Johnson, L. (1977) Performance and mood during and after gradual sleep reduction. *Psychophysiology,* **14**, 245-250. (61, 62)

Fröberg, J.E. (1977) Twenty-four-hour patterns in human performance, subjective and physiological variables and differences between morning and evening active subjects. *Biological Psychology,* **5**, 119-134. (33, 68)

Fröberg, J.E. (1978) *Task Complexity and 24-hr Performance Patterns in Morning and Evening Active Subjects.* Stockholm, Forsvarets Forskningsanstalt FOA rapport C52001–H6. (69, 72)

Fröberg, J.E. (1979) *Performance in Tasks Differing in Memory Load and its Relationship with Habitual Activity Phase and Body Temperature.* Stockholm, Forsvarets Forskningsanstalt FOA rapport C52002–H6. (71)

Fröberg, J., Karlsson, C.G. and Levi, L. (1972) Shift work: A study of catecholamine excretion, self-ratings and attitudes. *Studia Laboris et Salutis,* **11**, 10-20. (8, 192)

Fröberg, J., Karlsson, C.G., Levi, L. and Lidberg, L. (1972) Circadian variations in performance, psychological ratings, catecholamine excretion and diueresis during prolonged sleep deprivation. *International Journal of Psychology,* **2**, 23-36. (8)

Fröberg, J., Karlsson, C.G., Levi, L. and Lidberg, L. (1975a) Circadian rhythms of catecholamine excretion, shooting range performance and selfratings of fatigue during sleep deprivation. *Biological Psychology,* **2**, 175-188. (67, 196)

Fröberg, J.E., Karlsson, C.G., Levi, L. and Lidberg, L. (1975b) Psychological circadian rhythms during a 72-hour vigil. *Forsvarsmedicin,* **11**, 192-201. (67, 196)

Gadbois, C. (1981) Women on night shift: Interdependence of sleep and off-the-job activities. In A. Reinberg, N. Vieux and P. Andlauer (eds), *Night and Shift Work: Biological and Social Aspects,* Oxford, Pergamon Press, pp. 223-227. (224, 230)

Gale, A. (1969) 'Stimulus hunger': Individual differences in operant strategy in a button-pressing task. *Behaviour Research and Therapy,* **7**, 265-274. (128)

Gale, A., Bull, R., Penfold, V., Coles, M. and Barraclough, R. (1972) Extroversion, time of day, vigilance performance and physiological arousal: Failure of replicate traditional findings. *Psychonomic Science,* **29**, 1-5. (128, 131)

Gale, A. and Lynn, R. (1972) A developmental study of attention. *British Journal of Educational Psychology,* **42**, 260-266. (129)

Gale, A., Morris, P.E., Lucas, B. and Richardson, A. (1972) Types of imagery and imagery types: An EEG study. *British Journal of Psychology,* **63**, 523-531. (128)

Gamberale, F., Strindberg, L. and Wahlberg, I. (1975) Female work capacity during the menstrual cycle: Physiological and psychological reactions. *Scandinavian Journal of Work Environment and Health,* **1**, 120-127. (93)

Gange, J.J., Geen, R.G. and Harkins, S.G. (1979) Autonomic differences between extroverts and introverts during vigilance. *Psychophysiology,* **16**, 392-397. (128)

Garvey, W.G., Taylor, F.V. and Newlin, E.P. (1959) *The Use of 'Artificial Signals' to Enhance Monitoring Performance.* US Naval Research Laboratory, Engineering Psychol. Branch, Applications Research Division NRL Report 52569. (141)

Gates, A.I. (1916) Variations in efficiency during the day, together with practise effects, sex differences, and correlations. *University of California Publications in Psychology,* **2**, *1*, 1-156. (39)

Gatherum, D.P., Harrington, G. and Pomeroy, R.W. (1959) Visual judgements of quality in meat. *Journal of Agricultural Science,* **52**, 320-331. (139)

Gatherum, D.P., Harrington, G. and Pomeroy, R.W. (1960) Visual judgements of quality in meat. *Journal of Agricultural Science,* **54**, 145-157. (139)

Gatherum, D.P., Harrington, G. and Pomeroy, R.W. (1961) Visual judgements of quality in meat. *Journal of Agricultural Science,* **57**, 401-417. (139)

Gillberg, M. and Akerstedt, T. (1981a) Sleep deprivation in normals — some psychological and biochemical data from three studies. In W.P. Koella (ed.), *Sleep 1980,* Basle, Karger. (68, 81)

Gillberg, M. and Akerstedt, T. (1981b) Possible measures of 'sleepiness' for the evaluation of disturbed and displaced sleep. In A. Reinberg, N. Vieux and P. Andlauer (eds), *Night and Shift Work: Biological and Social Aspects,* Oxford, Pergamon Press, pp. 155–160. (81, 196)

Gillberg, M. and Akerstedt, T. (1982a) Temperature and sleep at different times of the day. *Sleep,* **5**, 378-388. (55, 195)

Gillberg, M. and Akerstedt, T. (1982b) The circadian pattern of unrestricted sleep and its relation to body temperature, hormones and alertness. In L.C. Johnson, D.I. Tepas, W.P. Colquhoun and M.J. Colligan (eds), *Biological Rhythms, Sleep and Shift Work.* New York, SP Medical and Scientific Books, pp. 481-498. (195)

Gillberg, M. (1984) The effects of two alternative timings of a one-hour nap on early morning performance. *Biological Psychiatry,* **19**, 45-54. (82, 83, 84).

Gillies, G.J. (1975) Glass nspection. In C.G. Drury and J.G. Fox (eds), *Human Reliability in Quality Control,* London, Taylor & Francis, pp. 273-287. (137, 142)

Globus, G.G., Drury, R.L., Phoebus, E.C. and Boyd, R. (1971) Ultradian rhythms in human performance. *Perceptual and Motor Skills,* **33**, 1171-1174. (103)

Golembiewski, R.T., Hillies, R. and Kagno, M.S. (1974) A longitudinal study of flex-time effects: Some consequences of an OD structural intervention. *Journal of Applied Behavioral Science,* **10**, 503-532. (156, 161)

Golembiewski, R.T. and Proehl, C.W. jr (1978) A survey of the empirical literature on flexible workhours: Character and consequences of a major innovation. *Academy of Management Review,* **3**, 823-853. (153, 155)

Golub, S. (1976) The effect of premenstrual anxiety and depression on cognitive function. *Journal of Personality and Social Psychology,* **34**, 99-104. (89, 95)

Gopher, D. and Lavie, P. (1980) Short term rhythms in the performance of a simple motor task. *Journal of Motor Behavior,* **12**, 207-219. (103)

Graeber, R.C. (1982) Alterations in performance following rapid transmeridian flight. In F.M. Brown and R.C. Graeber, (eds), *Rhythmic Aspects of Behavior,* Hillsdale, and London, Lawrence Erlbaum Associates, pp. 173-212. (274)

Graf, O., Pirtkien, R., Rutenfranz, J. and Ulich, E. (1958) *Nervose Belastung im Betrieb. I. Nachtarbeit und Nervose Belastung.* Cologne and Opladen, Westdeutscher Verlag. (190)

Grandjean, E. (1968) Fatigue: Its physiological and psychological significance. *Ergonomics,* **11**, 427-436.

Grant, C. and Pryse-Davies, J. (1968) Effects of oral contraceptives on depressive mood changes and on endometrial monoamine oxidase and phosphates. *British Medical Journal,* **28**, 777-780. (90)

Green, D.M. and Swets, J.A. (1966) *Signal Detection Theory and Psychophysics.* New York, Wiley. (109, 138)

Griefahn, B., Jansen, G. and Klosterkotter, W. (1976) Zur Problematick larmbedingter Schlafstorungen — eine Auswertung von Schlaf-Literatur. Berlin, Berichte des Umweltbundesamtes Berlin 4/1976. (207)

Gulevich, G., Dement, W. and Johnson, L.C. (1966) Psychiatric and EEG observations on a case of prolonged (264 hours) wakefulness. *Archives of General Psychiatry,* **15**, 29-36. (58, 61)

Gundy, R.F. (1961) Auditory detection of an unspecified signal. *Journal of Acoustical Society of America,* **33**, 1008-1012. (138)

Guralnick, R.F. (1972) Observing responses and decision processes in vigilance. *Journal of Experimental Psychology,* **93**, *2,* 239-244. (116, 117, 143)

Guralnick, M.J. and Harvey, K.G. (1970) Response requirement and performance in a visual vigilance task. *Psychonomic Science,* **20**, 215-217. (110)

Hacker, W. and Macher, F. (1977) Grundlagen und Moglichkeiten der projektierenden und korrigierenden Gestaltung von Arbeitstatigkeiten. *Universitatsreden 'Technische Universitat Dresden',* 5–32. (201)

Haider, M., Kundi, M. and Koller, M. (1981) Methodological issues and problems in shift work research. In L.C. Johnson, D.I. Tepas, W.P. Colquhoun and M.J. Colligan (eds), *Biological Rhythms, Sleep and Shift Work,* New York, SP Medical and Scientific Books, pp. 145–163. (203)

Halberg, F. (1967) Physiologic considerations underlying rhythmometry, with special reference to emotional illness. In J. Ajuriaguerra (ed.), *Cycles Biologiques et Psychiatrie,* Geneva, Symposium Bel-Air II, pp. 73-126. (98)

Halberg, F. (1978) Obituary: Professor John Mills. *Chronobiologia,* **5**, 91-93. (6)

Halberg, F., Carandente, F., Cornelissen, G. and Katinas, G.S. (1977) Glossary of chronobiology. *Chronobiologia,* **4**, Suppl. 1. (6)

Halberg, F. and Katinas, G.S. (1973) Chronobiologic glossary. *International Journal of Chronobiology,* **1**, 31-63. (6)

Halberg, F., Nelson, W. and Cadotte, L. (1975) Increased mortality in mice exposed to weekly 180°-shifts if lighting regimen LD 12:12 beginning at one year of age. *Chronobiologia,* **2**, Suppl. 1, 26. (275)

Halcomb, C.G. and Kirk, R.E. (1965) Organisational variables as predictors of vigilance behavior. *Perceptual and Motor Skills,* **21**, 547-552. (131)

Hamburg, D.A. (1966) Effects of progesterone on behavior. *Endocrines and the Central Nervous System,* **43**, 251-265. (92)

Hanhart, A. (1954) *Die Arbeitspause in Beitrieb.* Zurich, Oesch-Verlag. (144)

Harkins, S.G. and Geen, R.G. (1975) Discriminability and criterion differences between extraverts and introverts during vigilance. *Journal of Research in Personality,* **9**, 335-340. (126)

Harrington, J.M. (1978) *Shift work and health. A critical review of the literature.* London, HMSO. (13, 201, 203)

Harris, D.H. (1966) Effect of equipment complexity on inspection performance. *Journal of Applied Psychology,* **50**, 236-237. (137, 140)

Harris, W. and Mackie, R.R. (1972) *A Study of the Relationships Among Fatigue, Hours of Service, and Safety of Operation of Truck and Bus Drivers.* (Tech. Rep. 1727 2.) Goleta, Cal. Human Factors Research, Inc.

Hartley, L.R. (1974) A comparison of continuous and distributed reduced sleep schedules. *Quarterly Journal of Experimental Psychology,* **26,** 8-14. (73, 85)

Hartley, L.R., Olsson, R. and Ingleby, J.D. (1973) Visual assistance in an auditory detection task. Cited in E.C. Poulton (1973) The effects of fatigue upon inspection work. *Applied Ergonomics,* **4,** 73-83. (125)

Haslam, D.R. (1982) Sleep loss, recovery sleep, and military performance. *Ergonomics,* **25,** 163-178. (73)

Hassleman, M., Schaff, G. and Metz, B. (1960) Influences respectives du travail, de la temperature ambiante et de la privation de sommeil sur l'excretion urinaire de catecholamioines chez l'homme normal. *Comptes Rendus des Seances de la Societe de Biologie,* **154,** 197-201. (74)

Hastrup, J.L. (1979) Effects of electrodermal lability and introversion on vigilance decrement. *Psychophysiology,* **16,** 302-310. (127, 129)

Hatfield, J.L. and Loeb, M. (1968) Sense mode and coupling in a vigilance task. *Perception and Psychophysics,* **4,** 29-36. (125)

Hatfield, J.L. and Soderquist, D.R. (1970) Coupling effects and performance in vigilance tasks. *Human Factors,* **12,** 351-359. (125)

Hayes, A.S. (1950) Control of visual inspection. *Industrial Quality Control,* **6,** 73-76.

Henry, J.P. (1980) In R. Usdin *et al.* (eds), *Catecholamines and Stress: Recent Advances,* Amsterdam, North-Holland. (57)

Herrmann, H. (1982) Bedeutung und bewertung der nachtarbeit — gedanken zur erstellung eines berufs — genossenschaftlichen grundsatzes-. In *Kombinierte Belastungen am Arbeitsplatz. Der chromisch Erkrankte im Betrieb. Bericht uber die 22, Jahrestagung der Deutschen Gesellschaft fur Arbeitsmedizin e. V., Ulm/Neu-Ulm 27. -30.4.82. III. Arbeitsmedizinisches Kolloquium,* Gentner Verlag, Stuttgart, pp. 61–70. (208)

Hiatt, J.F. and Kripke, D.F. (1972) Ultradian rhythms in waking gastric activity. *Psychosomatic Medicine,* **37,** 320-325. (99)

Hickey, J.L.S. and Reist, P.C. (1977) Application of occupational exposure limits to unusual work schedules. *American Industrial Hygiene Association Journal,* **38,** 621-631. (160)

Hickey, J.L.S. and Reist, P.C. (1979) Adjusting occupational exposure limits for moonlighting, overtime and environmental exposures. *American Industrial Hygiene Association Journal.* **40,** 727-733. (160)

Hildebrandt, G. (1980) Survey of current concepts relative to rhythms and shift work. In L.E. Scheving and F. Halberg (eds), *Chronobiology: Principles and Applications to shifts in Schedules,* Sijthof and Noordhoff: Alphen a.d. Rijn, pp. 261-292. (34)

Hildebrandt, G., Rohmert, W. and Rutenfranz, J. (1974) Twelve and 24 hour rhythms in error frequency of locomotive drivers and the influence of tiredness. *International Journal of Chronobiology,* **2,** 97-110. (41, 242, 243)

Hildebrandt, G., Rohmert, W. and Rutenfranz, J. (1975) The influence of fatigue and rest period on the circadian variation of error frequency in shift workers (engine drivers). In P. Colquhoun, S. Folkard, P. Knauth and J. Rutenfranz (eds), *Experimental Studies of Shift Work,* Opladen, Westdeutscher Verlag, pp. 174-187. (42)

Hildebrandt, G. and Strattman, I. (1979) Circadian system response to night work in relation to the individual circadian phase position. *International Archives for Occupational and Environmental Health.* **3,** 73-83. (33, 235)

Hockey, G.R.J. (1970) Changes in attention allocation in a multi component task under loss of sleep. *British Journal of Psychology,* **61,** 473-480. (70)

Hockey, G.R.J. (1983) Varieties of attentional state: The effects of environment. In R. Parasuraman and D.R. Davies (eds), *Varieties of Attention,* New York, Academic Press. (128)

Hockey, G.R.J., Davies, S. and Gray, M.M. (1972) Forgetting as a function of sleep at different times of day. *Quarterly Journal of Experimental Psychology,* **24,** 386-393. (43, 44)

Hohmann-Beck, B. (1981) Verflegung von Nacht- und Schichtarbeitern. *Ernahrungs — Umschau,* **28,** 385-388. (209)

Holland, J.G. (1958) Human vigilance. *Science,* **128,** 61-67. (113)

Horne, J.A. (1976) Recovery sleep following different visual conditions during total sleep deprivation in man. *Biological Psychology,* **4,** 107-118. (61, 65)

Horne, J.A. (1977) Factors relating to energy conservation during sleep in mammals. *Physiological Psychology,* **5,** 403-408. (54)

Horne, J.A. (1978) A review of the biological effects of total sleep deprivation on man. *Biological Psychology,* **7,** 55-102. (57, 58)

Horne, J.A. (1983a) Human sleep and tissue restitution: some qualifications and doubts. *Clinical Science,* **65,** 569-578. (54, 58)

Horne, J.A. (1983b) Mammalian sleep function with particular reference to man. In A. Mayes (ed.), *Sleep Mechanisms and Functions,* UK, Van Nostrand, pp. 262-312. (54, 58)

Horne, J.A. (1985) Restitution and sleep — an update on the main issues. *Annals of Clinical Research,* in press. (58)

Horne, J.A., Anderson, N.R. and Wilkinson, R.T. (1983) The effects of sleep deprivation on signal detection measures of vigilance: Implications for sleep function. *Sleep,* **6,** 347-358. (60)

Horne, J.A., Brass, C.G. and Pettit, A.N. (1980) Circadian performance differences between morning and evening 'types'. *Ergonomics,* **23,** 129-36. (33)

Horne, J.A. and Ostberg, O. (1976) A self-assessment questionnaire to determine morningness-eveningness in human circadian rhythms. *International Journal of Chronobiology,* **4,** 97-110. (30, 33, 234, 235)

Horne, J.A. and Minard, A., (1985) Sleep and sleepiness following a behaviourally "active" day. *Ergonomics,* in press. (65)

Horne, J.A. and Ostberg, O. (1977) Individual differences in human circadian rhythms. *Biological Psychology,* **5,** 179-190. (30)

Horne, J.A. and Pettit, A.N. (1984) High incentive effects on vigilance performance during 72h of total sleep deprivation. *Acta Psychologica* (in press). (60, 61)

Horne, J.A. and Pettit, A.N. (1984) Sleep deprivation and the phsiological response to exercise under steady state conditions in untrained subjects. *Sleep,* **7,** 168-179. (57)

Horne, J.A. and Staff, L.H.E. (1983) Exercise and sleep: Body heating effects. *Sleep.* **6,** 36-46. (65)

Horne, J.A. and Wilkinson, S. (1984) Chronic sleep reduction: Daytime vigilance performance and EEG measures of sleepiness, with particular reference to 'practice' effects. *Psychophysiology* (in press). (61)

Howell, W.C., Johnston, W.A. and Goldstein, I.L. (1966) Complex monitoring and its relation to the classical problem of vigilance. *Organizational Behavior and Human Performance,* **1,** 129-150. (112, 140)

Hughes, D.G. and Folkard, S. (1976) Adaptation to an 8-h shift in living routine by members of a socially isolated community. *Nature,* **264,** 232-234. (40, 245, 260)

Hume, K.I. (1980) Sleep adaptation after phase shifts of the sleep-wakefulness rhythm in man. *Sleep,* **2,** 417435. (191)

Hume, K.I. and Mills, J.N. (1977) Rhythms of REM and slow wave sleep in subjects living on abnormal time schedules. *Waking and Sleeping,* **3,** 291-296. (63)

Hunter, S., Shraer, R., Landers, D.M., Buskirk, E.R. and Harris, D.V. (1979) The effects of total oestrogen concentration and menstrual-cycle phase on reaction time performance. *Ergonomics,* **22,** 263-268. (93)

ILO (1978) *Management of Working Time in Industrialised Countries.* Geneva, ILO. (168, 174)

Ivey, M.E. and Bardwick, J.M. (1968) Patterns of affective fluctuation in the menstrual cycle. *Psychosomatic Medicine,* **30,** 336-345. (90, 93)

Jacobsen, H.J. (1952) A study of inspector accuracy. *Industrial Quality Control,* **9,** 16-25. (137, 138)

Jaeger, H. (1981) Uber die Korperwarme des gesunden Menschen. *Deutsches Archiv fur Klinische Medizin,* **29,** 516-536. (188)

Jenkins, H.M. (1958) The effects of signal rate on performance in visual monitoring. *American Journal of Psychology,* **71,** 647-651. (111, 112, 113, 124, 131, 135, 144)

Jerison, H.J. (1967) Activation and long term performance. In A.F. Sanders (ed.), *Attention Performance I,* Amsterdam, North-Holland, pp. 373-389. (111, 113)

Jerison, H.J. (1970) Vigilance, discrimination and attention. In D.I. Mostofsky (ed.), *Attention: Contemporary Theory and Analysis,* New York, Appleton-Century-Crofts, pp. 127-147. (115)

Jerison, H.J. (1977) Vigilance: Biology, Psychology, theory and practice. In R.R. Mackie (ed.), *Vigilance: Theory, Operational Performance and Physiological Correlates,* New York, Plenum. (123)

Jerison, H.J. and Pickett, R.M. (1963) Vigilance: A review and re-evaluation. *Human Factors,* **5,** 211-238. (141)

Jerison, H.J., Pickett, R.M. and Stenson, H.H. (1965) The elecited observing rate and decision processes in vigilance. *Human Factors,* **7,** 107-128. (112, 115, 135)

Johnson, L.C. (1982) Sleep deprivation and performance. In W.B. Webb (ed.), *Biological Rhythms, Sleep and Performance,* New York, Wiley, pp. 111-141. (58, 59, 115)

Johnson, L.C. and MacLeod, W.L. (1973) Sleep and awake behaviour during gradual sleep reduction. *Perceptual Motor Skills,* **36,** 87-97. (61)

Johnson, L.C., Slye, E.S. and Dement, W.C. (1965) Electro-encephalographic and autonomic activity during and after prolonged sleep deprivation. *Psychosomatic Medicine,* **27,** 415-423. (58, 61)

Jones, H.S. and Oswald, I. (1968) Two cases of healthy insomnia. *Electroencephalography and Clinical Neurophysiology,* **24,** 378-380. (64)

Kabaj, M. (1968) Shift work and employment expansion: Towards an optimum pattern. *International Labour Review,* **98,** 245-274. (169)

Kanabrocki, E.L., Scheving, L.E., Halberg, F., Brewer, R.L. and Bird, T.J. (1973) Circadian variation in presumably healthy men under conditions of peace-time army reserve unit training. *Space Life Science,* **4,** 258-270. (5)

Kane, F.J., Lipton, M.A. and Ewing, J.A. (1969) Hormonal influences in female sexual response. *Archives of General Psychiatry,* **20,** 202-209. (91)

Kappauf, W.E. and Powe, W.E. (1959) Performance at an audio-visual checking task. *Journal of Experimental Psychology,* **57,** 49-56. (131)

Karacan, I., Finley, W.W., Williams, R.L. and Hursch, C.J. (1970a) Changes in stage 1-REM and stage 4 sleep during naps. *Biological Psychiatry,* **2,** 261-265. (63)

Karacan, I., Williams, R.L., Finley, W.W. and Hursch, C.J. (1970b) The effects of naps on nocturnal sleep: Influence on the need for stage 1-REM and stage 4 sleep. *Biological Psychiatry,* **2,** 391-399. (63)

Karvonen, M.J. (1979) Ergonomic criteria for occupational and public health surveys. *Ergonomics,* **22,** 641-650.

Katkin, E.S. and McCubbin, R.J.C. (1969) Habituation of the orienting response as a function of individual differences in anxiety and autonomic lability. *Journal of Abnormal Psychology,* **74,** 54-60. (128)

Kelly, R.J. and Schneider, M.F. (1983) The twelve-hour shift revisited: Recent trends in the electric power industry. *Journal of Human Ergology* (in press)

Kennedy, R.S. (1971) Comparison of performance on visual and auditory vigilance tasks. *Human Factors,* **13,** 93-98. (124)

Kennedy, R.S. (1977) The relationship between vigilance and eye movements induced by vestibular stimulation. In R.R. Mackie, (ed.), *Vigilance: Theory, Operational Performance and Physiological Correlates,* New York, Plenum. (128, 129)

Kerkhof, G.A. (1982) Event-related potentials and auditory signal detection: Their diurnal variation for morning-type and evening-type subjects. *Psychophysiology,* **19,** 94-103. (33)

Kerkhof, G.A. (1984). A Dutch-language questionnaire for the selection of morning type and evening type individuals (in Dutch). *Nederlands Tijdschrift voor de Psychologie,* **39,** 281-294. (30)

Kerkhof, G.A. (1985) Inter-individual differences in the human circadian system: A review. *Biological Psychology* (in press). (30, 33)

Kerkhof, G.A., Willemse-v. D. Geest, H.M.M., Korving, H.J. and Rietveld, W.J. (1981) Diurnal differences between morning-type and evening-type subjects in some indices of central and autonomous nervous activity. In A. Reinberg, N. Vieux and P. Andlauer (eds), *Night and Shift Work: Biological and Social Aspects,* Oxford, Pergamon Press, pp. 457-464. (34)

Khaleque, A. and Rahman, A. (1982) Sleep disturbances and health complaints of shift workers. Proceedings of the 6th International Symposium on Night and Shift Work. *Journal of Human Ergology,* **11,** Suppl. (169, 170)

Khaleque, A. and Verhaegen, P. (1981) Circadian effects in short-cycle repetitive work in a two-shift system. In A. Reiberg, N. Vieux and P. Andlauer (eds), *Night and Shift Work: Biological and Social Aspects,* Oxford, Pergamon Press. (242)

Kirchner, G.L. and Knopf, I.J. (1974) Vigilance performance of second grade children as related to sex and achievement. *Child Development,* **45,** 490-495. (131)

Kishida, K. (1973) Temporal change of subsidiary behavior in monotonous work. *Journal of Human Ergology,* **2,** 75-89. (114)

Kjellberg, A. (1977a) Sleep deprivation, arousal and performance. In R.R. Mackie (ed.), *Vigilance,* New York, Plenum Press, pp. 529-535. (58, 72, 115)

Kjellberg, A. (1977b) Sleep deprivation and some aspects of performance. *Waking and Sleeping,* **1,** 149-153. (73)

Klein, K.E., Herrmann, R., Kuklinski, P. and Wegmann, H.M. (1977) Circadian performance rhythms: Experimental studies in air operations. In R.R. Mackie (ed.), *Vigilance: Theory, Operational Performance and Physiological Correlates,* New York and London, Plenum Press, pp. 111-132.

Klein, K.E. and Wegmann, H.M. (1974) The resynchronization of human circadian rhythms after transmeridian flights as a result of flight direction and mode of activity. In L.E. Scheving, F. Halberg and J.E. Pauly, (eds), *Chronobiology,* Tokyo, Igaka Shoin, pp. 564-570. (194)

Klein, K.E. and Wegmann, H.M. (1980a) *Significance of Circadian Rhythms in Aerospace Operations.* AGARDograph no. 247. NATO-AGARD, Neuilly-sur-Seine. (265, 270, 274)

Klein, K.E. and Wegmann, H.M. (1980b) The effect of transmeridian and transequatorial air travel on psychological well-being and performance. In L.E. Scheving and F. Halberg (eds), *Chronobiology: Principles and Applications to Shifts in Schedules,* Alphen aan den Rijn, Sijthoff and Noordhoff, pp. 339-352. (265, 272)

Klein, K.E., Wegmann, H.M., Athanassenas, G., Hohlweck, H. and Kuklinski, P. (1976) Air operations and circadian performance rhythms. *Aviation, Space and Environmental Medicine,* **47,** 221-230. (272)

Klein, K.E., Wegmann, H.M. and Hunt, B.I. (1972) Desynchronization of body temperature and performance circadian rhythm as a result of outgoing and homegoing transmeridian flights. *Aerospace Medicine,* **43,** 119-132. (40, 271, 273)

Kleitman, N. (1949) The sleep–wakefulness cycle of submarine personnel. In *Human Factors in Undersea Warfare,* Washington, DC, National Research Council, pp. 329-341. (255, 256, 258)

Kleitman, N. (1963) *Sleep and Wakefulness.* University of Chicago Press. (39, 99)

Kleitman, N. (1970) Implications of the rest activity cycle: E. Hartman (ed.), *Sleep and Dreaming,* Boston, Little, Brown & Co., pp. 3-20. (105)

Kleitman, N. and Jackson, D.P. (1950a) Variations in body temperature and in performance under different watch schedules. Project NM 004 005.01.02. Bethesda, Md., Naval Medical Research Institute, National Naval Medical Center. (244, 256, 258)

Kleitman, N. and Jackson, D.P. (1950b) Body temperature and performance under different routines. *Journal of Applied Physiology,* **3**, 309-328. (40, 190, 244, 256, 257, 258)

Knauth, P., Eichhorn, B., Lowenthal, I., Gartner, K.H. and Rutenfranz, J. (1983) Reduction of nightwork by re-designing of shift-rotas. *International Archives of Occupational and Environmental Health,* **51**, 371-379. (209)

Knauth, P., Emde, E., Rutenfranz, J., Kiesswetter, E. and Smith, P. (1981) Re-entrainment of body temperature in field studies of shift work. *International Archives of Occupational and Environmental Health,* **49**, 137-149. (171, 189, 193)

Knauth, P., Landau, K., Droge, C., Schwitteck, M., Widynski, M. and Rutenfranz, J. (1980) Duration of sleep depending on the type of shift work. *International Archives of Occupational and Environmental Health,* **46**, 167-177. (181, 191, 196, 201)

Knauth, P., Rohment, W. and Rutenfranz, J. (1979) Systematic selection of shift plans for continuous production with the aid of work — physiological criteria. *Applied Ergonomics,* **10**, 9-15. (173, 175, 197)

Knauth, P., Romahn, R., Kuhlmann, W., Klimmer, F. and Rutenfranz, J. (1975) Analyse de Verteilung Verschiedener Tageselemente bei kontinuierlicher Arbeitsweise mit Hilfe von 'time-budget-studies'. In F. Nachreiner *et al.* (eds), *Schichtarbeit bei Kontinuierlicher Produktion,* Wilhelmshaven, Wirtschaftsverlag Nordwest, pp. 17-82. (207)

Knauth, P. and Rutenfranz, J. (1972a) Untersuchungen zum Problem Schlafverhaltens bei experimenteller Schichtarbeit. *Internationales Archiv fur Arbeitsmedizin,* **30**, 1-22. (191, 202, 207)

Knauth, P. and Rutenfranz, J. (1972b) Untersuchungen uber die Beziehungen zwischen Schichtform und Tagesaufteilung. *Internationales Archiv fur Arbeitsmedizin,* **30**, 173-191. (202, 207)

Knauth, P. and Rutenfranz, J. (1975) The effects of noise on the sleep of night-workers. In P. Colquhoun, S. Folkard, P. Knauth and J. Rutenfranz (eds), *Experimental Studies of Shift Work,* Opladen, Westdeutscher Verlag, pp. 57-65. (207)

Knauth, P. and Rutenfranz, J. (1981) Duration of sleep related to the type of shift work. In A. Reinberg, N. Vieux and P. Andlauer (eds), *Night and Shift Work: Biological and Social Aspects,* Oxford, Pergamon Press. (181, 212)

Knauth, P. and Rutenfranz, J. (1982) Development of criteria for the design of shiftwork systems. Proceedings of the 6th International Symposium on Night and Shift Work. *Journal of Human Ergology,* **11**, Suppl. (178)

Knauth, P., Rutenfranz, J., Herrmann, G. and Poppel, S.J. (1978) Re-entrainment of body temperature in experimental shift work studies. *Ergonomics,* **21**, 775-783. (186, 187, 190)

Knauth, P., Rutenfranz, J., Schulz, H., Bruder, S., Romberg, H.P., Decoster, F. and Kiesswetter, F. (1980) Experimental shift work studies of permanent night, and rapidly rotating, shift systems. *International Archives of Occupational and Environmental Health,* **46**, 111-125. (181, 196)

Knauth, P., Schwarzenu, P., Brockman, W. and Rutenfranz, J. (1983) Computerized construction of shift systems for continuous production which meet physiological, social and legal requirements. *Journal of Human Ergology* (in press). (209)

Kogi, K. (1971) Social aspects of shift work in Japan. *International Labour Review,* **104,** 415-433. (171, 173)

Kogi, K. (1976) Effects of industrialization on working schedules. *Journal of Human Ergology,* **5,** 133-143. (169)

Kogi, K. (1977) Shift work in developing countries. *Philippine Labour Review,* **2,** *4,* 29-40. (169)

Kogi, K. (1981a) Research motives and methods in field approaches to shift work. In L.C. Johnson, D.I. Tepas, W.P. Colquhoun and M.J. Colligan, (eds), *Biological Rhythms, Sleep and Shift Work,* New York, Spectrum Publications. (172, 180)

Kogi, K. (1981b) Comparison of resting conditions between various shift rotation systems for industrial workers. In A. Reinberg, N. Vieux and P. Andlauer (eds), *Night and Shift Work: Biological and Social Aspects,* Oxford, Pergamon Press, pp. 417-424. (181, 182, 209)

Kogi, K. (1983) *Gendaijin to Hiro.* Tokyo, Kinokuniya. (181)

Kogi, K., Miura, T. and Saito, H. (1982) Proceedings of the 6th International Symposium on Night and Shift Work. *Journal of Human Ergology,* **11,** Suppl. (183)

Kogi, K. and Ohta, T. (1975) Incidence of near accidental drowsing in locomotive driving during a period of rotation. *Journal of Human Egology,* **4,** 65-76. (192)

Kojima, A. and Niiyama, Y. (1965) Diurnal variations of 17-ketogenic steroid and catecholamine excretion in adolescent and middle-aged shift workers with special reference to adaptability to night work. *Industrial Health,* **3,** 9-19. (190)

Koller, M. (1983) Health risks related to shift work. An example of time-contingent effects of long-term stress. *International Archives of Occupational and Environmental Health,* **53,** 59-75. (204)

Koller, M., Kundi, M. and Cervinka, R. (1978) Field studies of shift work at an Austrian oil refinery. I. Health and psycholosocial wellbeing of workers who drop out of shiftwork. *Ergonomics,* **21,** 835-847. (172, 203)

Kolmodin-Hedman, B. and Swensson, A. (1975) Problems related to shift work. A field study of Swedish railroad workers with irregular work hours. *Scandinavian Journal of Work Environment and Health,* **1,** 254-262. (190)

Konz, S. and Osman, K. (1977) Team efficiencies on a paced visual inspection task. *Journal of Human Ergology,* **6,** 111-119. (139)

Kopell, B.S. (1969) The role of progestins and progesterone in brain functions and behavior. In *Metabolic Effects of Gonadal Hormones and Contraceptive Steroids,* Plenum Press, New York, pp. 649-667. (92, 93)

Kopell, B.S., Lunde, D.T., Clayton, R.B. and Moos, R.H. (1969) Variations in some measures of arousal during the menstrual cycle. *Journal of Nervous and Mental Diseases,* **148,** 180-187. (93)

Kornetsky, C., Mirsky, A.F., Kessler, E.K. and Dorff, J.E. (1959) The effects of dextroamphetamine on behavioral deficits produced by sleep loss in human. *Journal of Pharmacology and Experimental Therapy,* **127,** 46-50. (75)

Kostyo, J.L. and Nutting, D.F. (1974) Growth hormone and protein metabolism. *American Physiological Society Handbook of Physiology,* **7,** 187-210. (55)

Kreiger, D.T., Kreuzer, J. and Rizzo, F.A. (1969) Constant light: Effect on circadian pattern and phase reversal of steroid and electrolyte levels in man. *Journal of Clinical Endocrinology,* **29,** 1634-1638. (188)

Kripke, D.F. (1972) An ultradian biologic rhythm associated with perceptual deprivation and REM sleep. *Psychosomatic Medicine,* **3,** 221-234. (99, 100)

Kripke, D.F., Cook, B. and Lewis, O.F. (1971) Sleep of night workers: EEG recordings. *Psychophysiology,* **7**, 377-384. (191)

Kripke, D.F., Lavie, P. and Hiatt, F. (1975) Psychoendocrinal ultradian oscillators. *Chronobiologia Supplement,* **1**, 39. (103)

Kripke, D.F. and Sonnenschein, D. (1978) A biologic rhythm in waking fantasy. In D. Pope and J.L. Singer (eds.), *The Stream of Consciousness,* New York, Plenum Press, pp. 321-332. (100)

Krulewitz, J.E. and Warm, J.S. (1977) The event rate context in vigilance: Relation to signal probability and expectancy. *Bulletin of the Psychonomic Society,* **10**, 429-432. (113)

Krulewitz, J.E., Warm, J.S. and Wohl, T.H. (1975) Effects of shifts in the rate of repetitive stimulation on sustained attention. *Perception and Psychophysics,* **18**, 245-249. (112)

Kuhn, E., Rysanek, K., Kujalova, V., Brodan, V., Valek, J. and Rotreki, J. (1973) Diurnal rhythms of excretion of catecholamine metabolites during sleep deprivation. *Activitas Nervosa Superior,* **15**, 129-131. (57)

Kundi, M., Koller, M., Cervinka, R. and Haider, M. (1979a) Consequences of shift work as a function of age and years on shift. *Chronobiologia,* **6**, 123. (203, 204)

Kundi, M., Koller, M., Cervinka, R. and Haider, M. (1979b) field studies of shift work at an Austrian oil refinery. III. Consequences of shift work as a function of age and years on shift. Paper presented at the XIV International Conference on Chronobiology, Hanover. (203, 204)

Kundi, M., Koller, M., Cervinka, R. and Haider, M. (1981) Job satisfaction in shift workers and its relation to family situation and health. In A. Reinberg, N. Vieux and P. Andlauer (eds.), *Night and Shift Work: Biological and Social Aspects.* Oxford, Pergamon Press, pp. 237-244. (203)

Küpper, R., Rutenfranz, J., Knauth, P., Romahn, R., Undeutsch, K. and Lowenthal, I. (1980) Wechselwirkungen zwischen larmbedingten Storungen des Tagschlafs und der Haufigkeit verschiedener Beschwerden bei Schichtarbeitern. In W. Brenner, J. Rutenfranz, E. Baumgartner and M. Haider (eds.), *Arbeitsbedingte Gesundheitsschaden — Fiktion oder Wirklichkeit?* Stuttgart, Gentner Verlag, pp. 165-170. (207)

Lacey, J.I. (1967) Somatic response patterning and stress: Some revisions of activation theory. In M.H. Appley and R. Trumbull (eds.), *Psychological Stress,* New York, Appleton-Century-Crofts, pp. 14-37. (115)

Lacey, J.I. and Lacey, B.C. (1958) The relationship of resting autonomic activity to motor impulsivity. *Research Publications of the Association for Nervous and Mental Disease,* **36**, 144-209. (128)

Lader, M.H. and Wing, L. (1966) *Physiological measures, sedative drugs and morbid anxiety.* Oxford University Press. (128)

Laird, D.A. (1925) Relative performance of college students as conditioned by time of day and day of week. *Journal of Experimental Psychology,* **8**, 50-63. (39, 43, 46, 47)

Lambert, L. and Hart, S. (1976) Who needs a father? *New Society,* **37**, 80. (215)

Langenfelt, G. (1974) *The Historic Origin of the Eight Hours Day.* Westport, Conn., Greenwood Press. (149, 157)

Lavernhe, J. (1970) Wirkungen der Zeitverschiebung in der Luftfahrt auf das Flugpersonal. *Munchener Medizinische Wochenschrift,* **39**, 1746-1752. (275)

Lavie, P. (1976) There are 100-min rhythms in the perception of apparent motion. *Chronobiologia,* **3**, 214-218. (102)

Lavie, P. (1977) Nonstationarity in human perceptual ultradian rhythms. *Chronobiologia,* **4**, 38-48. (102)

Lavie, P. (1979) Ultradian rhythms in alertness — a pupillographic study. *Biological Psychology,* **9,** 49-62. (101)

Lavie, P., Gopher, D., Fogel, R. and Zomer, J. (1981) In L.C. Johnson, D.I. Tepas, W.P. Colquhoun and M.J. Colligan (eds), *Advances in Sleep Research,* vol. 7, *Biological Rhythms, Sleep and Shift Work,* New York, Spectrum Publications, pp. 133-145. (103)

Lavie, P. and Kripke, D.F. (1977) Ultradian rhythm in urine flow in waking humans. *Nature,* **269,** 142-144. (99)

Lavie, P. and Kripke, D.F. (1981) Ultradian circa 1.5 hour rhythms: A multioscillatory system. *Life Science,* **29,** 2445-2450. (104)

Lavie, P., Kripke, D.F., Hiatt, J.F. and Harrison, J. (1978) Gastric rhythms during sleep. *Behavioral Biology,* **23,** 526-530. (99)

Lavie, P., Levy, C.M. and Coolidge, F.L. (1975) Ultradian rhythms in the perception of the spiral aftereffect. *Physiological Psychology,* **3,** 144-146. (102)

Lavie, P., Lord, J.W. and Frank, A.R. (1974) Basic rest–activity cycle in the perception of the spiral aftereffect: A sensitive detector of a basic biological rhythm. *Behavioral Biology,* **11,** 373-378. (102)

Lavie, P., Oksenberg, A., Kedar, S., Luboshitzky, R. and Shen-Orr, Z. (1979) Nocturnal secretion of urine flow — peculiar reaction with REM sleep. *Sleep Research,* **8,** 63. (100)

Lavie, P. and Scherson, A. (1981) Ultrashort sleep–wake schedule: Evidence of ultradian rhythmicity in 'sleep-ability'. *Electroencephalography and Clinical Neurophysiology,* **52,** 163-174. (101, 103, 104)

Lawshe, C.H. and Tiffin, J. (1945) The accuracy of precision instrument measurement in industrial inspection. *Journal of Applied Psychology,* **29,** 413-419. (139)

Lee, K.W. (1978) *Shiftwork and Time Geography.* Research Papers in Geography no. 16. New South Wales, University of Newcastle. (212)

Levine, J.M. (1966) The effects of values and costs on the detection and identification of signals in auditory vigilance. *Human Factors,* **8,** 525-537. (143)

Levine, J.M., Romashko, T. and Fleishman, E.A. (1973) Evaluation of an abilities classification system for integrating and generalising human performance research findings: an application to vigilance tasks. *Journal of Applied Psychology,* **58,** 149-157. (118)

Levitan, S.A. and Belous, R.S. (1977) *Shorter Hours, Shorter Weeks: Spreading the Work to Reduce Unemployment.* Baltimore, Md., Johns Hopkins University Press. (157)

Lewis, B.D., Kripke, D.F. and Bowden, D.M. (1977) Ultradian rhythms in hand–mouth behavior of the rhesus monkey. *Physiology and Behavior,* **18,** 283-286. (104

Lille, F. (1967) Le sommeil de jour d'un groupe de travailleurs de nuit. *Travail Humain,* **30,** 85-97. (181, 191)

Lille, F., Sens-Salis, D., Ullsperger, P., Cheliot, F., Borodulin, L. and Burnod, Y. (1981) Heart rate variations in air traffic controllers during day and night work. In A. Reinberg, N. Vieux and P. Andlauer (eds), *Night and Shift Work: Biological and Social Aspects,* Oxford, Pergamon Press, pp. 391-398. (190)

Lipsett, S.M., Trow, M. and Coleman, J. (1962) *Union Democracy.* New York, Anchor. (218, 223)

Lisper, H.O. and Kjellberg, A. (1972) Effects of 24-hour sleep deprivations on rate of decrement in a 10-minute auditory reaction time task. *Journal of Experimental Psychology,* **96,** 287-290. (69, 70)

Little, B.C. and Zahn, T.P. (1974) Changes in mood and autonomic functioning during the menstrual cycle. *Psychophysiology,* **11,** 579-590. (93)

Livingstone, M.S. and Hubel, D.H. (1981) Effects of sleep and arousal on the processing of visual information in the cat. *Nature,* **291,** 554-561. (65)

Lobban, M.C. (1963) Human diurnal rhythms in an arctic mining community. *Journal of Physiology,* **165,** 75-76. (194)

Lobban, M.C. and Tredre, B.E. (1966) Daily rhythm of renal excretion in human subjects with irregular hours of work. *Journal of Physiology,* **186,** 139-140. (190)

Loeb, M. and Binford, J.R. (1968) Variation in performance on auditory and visual monitoring tasks as a function of signal and stimulus frequencies. *Perception and Psychophysics,* **4,** 361-367. (112, 113)

Loeb, M. and Binford, J.R. (1971) Modality, difficulty and coupling in vigilance behavior. *American Journal of Psychology,* **84,** 529-541. (124, 125)

Loskant, H. (1970) Der Einfluß verschiedener Schichtformen auf die Gesundheit und das Wohlbefinden des Wechselschichtarbeiters. *Zbl. Arbeitsmed.,* **20,** 133-144. (207)

Loskant, H. and Knauth, P. (1976) Kriterien zur Gestaltung der Schichtarbeit. In W. Brenner, W. Rohmert and J. Rutenfranz (eds), *Ergonomische Aspekte der Arbeitsmedizin,* Stuttgart, A.W. Gentner Verlag, pp. 231-240. (208)

Lubin, A., Hord, D.J., Tracy, M.L. and Johnson, L.C. (1976) Effects of exercise, bedrest and napping on performance decrement during 40 hours. *Psychophysiology,* **13,** 334-339. (73, 75, 84)

Luboshitzky, R., Lavie, P., Sok, Y., Glick, S.M., Leroith, D., Shen-Orr, Z. and Barzilai, D. (1978) Antidiuretic hormone secretion and urine flow in aged catheterized patients. *T.I.T. Journal of Life Sciences,* **8,** 95-103. (100)

Lucaccini, L.F., Freedy, A. and Lyman, J. (1968) Motivational factors in vigilance: Effects of instruction on performance in a complex vigilance task. *Perceptual and Motor Skills,* **26,** 783-786. (143)

Luschen, M.E. and Pierce, D.M. (1972) Effect of the menstrual cycle on mood and sexual arousability. *Journal of Sex Research,* **8,** 41-47. (92)

Lybrand, W.A., Andrews, T.G. and Ross, S. (1954) *American Journal of Psychology,* **67,** 704. (74)

Lyddan, J.M., Morgan, B.B. and Brown, B.R. (1974) Studies of performance assessment and enhancement: Final report of progress on research supported by project Themis. Performance Research Laboratory, University of Louisville, Progress Report number PR–74–30. (74)

McCornack, P.D. (1959) Performance in a vigilance task with and without knowledge of results. *Canadian Journal of Psychology,* **13,** 68-71. (142)

McCornack, P.D. (1962) A two-factor theory of vigilance. *British Journal of Psychology,* **54,** *4,* 357-363. (110, 111, 113, 142)

McCornack, P.D. (1967) A two-factor theory of vigilance in the light of recent studies. In A.F. Sanders (ed.), *Attention and Performance I,* Amsterdam, North-Holland, pp. 400-409. (110, 142)

McCornack, P.D. and Prysiazniuk, A.W. (1961) Reaction time and regularity of inter-stimulus interval. *Perceptual and Motor Skills,* **13,** 15-18. (113)

McCormack, R.L. (1961) Inspector accuracy, a study of literature. *Sandia,* SCTM 53–61 (14). (137)

McEwan Young, W. (1980) Shift work and flexible schedules: Are they compatible? *International Labour Review,* **119,** 1-19. (222)

McGann, B. (1971) *Psychological Aspects of Transmeridian Flying.* Dublin, Institute of Psychology.

McGrath, J.J. (1960) *The Effect of Irrelevant Environmental Stimulation on Vigilance Performance.* Technical Report 206–6. Los Angeles, Human Factors Research, Inc. (114)

McGrath, J.J. (1963a) Irrelevant stimulation and vigilance performance. In D.N. Buckner and J.J. McGrath (eds.), *Vigilance: A Symposium,* New York, McGraw-Hill, pp. 3-19. (144)

McGrath, J.J. (1963b) Cross-validation of some correlates of vigilance performance. In D.N. Buckner and J.J. McGrath (eds.), *Vigilance: A Symposium,* New York, McGraw-Hill. (131)

McGrath, J.J. and Harabedian, A. (1963) Signal detection as a function of intersignal-interval duration. In D.N. Buckner and J.J. McGrath (eds.), *Vigilance: A Symposium,* New York, McGraw-Hill, pp. 102-109. (113)

McGrath, J.J., Harabedian, A. and Buckner, D.N. (1960) *Review and critique of the literature on vigilance performance.* Technical Report No. 1 Los Angeles, Human Factors Research Inc. (131)

McGrath, J.J. and Hatcher, J.F. (1961) *Irrelevant Stimulation and Vigilance under Fast and Slow Stimulus Rates.* Technical Report 206-7. Los Angeles, Human Factors Research Inc. (112, 114)

McGrath, J.J., Maag, C.H., Hatcher, J.F. and Breyer, W.P. (1962) *Human Performance during Five Days Confinement.* Technical Memo 206-14. Los Angeles, Human Factors Research Inc. (117)

McKenzie, R.M. (1958) On the accuracy of inspectors. *Ergonomics,* **1**, 258-272. (136, 138, 143)

Maasen, A. (1978) The family life of shift workers and the school career of their children. In *The Effects of Shiftwork on Health, Social and Family Life,* Dublin, European Foundation for the Improvement of Living and Working Conditions. (215, 218)

Mackworth, J.F. (1970) *Vigilance and Attention.* Harmondsworth, Middx, Penguin Books. (142)

Mackworth, N.H. (1950) *Researches on the Measurement of Human Performance.* Medical Research Council Special Report, no. 268. London, HMSO. (110, 111, 124, 131, 143, 144)

Mackworth, N.H. (1957) Vigilance. *Advancement of Science,* **53**, 389-393. (134, 135)

Mackworth, N.H., Kaplan, I.T. and Metlay, W. (1964) Eye movement during vigilance. *Perceptual and Motor Skills,* **18**, 397-402. (110, 117)

MacMahon, B. and Pugh, T.F. (1970) *Epidemiology. Principles and Methods.* Boston, Little, Brown & Co. (201)

Mangan, G.L. and O'Gorman, J.G. (1969) Initial amplitude and rate of habituation of orienting reaction in relation to extroversion and neuroticism. *Journal of Experimental Research in Personality,* **3**, 275-282. (128)

Mann, F.C. and Hoffman, L.R. (1960) *Automation and the Worker.* New York, Henry Holt. (218)

Martin, B.J. (1981) Effect of sleep deprivation on tolerance of prolonged exercise. *European Journal of Applied Psychology,* **47**, 345-354. (57)

Martin, B.J. and Gaddis, G.M. (1981) Exercise after sleep deprivation. *Medicine and Science in Sports and Exercise,* **13**, 220-223. (57)

Martin, C.R. (1977) *Textbook of Endocrine Physiology,* Baltimore, Williams & Wilkins. (55)

Matsumoto, K. (1978) Sleep patterns in hospital nurses due to shift work: An EEG study. *Waking and Sleeping,* **2**, 169-173. (190)

Matsumoto, K., Matsui, T., Kawamori, M. and Kogi, K. (1982) Effects of night time naps on sleep patterns of shiftworkers. Proceedings of 6th International Symposium on Night and Shift Work. *Journal of Human Ergology,* **11**, Suppl. (182)

Maurice, M. (1975) *Shift Work.* Geneva, International Labour Office. (168, 216, 218)

Meers, A. (1975) Performance on different turns of duty within a three-shift system and its relation to body temperature — two field studies. In P. Colquhoun, S. Folkard, P. Knauth and J. Rutenfranz (eds), *Experimental Studies of Shift Work*, Opladen, Westdeutscher Verlag, pp. 188-205. (190, 242)

Meers, A., Maasen, A. and Verhaegen, P. (1978) Subjective health after six months and after four years of shift work. *Ergonomics*, **21**, 857-859. (231, 234)

Megaw, E.D. (1977) *The Analysis of Visual Search Strategies to Improve Industrial Inspection.* Science Research Council Contract B/RG/7380, Second Progress Report. (134, 136)

Menzel, W. (1962) *Menschliche Tag-Nacht-Rhythmik und Schichtarbeit.* Basle, Benno Schwabe. (171, 190, 201, 205)

Merimee, T.J. (1979) Growth hormone secretion and action. In L.J. DeGroot *et al.* (eds), *Endocrinology*, vol. 1, New York, Grune & Stratton, pp. 123-132. (55)

Messent, P.R. (1976) Female hormones and behaviour. In B. Lloyd and J. Archer (eds), *Exploring Sex Differences*, London, Academic Press, pp. 185-212. (92)

Michael, R.P. (1971) Neuroendocine factors regulating primate behaviour. In L. Martini and W.F. Ganong (eds), *Frontiers in Neuroendocrinology*, New York, University Press. (91)

Migeon, C.J., Tyler, F.H., Mahoney, J.P., Florentin, A.A., Castle, H., Bliss, E.L. and Samuels, L.T. (1956) The diurnal variation of plasma levels and urinary excretion of 17-hydroxycorticosteroids in normal subjects, night workers, and blind subjects. *Journal of Clinical Endocrinology and Metabolism*, **16**, 622-633. (189)

Millar, K., Styles, B.C. and Wastell, D.G. (1980) Time of day and retrieval from long-term memory. *British Journal of Psychology*, **71**, 407-414. (45)

Mills, J.N., Minors, D.S. and Waterhouse, J.M. (1977) The physiological rhythms of subjects living on a day of abnormal length. *Journal of Physiology*, **268**, 803-826. (12)

Mills, J.N., Minors, D.S. and Waterhouse, J.M. (1978a) The effect of sleep upon human circadian rhythms. *Chronobiologia*, **5**, 14-27. (8, 194)

Mills, J.N., Minors, D.S. and Waterhouse, J.M. (1978b) Adaptation to abrupt shifts of the oscillators controlling human circadian rhythms. *Journal of Physiology*, **285**, 455-470. (14, 194)

Mills, R. and Sinclair, M.A. (1976) Aspects of inspection in a knitwear company. *Applied Ergonomics*, **7**, *2*, 97-107. (136)

Minors, D.S. and Waterhouse, J.M. (1981a) *Circadian Rhythms and the Human.* Bristol, Wright PSG. (2, 7, 11, 14)

Minors, D.S. and Waterhouse, J.M. (1981b) Anchor sleep as a synchronizer of rhythms on abnormal routines. In L.C. Johnson, D.I. Tepas, W.P. Colquhoun and M.J. Colligan (eds), *Advances in Sleep Research*, vol. 7, *Biological Rhythms, Sleep and Shift Work*, New York, Spectrum Publications, pp. 399-414. (2, 7, 13, 182, 197)

Minors, D.S. and Waterhouse, J.M. (1981c) Endogenous rhythms during anchor sleep experiments. In A. Reinberg, N. Vieux and P. Andlauer (eds), *Night and Shift Work: Biological and Social Aspects*, Oxford, Pergamon Press, pp. 169-170. (194, 197)

Minors, D.S. and Waterhouse, J.M. (1983a) Does 'anchor sleep' entrain circadian rhythms? Evidence from constant routine studies. *Journal of Physiology*, **345**, 451-467. (13)

Minors, D.S. and Waterhouse, J.M. (1983b) Masking effects during night work. *Chronobiologia*, **10**, 142. (14)

Mitchell, J.H. (1935) Subjective standards in inspection for appearance. *Human Factor*, **9**, 235-239. (136)

Mitten, L.G. (1952) Research team approach to an inspection operation. In C.W. Churchman, R.L. Ackoff and E.L. Arnoff (eds), *Introduction to Operations Research*, New York, Wiley. (143)

Mohler, S.R. (1976) Physiological index as an aid in developing airline pilot scheduling patterns. *Aviation, Space and Environmental Medicine,* **47**, 238-247. (269)
Monk, T.H. and Conrad, M.C. (1979) Time of day effects in a range of clerical tasks. *Human Factors,* **21**, **2**, 191-194. (52)
Monk, T.H. and Embrey, D.E. (1981) A field study of circadian rhythms in actual and interpolated task performance. In A. Reinberg, N. Vieux and P. Andlauer (eds), *Advances in the Biosciences,* vol. 30, *Night and Shift Work: Biological and Social Aspects,* London, Pergamon Press, pp. 473-480. (249, 250)
Monk, T.H. and Folkard, S. (1978) Concealed inefficiency of late night study. *Nature,* **273**, 296-297. (249)
Monk, T.H. and Folkard, S. (1983) Circadian rhythms and shiftwork. In G.R.J. Hockey (ed.), *Stress and Fatigue in Human Performance,* Chichester, Wiley, pp. 97-121. (229)
Monk, T.H., Knauth, P., Folkard, S. and Rutenfranz, J. (1978) Memory based performance measures in studies of shiftwork. *Ergonomics,* **21**, 819-826. (245, 246, 278)
Monk, T.H. and Leng, V.C. (1982) Time of day effects in simple repetitive tasks: Some possible mechanisms. *Acta Psychologia,* **51**, 207-221. (49, 50)
Monk, T.H., Weitzman, E.D., Fookson, J.E. and Moline, M.L. (1984) Circadian rhythms in human performance efficiency under free-running conditions. *Chronobiologia* (in press). (51, 52)
Monk, T.H., Weitzman, E.D., Fookson, J.E., Moline, M.L., Kronauer, R.E. and Gander, P.H. (1983) Task variables determine which biological clock controls circadian rhythms in human performance. *Nature,* **304**, 543-545. (51)
Moog, R. (1981) Morning–Evening types and shiftwork. A questionnaire study. In A. Reinberg, N. Vieux and P. Andlauer (eds), *Night and Shift Work: Biological and Social Aspects.* Oxford, Pergamon Press. pp. 481-488. (235)
Moore, S.F. and Gross, S.J. (1973) Influence of critical signal regularity, stimulus event matrix and cognitive style on vigilance performance. *Journal of Experimental Psychology,* **99**, 137-139. (129)
Moore-Ede, M.C. and Sulzman, F.M. (1981) Internal temporal order. In J. Aschoff (ed.), *Handbook of Behavioral Neurobiology,* vol. **4**, *Biological Rhythms,* New York, Plenum Press, pp. 215-242. (195)
Moore-Ede, M.C. Sulzman, F.M. and Fuller, C.A. (1982) *The Clocks that Time Us.* Cambridge, Mass. and London, Harvard University Press. (9, 10, 11, 14, 265, 269)
Moos, R.H. (1968) The development of a menstrual distress questionnaire. *Psychosomatic Medicine,* **30**, 853-867. (89, 93, 95)
Moos, R.H. (1969) Typology of menstrual cycle symptoms. *American Journal of Obstetrics and Gynecology,* **103**, 390-402. (89)
Moos, R.H., Kopell, B.S., Melges, F.T., Yalom, I.D., Lunde, D.T., Clayton, R.B. and Hamburg, D.A. (1969) Fluctuations in symptoms and moods during the menstrual cycle. *Journal of Psychosomatic Research,* **13**, 37-44. (89, 92)
Morris, A.R. and O'Connor, A.R. (1970) Cyclic scheduling. *Hospitals,* **44**, 66-71. (162)
Morris, P.E. and Gale, A. (1974) A correlational study of variables related to imagery. *Perceptual and Motor Skills,* **38**, 659-665. (128)
Moses, J.M., Hord, D.J., Lubin, A., Johnson, L.C. and Naitoh, P. (1975) Dynamics of nap sleep during a 40 hour period. *Electroencephalography and Clinical Neurophysiology,* **39**, 627-636. (63)
Moses, J., Lubin, A., Naitoh, P. and Johnson, L.C. (1978) Circadian variation in performance, subjective sleepiness, sleep and oral temperature during an altered sleep–wake schedule. *Biological Psychology,* **6**, 301-308. (245)

Mott, P.E., Mann, F.C., McLoughlin, Q. and Warwick, D.P. (1965) *Shift Work: The Social, Psychological and Physical Consequences.* Ann Arbor, University of Michigan Press. (214, 215, 218, 219, 220)

Mullaney, D.J., Johnson, L.C., Naitoh, P., Friedman, J.K. and Globus, G.C. (1977) Sleep during and after gradual sleep reduction. *Psychophysiology,* **14,** 237-244. (62)

Murray, E.J. (1966) *Sleep Dreams and Arousal.* New York, Appleton-Century-Crofts. (65, 72)

Murrel, K.F.H. (1971) Industrial work rhythms. In W.P. Colquhoun (ed.), *Biological Rhythms and Human Performance,* London, Academic Press, pp. 241-242. (105)

Murrell, G.A. (1975) A reappraisal of artificial signals as an aid to a visual monitoring task. *Ergonomics,* **18,** 693-700. (141)

Näätänen, R. and Michie, P.T. (1979) Early selective-attention effects on the evoked potential: A critical review and reinterpretation, *Biological Psychology,* **8,** 81-136. (32)

Nachreiner, F. (1975) Role perceptions, job satisfaction and attitudes towards shiftwork of workers in different shift systems as related t situational and personal factors. In P. Colquhoun, S. Folkard, P. Knauth and J. Rutenfranz (eds), *Experimental Studies of Shiftwork,* Opladen, Westdeutscher Verlag, pp. 232-243. (206, 207, 231)

Nachreiner, F. (1977) Experiments on the validity of vigilance experiments. In R.R. Mackie (ed.), *Vigilance,* New York, Plenum, pp. 665-678. (135, 143)

Naitoh, P. (1976) Sleep deprivation. *Waking and Sleeping,* **1,** 53-60. (58, 59, 73)

Naitoh, P. (1981) Circadian cycles and restorative power of naps. In L.C. Johnson, D.I. Tepas, W.P. Colquhoun and M.J. Colligan (eds), *Biological Rhythms, Sleep and Shift Work,* New York, Spectrum Publications, pp. 553-580. (41, 73, 81, 82, 83, 84)

Naitoh, P. (1982) Chronobiologic approach for optimizing human performance. In F.M. Brown and R.C. Graeber (eds), *Rhythmic Aspects of Behaviour,* Hillsdale, NJ, Lawrence Erlbaum Associates, pp. 41-103. (182)

Naitoh, P., Beare, A.N., Biersner, R.J. and Englund, C.E. (1983) Altered circadian periodicities in oral temperature and mood in men on an 18-hour work/rest cycle during a nuclear submarine patrol. *International Journal of Chronobiology,* **8,** 149-173. (258)

Naitoh, P., Englund, C.E. and Ryman, D. (1982) Restorative power of naps in designing continuous work schedules. Proceedings of the 6th International Symposium on Night and Shift Work. *Journal of Human Ergology,* **11,** Suppl.

Naitoh, P., Pasnau, R.O. and Kollar, E.J. (1971) Psychophysiological changes after prolonged deprivation of sleep. *Biological Psychiatry,* **3,** 309-320. (58)

Nakagawa, Y. (1980) Continuous observation of EEG patterns at night and in daytime of normal subjects under restrained conditions. I. Quiescent state when lying down. *Electroencephalography and Clinical Neurophysiology,* **49,** 524-537. (191)

Nakano, Y., Miura, T., Hara, I., Aono, H., Miyano, N., Mayajima, K., Tabuchi, T. and Kosaka, H. (1982) The effect of shift work on cellular immune function. Proceedings of the 6th International Symposium on Night and Shift Work. *Journal of Human Ergology,* **11,** Suppl. (172)

Narayanan, V.K. and Nath, R. (1982) A field test of some attitudinal and behavioral consequences of flexitime. *Journal of Applied Psychology,* **67,** 214-218. (156)

Natsuhara, O. and Shimizu, A. (1982) Measures suggested for improving working life of shift workers in Japan. Proceedings of the 6th International Symposium on Night and Shift Work. *Journal of Human Ergology,* **11,** Suppl. (177)

Nelson, W., Tong, Y.L., Lee, J.K. and Halberg, F. (1979) Methods for cosinor-rhythmometry. *Chronobiologia,* **6,** 305-323. (4)

Nicely, P.E. and Miller, G.A. (1957) Some effects of unequal spatial distribution on the detectability of radar targets. *Journal of Experimental Psychology,* **53,** 195-198. (140)

Nicholson, A.N. (1972) Duty hours and sleep patterns in aircrew operating world-wide routes. *Aerospace Medicine,* **43,** 138-141. (269)

Nilsson, C. (1981) Social consequences of the scheduling of working hours. In A. Reinberg, N. Vieux and P. Andlauer (eds), *Night and Shift Work: Biological and Social Aspects,* Oxford, Pergamon Press. pp. 489-494. (215)

Nollen, S. (1979) *New Patterns of Work.* Scarsdale, New York, Work in America Institute. (157, 159)

Nollen, S.D. and Martin, V.H. (1978) *Alternative Work Schedules.* New York, American Management Association. (153)

Northrup, H.R., Wilson, J.T. and Rose, K.M. (1979) The twelve-hour shift in the petroleum and chemical industries. *Labor Relations Review,* **32,** 312-326. (157, 159)

Norton, R. (1970) The effects of acute sleep deprivation on selective attention. *British Journal of Psychology,* **61,** 157-162. (70)

Oginski, A., Kozlakowska-Swigon, L. and Pokorski, J. (1976) Diurnal and seasonal variations in industrial fatigue of shift workers. *Proceedings of the 6th Congress of the International Ergonomics Association and Technical Program for the 20th Annual Meeting of the Human Factors Society, July 11–16,* pp. 515-518. (251)

O'Hanlon, J. (1964) *Adrenaline, Noradrenaline and Performance in a Visual Vigilance Task.* Technical Report 750-5. Los Angeles, Human Factors Research Inc. (115)

Ohman, A. and Lader, M. (1977) Short-term changes of the human auditory evoked potential during repetitive stimulation. In J.E. Desmedt (ed.), *Auditory Evoked Potentials in Man. Psychopharmacology Correlates of ERPs,* Basle, Karger, pp. 93-118. (32)

Olree, H.D., Corbin, B., Dugger, G. and Smith, C. (1973) An evaluation of the effects of bedrest, sleep deprivation and discontinuance of training on the physical fitness of highly trained young men. NASA-CR-134044.N73-32008. Searcy, Arkansas. (72)

Ong, C.N. and Hong, B.T. (1982) Shiftwork in manufacturing industries in Singapore. Proceedings of the 6th International Symposium on Night and Shift Work. *Journal of Human Ergology,* **11,** Suppl. (170)

Oquist, O. (1970) Kartlaggning au individuella dygnsrytmer (Mapping of individual diurnal rhythms). Doctoral thesis. University of Göteberg. (234)

Orr, W., Hoffman, H. and Hegge, F. (1974) Ultradian rhythms in extended performance. *Aerospace Medicine,* **45,** 995-1000. (103)

Ostberg, O. (1973a) Interindividual differences in circadian fatigue patterns of shift workers. *British Journal of Industrial Medicine,* **30,** 341-351. (206)

Ostberg, O. (1973b) Circadian rhythms of food intake and oral temperature in 'morning' and 'evening' groups of individuals. *Ergonomics,* **16,** 203-209. (33, 234)

Ostberg, O. and McKnicholl, A.G. (1973) The preferred thermal conditions for 'morning' and 'evening' types of subjects during day and night. *Building International,* **6,** 147-157. (33)

Oswald, I., Merrington, J. and Lewis, H. (1970) Cyclical 'on demand' oral intake by adults. *Nature,* **225,** 959-960. (99)

Owen, J.D. (1979) *Working Hours: An Economic Analysis.* Lexington, Mass. D.C. Heath. (152)

Paige, K.E. (1971) Effects of oral contraceptives on affective fluctuations associated with the menstrual cycle. *Psychosomatic Medicine,* **33,** 515-537. (90)

Paige, K.E. (1973) Women learn to sing the menstrual blues. *Psychology Today,* **7,** 4-46. (89)

Palmblad, J., Cantell, K., Strander, H., Froberg, J., Karlsson, C.-G., Levi, L., Granstrom, M. and Unger, P. (1976) Stressor exposure and immunological response in man: Interferon-producing capacity and phagocytosis. *Journal of Psychosomatic Research,* **20,** 193-199. (57)

Palmblad, J., Petrini, B., Wasserman, J. and Akerstedt, T. (1979) Lymphocyte and granulocyte reactions during sleep deprivation. *Psychosomatic Medicine,* **41**, 373-378. (57)

Parasuraman, R. (1975) Response bias and physiological reactivity. *Journal of Psychology,* **91**, 390-413. (124, 129, 131)

Parasuraman, R. (1979) Memory load and event rate control sensitivity decrements in sustained attention. *Science,* **205**, 924-927. (118)

Parasuraman, R. (1984) The psychobiology of sustained attention. In J.S. Warm (ed.), *Sustained Attention in Human Performance,* New York, Wiley. (115)

Parasuraman, R. and Davies, D.R. (1977) A taxonomic analysis of vigilance performance. In R.R. Mackie (ed.), *Vigilance: Theory Operational Performance and Physiological Correlates,* New York, Plenum. (109, 117, 118, 126, 139)

Parlee, M.B. (1973) The premenstrual syndrome. *Psychological Bulletin,* **80**, 454-465. (89)

Parlee, M.B. (1974) Stereotypic beliefs about menstruation: A methodological note on the Moos menstrual distress questionnaire and some new data. *Psychosomatic Medicine,* **36**, 229-240. (89)

Pasnau, R.O., Naitoh, P., Stier, S. and Kollar, E.J. (1968) The psychological effects of 205 hours of sleep deprivation. *Archives of General Psychiatry,* **18**, 496-508. (58, 61)

Patkai, P. (1971a) The diurnal rhythm of adrenaline secretion in subjects with different working habits. *Acta Physiologica Scandinavica,* **81**, 30-34. (234)

Patkai, P. (1971b) Interindividual differences in diurnal variations in alertness, performance and adrenaline excretion. *Acta Physilogica Scandinavica,* **81**, 35-46. (33, 206, 234)

Patkai, P., Akerstedt, T. and Pettersson, K. (1977) Field studies of shift work: I. Temporal patterns in psychophysical activation in permanent night workers. *Ergonomics,* **20**, 611-619. (189, 193)

Patkai, P., Johansson, G. and Post, B. (1974) Mood, alertness and sympathetic-adrenal medullary activity during the menstrual cycle. *Psychosomatic Medicine,* **36**, 503-512. (94)

Patkai, P. and Pettersson, K. (1975) Psychophysiological correlates of premenstrual tension. Reports from the Department of Psychology, no. 448, University of Stockholm. (89)

Patty, R.A. and Ferrell, M.M. (1974) A preliminary note on the motive to avoid success and the menstrual cycle. *Journal of Psychology,* 173-177. (95)

Perkoff, G.T., Eiknes, K., Nugent, C.A., Fred, H.L., Nimer, R.A., Rush, L., Samuels, L.T. and Taylor, F.H. (1959) Studies of the diurnal variation of plasma 17-hydroxycorticosteroids in man. *Journal of Clinical Endrocrinology,* **19**, 432-444. (188)

Persky, H., Charney, N., Lief, H.I., O'Brien, C.P., Miller, W.R. and Strauss, D. (1978) The relationship of plasma estradiol level to sexual behavior in young women. *Psychosomatic Medicine,* **40**, 523-535. (91)

Pierson, W.R. and Lockhart, A. (1963) Effect of menstruation on simple reaction and movement time. *British Medical Journal,* **1**, 796-797. (93)

Pittendrigh, C.S. and Minis, D.H. (1972) Circadian systems — longevity as a function of circadian resonance in Drosophila Melanogaster. *Proceedings of the National Academy of Sciences,* **69**, 1537. (275)

Pokorny, M.L.I., Blom, D.H.J. and Van Leeuwen, P. (1981) Analysis of traffic accident data (from bus drivers) — an alternative approach (II). In A. Reinberg, N. Vieux and P. Andlauer (eds.). *Night and Shift Work: Biological and Social Aspects,* Oxford Pergamon Press, pp. 279-286.

Pope, L.T. and McKechnie, D.F. (1963) Correlation between visual and auditory vigilance performance. US Air Force, Aerospace Medical Research Laboratory Technical Report no. TR-63-57. (124)

Poor, R. (1970) Reporting a revolution in work and leisure: 27 4-day firms. In R. Poor (ed.), *4-days, 40 Hours,* Cambridge, Mass., Bursk & Poor, pp. 15-37. (149, 157, 158)

Post, W. and Gatty, H. (1931) *Around the World in Eight Days.* London, Hamilton. (265)

Poulton, E.C. (1977) Arousing stresses increase vigilance. In R.R. Mackie (ed.), *Vigilance,* New York, Plenum, pp. 423-459. (114)

Poulton, E.C., Edwards, R.S. and Colquhoun, W.P. (1972) Efficiency in heat after a night without sleep. Royal Naval Personnel Research Committee, Report OES 8/72. (115)

Poulton, E.C., Edwards, R.S. and Colquhoun, W.P. (1974) The interaction of the loss of a night's sleep with mild heat: Task variables. *Ergonomics,* **17,** 59-73. (115)

Preston, F.S. (1973) Further sleep problems in airline pilots on world-wide schedules. *Aerospace Medicine,* **44,** 775-782.

Prokop, O. and Prokop, L. (1955) Ermudung und Einschlafen am Steuer. *Zentralblatt fur Verkehrs-Medizin, Verkehrs-Psychologie und angrenzende Gebiete,* **1,** 19-30. (192, 242, 243)

Quilter, R.E., Giambra, L.M. and Benson, P.E. (1983) Longitudinal age changes in vigilance over an eighteen year interval. *Journal of Gerontology,* **38,** 51-54. (130)

Raphael, W.S. (1942) Some problems of inspection. *Occupational Psychology,* **16,** 157-163. (139)

Redgrove, J.A. (1971) Menstrual cycles. In W.P. Colquhoun (ed.), *Biological Rhythms and Human Performance,* London, Academic Press, pp. 211-240. (94, 95)

Reilly, T. and Walsh, T.J. (1981) Physiological, psychological and performance measures during an endurance record for a 5-a-side soccer play. *British Journal of Sports Medicine,* **15,** 122-128. (57)

Reinberg, A., Andlauer, P., De Prins, J., Malbec, W., Vieux, N. and Bourdeleau, P. (1984) Desynchronisation of the oral temperature circadian rhythm and intolerance to shift work. *Nature,* **308,** 272-274. (51)

Reinberg, A., Andlauer, P., Guillet, P., Nicolai, A., Vieux, N. and Laporte, A. (1980) Oral temperature, circadian rhythm amplitude, ageing and tolerance to shiftwork. *Ergonomics,* **23,** 55-64. (229, 235)

Reinberg, A., Vieux, N., Andlauer, P., Guillet, P., Laporte, A. and Nicolai, A. (1979) Oral temperature circadian rhythm amplitude, aging and tolerance to shiftwork (study 3). *Chronobiologia,* **6,** suppl. 1, 77-85. (206)

Reinberg, A., Vieux, N., Ghata, J., Chaumont, A.J. and Laporte, A. (1978) Circadian rhythm amplitude and individual ability to adjust to shift work. *Ergonomics,* **21,** 763-766. (22, 35, 206)

Reist, R.C. and Hickey, J.L.S. (1982) Coping with exposure limits for unusual work schedules. American Industrial Hygiene Association Annual Meeting, 1982. (160)

Rigby, L.V. and Swain, A.D. (1975) Some human-factor applications to quality control in a high technology industry. In C.G. Drury and J.G. Fox (eds), *Human Reliability in Quality Control,* London, Taylor & Francis, pp. 201-216. (137, 144)

Robinson, E.S. and Bills, A.G. (1926) Two factors in the work decrement. *Journal of Experimental Psychology,* **9,** 415-443. (114)

Robinson, M.F. (1938) The work decrement as affected by three kinds of meaningfulness. *Journal of Experimental Psychology,* **22,** 124-149. (110)

Rodin, J. (1976) Menstruation, re-attribution and competence. *Journal of Personality and Social Psychology,* **33,** 345-353. (95)

Ronen, S. (1981) *Flexible Working Hours: An Innovation in the Quality of Work Life.* New York, McGraw-Hill. (153, 161)

Ross, J.J. (1966) Neurological findings after prolonged sleep deprivation. *Archives of Neurology,* **12,** 399-403. (58)

Rosvold, H.E., Mirsky, A.F., Sarason, I., Bransome, E.D. and Beck, L.N. (1956) A continuous performance test of brain damage. *Journal of Counselling Psychology,* **20,** 343-350. (129)

Ruble, D.N. (1977) Premenstrual symptoms: A reinterpretation. *Science,* **197,** 291-292. (89)

Ruble, D.N., Brooks-Gunn, J. and Clarke, A. (1980) Research on menstrual-related psychological changes. In J.E. Parsons (ed.), *The Psychobiology of Sex Differences and Sex Roles,* New York, McGraw-Hill, pp. 227-243. (88, 89)

Rutenfranz, J. (1971) Problems der Schichtarbeit. *Werksarztliches,* **2,** *3,* 1-27. (205)

Rutenfranz, J. (1976) Arbeitsmedizinische Erwartungen an die Ergonomie. In W. Brenner, W. Rohmert and J. Rutenfranz, (eds), *Ergonomische Aspekte der Arbeitsmedizin,* Stuttgart, A.W. Gentner Verlag, pp. 31-37. (203)

Rutenfranz, J. (1982) Occupational health measures for night- and shiftworkers. Proceedings of the 6th International Symposium on Night and Shift Work. *Journal of Human Ergology,* **11,** Suppl. (180, 200)

Rutenfranz, J., Aschoff, J. amd Mann, H. (1972) The effects of a cumulative sleep deficit, duration of preceding sleep period and body temperature on multiple choice reaction time. In *Aspects of Human Efficiency: Diurnal Rhythm and Loss of Sleep,* London, English Universities Press, pp. 217-229. (248, 257, 258, 260)

Rutenfranz, J. and Colquhoun, W.P. (1978) Shiftwork: Theoretical issues and practical problems. *Ergonomics,* **21,** 737-874.

Rutenfranz, J., Colquhoun, W.P., Knauth, P. and Ghata, J.N. (1977) Biomedical and psychological aspects of shift work. *Scandinavian Journal of Work and Environmental Health,* **3,** 165-182. (171, 172, 173, 180, 228, 237)

Rutenfranz, J. and Helbruegge, T. (1957) Uber Tagesschwankungen der Rechengeschwindigkeit bei 11-jahrigen Kinder. *Zeitschrift Kinderheilk,* **80,** 65-82. (47)

Rutenfranz, J. and Knauth, P. (1982) *Schichtarbeit und Nachtarbeit. Probleme — Formen — Empfehlungen.* Bayerischen Staatsministerium fur Arbeit und Sozialordnung, Munchen. (201)

Rutenfranz, J., Knauth, P. and Angersbach, D. (1981) Shift work research issues. In L.C. Johnson, D.I. Tepas, W.P. Colquhoun and M.J. Colligan (eds), *Advances in Sleep Research,* vol. 7, *Biological Rhythms, Sleep and Shift Work,* New York, Spectrum Publications, pp. 165-196. (172, 180, 202, 203, 217)

Rutenfranz, J., Knauth, P. and Colquhoun, W.P. (1976) Hours of work and shiftwork. 6th Congress of the International Ergonomics Association 11–16 July, 1976, University of Maryland, USA. *Ergonomics,* **19,** 331-340. (171, 201)

Rutenfranz, J., Knauth, P., Hildebrandt, G. and Rohmert, W. (1974) Nacht- und Schichtarbeit von Triebfahrzeugfuhrern. 1. Mitt.: Untersuchungen uber die tagliche Arbeitszeit und die ubrige Tagesaufteilung. *Int. Arch. Arbeitsmed.,* **32,** 243-259. (207)

Rutenfranz, J., Knauth, P., Kupper, R., Romahn, R. and Ernst, G. (1981) Pilot project on the physiological and psychological consequences of shiftwork in some branches of the services sector. In *The Effects of Shiftwork on Health, Social and Family Life.* Dublin, European Foundation for the Improvement of Living and Working Conditions. (212)

Saito, H. (1954) *Rodo jikan, kyukei, kotaisei.* Tokyo, Institute for Science of Labour. (171)

Sakai, K., Kogi, K., Watanabe, A., Onishi, N. and Shindo, H. (1982) Location-and-time budget in working consecutive nightshifts. Proceedings of the 6th International Symposium on Night and Shift Work. *Journal of Human Ergology,* **11,** Suppl. (166, 182)

Sakamoto, H. and Matsui, K. (1972) Time taken for familiarization with boarding life. *Journal of Human Ergology,* **1,** 189-194. (183)

Salaman, G. (1974) *Community and Occupation.* Cambridge University Press. (218, 223)

Saldanha, E. (1957) Alternating an exacting visual task with either rest or similar work. Medical Research Council Applied Psychology Research Unit Report, no. 289/57. (144)

Sassin, J.F. (1970) Neurological findings following short-term sleep deprivation. *Archives of Neurology,* **22**,54-56. (58)

Sato, S., Dreifuss, F.E. and Penry, J.K. (1975) Photic sensitivity of children with absence seizures in slow wave sleep. *Electroencephalography and Clinical Neurophysiology,* **39,** 479-489. (65)

Schaeffer, K.E., Kerr, C.M., Buss, D. and Haus, E. (1979) Effect of 18-h watch schedules on circadian cycles of physiological functions during submarine patrols. *Undersea Biomedical Research, Submarine Supplement,* **6,** S81-S90. (258)

Scherrer, J. (1981) Man's work and circadian rhythm through the ages. In A. Reinberg, N. Vieux and P. Andlauer (eds), *Night and Shift Work: Biological and Social Aspects,* Oxford, Pergamon Press, pp. 1-10. (149)

Scheving, L.E. (1959) Mitotic rhythm in the human epidermis. *Anatomical Record,* **135,** 7-20. (56)

Schoonard, J.W., Gould, J.D. and Miller, L.A. (1973) Studies of visual inspection. *Ergonomics,* **16,** 365-379. (137)

Schreiner-Engel, P., Schiavi, R., Smith, H. and White, D. (1981) Sexual arousability and the menstrual cycle. *Psychosomatic Medicine,* **43,** 199-214. (91)

Self, H.C. and Rhodes, F. (1964) The effect of simulated aircraft speed on detecting and identifying targets from side-looking radar imagery. Aerospace Medical Research Laboratories, AMRL TDR 64-40. (137)

Sergean, R. (1971) *Managing Shift Work.* London, Gower Press and Industrial Society. (174, 213)

Shapcott, M. and Steadman, P. (1978) Rhythms of urban activity. In T. Carlstein, D. Parkes and N. Thrift (eds), *Timing Space and Spacing Time,* London, Edward Arnold. (211)

Sheehan, J.J. and Drury, C.G. (1971) The analysis of industrial inspection. *Applied Ergonomics,* **2,** 74-78. (130, 136, 139)

Sherif, C.W. (1980) A social psychological perspective on the menstrual cycle. In J.E. Parsons (ed.), *The Psychobiology of Sex Differences and Sex Roles,* New York, McGraw-Hill, pp. 245-268. (88)

Shift Work Committee, Japan Association of Industrial Health (1979) Opinion on night work and shift work. *Journal of the Science of Labour,* **5,** *8,* Part II, 1-36. (171, 174, 178, 179)

Shri Ram Centre for Industrial Relations (1970) *Human problems of shift work.* New Delhi, New India Press. (169)

Siddle, D.A.T. (1972) Vigilance decrement and speed of habituation of the G.S.R. component of the orienting response. *British Journal of Psychology,* **63,** 191-194. (129)

Siesjo, B.K. (1978) *Brain Energy Metabolism.* New York, Wiley. (65)

Silbergeld, S., Brast, N. and Noble, E.P. (1971) The menstrual cycle: A double-blind study of symptoms, mood and behavior, and biochemical variables using Enovid and placebo. *Psychosomatic Medicine,* **33,** 411-428. (92)

Singer, I. and Singer, J. (1972) Periodicity of sexual desire in relation to time of ovulation in women. *Journal of Biosocial Science,* **4,** 471-481. (92)

Sipowicz, R.R. and Baker, R.A. (1961) Effects of intelligence on vigilance: A replication. *Perceptual and Motor Skills,* **13**, 398. (131)

Smith, L.A. and Barany, J.W. (1970) An elementary model of human performance on paced visual inspection tasks. *AIIE Transactions,* **2**, 298-308. (143)

Smith, P. (1979) A study of weekly and rapidly rotating shift workers. *International Archives of Occupational and Environmental Health,* **46**, 111-125. (190)

Smith, P.A. (1972) Oral temperature rhythms in two groups of industrial shift workers. *Studia Laboris et Salutis,* **11**, 66-78.

Smith, R.L. and Lucaccini, L.F. (1969) Vigilance research: Its application to industrial problems. *Human Factors,* **11**, 149-156. (136)

Smith, R.P. (1961) The effects of signal intensity and signal variability in the efficiency of human vigilance. PhD dissertation, Emory University. (141)

Smith, R.P., Warm, J.S. and Alluisi, E.A. (1966) Effects of temporal uncertainty on watchkeeping performance. *Perception and Psychophysics,* **1**, 293-299. (113)

Smith, S.L. (1975) Mood and the menstrual cycle. In E.J. Sachar (ed.), *Topics in Psychoendocrinology,* New York, Grune & Stratton. (89)

Smolensky, M.H. (1981) The chronoepidemiology of occupational health and shift work. In A. Reinberg, N. Vieux and P. Andlauer (eds), *Night and Shift Work: Biological and Social Aspects,* Oxford, Pergamon Press, pp. 51-65. (195)

Snyder, S. (1983) Isolated sleep paralysis after rapid time zone change ('jet lag') syndrome. *Chronobiologia,* **10**, 377-379. (248)

Sommer, B. (1973) The effect of menstruation on cognitive and perceptual-motor behavior: A review. *Psychosomatic Medicine,* **35**, 515-534. (88, 89, 94, 95)

Sommer, B. (1978) Stress and menstrual distress. *Journal of Human Stress,* **4**, 5-11. (89, 91, 94)

Sostek, A.J. (1978) Effects of electrodermal lability and payoff instructions on vigilance performance. *Psychophysiology,* **15**, 561-568. (128, 129)

Spitz, C.J., Gold, A.R. and Adams, D.B. (1975) Cognitive and hormonal factors affecting coital frequency. *Archives of Sexual Behavior,* **4**, 249-263. (91)

Sterman, M.B., Lucas, E.A. and MacDonald, L.R. (1972) Periodicity within sleep and operant performance in the cat. *Brain Research,* **38**, 327-341. (99)

Stocker, G. and Jovanovic, U.J. (1973) The significance of prolonged sleep deprivation in road traffic. In U.J. Jovanovic (ed.), *The Nature of Sleep,* Stuttgart, Gustave Fischer. (69)

Stuss, D. and Broughton, R. (1978) Extreme short sleep: Personality problems and a case of sleep requirement. *Waking and Sleeping,* **2**, 101-105. (64)

Sverko, B. (1968) Intermodal correlations in vigilance performance. In *Proceedings of the 16th International Congress of Applied Psychology.* Amsterdam, Svets & Zeitlinger. (124, 125)

Swain, A.D. and Guttmann, H.E. (1980) *Handbook of Human Reliability Analysis with Emphasis on Nuclear Power Plant Applications.* NUREG/CR-1278. Albuquerque, New Mexico, Sandia Laboratories.

Swart, J.C. (1977) *A Flexible Approach to Working Hours.* New York, AMACOM, American Management Association. (153)

Sykes *et al.* (1973) Sustained attention in hyperactive children. *Journal of Child Psychology and Child Psychiatry,* **14**, 213-221. (129, 131)

Talland, G.A. (1966) Visual signal detection as a function of age, input rate and signal frequency. *Journal of Psychology,* **63**, 105-115. (130)

Tarriere, C. and Wisner, A. (1962) Effets des bruits significatifs ou non significatifs au cours d'une epreuve vigilance. *Le Travail Humain,* **25**, 1-28. (114, 144)

Tassinari, C.A., Coccagna, E., Mantovani, M., Della Bernardina, B., Spric, J.P., Marcia, D., Vela, A. and Vallicioni, P. (1973) Duodenal EMG activity during sleep in man. In U.J. Jovanovic (ed.), *The Nature of Sleep,* Stuttgart, Gustav Fischer, pp. 55-58. (99)

Tasto, D.L. and Colligan, M.J. (1978) *Health Consequences of Shiftwork.* Melo Park California, Stanford Research Institute, Project URU-4426 Technical Report. (230)

Taub, H.A. and Osborne, F.H. (1968) Effects of signal and stimulus rates on vigilance performance. *Journal of Applied Psychology,* **52,** 133-138. (113)

Taub, J.M. (1971) The sleep–wakefulness cycle in Mexican adults. *Journal of Cross-Cultural Psychology,* **4. (78, 79, 80)**

Taub, J.M. (1978) Behavioral and psychophysical correlates of irregularity in chronic sleep routines. *Biological Psychology*, **4.** (78, 79, 80)

Taub, J.M. (1979) Effects of habitual variations in napping on psychomotor performance, memory and subjective states. *International Journal of Neuroscience,* **9,** 97-112. (80, 81)

Taub, J.M. and Berger, R.J. (1976) The effects of changing the phase and duration of sleep. *Journal of Experimental Psychology, Human Perception and Performance,* **2,** *1,* 30-41. (248)

Taub, J.M., Hawkins, D.R. and Van de Castle, R.L. (1978) Personality characteristics associated with sustained variations in the adult human sleep–wakefulness rhythms. *Waking and Sleeping,* **2,** 7-15. (34)

Taub, J.M., Tanguay, P.E. and Rosa, R.R. (1977) Effects of afternoon naps on physiological variables performance, and self-reported activation. *Biological Psychology,* **5,** 191-210. (80, 81, 82)

Taylor, P.J. (1968) Personal factors associated with sickness absence. *British Journal of Industrial Medicine,* **25,** 106-118. (208)

Taylor, P.J. and Pocock, S.J. (1972) Mortality of shift and day workers 1956–68. *British Journal of Industrial Medicine,* **29,** 201-207. (203)

Taylor, P.J., Pocock, C.J. and Sergean, R. (1972) Absenteeism of shift and day workers. *British Journal of Industrial Medicine,* **29,** 208-213. (172)

Teel, K.S., Springer, R.M. and Sadler, E.E. (1968) Assembly and inspection of microelectronic systems. *Human Factors,* **10,** *3,* 217-224. (140)

Teichner, W.H. (1974) The detection of a simple visual signal as a function of time of watch. *Human Factors,* **16,** 339-353. (136)

Tejmar, J. (1976) Shift work round the clock in supervision and control; schedules of rewarded and unrewarded time. *Applied Ergonomics,* **7,** 66-74; 1-17. (222)

Tepas, D.I. (1976) Methodological pitfalls of shift work research. In *Shift Work and Health, HEW Publications No. (NIOSH) 76-203, Washington, pp. 218-228. (156)*

Tepas, D.I. (1982) Work/sleep time schedules and performance. In W.B. Webb (ed.), Biological Rhythms, Sleep and Performance, New York, Wiley, pp. 175-204. (159)

Tepas, D.I. and Tepas, S.K. (1982) *Alternative Work Schedules Practice in the United States.* Chicago, Work Systems Research. (149)

Tepas, D.I., Walsh, J.K. and Armstrong, D.R. (1981a) Comprehensive study of the sleep of shift workers. In L.C. Johnson, D.I. Tepas, W.P. Colquhoun and M.J. Colligan, (eds), *Biological Rhythms, Sleep and Shift Work,* New York, Spectrum Publications, pp. 347-356. (183, 191, 250)

Tepas, D.I., Walsh, J.K., Moss, P.D. and Armstrong, D. (1981b) Polysomnographic correlates of shift work performance in the laboratory. In A. Reinberg, N. Vieux and P. Andlauer (eds), *Night and Shift Work: Biological and Social Aspects,* Oxford, Pergamon Press, pp. 179-186. (250)

Testu, F. (1982) *Les Variations Journalieres et hebdomadaires de l'activite intellectuelle de l'eleve.* Monographies Francaises de Psychologie no. 59. Paris, Edition du CNRS. (49)

Thackray, R.I., Bailey, J.P. and Touchstone, R.M. (1977) Physiological, subjective, and performance correlates of reported boredom and monotony while performing a simulated radar control task. In R.R. Mackie (ed.), *Vigilance,* New York, Plenum. (116)

Thackray, R.I., Jones, K.N. and Touchstone, R.M. (1974a) Personality and physiological correlates of performance decrement on a monotonous task requiring sustained attention. *British Journal of Psychology,* **65,** 351-358. (127)

Thackray, R.I., Jones, K.N. and Touchstone, R.M. (1974b) Self-estimates of distractibility as related to performance decrement on a task requiring sustained attention. *Ergonomics,* **16,** 141-152. (117)

Tharp, V.K. (1978) Sleep loss and stages of information processing. *Waking and Sleeping,* **2,** 29-33. (70)

Thierry, H., Hoolwerf, G. and Drenth, P.J.D. (1975) Attitude of permanent day and shift workers towards shiftwork; a field study. In W.P. Colquhoun, S. Folkard, P. Knauth and J. Rutenfranz (eds), *Experimental Studies of Shift Work,* Opladen, Westdeutscher Verlag. (183)

Thiis-Evensen, E. (1958) Shift work and health. *Industrial Medicine and Surgery,* **27,** 493-497. (190, 192, 205)

Thompson, L.W., Opton, E.M. and Cohen, L.D. (1963) Effects of age, presentation speed and sensory modality on performance of a 'vigilance' task. *Journal of Gerontology,* **18,** 366-369 (130)

Thorndike, E.L. (1926) *Educational Psychology,* vol. III, *Mental Work and Fatigue, and Individual Differences and Their Causes.* New York, Teachers College, Columbia University. (110)

Thurstone, L.L. and Jeffrey, T.E. (1956) *Flags: A test of space thinking.* Chicago, Education Industry Service. (49)

Tiffin, J. and Rogers, H.B. (1941) The selection and training of inspectors. *Personnel,* **18,** 14-31. (137)

Tilley, A. and Warren, P. (1983) Retrieval from semantic memory at different times of day. *Journal of Experimental Psychology: Learning, Memory and Cognition,* **9,** 718-724. (45, 46)

Tilley, A. and Warren, P. (1984) Retrieval from semantic memory during a night without sleep. *Quarterly Journal of Experimental Psychology,* (in press). (46)

Tilley, A.J., Wilkinson, R.T. and Drud, M. (1981) Night and day shifts compared in terms of the quality and quantity of sleep recorded in the home and performance measured at work: A pilot study. In A. Reinberg, N. Vieux and P. Andlauer (eds), *Night and Shift Work: Biological and Social Aspects,* Oxford, Pergamon Press, pp. 187-196. (190)

Tilley, A.J., Wilkinson, R.T., Warren, P.S.G., Watson, B. and Drud, M. (1982) The sleep and performance of shift workers. *Human Factors,* **24,** 629-641. (251)

Tolin, P. and Fisher, P.G. (1974) Sex differences and effects of irrelevant auditory stimulation on performance of a visual task. *Perceptual and Motor Skills,* **39,** 1255-1262. (131)

Tolle, R. (1981) Sleep deprivation and sleep treatment. In H.M. van Praag (ed.), *Handbook of Biological Psychiatry,* Part VI, New York and Basle, Marcel Dekker, pp. 473-495. (205)

Tooraen, L.A. (1972) Physiological effects of shift rotation on ICU nurses. *Nursing Research,* **21,** 398-405. (190)

Torsvall, L. and Akerstedt, T. (1980) A diurnal type scale. *Scandinavian Journal of Work and Environmental Health,* **6,** 283-290. (235)

Torsvall, L., Akerstedt, T. and Gillberg, M. (1981) Age, sleep and irregular workhours: A field study with EEG recording, catecholamine excretion and self-ratings. *Scandinavian Journal of Work and Environmental Health,* **7,** 196-203. (190, 191)

Toulouse, E. and Pieron, H. (1907) Le Mecanisme de l'inversion chez l'homme du rhythme nychthemeral de la temperature. *Journal de Physiologie et de Pathologie Generale,* **9,** 425-440. (188)

Tune, G.S. (1966a) Errors of commission as a function of age and temperament in a type of vigilance task. *Quarterly Journal of Experimental Psychology,* **18,** 358-361. (130)

Tune, G.S. (1966b) Age difference in errors of commission. *British Journal of Psychology,* **57,** 391-392. (130)

Tune, G.S. (1969a) Sleep and wakefulness in a group of shift workers. *British Journal of Industrial Medicine,* **26,** 54-58. (192)

Tune, G.S. (1969b) The influence of age and temperament on the adult human sleep–wakefulness pattern. *British Journal of Psychology,* **60,** 431-441. (34)

Tyler, D.M., Waag, W. and Halcomb, C.G. (1972) Monitoring performance across sense modes: An individual differences approach. *Human Factors,* **14,** 539-549. (125)

Udry, J.R. and Morris, N.M. (1968) Distribution of coitus in the menstrual cycle. *Nature,* **200**, 593–596 (91)

Udry, J.R. and Morris, N.M. (1970) The effect of contraceptive pills on the distribution of sexual activity in the menstrual cycle. *Nature,* **227,** 502-503. (92)

Uexkull, von J. and Kriszat, G. (1956) *Streifzuge durch die Umwelt von Tieren und Menschen.* Hamburg, Rowohlt.

Utterback, R.A. and Ludwig, G.D. (1949) A comparative study of schedules for standing watches aboard submarines based on body temperature cycles. Project NM 004 003, Report No. 1. Bethesda, Md., Naval Medical Research Institute, National Naval Medical Center. (255, 258)

Valk, I.M. and Bosch, J.S.G. van den (1978) Intra daily variation of the human ulnar length and short term growth – a longitudinal study in eleven boys. *Growth,* **42,** 107-111. (56)

Van Loon, J.H. (1963) Diurnal body temperature curves in shift workers. *Ergonomics,* **6,** 267-273. (171, 188, 193)

Verdone, P. (1968) Sleep satiation: Extended sleep in normal subjects. *Electroencephalography and Clinical Neurophysiology.* **24,** 417-423. (62)

Vickers, D. (1979) *Decision Processes in Visual Perception.* London, Academic Press. (120)

Vickers, D. and Leary, J.N. (1983) Criterion control in signal detection. *Human Factors,* **25,** 283-296. (120)

Vickers, D., Leary, J. and Barnes, P. (1977) Adaptation to decreasing signal probability. In R.R. Mackie (ed), *Vigilance: Theory, Operational Performance, and Physiological Correlates,* New York, Plenum, pp. 679-703. (120)

Vieux, N., Ghata, J., Laporte, A., Migraine, C., Nicolai, A. and Reinberg, A. (1979) Adjustment of shift workers adhering to a three-to-four-day rotation. *Chronobiologia,* **6,** 1, 37-44. (190)

Vogel, W., Broverman, D.M. and Klaiber, E.L. (1971) EEG responses in reguarly menstruating women and in amenorrheic women treated with ovarian hormones. *Science,* **172,** 388-391. (94)

Vokac, Z., Gundersen, N., Magnus, P., Jebens, E. and Bakka, T. (1980) Circadian rhythmicity of the urinary excretion of mercury, potassium and catecholamines in unconventional shift-work systems. *Scandinavian Journal of Work and Environmental Health,* **6,** 188-196. (259)

Vokac, Z., Magnus, P., Jebens, E. and Bakka, T. (1979) A field study of circadian patterns in a continuous 6-h shift. *Chronobiologia,* **6,** 168 (Abstract). (259)

Vokac, Z., Magnus, P., Jebens, E. and Gundersen, N. (1981) Apparent phase-shifts of circadian rhythms (masking effects) during rapid shift rotation. *International Archives of Occupational and Environmental Health,* **49,** 53-65. (190)

Vokac, Z. and Rodahl, K. (1975) A field study of rotating and continuous night shifts in a steel mill. In P. Colquhoun, S. Folkard, P. Knauth and J. Rutenfranz, (eds), *Experimental Studies of Shift Work*, Opladen, Westdeutscher Verlag, pp. 168-173. (190)

Volle, M., Brisson, G.R., Perusse, M., Tanaka, M. and Doyon, Y. (1979) Compressed work-week; psychophysiological and physiological repercussions. *Ergonomics*, **22**, 1001-1010. (159)

Vrancianu, R., Filcescu, V., Ionescu, V., Groza, P., Persson, J., Kadefors, R. and Petersen, I. (1982) The influence of day and night work on the circadian variations of cardiovascular performance. *European Journal of Applied Physiology*, **48**, 11-23. (190)

Vroom, V.H. (1964) *Work and Motivation*, London, Wiley. (213)

Waag, W.L., Tyler, D.M. and Halcomb, C.G. (1973) Sex differences in monitoring performance. *Journal of Applied Psychology*, **58**, 272-274. (131)

Wada, T. (1922) An experimental study of hunger and its relation to activity. *Archives of Psychology Monography*, **8**, 1-65. (99)

Wade, M. (1974) *Flexible Working Hours in Practice*. New York, Wiley. (149, 153, 158)

Walker, J. (1966) Frequent alteration of shift on continuous work. *Occupational Psychology*, **40**, 215-225. (222)

Walker, J. (1978) *The Human Aspects of Shiftwork*. London, Institute of Personnel Management. (223)

Walker, J. and De la Mare, G. (1971) Absence from work in relation to length and distribution of shift hours. *British Journal of Industrial Medicine*, **28**, 36-44. (220)

Ware, J.R. (1961) Effects of intelligence on signal detection in visual and auditory monitoring. *Perceptual and Motor Skills*, **13**, 99-102. (131)

Ware, J.R., Baker, R.A. and Sibowicz, R.R. (1962) Performance of mental deficients on a simple vigilance task. *American Journal of Mental Deficiency*, **66**, 647-650. (131, 142)

Ware, J.R., Kowal, B. and Baker, R.A. (1964) The role of experimental attitude and contingent reinforcement in a display. *Human Factors*, **6**, 111-115. (114)

Warm, J.S. (1977) Psychological processes in sustained attention. In R.R. Mackie (ed.), *Vigilance*, New York, Plenum, pp. 623-644. (111, 142)

Warm, J.S., Epps, B.D. and Ferguson, R.P. (1974) Effects of knowledge of results and signal regularity on vigilance performance. *Bulletin of the Psychonomic Society*, **4**, 272-274. (142)

Warner, M.D. (1976) Scheduling nursing personnel according to nursing preference: A mathematical programming approach. *Operations Research*, **24**, 842-856. (162)

Warren, N. and Clark, B. (1937) Blocking in mental and motor tasks during a 65-hour vigil. *Journal of Experimental Psychology*, **21**, 97-105. (115)

Waterlow, J.C., Garlick, P.J. and Millward, D.J. (1978) *Protein Turnover in Mammalian Tissues and in the Whole Body*. Amsterdam, Elsevier. (56)

Webb, W.B. and Agnew, H.W. (1970) Sleep stage characteristics of long and short sleepers. *Science*, **168**, 146-147. (63, 64)

Webb, W.B. and Agnew, H.W. (1971a) Stage 4 sleep: Influence of time-course variables. *Science*, **174**, 1354-1356. (63)

Webb, W.B. and Agnew, H.W. Jr. (1971b) Variables associated with split-period sleep regimes. *Aerospace Medicine*, **42**, 847-850.

Webb, W.B. and Agnew, H.W. (1973) Effects on performance of high and low energy-expenditure during sleep deprivation. *Perceptual and Motor Skills*, **37**, 511-514. (75)

Webb, W.B. and Agnew, H.W. (1974a) The effects of a chronic limitation of sleep length. *Psychophysiology*, **11**, 265-274. (61)

Webb, W.B. and Agnew, H.W. (1974b) Regularity in the control of the free-running sleep–wakefulness rhythm. *Aerospace Medicine,* **45**, 701-704. (194)
Webb, W.B. and Agnew, H.W. (1975) Are we chronically sleep deprived? *Bulletin of the Psychonomic Society,* **6**, 47-48. (62)
Webb, W.B. and Agnew, H.W. (1977) Analysis of the sleep stages in sleep wakefulness regimes of varied length. *Psychophysiology,* **14**, 445-450. (105)
Webb, W.B. and Agnew, H.W. (1978) Effects of rapidly rotating shifts on sleep patterns and sleep structure. *Aviation, Space and Environmental Medicine,* **49**, 384-389. (191)
Webb, W.B. and Bonnet, M.H. (1978) The sleep of 'morning' and 'evening' types. *Biological Psychology,* **7**, 29-35. (30)
Webb, W.B. and Dube, G. (1981) Temporal characteristics of sleep. In J. Aschoff (ed.), *Biological Rhythms,* New York, Plenum Press, pp. 499-517. (98)
Webb, W.B. and Friel, J. (1971) Sleep stages and personality characteristics of 'natural' long and short sleepers. *Science,* **171**, 587-588. (64)
Wedderburn, A.A.I. (1967) Social factors in satisfaction with swiftly rotating shifts. *Occupational Psychology,* **41**, 85-107. (172, 222)
Wedderburn, A.A.I. (1975) *Studies of Shift Work in the Steel Industry.* Edinburgh, Department of Business Organization, Heriot-Watt University. (218, 220)
Wedderburn, A.A.I. (1981) Is there a pattern in the value of time off work? In A. Reinberg, N. Vieux and P. Andlauer (eds), *Night and Shift Work: Biological and Social Aspects,* Oxford, Pergamon Press. (213)
Wegmann, H.M., Conrad, B. and Klein, K.E. (1983) Flight, flight duty and rest times: A comparison between the regulations of different countries. *Aviation, Space and Environmental Medicine,* (in press). (269)
Wegmann, H.M. and Klein, K.E. (1973) Internal dissociation after transmeridian flights. In *XXI International Congress of Aviation and Space Medicine, Munchen,* pp. 334-337. (269, 273, 274)
Wegmann, H.M. and Klein, K.E. (1981) Sleep and air travel. In D. Wheatley (ed.), *Psychopharmacology of Sleep,* New York, Raven Press, pp. 95-115. (275)
Wegmann, H.M. and Klein, K.E. (1982) Prediction of circadian rhythm resynchronization after time-zone flights. In *Preprints of Scientific Program, Aerospace Medical Association,* Bal Harbour, pp. 309-310: (269, 273)
Wegmann, H.M., Klein, K.E., Conrad, B. and Esser, P. (1983) A model for prediction of resynchronization after time-zone flights. *Aviation, Space and Environmental Medicine,* pp. 424–427. (273).
Wehr, T.A. and Goodwin, F.K. (1981) Biological rhythms and psychiatry. In S. Arieti and H.K.H. Brody (eds), *American Handbook of Psychiatry,* vol. 7, New York, Basic Books, pp. 47-74. (251)
Wehr, T.A., Wirz-Justice, A., Goodwin, F.K., Duncan, W. and Gillin, J.C. (1979) Phase advance of the circadian sleep–wake cycle as an antidepressant. *Science,* **206**, 710-713. (35)
Weidenfeller, E.W., Baker, R.A. and Ware, J.R. (1962) Effects of knowledge of results (true and false) on vigilance performance. *Perceptual and Motor Skills,* **14**, 211-215. (142)
Weitzman, E.D. and Kripke, D.F. (1981) Experimental 12-hour shift of the sleep–wake cycle in man: Effects on sleep and physiologic rhythms. In L.C. Johnson, D.I. Tepas, W.P. Colquhoun and M.J. Colligan (eds), *Advances in Sleep Research,* vol. 7, *Biological Rhythms, Sleep and Shift Work,* New York, Spectrum Publications, pp. 93-110. (186, 187, 194)
Weitzman, E.D., Kripke, D.F., Goldmacher, D., McGregor, P. and Nogeire, C. (1970) Acute reversal of the sleep–wake cycle in man. *Archives of Neurology,* **22**, 483-489. (191)

Weitzman, E.D., Moline, M.L., Czeisler, C.A. and Zimmerman, J.C. (1982) Chronobiology of aging, temperature, sleep/wake rhythms and entrainment. *Neurobiology of Aging,* **3**, 299-309. (34, 229, 244)

Weitzman, E.D., Nogeire, C., Perlow, M., Fukushima, D., Sassin, J. McGregor, P., Gallagher, T.F. and Hellman, L. (1974) Effects of a prolonged 3-hour sleep–wake cycle on sleep stages, plasma cortisol, growth hormone and body temperature in man. *Journal of Clinical Endocrinology and Metabolism,* **34,** 1018-1030. (84)

Wendt, H.W. (1977) Population, sex and constitution in typologies based on individual circadian rhythms. *Journal of Interdisciplinary Cycle Research,* **8,** 286-290. (235)

Wever, R.A. (1975a) The circadian multi-oscillator system of man. *International Journal of Chronobiology,* **3,** 19-55. (24)

Wever, R.A. (1975b) Autonomous circadian rhythms in man: Singly versus collectively isolated subjects. *Naturwissenschaften,* **62,** 443-444. (17)

Wever, R.A. (1979a) *The Circadian System of Man. Results of Experiments under Temporal Isolation.* New York, Springer Verlag. (10, 16, 19, 23, 32, 50, 51, 196, 273)

Wever, R.A. (1979b) Influence of physical workload on freerunning circadian rhythms in man. *Pflugers Archiv,* **381,** 119-126. (17)

Wever, R.A. (1980a) Phase shifts of human circadian rhythms due to shifts of artificial zeitgebers. *Chronobiologia,* **7,** 303-327. (21, 35, 186, 274)

Wever, R.A. (1980b) Circadian rhythms of finches under bright light: is self-sustainment a precondition for circadian rhythmicity? *Journal of Comparative Physiology,* **A140,** 113-119. (20)

Wever, R.A. (1981) On varying work–sleep schedules: the biological rhythm perspective. In L.C. Johnson, D.I. Tepas, W.P. Colquhoun and M.J. Colligan (eds), *Biological Rhythms, Sleep and Shift Work,* New York, Spectrum Publications, pp. 35–60. (19, 275)

Wever, R.A. (1982) Behavioral aspects of circadian rhythmicity. In F.M. Brown and R.C. Graeber (eds), *Rhythmic Aspects of Behavior,* Hillsdale, N.J. Lawrence Erlbaum Associates, pp.105-171. (18, 24, 274)

Wever, R.A. (1983a) Fractional desynchronization of human circadian rhythms: A method for evaluating entrainment limits and functional interdependencies. *Pflugers Archiv,* **396,** 128-137. (26)

Wever, R.A. (1983b) Organization of the human circadian system: Internal interactions. In T.A. Wehr and F.K. Goodwin (eds), *Circadian Rhythms in Psychiatry,* Los Angeles, Boxwood Press, pp. 17-32. (17)

Wever, R.A. (1984a) Properties of human sleep–wake cycles: Parameters of internally synchronized freerunning rhythms. *Sleep,* 7, 27-51. (19, 23).

Wever, R.A. (1984) Sex differences in human circadian rhythms: Intrinsic periods and sleep fractions. *Experientia,* (in press). (23, 34)

Wever, R.A., Polasek, J. and Wildgruber, C.M. (1983) Bright light affects human circadian rhythms. *Pflugers Archiv,* **396,** 85-87. (26)

Wheeler, K.E., Gurman, R. and Tarnowieski, D. (1972) *The Four-Day Week.* New York, American Management Association. (157, 158, 159)

Whitehead, W.E., Robinson, T.M., Wincor, M.Z. and Rechtschaffen, A. (1969) The accumulation of REM sleep need during sleep and wakefulness. *Communications in Behavioural Biology,* **4,** 195-201. (63)

Whittenburg, J.A., Ross, S. and Andrews, T.G. (1956) Sustained perceptual efficiency as measured by the Mackworth 'Clock' test. *Perceptual and Motor Skills,* **6,** 109-116. (110)

Wieneman, E.W. (1971) Autonomic balance changes during the human menstrual cycle. *Psychophysiology,* **8,** 1-6. (94)

Wiener, E.L. (1964) Transfer of training in monitoring: Signal amplitude. *Perceptual and Motor Skills,* **18,** 104. (111)
Wiener, E.L. (1975) Individual and group differences in inspection. In C.G. Drury and J.G. Fox (eds), *Human Reliability in Quality Control,* London, Taylor & Francis, pp. 101-122. (142)
Weiner, H. and Ross, S. (1962) The effects of unwanted signals and d-amphetamine sulphate on observer response. *Journal of Applied Psychology,* **46,** 135-141. (117)
Wilcoxon, L.A., Schrader, S.L. and Sherif, C.W. (1976) Daily self-reports on activities, life events and somatic changes during the menstrual cycle. *Psychosomatic Medicine,* **38,** 399-417. (89, 90)
Wilkinson, R.T. (1958) The effects of sleep loss on performance. *Medical Research Council Applied Psychology Unit Research Report, no. 323/58.* (59, 115)
Wilkinson, R.T. (1961a) Interaction of lack of sleep with knowledge of results, repeated testing and individual differences. *Journal of Experimental Psychology,* **62,** 263-271. (59, 72, 131)
Wilkinson, R.T. (1961b) Comparison of paced, unpaced, irregular and continuous displays in watchkeeping. *Ergonomics,* **4,** 259-267.
Wilkinson, R.T. (1962) Muscle tension during mental work under sleep deprivation. *Journal of Experimental Psychology,* **64,** 565-571. (59)
Wilkinson, R.T. (1963) Interaction of noise with knowledge of results and sleep deprivation. *Journal of Experimental Psychology,* **66,** 332-337. (75)
Wilkinson, R.T. (1964a) Effects of up to 60 hours sleep deprivation on different types of work. *Ergonomics,* **7,** 175-186. (59, 68, 70, 71)
Wilkinson, R.T. (1964b) Artificial 'signals' as an aid to an inspection task. *Ergonomics,* **7,** 63-72. (72, 141, 142)
Wilkinson, R.T. (1965) Sleep deprivation. In O.G. Edholm and A.L. Bacharach (eds), *The Physiology of Human Survival,* New York, Academic Press. (58, 59, 72, 75, 115)
Wilkinson, R.T. (1969) Some factors influencing the effect of environmental stress on performance. *Psychological Bulletin,* **72,** 260-272. (69)
Wilkinson, R.T. (1971) Hours of work and the twenty-four hour cycle of rest and activity. In P.B. Warr (ed.), *Psychology at Work,* Harmondsworth, Middx, Penguin Books, pp. 31-54. (259)
Wilkinson, R.T. (1972) Sleep deprivation — eight questions. In W.P. Colquhoun (ed.), *Aspects of Human Efficiency,* London, English Universities Press, pp. 25-30. (115)
Wilkinson, R.T. (1982) The relationship between body temperature and performance across circadian phase shifts. In F.M. Brown and R.C. Graeber (eds), *Rhythmic Aspects of Behaviour,* Hillsdale, NJ, Lawrence Erlbaum Associates, pp. 213-240. (259)
Wilkinson, R.T. and Edwards, R.S. (1968) Stable hours and varied work as aids to efficiency. *Psychonomic Science,* **13,** 205-206. (244, 259)
Wilkinson, R.T., Edwards, R.S. and Haines, E. (1966) Performance following a night of reduced sleep. *Psychonomic Science,* **5,** 471-472. (248)
Wilkinson, R.T., Tyler, P.D. and Varey, C.S. (1975) Duty hours of young hospital doctors: Effects on the quality of work. *Journal of Occupational Psychology,* **48,** 219-229.
Williams, H.L. (1973) Effects of noise on sleep: A review. In *Proceedings of the International Congress on 'Noise as a Public Health Problem', Dubrovnik,* Washington, DC, Environmental Protection Agency, pp. 501-511. (207)
Williams, H.L., Hammack, J.T., Daly, R.L., Dement, W.C. and Lubin, A. (1964) Responses to auditory stimulation, sleep loss and the EEG stages of sleep. *Electroencephalography and Clinical Neurophysiology,* **16,** 269-279. (61)

Williams, H.L., Lubin, A. and Goodnow, J.J. (1959) Impaired performance with acute sleep loss. *Psychological Monographs,* **73**, 1-26. (59, 69, 72, 115)

Williams, H.L. and Williams, C.L. (1966) Nocturnal EEG profiles and performance. *Psychophysiology,* **3**, 164-175. (71)

Williges, R.C. (1969) Within-session criterion changes compared to an ideal observer criterion in a visual monitoring task. *Journal of Experimental Psychology,* **81**, 61-66. (140)

Williges, R.C. (1971) The role of payoffs and signal ratios in criterion changes during a monitoring task. *Human Factors,* **13**, 261-267. (143)

Williges, R.C. (1973) Manipulating the response criterion in visual monitoring. *Human Factors,* **15**, 179-185. (140)

Williges, R.C. (1976) The vigilance increment: An ideal observer hypothesis. In T.B. Sheridan and G. Johannsen (eds), *Monitoring Behavior and Supervisory Control,* New York, Plenum, pp. 181-190. (120)

Williges, R.C. and North, R.A. (1972) Knowledge of results and decision making performance in visual monitoring. *Organizational Behavior and Human Performance,* **8**, 44-57. (142)

Wojtczak-Jaroszowa, J., Makowsa, Z., Rzepecki, H., Banaszkiewicz, A. and Romejko, A. (1978) Changes in psychomotor and mental task performance following physical work in standard conditions and in a shift-working situation. *Ergonomics,* **21**, 801-810. (249)

Wojtczak-Jaroszowa, J. and Pawlowska-Skyba, K. (1967) Night and shift work I: Circadian variations in work. *Medycyna Pracy,* **18**, 1. (41, 242, 243)

Wolf, S., Almy, T.P., Bachrach, W.H., Spiro, H.M., Sturdevant, R.A.L. and Weiner, H. (1979) The role of stress in peptic ulcer disease. *Journal of Human Stress,* **5**, *2*, 27-37. (203)

Wong, S. and Tong, J.E. (1974) Menstrual cycle and contraceptive hormonal effects on temporal discrimination. *Perceptual and Motor Skills,* **39**, 103-108. (93)

Wongphanich, M., Karnasuta, K., Saito, H., Kogi, K., Temmyo, Y. and Sakai, K. (1982) *A Comparative Study of Women Workers in the Textile Industry of Japan and Thailand: A Socio-economic Profile.* Faculty of Public Health, Mahidol University, Bankok. (170)

Wright, L. (1968) *Clockwork Man.* London, Elek Books. (161)

Wyatt, S. and Langdon, J.N. (1932) Inspection processes in industry. MRC IHRB no. 63. HMSO. (141, 144)

Wyatt, S. and Marriott, R. (1953) Night work and shift changes. *British Journal of Industrial Medicine,* **10**, 164-177. (192)

Yerushalmy, J. (1969) The statistical assessment of the variability in observer perception and description of roentgenographic pulmonary shadows. *Radiological Clinics of America,* **7**, 381-392. (137)

Yerushalmy, J., Harkness, J.T., Cope, J.H. and Kennedy, B.R. (1950) The role of dual reading in mass radiography. *American Review of Tuberculosis,* **61**, 443-464. (139)

Young, J. and Willmott, P. (1973) *The Symmetrical Family.* London, Routledge & Kegan Paul. (217)

Young, J.P., Giovannetti, P., Lewison, D. and Thoms, M.L. (1981) *Factors Affecting Nurse Staffing in Acute Care Hospitals: A Review and Critique of the Literature.* DHEW Publication No. HRA 81-10, Washington. (162)

Zimmerman, E. and Parlee, M.B. (1973) Behavioral changes associated with the menstrual cycle. An experimental investigation. *Journal of Applied Social Psychology,* **3**, 335-344. (93)

Zomer, Y. and Lavie, P. (1981) Variations in daytime 'sleepability'. I. Circadian modulation of ultradian rhythmicity. *Sleep Research*, **10**, 302. (102)

Zuercher, J.D. (1965) The effects of extraneous stimulation on vigilance. *Human Factors*, **7**, 101-105. (114)

Zulley, J. (1979) *Der Einfluss von Zeitgebern auf den Schlaf des Menschen.* Frankfurt am Main, Rita G. Fischer Verlag. (195)

Zulley, J. and Wever, R.A. (1982) Interaction between the sleep–wake cycle and the rhythm of rectal temperature. In J. Aschoff, S. Daan and G. Groos (eds), *Vertebrate Circadian Systems: Structure and Physiology*, Berlin and Heidelberg, Springer Verlag, pp. 253-261. (24)

Zulley, J., Wever, R. and Aschoff, J. (1981) The dependence of onset and duration of sleep on the circadian rhythm of rectal temperature. *Pflugers Archiv*, **391**, 314-318. (195)

Subject Index